Design Through Discovery

fourth edition

Marjorie Elliott Bevlin

Holt Rinehart Winston

New York Chicago San Francisco
Philadelphia Montreal Toronto London
Sydney Tokyo Mexico City Rio de Janeiro Madrid

Publisher: Susan Katz
Acquiring Editor: Karen Dubno
Project Editor: Lisa Owens
Picture Editor: Joan Scafarello
Picture Research: Marion Geisinger
Production Manager: Nancy Myers
Composition and camera work: York Graphic Services
Color separations: The Lehigh Press, Inc.
Printing and binding: Von Hoffmann Press, Inc.

Reproduced on the cover:
Nancy Crow, *High Spirits.* 1982.
Quilt (cotton and cotton blends),
5′5″ × 5′5″ (1.65 × 1.65 m).
Collection of the artist.

Library of Congress Cataloging in Publication Data

Bevlin, Marjorie Elliott.
Design through discovery.

Bibliography: p. 416
Includes index. p. 420
1. Design. I. Title.
NK1510.B53 1983 745.4 83–18387

ISBN 0-03-062148-8

Address correspondence to:
383 Madison Avenue
New York, N.Y. 10017

Printed in the United States of America
Published simultaneously in Canada

4 5 6 7 032 9 8 7 6 5 4 3 2

CBS COLLEGE PUBLISHING

Holt, Rinehart and Winston
The Dryden Press
Saunders College Publishing

TO RUSS
who might have used it.

Preface

Although the various editions of DESIGN THROUGH DISCOVERY have witnessed a world of increasing complexity and concern, the basic elements and principles of effective design have remained the same. Primitive African sculpture and a painting by a Renaissance master, a jar from Crete and a skyscraper in an American city—all are based on the same universal guidelines governing aesthetic validity. Perhaps in emphasizing this universality, more than in any other feature, lies the true value of DESIGN THROUGH DISCOVERY.

As each edition has reflected sweeping changes in the universe and in the role of the designer, the discovery for the student has become one of self, and of an individual role in a chaotic world. By enlightened selection as well as by creation, we become designers of the environment in which we live, of our lives and of the products that comprise it. It is when we are surrounded by things we appreciate and love that we find our sense of home, whether the things be guitar music, mountains, people, or beautiful weaving. The student, by learning the processes of design, discovers a basis for discriminating choice, gradually assimilating preferences into an individual role, just as the designer assimilates elements and principles into a personal style of work.

Like its predecessors, the fourth edition represents a totally rewritten text, introducing new alignments and new emphases and, in some cases, new materials. As before, Part One establishes the place of design in the universe and in human life, analyzing design as a creative process. It sets forth the elements and principles in an order that seems more logical than in previous editions. Both two-dimensional and three-dimensional design are emphasized, and a firm effort is made to distinguish between art and design and between artist and designer.

Part Two is concerned with tools, materials, and expressive forms, in which we have included structural and decorative design. The most radical change from the previous edition occurs here, where the information about materials and processes has been compressed into two chapters instead of being distributed among separate chapters on weaving, pottery, glass, and so on. It is hoped that in this way the information will be easily available. Where applicable, the information is discussed further in other contexts throughout the book.

In Part Three we show symbolism as the alphabet of visual communication. In this section we demonstrate how a framework of design underlies, often symbolically, the various areas of the fine arts, directing their form and structure into integrated aesthetic entities that can nevertheless be distinguished from designs as such. We thus establish the fundamental yet subtle relationship between design and art, while attempting to clarify the difference.

Part Four brings all the previous material into focus as the setting for human life. In this section we discuss those areas that touch us most intimately—the design of what we wear and use for everyday living, the settings in which we carry on our activities, and the total environment in which all these are set. Following these chapters is a Glossary of design terms to clarify the reader's understanding and an updated Bibliography for those who wish to pursue certain subjects in greater depth.

Acknowledgments

I have been given immeasurable help by a diversified group of professors who have taken the time and painstaking effort to assess the manuscript in detail, in the light of their own students' needs. It would be impossible to express how much the present edition is indebted to their perceptive comments and suggestions. My sincere appreciation goes to Timothy T. Blade, University of Minnesota, Twin Cities; Mel Casas, San Antonio College, Texas; William Holley, East Carolina University, North Carolina; Jo A. Lonam, California State University, Sacramento; Lon Nuell, Middle Tennessee State University, Murfreesboro; Harper T. Phillips, Bergen Community College, New Jersey; Carol S. Robertson, Bauder Fashion College, Georgia; Rick Rodrigues, City College of San Francisco; Patricia Terry, The University of Southwestern Louisiana; Mary VanRoekel, North Dakota State University, Fargo; Nicholas H. von Bujdoss, Smith College, Massachusetts; and Lee Wright, The University of Texas, Arlington.

I am indebted as well to Dr. Donald R. Woods of McMaster University for his suggestions in the area of problem solving.

My very special thanks go to Karen Dubno, Art Editor, and Lisa Owens, Project Editor, at Holt, Rinehart and Winston, who guided the production of the book from start to finish, providing guidance while still allowing me to make the book my own, a feat requiring a rare combination of tact, understanding, and editorial skill. I am also much indebted to Joan Scafarello, who was in charge of obtaining illustrations, and Marion Geisinger, who spent long hours at the task, a tedious and frequently frustrating undertaking.

Living on an island places the creation of a book, like all other aspects of living, on a personal basis, since the services readily available in cities are not taken for granted. Thus it is that I feel special appreciation for Cele Westlake and her trusty copying machine and for Kathy Strutz, who brought interest and intelligence to the typing of the final manuscript.

Finally, my thanks go to my family for their support and encouragement, and to the many friends who bore with me during my preoccupation, several of whom contributed helpful research material. Among the last, I would especially mention Michael Boyd, Clara Chapman, Barbara Meyer, Father Johnson West, Peg Ferguson, Gladys and Al Walker, and Fred Carr.

M.E.B.

Cragbourne
Orcas Island, Washington
July 1983

Contents

Part One

Part Three

Design for Environment 331

Part One

Design as Universal Reality Design as Universal Reality Design as Universal Reality Design as Universal Reality Design as Universal Reality Design as Un

1 The Essence of Design

Design is the organization of parts into a coherent whole. Although it is considered to be a human expression, design is in reality the underlying process by which the universe was formed through orderly procedures of selection and evolution. The resulting phenomena often reveal a perfection far beyond the capabilities of human designers, yet they have the potential to offer limitless inspiration (Fig. 1).

The incredibly complex design of our universe continues to baffle scientists. No choreographer could plot a network of movements as intricate as the revolution of moons around planets, planets around their stars, stars whirling in their galaxies, and galaxies interrelated in a system whose limits we have only begun to explore. On our own Earth—a small planet belonging to a small star, the Sun—we can identify a complicated design of water and land, mountains and deserts, forests and plains. What through the centuries has been erected over this topography seems to be the creation solely of human designers—a superficial pattern laid upon the surface of the land. Actually these human constructions, farms, cities, and nations, were determined largely by the natural design that existed before them. Areas of fertility yield patches of growth (Fig. 2); rivers and natural harbors form obvious sites for the construction of cities; and mountain ranges, rivers, and other bodies of water mark the boundaries between nations. In contrast, deserts, towering mountains, and dense jungles retain their primal character by defying the possibility of any human imprint. Even the seacoasts, pounded by surf, retain a stark beauty, having triumphed over human invasion. The repetition of natural forms in eroded rock and ebbing

1
Victor B. Scheffer. Green sea anemone, *Anthopleura xanthogrammica,* Olympic seacoast, Washington. Photograph.

2
Aerial photo of terraced farms in central Peru.

3

4

tide creates a continually changing masterpiece of design (Fig. 3). Taken in its totality then, our environment, both constructed and natural, can be considered the actual character of the earth, the result of the natural forces inherent in its composition.

Other designs of astonishing complexity appear in the food chains of animals and fish and in the interdependence of insects and plants (Fig. 4). The mechanisms of organisms are functional designs of a high order. Most sophisticated of all is the human body, with its neurological, muscular, circulatory, digestive, eliminative, and reproductive functions all evolved to a high degree.

With such order underlying every aspect of our universe, it is not surprising that the desire for order should have become a basic human characteristic. In every culture, every mythology, and every religion, the world began when order was created out of chaos. The book of Genesis, the foundation stone of the Judeo-Christian tradition, reads like a classic design scheme (Fig. 5). Greek mythology is founded upon a process in which the entire complicated genealogy of the gods can be traced back to the ancestors who sprang from chaos and then sorted the universe into categories, giving Zeus dominion over the land, Poseidon over the seas, and Hades over the underworld. Further subdivisions allocated the Dawn, the Harvest, the Hunt, Love, and so forth. Both the ancient Chinese and the ancient Egyptians believed in a nebulous state that existed before the earth came into being. In all these versions the world as we know it began only when confusion or nothingness gave way to form and order—in other words, to design.

The great religions of the world have carried design further, into the systems of ethics by which people can live in harmony with one another and the universe. The Hebrew Torah, the writings of Confucius and Lao-Tse, the Hindu Vedas, the New Testament, and the Muslim Koran are all bodies of instruction seeking to create order in both individual and collective human lives.

3
Victor B. Scheffer. *Surf at South Point, Island of Hawaii.* Photograph.

4
David Cavagnaro. *Orb Weaver Spider Web.* 1970. Photograph.

5
The Creation of the World. 13th century. Vault mosaic. St. Mark's Cathedral, Venice.

6
Moraine Lake, near Banff, Alberta, Canada.

The quest for order did not stop with the arrangement of philosophical priorities, however. It continued in the establishment of nations, the formation of medieval guilds, and the design of planned communities. Today the process gives rise to such diversified groups as the proponents of Esperanto (the international language), the European Common Market, the Arab League, and the Women's Movement, all designed to sort out areas of increasing importance and to place them in an orderly context with existing practices and organizations.

In nature, the endless cycle of birth, death, and renewal can result in what appears to be a chaotic tangle . Taming the wilderness, the traditional beginning for pioneers moving onto a new frontier, meant the ordering of such chaos for human use. Today, in a world threatened with overpopulation and destructive technology, we see the wilderness rather as a treasure to be protected. This idea inspired one of the most vital and sensitive of designs, the creation of national parks and wilderness areas. In all parts of the earth, regions of particular scenic or ecological interest have now been set aside for preservation, scientific study, and human enjoyment. In Italy, India, and Africa national parks provide protection for animals, from the chamois to the Asian lion, while the first national park in the United States was established to protect the geysers, hot springs, and other phenomena unique to the Yellowstone region of Wyoming. All such parks are carefully designed to maintain a delicate balance between human enjoyment and ecological preservation. Roads are unobtrusive, and inns, lodges, shops, and cabin accommodations are designed in rustic styles that blend with the natural surroundings. Miles of trails lead to lakes and mountain tops and strategically located campsites make an extended visit possible. While the emphasis is placed on the preservation of natural beauty and wildlife, human needs are served in a variety of ways (Fig. 6).

5

6

Increased emphasis on human needs is obvious in the design of model cities, apartment complexes, and shopping malls. The World Trade Center in Dallas (Fig. 7) is the last in a six-building complex comprising the Dallas Market Center, a 125-acre (50-hectare) beehive of trade shops. In planning the World Trade Center, the builders wished to erect a structure that would be usable year-round, even in Dallas' hot climate; that would provide for easy passage within the building and to the others in the complex; that would categorize certain types of shops; and, finally, that would give the feeling of a town square.

Architects Beran and Shelmire solved all these problems with a soaring, open-core structure of seven floors (eventually to be twenty). Since the entire facility is enclosed, climate can be regulated to a comfortable springlike atmosphere. All the shops open from balconies located mostly around the central courtyard. The various floors are connected by high-speed escalators and glass-enclosed elevators, while carpeted halls lead to the other buildings. Each level has been assigned to an individual type of shop, with gifts on the second floor, fabrics on the third, and so forth. Best of all, the core of the building succeeds beautifully at creating the effect of a pleasant city plaza. The floor is cobbled, trees and plants abound, a central pool-fountain provides a gathering point for people, and the whole is lighted by an immense natural skylight. In all respects, the World Trade Center has been pronounced a resounding success.

We have mentioned designs that involve economic considerations, moral values, and philosophical beliefs. In the last two examples discussed, national parks and the World Trade Center, function and visual pleasure are inseparable. This is not unusual. Most designs that function well are visually satisfying. A town that has grown up serving the needs of its inhabitants usually presents an orderly and attractive appearance (Fig. 8). A book, a pot, a skyscraper, or a stage set that is functionally successful will almost certainly be satisfying to the eye as well.

In visual design, satisfying the eye is an important aspect of function. The effectiveness of any work of art lies in certain elements and principles that govern its creation and in the impact these have on our senses and emotions. This is true of the work of the writer and musical composer as well as of the work of the visual artist. To put it simply, music enters the consciousness through the sense of hearing, from which point it can involve our emotions, often affecting us deeply. We can be just as deeply affected by experiences that enter our consciousness through the sense of sight. Visual experiences can arouse our curiosity or simply inform us. It is with these visual experiences that we are primarily concerned.

The Psychology of Seeing

Fundamental to either creating or appreciating a visual design is the process of *seeing.* Sensations enter the human eye through the *lens,* a flattened sphere constructed of numerous transparent fibers, which flattens or becomes more spherical depending upon its distance from the object to be viewed. The lens brings images of such objects to the light-sensitive *retina* where the images are registered; in fact, the retina of an eye removed from either a human being or an animal will frequently show a complete image of the world toward which the eye had been turned.

What happens after the image reaches the retina has long been a subject

7
Beran and Shelmire. Hall of Nations in the World Trade Center, Dallas Market Center, Texas. Completed 1974.

8
Aerial view of San Gimignano, Italy, a medieval town.

of philosophical and psychological debate. The ancient Greeks tended to stress the unreliability of the senses generally, since individuals react differently to sounds and tastes and see shapes and colors differently. The realization that a stick dipped in water looked broken and the edges of a road seemed to meet in the distance when they knew this was not true only reinforced their distrust of the human eye. As a result, one of the functions of the intellect was assumed to be the correction of the senses in order to establish the truth. Reason was called upon to be the guide in evaluating perception.

Later thinkers, including Leonardo da Vinci, felt that the eye had power to extend rays to the object viewed as well as to take in images emanating from it. Contemporary thought might conceivably be considered a philosophical extension of this theory, for experiments have proven that perception is not a simple, purely sensory mirroring but a process involving selective acts of considerable intricacy. The word *Gestalt,* which translates from the German as "form," is used to describe the fact that we tend to seize our visual experiences as total unified configurations. This is achieved through a sequence of phases in which our individual brains perform the act of *closure,* unifying our perceptions into an order in which our intelligence, memory, and visual perceptions are refined to acknowledge a specific shape, size, or color. We see four lines and perceive that they are a square because by the act of closure we have imposed our own order upon them. Color, too, is perceived through a series of reactions to the light that is admitted to the brain as electromagnetic energy (see Chapter 7).

Studies have shown that the act of seeing is influenced not only by the viewer's intelligence and memory but by race, cultural group, and amount

7

8

9

of training. Seeing, therefore, becomes a personal experience conditioned by thought processes, memory, and associations, leading to widely differing interpretations of any given subject (p. 17).

With this brief consideration of what is involved in the process of seeing, we will now explore the characteristics of visual design.

Definition of Visual Design

In order to understand what we mean by a visual design, we must first make a distinction between art and design. *Art is concerned with the creation of a work that will arouse an aesthetic response.* "Aesthetic" derives from the Greek *aisthetikos,* pertaining to sense perception, and although for centuries this meant that art was expected to be beautiful, today we extend the range of response to include the entire gamut of human reaction. What we perceive with our eyes—in paintings, sculpture, drawings, prints, and photographs—may result in our feeling delight, admiration, shock, rapture, intrigue, disquiet, revulsion, or even disinterest. The important point is that the aesthetic experience is the work's primary purpose. The artist also undergoes an aesthetic experience in creating the work. In this context, art is a form of communication: the artist expresses and the viewer responds. To carry the definition a step further, it could be said that art rises above the utilitarian aspects of everyday living to spiritual levels.

A design has an explicit purpose. We have already discussed the broad application of the term *design* in the world of nature and human relationships, noting reasons for designs in these areas. A visual design has many possible reasons for being, or *purposes,* ranging from household efficiency to the encouragement of self-esteem. In the pages that follow we will discover a fascinating range of such possibilities.

It is of the utmost importance that we understand that art and design, while representing two distinct fields of activity, are in their fundamental aspects closely related. A work of art depends upon a framework of design in order to achieve its aesthetic character. A design, in turn, may have a strong aesthetic quality. In their own distinctive ways, both a motorcycle and a painting can be beautiful.

9
Piet Mondrian's studio in New York, 1940s.
10
Piet Mondrian.
Composition with Red, Yellow, and Blue.
1939–42. Oil on canvas, 28⅝ × 27¼" (72.4 × 69.2 cm). Tate Gallery, London.

This relationship is not accidental. It is the result of a body of specific elements and principles governing the creation of both works. The elements—line, shape and mass, space, texture, and color—are the ingredients with which the artist or designer works. The principles—unity and variety, balance, emphasis, rhythm, proportion, and scale—provide the means by which the elements can be combined in an aesthetic way. The purpose of this book is to show how these elements and principles operate, not only in design but in the field of art, and to illustrate the basic importance of these elements and principles in all creative activity.

In visual terms, design is the *organization* of *materials* and *forms* in such a way as to fulfill a specific *purpose.* There are four ideas here: organization or order, materials, form, and purpose. Although they are interwoven in the creation of any effective design, we will discuss each one separately.

A Plan for Order

Throughout the height of his career, the Dutch artist Piet Mondrian created paintings that consist of precise squares and rectangles in black, white, and the primary colors (red, yellow, and blue). It would be difficult to find more ordered works of art than these. Although Mondrian's sense of organization carried him to extremes of method, we can learn much about the way an artist organizes a composition by studying his working habits.

Figure 9 shows Mondrian's studio in New York, where he moved toward the end of his life. On the walls are fixed rectangles in different sizes of black, white, and colors. According to his biographers, it was the artist's custom to arrange and rearrange these rectangles on the wall constantly until he had arrived at a pattern that satisfied him. Similar relationships can be found in his precise, geometric paintings (Fig. 10).

Many times artists follow this procedure to plot out a design, working perhaps with scraps of paper or pieces of fabric. Preliminary drawings for a painting or sculpture do the same job, as do architects' sketches and scale models. All of these are plans for order—the first step in creative design.

10

11

Expression of Materials

Much of the impact of a design will depend upon the way the artist uses particular materials. Oil paints can be laid on in transparent glazes, or they can be applied with a palette knife in a thick plastic buildup known as *impasto.* Wood can be finished until it is almost as smooth as glass, or left rough, in the manner of driftwood.

The two sculptures shown in Figures 11 and 12 are the work of a single artist, Auguste Rodin. The strikingly different treatment of forms, surface, and modeling can be attributed at least in part to Rodin's feelings about two different materials—marble and bronze. In the marble *Danaïd* (Fig. 11) we see a smoothly polished, luminous interpretation of the nude. Every bone, every muscle, is beautifully expressed, and the figure's flesh almost seems as though it would be warm to the touch. Rodin clearly was responding to the pure sensuousness of the marble in designing this work. The bronze *Balzac* (Fig. 12) is quite another matter. Here the artist wished to create an impression of overwhelming monumentality, of sheer power, in the personality of the French writer. Physical characteristics yield to the dynamic flow of Balzac's cloak, a movement culminating in a head whose features are highly stylized. The character's essential dynamism is depicted through the inherent strength and force of the bronze itself.

Some artists construct forms specifically to exploit the characteristics of a chosen material. Michelangelo loved the beauty of the marble in the hills of his native Italy, and he used it for his sculpture whenever possible. He blocked out the stone while it was still in the quarry, directing the workmen to cut pieces in which he saw particular beauty. When asked how he had carved the magnificent *David* (Fig. 13), he replied that he had simply chiseled away the stone until the figure was liberated. To him, the stone was a living entity and each block unique, with a form waiting inside to be released.

In the years following World War II, several sculptors became intrigued

11
Auguste Rodin. *The Danäid.* 1885. Marble, 13¾ × 28½ × 22½" (34.9 × 72.4 × 57.2 cm). Rodin Museum, Paris.

12
Auguste Rodin. *Monument to Balzac.* 1897–98. Bronze (cast 1954), height 8'10" (2.69 m), at base 48¼ × 41" (1.23 × 1.04 m). Museum of Modern Art, New York (presented in memory of Curt Valentin by his friends).

13
Michelangelo. *David.* 1501–04. Marble, height 18' (5.48 m). Academy, Florence.

14
David Smith. *Zig IV.* 1961. Steel, painted yellow-gold; 7'9⅜" × 7¼" × 6'4" (2.37 × 2.14 × 1.93 m). Vivian Beaumont Theater, Lincoln Center for the Performing Arts, New York (purchased with funds contributed by Howard and Jean Lipman).

12

13

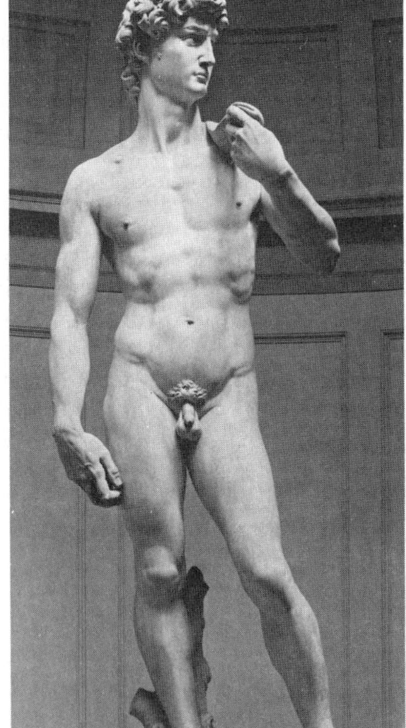

by the possibilities of metal. These artists saw welding techniques as a means to tremendous freedom of expression, and they began to experiment with forms that were cut from sheets of steel and other metals. Within a few years the entire concept of sculpture had been altered (Fig. 14).

Designers approach their work in different ways. Some *plan* a specific object with its purpose in mind, and all other considerations are secondary. Many designers, however, visualize first in terms of form. They have an idea, and they choose a medium in which to express it, just as a sculptor who creates a portrait bust has a choice of working in bronze, stone, plaster, clay, acrylic, wood, or even fiber. The selection of the material is a major decision in terms of how it will best realize the specific form.

Form

The world around us is composed of *physical* forms, from the pebble that can be held in the hand to the mountain that requires days to climb. Trees that at a distance are flatly silhouetted against the horizon become at close range three-dimensional forms that can be walked around and viewed from all sides. Form, however, is not a synonym for mass or volume. A two-dimensional object can have form just as a three-dimensional one does. When shape is governed by structural considerations, it becomes form. In other words, the silhouetted tree is still a form because its shape is determined by the structure of the tree. It is only our perception and the conditions governing it that transform the tree into a flat shape. A round shadow on a wall is a shape, but the street sign casting the shadow is a form. Form, then, is the shape and structure of an object.

14

The term *form* may also refer to medium or subject matter in a work of art. A sculptor's work may be in the form of stone; a painter's canvases may be in the form of landscapes. There are other uses of the term, for instance, form as the physical being of an object (the female form) or as its physical composition (a solid or a vaporous form).

From the standpoint of the designer, form is the particular combination of sizes, shapes, and masses that compose a work and cause that work to exist in the space around it. The artist organizes these elements into an integrated entity. As the artist works with the elements and principles of design, form emerges, a material embodiment of the message of the senses and emotions.

Form can spring entirely from the artist's imagination (Fig. 15) or it can be controlled to some extent by tradition. Christian tradition, for instance, requires that a church be adorned in some way with a cross. The Mohammedan religion forbids the use of the human figure, so Islamic art is rich in geometric and abstract forms.

Form is dictated by the purpose a designed object must serve. A chair must have a horizontal plane for sitting, a cup must be hollow to contain liquids, a bracelet must fit an arm or ankle. These considerations bring us to the fourth concern in our definition of visual design.

15

15
Joan Miró. *Self-Portrait I.* 1937–38. Pencil, crayon, and oil on canvas; 4′9½″ × 3′2¼″ (1.46 × .97 m). Museum of Modern Art, New York. James Thrall Soby Bequest.

16
Blickensderfer electric typewriter. 1902. Courtesy British Typewriter Museum, Bournemouth, England.

17
Olivetti ET 225 electronic typewriter.

18
Totem pole, Stanley Park, Vancouver, B.C.

16

17

18

Fulfillment of Purpose

Although intuition and other personal qualities play a large part in the design process, concern for the purpose of the design must be the first priority of any designer. In utilitarian objects—home furnishings, utensils, clothing—this purpose is clear, yet there are many ways in which a design problem can be handled. The diversity of possibilities can be seen in the two typewriters shown in Figures 16 and 17. Both are electric, designed for the same purpose, yet the span of three-quarters of a century separating the designs has resulted in dramatic refinements in the concept of how a typewriter should look. In creating the 1902 model, the designer was obviously concentrating on the utilitarian aspects of an invention that was less than thirty years old. Seventy-five years later, the designer could take function more or less for granted, freeing the attention to consider such elements as proportion, color, line, and texture. This in no way implies that the later machine is a better design; the modern typewriter simply incorporates more varied considerations.

Some works serve purposes on several levels. The totem poles carved by the Indians of the Pacific Northwest (Fig. 18) are strong in design quality, yet they have as their purpose the keeping of tribal records. Stylized characters representing the Indians' animal companions of land and sea and air are carved in exciting variety into the huge pole of Northwest cedar, adding visual drama and meaning to the depiction of the clan's

19

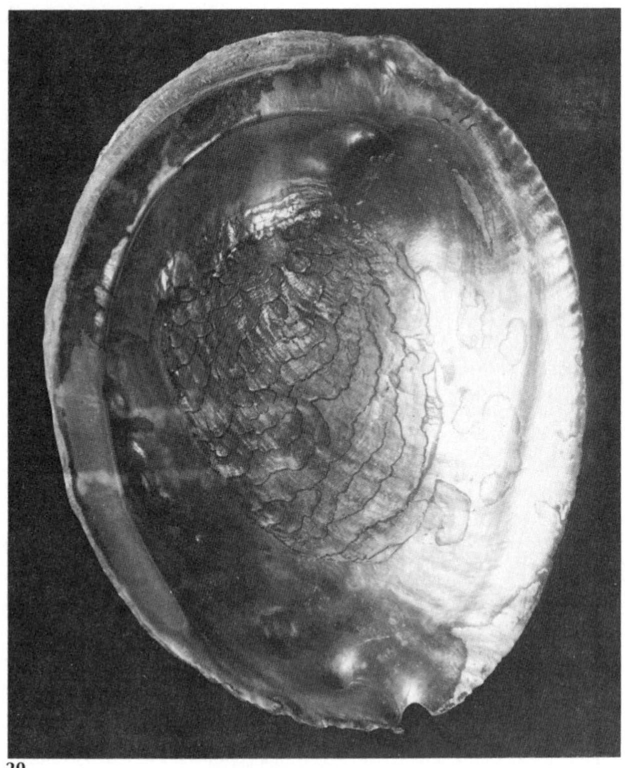

20

history. Remaining visible under the sculpture and paint, the majestic tree narrates the personal and familial legend of the chief of the clan and records the social and religious philosophy of a people. Even to the casual viewer, however, the totem pole is a work of striking design. Appreciation of this fact operates independently of any knowledge of Indian symbolism.

The Role of the Designer

The designer brings two important ingredients to any creative work: *inspiration,* which gives birth to a particular design, and *originality,* which sets it apart from other designs.

Inspiration

The creative designer observes the universe with sensitivity, absorbing impressions from all around. These impressions drop into the subconscious mind like cells that divide and combine to form new entities, which could never be constructed by conscious effort. Often when one least expects it, one becomes aware of new relationships and, seeing them in unique terms, works to give them a form that will make them apparent to others. This, in essence, is the phenomenon known as *inspiration.*

Looking at June Schwarcz' enamel bowl in Figure 19, we can see a striking resemblance to the haliotis shell (Fig. 20). The roughness of the exterior and the iridescent quality of the inside of the bowl are both strongly reminiscent of the shell. The fluted appearance of the interior of

19
June Schwarcz. Electroformed enamel bowl 571. 1970. Copper enamel; diameter 11" (28 cm), height 2¾" (7 cm). Courtesy Mrs. K. Reichert, San Diego, Calif.

20
Haliotis fulgens, a shell found on the beaches of California.

21
Clitocybe dealbata, subspecies *sudorifica.* Toadstools.

the bowl is strikingly like a toadstool (Fig. 21) or like other forms of sea life (Fig. 177, p. 137). The artist had no intention of *imitating* any of these objects, but in delving into her personal experience she, consciously or unconsciously, combined characteristics of two things she had found interesting. Her reactions to these natural forms and her ability to see their characteristics in a totally new relationship provided the inspiration for her bowl.

Since inspiration is nourished by impressions, it becomes imperative that the artist absorb through the senses as much of the world as possible. One designer may find motivation in travel to other lands, another in films of space flight, yet another in the sight of a familiar weed. Some artists draw their ideas directly from their own memories and experiences. Generally speaking, the more one is exposed to sights, sounds, smells, and textures, the more one learns of the arts of theater, dance, poetry, and music; and to the extent one attempts to understand the workings of science and technology, one is likely to arrive at designs that will awaken response in a variety of people.

The New Mexico-based artist Georgia O'Keeffe has executed a series of paintings based on flowers (Pl. 1, p. 21). Her particular approach causes her to move in very close on the subject, so that the flowers open up and expand to create a whole universe. Seeing these natural forms through O'Keeffe's eyes, we become aware of them as shapes and patterns as well as living personalities. Inspiration was derived from a delicate botanical specimen, but the artist's unique viewpoint gave this sensitive expression of beauty a feeling of monumentality.

Originality

Originality of design results from individuality in the designer. Today there is increased emphasis on individuality in reaction to computerized civilization and worldwide standardization. Ease of transportation has brought widely separated cultures together, made possible instant communication, and caused formerly isolated cultures to be invaded and in some cases destroyed. In a world where it is possible to eat hamburgers in Tokyo and sukiyaki in New York, the potential for uniqueness in a human being is not something to be taken for granted.

21

22

In former generations of children, the first five highly impressionable years could be filled with a wealth of personal exploration, uninhibited fantasy, and rich associations derived from family experiences and imaginative reactions to stories. The advent of television, however, has bombarded the child with a conformity of influences almost as soon as that child learns to focus. Thus, kindergarten classmates have a store of reference material in common with children all over the nation, if not the world. Since characters, settings, and other data are presented on television with all details visually complete, the imaginative efforts of children are not called upon to create but must be exercised in the adaptation and expansion of things already seen. Fortunately, imagination is a strong trait in most children, and in spite of this narrowing band of experience their imagination will express itself in daydreaming and play.

Imagery

The Dutch artist M. C. Escher (Fig. 22) describes his work as an effort to communicate ideas springing from his amazement and wonder at the laws of nature that operate in the world around us. Although his works involve a wide variety of subjects and forms, any one of them immediately proclaims itself as the creation of this particular artist, for it is the result of a highly personal *imagery* expressed in personal stylization.

Imagery lies behind any work of art, for it is in translating a personal image that the artist achieves artistic expression. In another sense, imagery can be defined as the *act* of making images, as in drawing or painting. Images can be direct representations of people, places and things, but they can also become *symbols,* evoking other things and ideas. The concept of imagery may become clearer when we contrast two types: *perceptual* and *conceptual.*

22
M. C. Escher.
Concave and Convex. 1955.
Lithograph, 10⅞ × 13⅛″
(27.5 × 33.5 cm).
Haagsgemeentemuseum, The Hague.

23
John Marin.
Woolworth Building, New York, No. 3.
1913. Etching, 12⅞ × 10½″
(33.02 × 26.6 cm). Brooklyn
Museum (Dick S. Ramsay Fund).

24
Joseph Stella. *Skyscrapers.*
1922. Mixed media on canvas,
8′3¾″ × 4′6″ (2.53 × 1.37 m).
Newark Museum, N.J.

Perceptual Imagery

Perception relates to *real things* that actually exist or that actually did exist and survive in memory. No two people perceive in exactly the same way, as we noted in discussing the psychology of seeing (p. 6). Even artists who strive for realistic representation of what they see will necessarily be influenced by a personal perception.

We can understand this by looking at two remarkably different interpretations of the New York City skyline. Neither artist in this case was striving for realistic representation, yet perception was the starting point for both interpretations.

John Marin, an early twentieth-century American watercolorist, was especially sensitive to atmospheric effects. In his etching of the *Woolworth Building* (Fig. 23) this sensitivity is translated into the image of a skyscraper being tossed about by the wind. Millions of people have seen the Woolworth Building from the exact spot where Marin stood, and many on just such a windy day. However, it was Marin's special *perception* of the scene that led to this particular *imagery.*

A more conventional attitude toward skyscrapers, though not necessarily a conventional image, appears in Joseph Stella's painting (Fig. 24). Here the image is one of strict geometry, soaring verticality, buildings reaching up to the skies. Stella's skyscrapers would never bend before the wind. They are instead closely spaced spires, almost like the spires on a cathedral, perhaps signaling the new religion of technology. Again, the artist builds his imagery from his own perceptions of a subject.

23

24

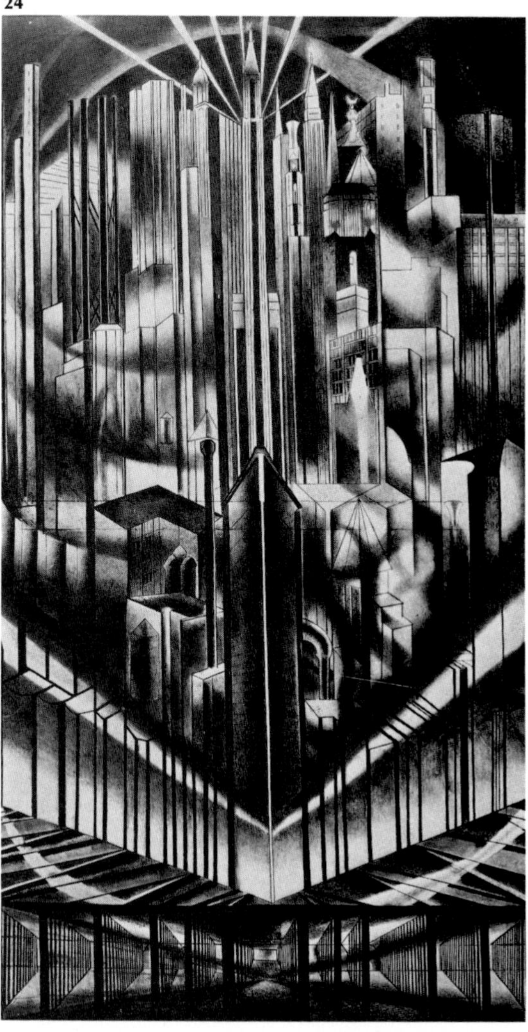

Conceptual Imagery

A conceptual image is a kind of symbol, a shape or form that represents something in the artist's mind rather than what is actually seen. In other words, it is the artist's personal concept of a subject. Conceptual imagery derives from emotion, fantasy, or invention.

One thinks of the eye as being like a camera, but the human eye does not actually record complete and separate pictures except for the fraction of a second when a given image is registered on the retina. The moment the eyeball moves, a new image is registered, with the result that impressions recorded over a period of a few minutes become a continually changing kaleidoscope of images, colors, shapes, sizes, textures, and lines, many of which are superimposed on others or rearranged from the order in which they originally appeared. To these may be added memory, fantasy, pleasant dreams, nightmares, and personal visions. All of these make up the raw material for conceptual imagery. The individual response to them creates the unique expression that frequently results.

The fantastic creations of Hieronymus Bosch resemble nothing on this earth. His *Tree Man in a Landscape* (Fig. 25), for instance, shows a form based on a tree but with humanoid characteristics. The Tree Man is standing, for no apparent reason, in two little boats in the water, and a group of people are having dinner inside his body. On his head rests a jug, from which emerges a ladder being climbed by a tiny man. It is characteristic of Bosch's work that his inventions manage to seem at once whimsical and disquieting. All, however, are interwoven in a composition that unifies his conceptual imagery.

Now that we have explored the nature of design, we are ready to deal with the practical and specific ways of approaching the subject, both as designer and as one who uses, judges, and appreciates design. In Chapter 2 we will see how each of us is, in essence, a designer.

25

25
Hieronymus Bosch.
Tree Man in a Landscape.
c. 1500. Pen and brown ink,
$10^{15}/_{16} \times 8^{3}/_{8}''$ (27.54 × 21.59 cm).
Albertina Gallery, Vienna.

2 The Individual as Designer

Nearly everyone is a designer. We design when we plan our days with a balance of work and recreation. We design again when we organize the contents of a desk or dresser, arrange furniture or place books on a shelf in an orderly fashion. A person who hangs laundry on a line with garments grouped according to size and shape is creating a unified visual design. There is no better example of design than a workshop arranged with an assemblage of tools neatly placed for immediate accessibility (Fig. 26).

Design by Selection

We are also continual *critics* of design. Every time we make a purchase from among a selection of items we exercise judgment in matters of appearance and function.

For fifty thousand years people have used a sharp edge for cutting. Today we select our cutting edges from hundreds of varieties of scissors and knives. The knives differ in width and length of blade, in size, shape, and material of handle, and in the potential for retaining a keen cutting edge without continual sharpening. Even the choice of a knife for kitchen use presents a formidable exercise in selection (Fig. 27). The choice of a vessel for drinking means choosing from hundreds of possible designs,

26

27

26
Workshop of E. L. Walker. Renton, Washington.

27
Selection of kitchen knives.

28

29

ranging from traditional forms seasoned by centuries of use (Fig. 28) to models that are frankly contemporary (Fig. 29). Each choice involves judgment of available models to find the one that best suits a particular need.

When we select home furnishings, clothes, or a car, we do not make a simple choice of an individual object. Consciously or not, we are choosing an element of our personal world, a symbol of who we are and how we want to live. Every selection contributes to the design of our way of life, from the style of furniture to the colors on the walls. The relative emphasis we place on appearance or practicality provides a basic clue to our personality. Even more intimately, our clothes indicate a personal style, a costume for the role we play. Here again, durability and ease of upkeep are variable considerations, depending upon our needs, our financial capabilities, and our outlook. In the selection of a car the priorities may be reversed. Most people hope first for maximum dependability and economy of operation, yet want a model and color they can enjoy. In every choice we make, we are exercising design preferences. This selective process is very much like the first step in *creating* a design.

28
Egyptian Lotiform Cup.
19th–20th Dynasty Faïence.
Metropolitan Museum of Art,
New York, Carnarvon Collection
(gift of Edward S. Harkness,
1926).

29
Contemporary wine goblets.

The Design Process: Problem Solving

The most original designs are conceived intuitively, yet the complete design process is both conscious and unconscious. Intuition presents a concept that sparks the designer's interest, and then the mind enters the

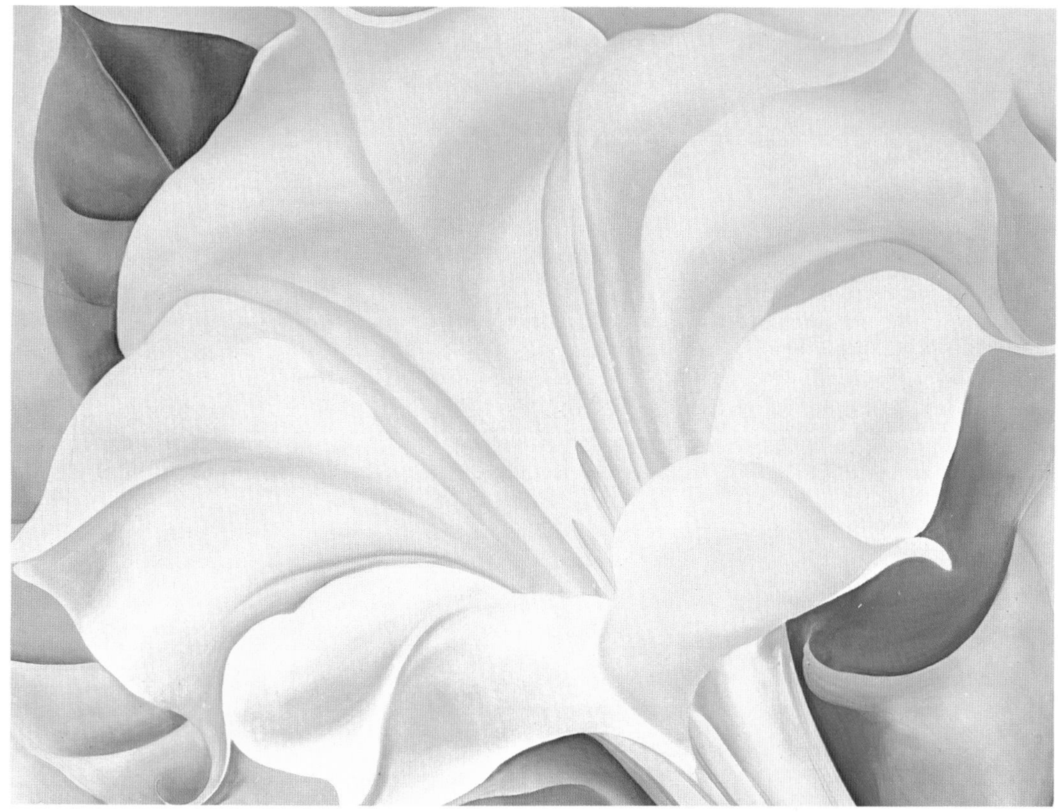

Plate 1
Georgia O'Keeffe. *White Trumpet Flower.* 1932. Oil on canvas, 30 × 40″ (76 × 102 cm). San Diego Museum of Art (gift of Mrs. Inez Grant Parker).

Plate 2
Jane Hamilton-Merritt. *Night Fighting: South Vietnam.* 1969. Photograph.

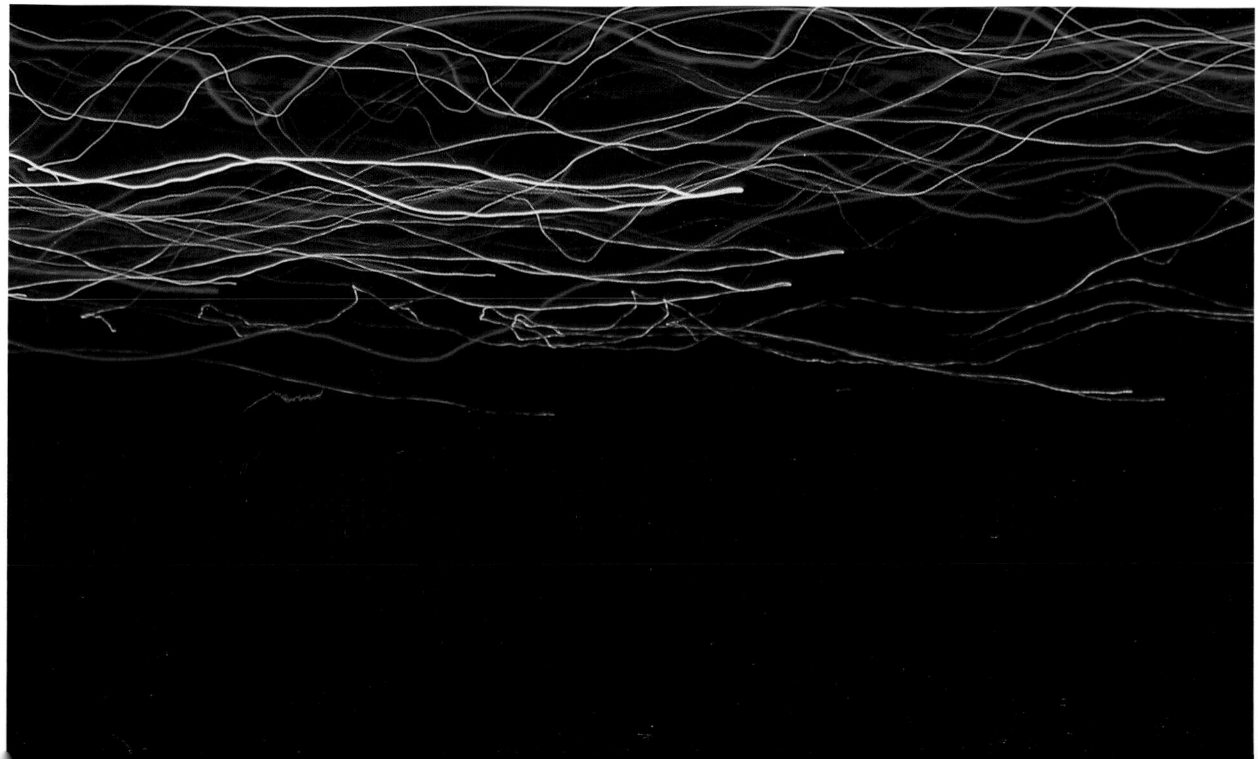

Plate 3
Richard Anuszkiewicz.
Blue to Red Portal. 1977.
Screenprint on Masonite, 7 × 4′
(2.1 × 1.2 m). Courtesy Editions
Lassiter-Meisel, New York.
Collection of the artist.

31

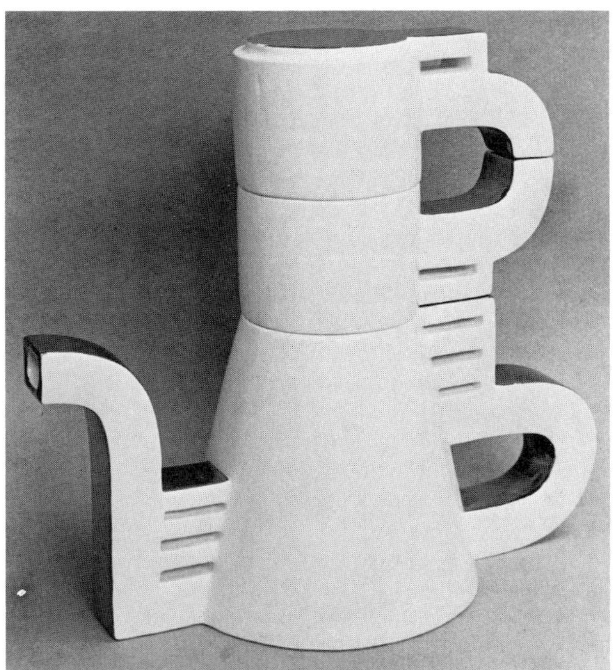
30

32

30
Anne Currier. *Teapot with Two Cups.* 1975. Slip-cast earthenware with slab-built handles and spout, luster glaze; height 9" (22.86 cm). Courtesy the artist.

31
Wilhelm Wagenfeld. *Teapot.* 1932. Heat-resistant glass, height 4⅜" (11.43 cm). Mfr.: Jensor Glaswerk Schutt & Gen, Germany. Museum of Modern Art, New York (gift of Philip Johnson and Fraser's Inc., New York).

32
Marianne Brandt. *Teapot.* 1924. Nickel silver and ebony, height 3⅝" (8.89 cm). Mfr.: Bauhaus Metal Workshop, Germany. Museum of Modern Art, New York (Phyllis B. Lambert Fund).

process by sorting out the possible approaches. Even the most seemingly straightforward design presents a wide range of possibilities.

If the object to be designed is a teapot, for instance, one might think there are few decisions to be made. Over the centuries, the teapot shape has assumed a fairly standard form, determined by the requirements for brewing and serving tea. It must be a hollow container with a lid and have a spout for pouring, a handle, and often a strainer for the tea leaves. The aim of a new design, however, is to create something different from what existed before—a more beautiful or interesting appearance, a more functional shape.

One of the first decisions in designing a teapot would concern the material. Traditionally most teapots are ceramic, which holds the heat well (Fig. 30). Some, however, are glass, allowing one to watch the brewing process (Fig. 31). A teapot can also be metal, as many fine ones have been (Fig. 32). The spout should pour without dripping or spilling: a straight or curved spout will do this equally well. Frequently the handle reaches across the top of the pot, but if the overall form is carefully balanced, it can be placed on the side. Teapots generally have flat bottoms, but since they are rarely used directly on the stove, this is a matter of tradition rather than of function. A built-in stand to insulate the table from heat might be a practical innovation. There remains the potential for decoration, in which the choices are even wider. Through the creative process, the designer seeks entirely new solutions.

We mention the possibilities above to emphasize the fact that creating a

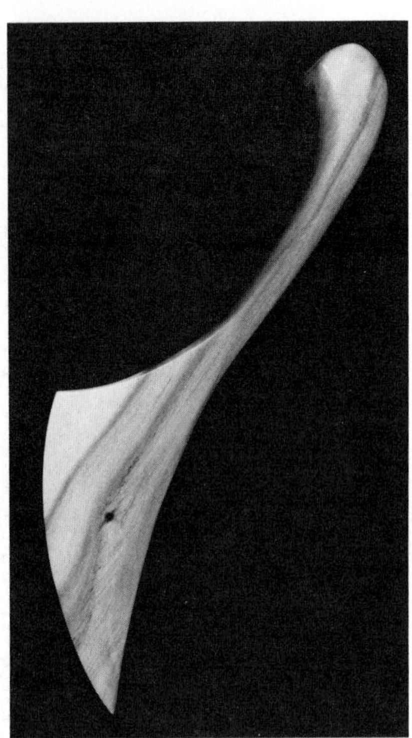

33

design is not a mysterious process. It is instead a series of choices similar to those we make every day. Designers approach the choices in a variety of ways. A weaver sees a skein of beautiful fiber and envisions a design to make the most of the texture and color. At another time the same weaver may want to create a runner for a table in a specific room and will set about finding appropriate fibers to complement the setting. An interesting block of wood has inspired many an artist to find a use that would exploit the grain (Fig. 33), whereas a commission for a chest or wall panel will necessitate searching for the proper wood to fulfill the purpose. Design evolves in many ways.

Scientists and engineers pursue results through orderly processes, usually based on mathematics. Art is considered to be more intuitive in nature, yet the process of design follows orderly procedures not unlike those used in the sciences. In either case, the development of a solution is fundamentally a matter of *problem solving.*

Expert problem solvers in all fields appear to work through certain mental stages. These stages, the steps in any creative work, could be identified as *definition, creativity, analysis, production,* and *clarification.* The stages do not necessarily occur in a fixed sequence but are named primarily for the purpose of identifying a mental attitude at a specific point in the development of a work.

There are many ways of approaching the *definition* of a problem. Some people use diagrams and sketches, laying out aspects of the problem in visual symbols. In designing the teapot mentioned already, for instance, one might sketch the essential elements simply as diagrams of what is involved. Next, one would visualize the working process—the finished object in use and the demands that would be made upon it. These could be set down in a few phrases beside the sketches. A methodical person might jot down the word "Given" and list the essential needs, then the word "Find" with the solutions to be worked out listed under it. As a starting point, the definition of the problem can be a reassuring step, helping the solver to be emotionally calm, confident, and creative. Two interior designers make statements that can help us to understand what is involved here. Tonny Foy says: "The kind of contemporary design I do is changing the function of space . . . rearranging rooms to suit the rhythms of a person's life."[1] Designer Jay Spectre states: "Most of my interiors seem to work best at night, because they are apartments in the city and the residents are usually out most of the day."[2] Each of these designers has arrived at a basic definition of his work in general. From this point, each commission can be approached with a specific definition of the individual problem.

Creativity describes the stage at which the imagination soars. Some designers fantasize to the extreme, pushing originality beyond the obvious solutions to discover surprising results. The construction in Figure 34 is an excellent example. What might have begun as a wall hanging evolved through imaginative use of materials and forms into a unique work, one that did not simply decorate a wall but formed a dynamic wall in itself.

Analysis is the direct opposite. It means applying preset rules of judgment and taking account of constraints of time, economy, and purpose. Analysis employs logic, integrity, and the consideration of potential problems. If some aspect of the project appears to be an insurmountable

33
Tony Howard. *Spreader.* 1983. Madrona, 11¼ × 2¼" (28.58 × 5.72 cm).

34
Patricia Campbell.
Constructed Light Wall II. 1979.
Shellacked fabric, paper, cord, fabricated; 96 × 78 × 18" (2.44 × 1.98 × .46 m).
Collection of the artist.

35
Poster for Guggenheim Museum in New York.
Malcolm Grear Designers.

[1]Paige Rense, "People Are the Issue," *Architectural Digest,* May 1981, p. 24.

[2]Paige Rense, "People Are the Issue," *Architectural Digest,* September 1980, p. 24.

34

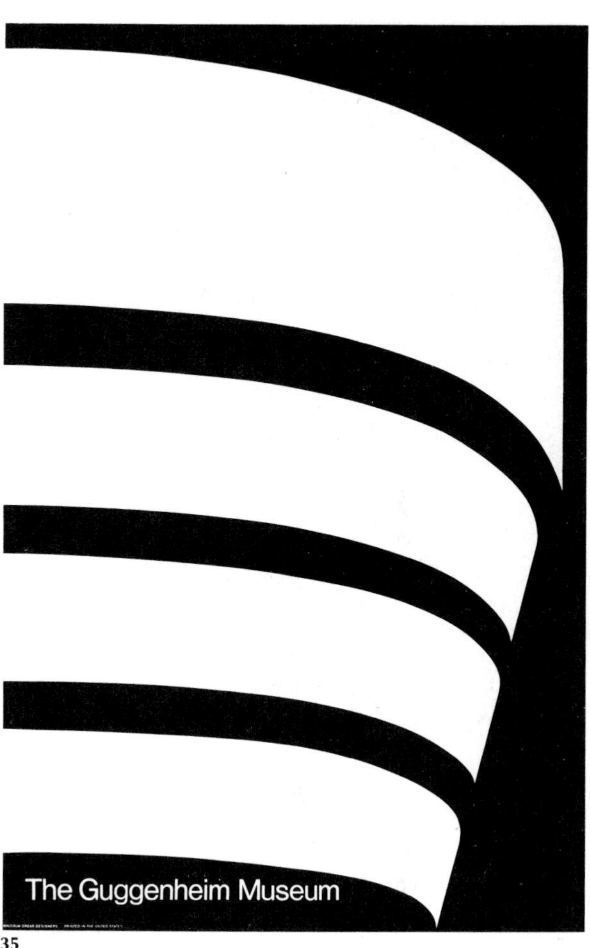

35

problem, it helps to isolate it. When dissected and viewed from different angles, obstacles sometimes disappear; if they don't, it is at the analytical stage that the necessary adjustments can be made.

Production of a work is not simply the carrying out of decisions made through definition and analysis. Throughout the actual construction, the designer must remain flexible in order to take advantage of unexpected implications in the material or in the evolving form. It is the degree of imagination with which the necessary choices are made that determines the ultimate character of a work.

In the poster in Figure 35 the designer was working with a flat rectangle in which a circular form was to be displayed. The problem was defined as one of communication, reaching the public with a reminder that the museum was there. Basic decisions concerned scale and placement. Numerous choices were possible. A medium-size depiction of the museum would have carried the message. The type could have been superimposed upon the image or placed at the top of the rectangle. The outstanding characteristic of the building, its dramatic spiral form, was chosen as the keynote of the design. Its monumental aspect was accentuated by the use of seven simple rectangles, slightly curved, diminishing in size, and alternating in light and dark. Through them, the spiral effect directs the eye to the startlingly simple block print at the bottom. Simplicity carries a potent impact.

36

The design process is a continuous unfolding in which each step determines those that follow, culminating in *clarification.* Regardless of the designer's methods, there comes a moment when the work is done, and the effort to appraise it must be made. Occasionally, the designer is elated with the results. Sometimes, looking at one's finished work is a disappointment. This is the stage at which an artist or designer grows, becoming critic and objective appraiser of an intensely personal effort. The person who can be objective enough to analyze the strengths and weaknesses of a particular piece will strive onward in a process of continuing improvement. This is the approach of the professional designer.

Integrity of Design

The quality that makes a design a unique expression of its time and of its creator can be described as *integrity.* Stemming from the Latin *integritas,* the word *integrity* has as one of its meanings the quality or state of being whole. In design, this means a unity in the artist's conception that makes a design a personal and original statement. There are several areas in which integrity contributes to the effectiveness of a design.

Before any design can be attempted, the designer should be aware of what *materials* are available and should be familiar with their advantages and limitations. The architect must know which materials are strong in compression (when pressed under weight) and which have more strength in tension (when stretched). The sculptor should understand which materials are capable of assuming certain forms, which will endure the longest, and how they will behave when exposed to weather. Painters will be better able to achieve effects they are seeking if they are familiar with the various painting media available. They must also be aware of a medium's potential for endurance. A painting whose surface cracks or flakes after a few months of hanging on a wall does not have integrity.

36
Folding telephone by Technidyne. 1982.

37
Lynda Benglis. *Adhesive Products.* 1971.
Nine individual configurations of black pigmented polyurethane,
13′6″ × 80′ × 15′ (4.11 × 24.38 × 4.6 m).
Walker Art Center, Minneapolis.

Materials should be used for their own qualities and for the purposes to which they are best suited. Industrial design today relies heavily on the materials that are especially of our own age—metal, plastic, and glass. In keeping with the qualities of these smooth, sleek materials, design tends to be clean and hard-edged, with a minimum of superficial ornament (Fig. 36). Forms are likely to express the function of an object, with the material implying efficiency, a "no-nonsense" approach.

In the first uses of plastics, manufacturers imitated familiar surfaces with vinyl or melamine, advertising the advantages of increased durability and ease of upkeep. Americans walk on vinyl floors patterned to imitate the ceramic tile of Europe and set their hot kettles on counters topped with melamine grained to look like wood or leather. The intrinsic qualities of the original materials are totally lost in imitation—the earthy quality of tile, the warmth and aroma of wood, the pliancy and fragrance of leather. Furthermore, in such imitations, designers miss the opportunity to create new designs appropriate to plastic. The unique qualities of plastic have been exploited by Linda Benglis in her *Adhesive Products,* shown in Figure 37. With no attempt at practical application, she has simply shown polyurethane as a flexible, flowing substance quite unlike any of the materials with which artists have worked in the past. Her nine imaginative configurations, with their fantastic organic quality, are an eloquent expression of integrity in the use of material.

During much of the twentieth century, the idea of *integrity in form* has been summed up in the phrase "form follows function." Emerging from the writings of the nineteenth-century American sculptor Horatio Greenough, this phrase is generally attributed, however, to the American architect Louis Sullivan. The concept has long been associated with the Bauhaus, a school of design founded in Weimar, Germany, in 1919. Among the major aims of the Bauhaus program was the development of designs suitable for machine production. Its faculty and staff concentrated on architecture, textiles, furniture, and household items, paring them down to essential form so they would become a direct indication of the function

37

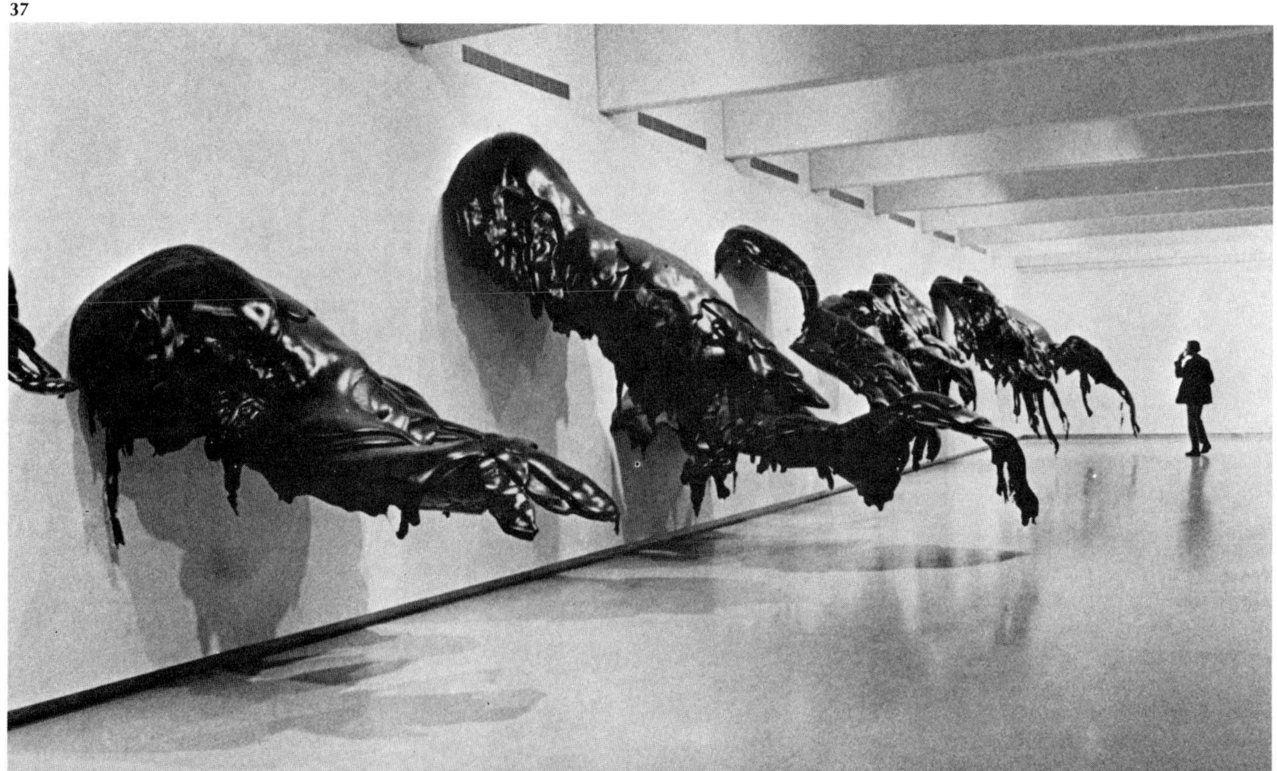

38

39

38
Marcel Breuer. *Armchair.* 1925. Chrome-plated steel tube and canvas, height 28″ (71 cm). Mfr.: Gebruder Thonet A. G., Germany. Museum of Modern Art, New York (gift of Herbert Bayer).

39
Gad-dam stilt tree house, Luzon Island, Philippines.

40
Stephen A. Foley. Spinning wheel. Black walnut, lignum vitae, with brass and steel hardware; 35¼ × 17 × 24″ (89 × 43 × 61 cm). Renwick Gallery of the National Collection of Fine Arts, Smithsonian Institution, Washington, D.C.

41
Salt basket from the Kagoshima Prefecture. Kyushu, Japan. Woven bamboo and vine. From *How to Wrap Five More Eggs* by Hideyuki Oka.

they were intended to fill (Fig. 38). Each design was to be expressive of its material and of the machine process that made it. A chair such as the one in Figure 38 must have seemed remarkable to the 1920s consumer accustomed to heavily carved oak and mahogany furnishings. The fact that it still looks "modern" today testifies to its purity of design.

Design in nature adheres rigidly to the principle of form following function in the nests of birds made from materials that blend with their surroundings, thus offering protection against predators. Beavers build their lodges from sticks and small logs under water, making it possible for them to swim in and out and still be protected. Examples are limitless.

Along the same line, but much more elaborate, are the tree houses in the Philippines (Fig. 39), which have been designed to cope with a hostile climate. Deep in the jungle, in an area plagued by high humidity, floods, insects, and dangerous animals, the tree house avoids all by its position 40 feet above the ground. This elevation also permits cooling breezes to flow under the house. A steeply pitched roof shuns the torrential rains that are common to this area, while minimum walls give the greatest possible ventilation. Truly, function is satisfied in the form of this ingenious design.

Although form for function is most obvious in such elemental designs as shelters, it can be equally important in more complicated ones, involving the performance of an active task. The spinning wheel is designed for the purpose of twisting animal, vegetable, or synthetic fibers to form threads that can be used for weaving, knitting, or sewing. For centuries, the only method of doing this was by twisting the fibers to be spun in one hand while spinning with the other. The spinning wheel emerged in the eighteenth century, using the foot pedal and spindles that transformed spinning into a smooth operation that could be accomplished by sitting at a bulky

40

41

three-legged piece of equipment. Stephen Foley has designed a contemporary version (Fig. 40) in which a delicately balanced form conserves space, and flowing lines seem a part of the act of spinning. The wheel and spindles, both circular, are the focal point, as always, but the form of the structure holding them is also curved, even where supports meet at right angles. The design and function become one.

A charming example of integrity of form can be seen in the Japanese salt basket in Figure 41. Basket weaving is an ancient craft that is still used by the Japanese for packaging. Few consumers would deny that such a package has considerably more appeal than the plastic bubble wrap so common in Western countries. The concept of a cone shape for a salt basket has a special integrity. Although it is easy to carry, this basket would not hold many apples or potatoes, for instance, and the bottom of the basket at the point of the cone would be wasted space with such cargo. Salt, however, can seep into every part of the cone, settling so the burden of weight is at the bottom; this allows for stability and total use of space. Such designs have no problems with integrity. Unhampered by distracting considerations, they provide for a need in the most direct and honest terms.

It is obvious from this discussion that, in general, integrity of form leads to integrity of *function.* The two are so interdependent that it is impossible to make a clear-cut separation between them even for purposes of discussion. Many of the irritations of modern life stem from objects lacking integrity of function. Furniture with drawers that do not run smoothly, automobiles that require a contortionist's skill to manipulate the seat belts, umbrellas that reverse under the slightest breeze—all of these are commonplace nuisances. We cannot help noting, however, that a problem with function usually stems from some fault in the form.

42

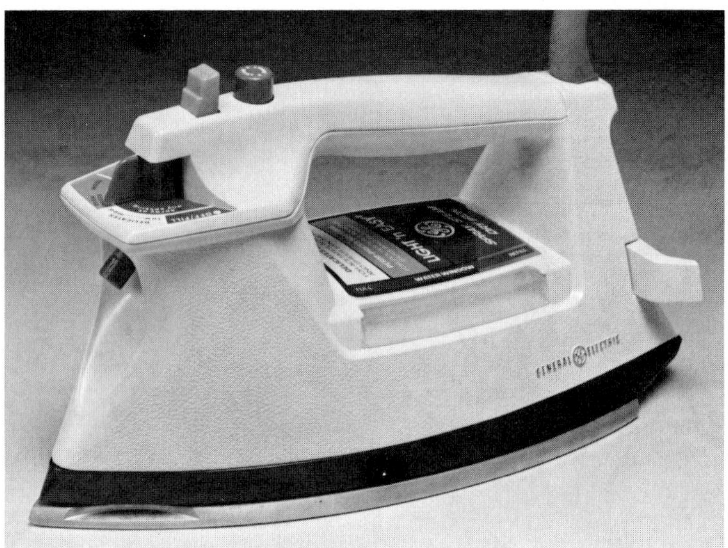

43

42
Flatiron. 19th century.

43
Modern electric iron.
General Electric Company.

44
Suzuki GS1100ESD. 1983.

Integrity of design plays a special role when the function of an object evolves from a prototype. When electric irons were first introduced, their design remained close to the heavy flatirons that had to be heated on top of a cast iron stove (Fig. 42). It was many years before manufacturers realized that weight was no longer a factor in the effectiveness of an iron. The iron in Figure 43 is lightweight and streamlined, yet it performs its function with far less effort than its predecessor. Similar comparisons can be made with vacuum cleaners and washing machines. No longer is it necessary to bear down on a heavy machine in order to suck soil from a carpet, or to scrub violently on a corrugated metal board to keep a family in clean clothing.

The Bauhaus concept of form following function was a reaction to many centuries of ornate decoration in architecture. The name comes from the German words for *construction* and *house* and originated when Walter Gropius constructed school classrooms and dormitories in a revolutionary style of unadorned steel, concrete, and glass. More than half a century later, we are swinging back to a less austere concept of design. The movement known as Post-Modernism is bringing a return to decorative, imaginative, and emotional elements in architecture, as well as in painting (see Chapters 16 and 25), realizing that sometimes there is legitimate function in simply pleasing the eye.

Some of the best designs we see today are found in products that are uniquely of our own time, especially in the fields of communication, transportation, and sports. When a designer undertakes to create something that has never existed before, the principal concern must be with integrity of function, since there are no preconceived ideas of how such an object should look. With widespread usage the function remains important, but adjustments to weight, speed, and appearance follow quickly. We see this in radios, stereo components, television sets, and motorbikes (Fig. 44), to cite only a few examples.

No discussion of integrity in design could be complete without mention of the integrity of the designer as a person concerned with the earth and the well-being of the people who live upon it, both now and in the future. In recent years we have become aware of countless designed objects that are dangerous, even life-threatening. Some are the result of using dangerous materials, such as the spray cans that endanger the quality of the air we breathe, buildings containing asbestos that can cause a form of cancer, synthetic materials used in home furnishings that can bring illness to those living with them. Others are faulty in form, such as buildings that collapse, bridges that go down in storms, airplanes that crash from a malfunction, and automobiles that cause fatal accidents because of errors in construction. Thus designers have a strong responsibility for knowledge of materials and of construction principles and for a sincere concern for all people who might in any way be affected by their design. For those who are not professional designers, it is vital to be aware of materials and forms, and particularly to document unsatisfactory experiences as guidance for those responsible for designing the world in which we live.

Design is a fundamental part of environment and of living. Now that we understand its relationship to each of us as designers through selection and as consumers of designed products, it will be well to approach the methods by which designs are created.

As mentioned earlier (p. 9), design is accomplished by the use of certain *elements,* which comprise the materials with which a designer or an artist works. These elements are combined according to certain *principles.* Together the elements and principles form an aesthetic framework that is essential to any design and to any work of art, be it visual, literary, or musical. We will explore these elements and principles as they apply to visual works of art and design; first the elements—line, space, shape and mass, texture and pattern, and color. Then we will consider the ways in which these elements are combined into a design through the use of the principles of unity, variety, balance, emphasis, rhythm, proportion, and scale. All of the elements and principles interact and many are interdependent, according to their function in an individual work. This interaction forms a fascinating study, which will occupy us for the next eight chapters.

44

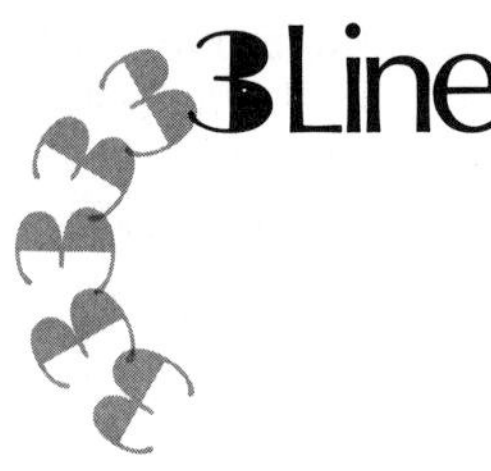

3 Line

The beginning of any drawing is a *point.* This is true whether it is a student's drawing, the working drawing of a professional designer, or a drawing that will ultimately become a work of art. A point is placed upon a piece of paper by a drawing tool, and the paper is no longer the same. Where that point goes can be one of the most important decisions involved in the entire work, for it is in the extension of the point, and in the determination of the direction of that extension, that *line* develops, and line is the most fundamental element of design.

Since civilization began, people have been fascinated by lines, using them to decorate primitive tools or the walls of caves. Few people can resist the urge to draw with a stick in wet sand, to doodle with a pen on paper, or to scratch with a piece of charcoal. Children draw lines on the sidewalk and invent games around them. It is almost as though it were a basic human need to draw a line, to leave one's mark.

We have mentioned lines drawn on a sheet of paper or on a canvas, but there are many kinds of lines, some created by human hands, some occurring naturally, even some that actually do not exist at all except as a consequence of human perception—a horizon line, for instance.

As an element of design, line cannot be discussed without reference to shape and space. The presence of one of these elements nearly always implies that the other two are involved. For example, a line necessarily carves out areas of space on either side of it (Fig. 45). At the same time, it is the *closure* of line that creates a shape. We cannot have shape without *edges* created by line, or without the space from which the line carves the shape. Because we recognize most things by their shapes, the lines that function as edges become particularly important. We are aware of the space within a building only because it has been demarcated by the presence of walls and a roof, in other words by the structural edges where two planes meet.

Each of these elements—line, shape, and space—is an important part of any design. Each will be discussed in a separate chapter. In this chapter we will look at the many roles line has in the visual world and at the different kinds of lines, to understand fully the possibilities of their use in the creation of designs.

Line in Nature

Lines fill every part of our world, from the dramatic line of lightning flashing across the sky to the filaments of an airborne seed (Fig. 46), from the soaring vertical lines of skyscrapers to the lines in a drawing or a painting. The natural world abounds in lines of every description.

One of the most basic natural lines is that of the human body. In a stark photograph of the Alwin Nikolais dance company (Fig. 47) our attention is directed to the line of the body in motion, extended and dramatized by lines surrounding it to create new shapes contingent upon the position of the body at any given moment. As each body moves, its surrounding lines and shapes change constantly. This use of lines to create a special choreographic effect emphasizes what every stage director or drill master knows—that the interplay of bodily lines in groups or masses can be of striking impact.

The word *line* can apply to an overall feeling or essential quality. The lines of a figure depend not only on its proportions but on the personality of

45
Aiko Miyawaki. *A Moment of Movement.* (*Utsurohi.*) 1980. Stainless steel wire; 12′10″ × 9′6″ × 13⅔″ (3.9 × 3 × 4.2 m). Collection Ichinomiya City, Aichi Prefecture, Japan.

46
David Cavagnaro. *Thistle Seed against the Sun. San Geronimo Valley, California.* Photograph.

47
The Nikolais Dance Theatre performing *Sanctum,* with Amy Broussard, Phyllis Lamhut, and Murray Louis.

the individual within. For instance, we have a graceful figure, a pompous figure, an athletic figure, and so on. Similarly, we speak of the majestic lines of a ship, the flowing lines of a gown, the undulating line of hills. The unique quality of an entity is expressed by the kind of *line* it presents to the human eye.

Frequently this use of line extends into symbolism. As we associate the lines of the body with different types of personality, so we may see the "sleek" lines of an aircraft not only as describing its basic form but also as hinting at its potential speed, its power, and its reflection of space-age technology.

45

46

47

48

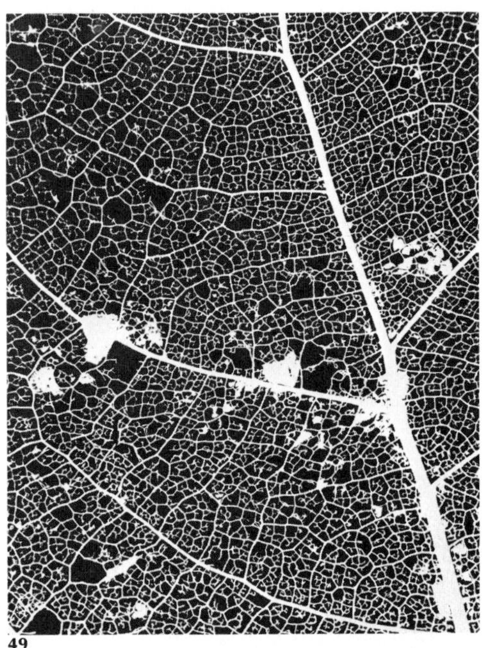
49

Nature presents an infinite variety of lines. Ripples on a pond create lines, as do grasses in a field, a pattern of pebbles on a beach, or a column of ants marching to their nest. The branches of bare trees trace magnificent patterns against a winter sky (Fig. 48), and the fallen leaf attacked by parasites exposes its own pattern of linear beauty (Fig. 49). The lines in Figure 50 change with the winds, varying from knife-edged outlines to smooth ripples extending in both directions. The curving lines of dunes terminate the long vertical line, and the strong horizontal background line is formed by mountains in the distance. If we study the world around us, we will find a wealth of natural lineal configurations.

Abstract Lines

No line of itself is abstract. A drawn line is essentially a symbol, as lines in nature are formed by human perception. In the third century B.C. Euclid used lines to develop the science of geometry, connecting points to develop theorems. Such lines are still used in engineering to calculate distances and elevations. We also use lines to plot the projected course of a spaceship. We use the term *abstract* for such lines because they are not actually visible until they are projected as symbols of knowledge we are attempting to determine or explain.

The term *abstract* may also be applied to lines that are visible only momentarily, such as those created in the water by the wake of a ship or in the sky by the jet trail that streaks behind a plane and then vanishes. The modern camera has provided us with the means of giving lasting form to abstract lines created by motion and energy. The striking linear design in Plate 2 (p. 21) was created by fighter planes in night combat over Vietnam, which the photographer caught in a long exposure.

48
David Cavagnaro. *Valley Oak,* Quercus lobata, *in a Winter Morning Ground Fog, near El Verano, California.* Photograph.

49
Wolf Strache. *Leaf Skeleton of Black Poplar.* 1956. Photograph.

50
Charles Moore. *Death Valley.* 1970. Photograph.

51
Facsimile of autograph manuscript of Ludwig van Beethoven's *Missa Solemnis,* page 25. Published by Hans Schneider (Tutzing).

Line as Symbol

A line becomes a *symbol* when a specific meaning is attached to it. As a symbol, it may delineate a shape that has meaning to the viewer, or it may express the reaction of the artist to the shapes, forms, and rhythms that he or she sees. Many lines do both. When two or more people agree about the meaning, the symbol can serve as a method of communication.

Sometimes the shortest lines have the most comprehensive symbolism. The lines that form letters and numbers can, in combination, represent all the knowledge that humanity has ever recorded. The symbolism of line encompasses not only all the alphabets of the world but mathematical formulas and musical scores as well (Fig. 51). Without such symbols we could not efficiently store or transmit knowledge.

50

51

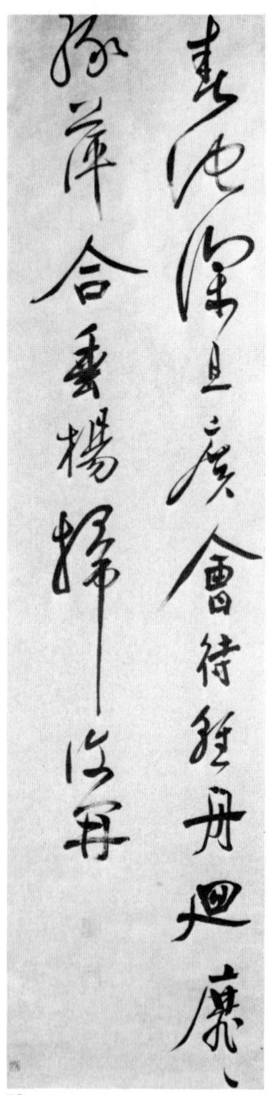

52

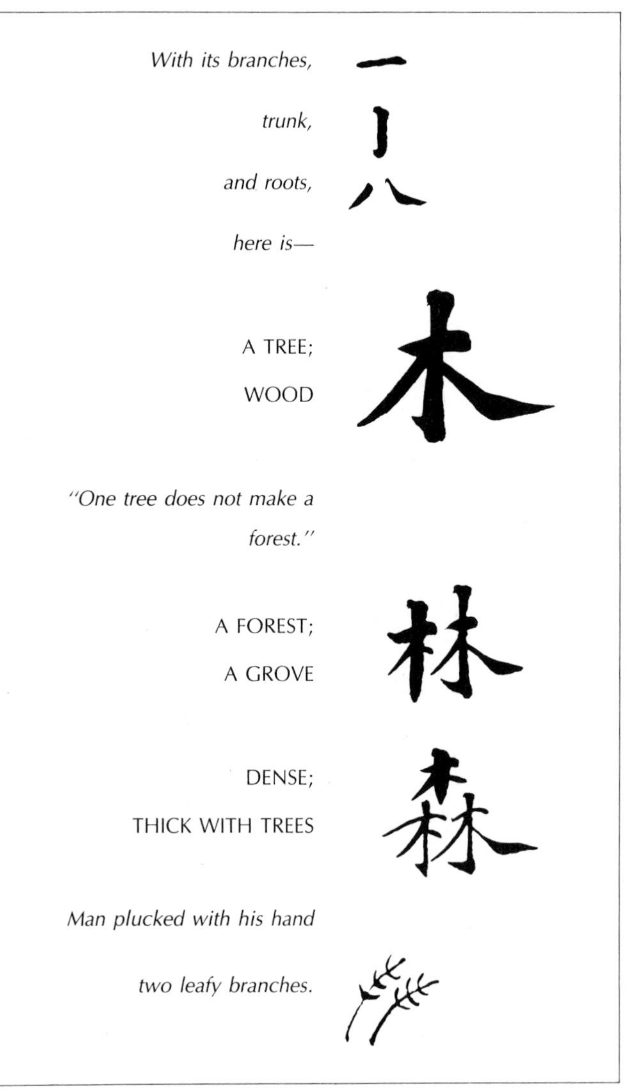

With its branches,
trunk,
and roots,
here is—
A TREE;
WOOD
木
"One tree does not make a forest."
A FOREST;
A GROVE
林
DENSE;
THICK WITH TREES
森
Man plucked with his hand
two leafy branches.

53

52
Hai Jui (Chinese, 1514–87).
Hanging scroll, India ink on paper;
6′10⅞″ × 1′8″ (2.11 × .5 m).
Collection John M. Crawford, Jr., New York.

53
Evolution of Chinese written characters from symbolic representations of actual objects.

54
Colin Cole, age 5.
Amy by the Gumball Machine at King Soopers.
Felt-tip pen drawing.

55
Lewis Knauss. *Rain on the Mediterranean.*
1981. Woven pile, knotted and tied;
hemp twine, linen, paint; 36 × 46″
(.92 × 1.17 m). Collection of the artist.

Nearly all civilizations have practiced a form of *calligraphy* (from the Greek for "beautiful writing"). Some of the most decorative calligraphy exists in the highly stylized brushstrokes of Oriental characters (Fig. 52). The Chinese or Japanese calligrapher is considered a master artist, who may spend years—even decades—perfecting the technique. Each element of the craft is ritualized, including the way the brush is held, the relationship of the hand to the paper, the preparation of the ink, and especially the movement of the brush's tip onto the paper and away from it.

The letters in the Roman alphabet that we use can be considered arbitrary symbols, for they are assigned to particular sounds in spoken language but have no visual meaning of their own. This is not true, however, of many forms of Oriental writing, which are *ideographic.* This means that the characters are abstracted images of what they represent; for example, the character that stands for "tree" is based on the form of a tree (Fig. 53).

Children are natural users of symbols. They will cover a sheet of paper with lines undecipherable to the adult eye and be able to explain each one. An entire experience can be translated into line (Fig. 54).

Line used as symbol becomes a powerful tool for the designer, for it permits the communication of abstract ideas or of immensely complicated associations with just a few lines or shapes. The fiberwork in Figure 55 depends on its linear quality for both symbolism and visual impact. A linear design without symbolism can be visually pleasing, but a design that makes use of symbols, whether they are personal, general, or universal, makes a much stronger impression on the viewer.

54

55

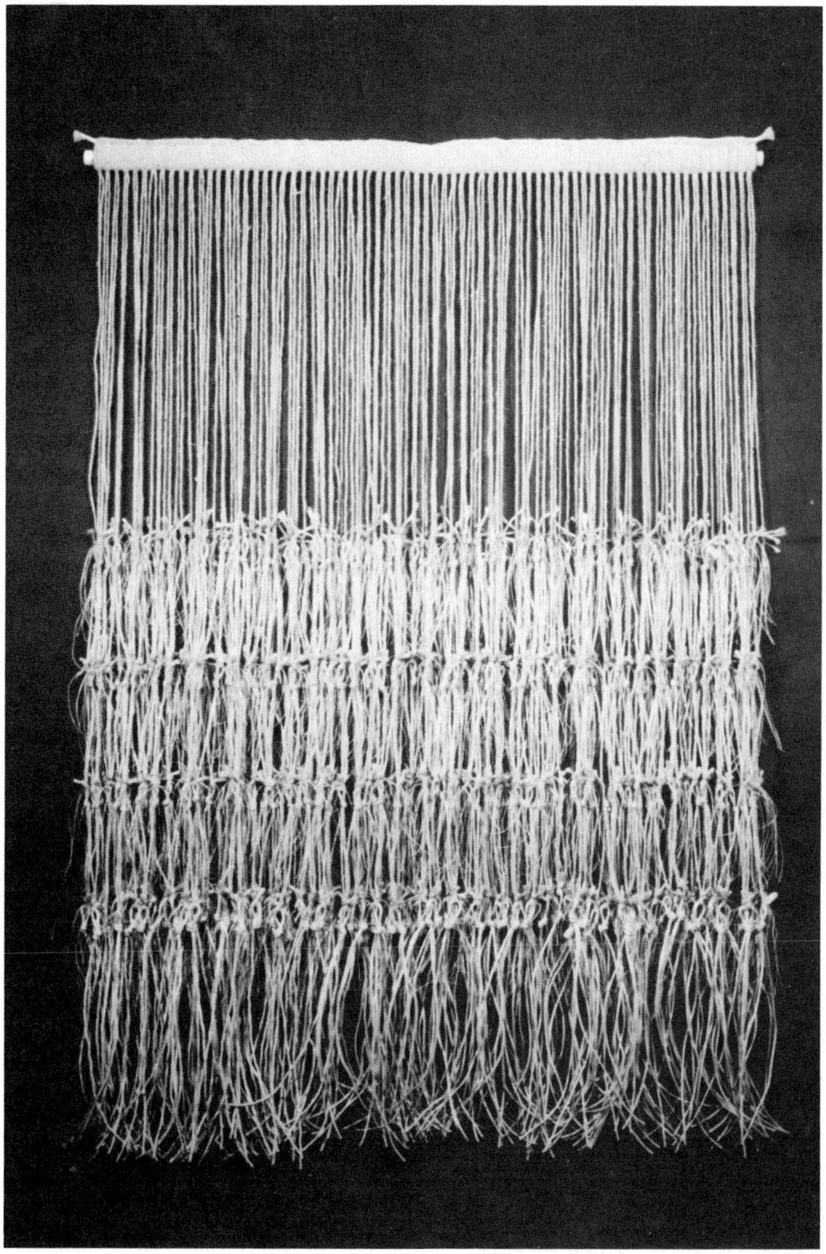

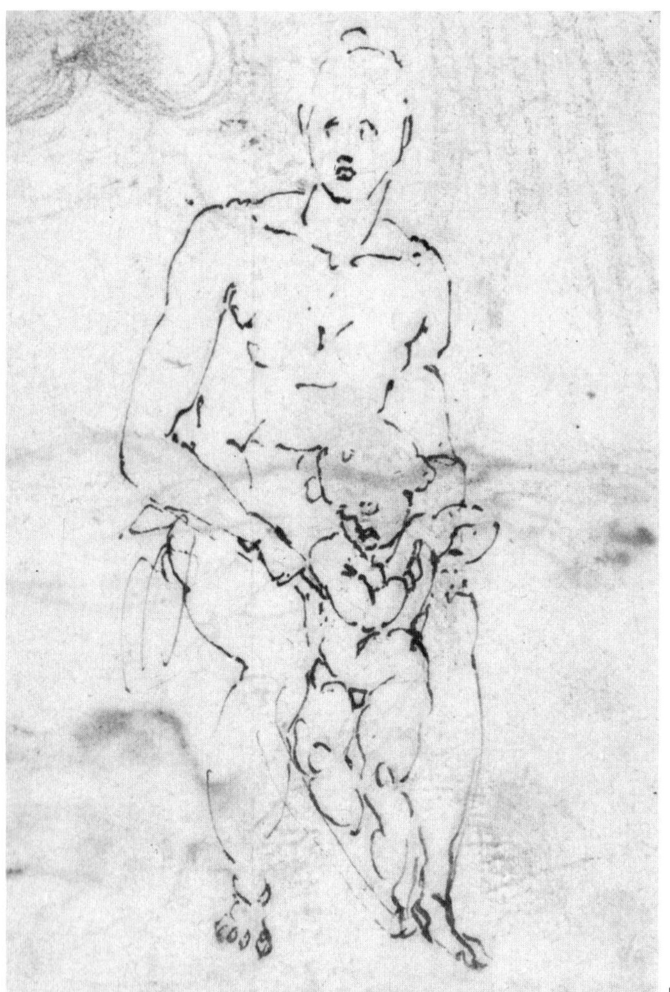

56

57

Line as Contour and Modeling

56
Michelangelo. Sketch for the *Madonna of Bruges* (detail). c. 1503. Pen and ink, 12½ × 11″ (31.5 × 27.8 cm). British Museum, London.

57
Pavel Tchelitchew. *Africa.* 1932. Black india ink and pen on white paper; 10½ × 8¼″ (26.7 × 20.9 cm). The Museum of Modern Art, New York. John S. Newberry Collection.

58
Alberto Giacometti. *Chariot.* 1950. Bronze, 4′9″ × 2′2″ × 2′4⅛″ (1.45 × .66 × .71 m). Museum of Modern Art, New York (purchase).

A contour line is a line that traces outline or overall shape. Existing on a two-dimensional surface, it does no more than carve that surface into two-dimensional shapes. In the hands of a skilled artist, however, a contour line can give a distinct sense of three-dimensional volume. The sketch in Figure 56 is a sketch that Michelangelo did while planning a sculpture to be executed in stone. It is interesting to note that the broken line is just as effective as a continuous one would be in delineating the forms of the figures, and at the same time, it seems to convey by its staccato character the action of the chisel as it will gouge into the stone.

The artist who wishes to convey more specifically the details of surface, feature, or different planes may use a *modeled line.* Such a line can be shaded, perhaps with the side of a pencil or a smudge of charcoal, or there may be closely spaced parallel lines (hatchings) or intersecting parallel hatchings (cross-hatchings) to mold the two-dimensional surface into a variety of planes and hollows (Fig. 57).

Line as Form

Sometimes line does not merely convey form but actually *is* form. We see this most readily in three-dimensional works such as sculpture or constructions, where wires and fibers are the means of building form. Alberto Giacometti's *Chariot* (Fig. 58) is really nothing more than an assembly of lines, in this case drawn in bronze. The subject matter is obvious, nevertheless, even the simplified figure of the charioteer.

58

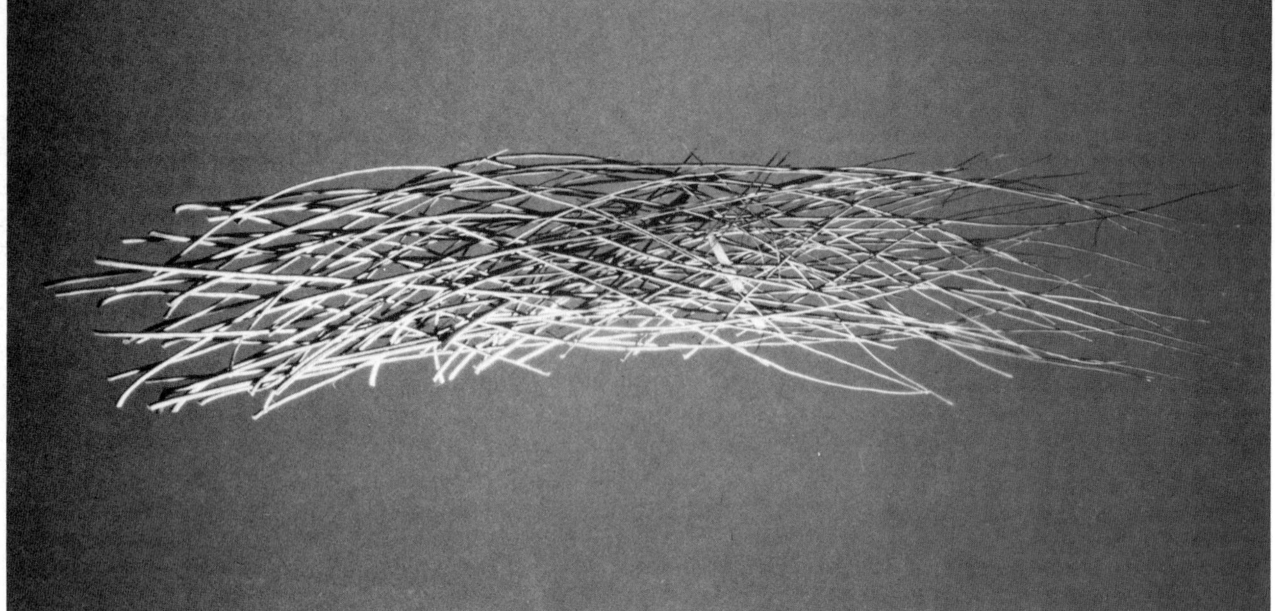
59

Concerned with the rhythms of the natural environment and the universal life force, Carol Shaw-Sutton has constructed a series of "space drawings," using the sucker shoots of willow and wild plum. These shoots build a linear construction composed of layers suggesting depths and ripples, with which she intersperses linen threads and washes of color. In *Dusk River Crossing* she seeks to express a personal experience by means of an intricate construction of lines (Fig. 59).

Light is an important tool in any area of design. Otto Piene uses it in polyethylene tubing for his *Manned Helium Sculpture* in Figure 60. The movement of the lines, with their highlights and gradations of color and shadow, becomes a kind of symbolic choreography in which the human eye continues the movement, arousing in the viewer a wealth of personal associations.

In Steven Weiss' table in Figure 61 the lines are actually the perimeters of sheets of Plexiglas cut in such a way that their edges catch the light. In a sense this work could be seen as an example of lines that do not actually exist, yet the lines are like the forms in Michelangelo's sculpture (Fig. 13) in that they are within the material, waiting for the imaginative artist to release them. Under proper lighting conditions, everything disappears except the tabletop and the compositions of lines supporting it, producing the dramatic illusion of a form that is purely linear.

59
Carol Shaw-Sutton. *Dusk River Crossing.* 1981. Fruitwood, linen, paint; 20 × 94 × 4″ (50.8 × 238.76 × 10.16 cm). Collection of Gary Austin.

60
Otto Piene. *Manned Helium Sculpture Stage 1* from *Citything Sky Ballet.* 1970. Helium-filled polyethylene tubing. Courtesy the artist.

61
Steven Weiss. "Infinity" table. Plexiglass.

62
Crystal glassware in the "twist" pattern, designed by Michael Boehm for Rosenthal Studio-Linie. 1973.

Line as Pattern or Texture

When lines are drawn close together or when similar lines are repeated in a composition, they may create a visual pattern or texture. We noted the use of closely placed lines to achieve modeling in the head in Figure 57.

Lines as decorative design are used in many different media. In a set of glasses designed by Michael Boehm (Fig. 62), a pattern of thin lines swirls upward in a diagonal movement from the base of each glass to the rim. The delicate linear design helps to emphasize the swell of the forms. The lines formed by a potter's fingers in throwing a clay pot provide the same kind of decorative design, as do the lines of a woodcarver's chisel.

60

61

62

63

Line as Direction and Emphasis

In any design, line can perform the important function of leading the eye and creating emphasis. Figures 63 and 64 show opposite aspects of the way in which line can lead the eye. In the painting by Al Held (Fig. 63), lines and forms are carried to the edge of the canvas and then chopped off abruptly so that the viewer's eye is continually pulled *out* of the painting and back *in* again. The impression is of an infinitely expanding universe. By contrast, the lines in Amédée Ozenfant's *Fugue* (Fig. 64) all curve inward and are contained by a basically rectangular format. Their swelling and tapering widths encourage us to follow them around in their rhythmic paths throughout the drawing. There is nothing static about this work; the lines keep our eyes moving continually. While it is obvious that the work depicts a collection of distinctive shapes, the lines become so dominant that the rhythm created by the flowing and interaction of the shapes seems far more important than the shapes themselves.

Line plays an important part in any *composition.* We use the term to mean the total structure or organization of any work of art or design, whether it is a drawing, a pot, or a building. In the painting in Figure 65, line is used to awaken an emotional response in the viewer. The entire composition seems in repose—the horizontal lines of clouds, the slightly swelling ground, the distant horizon. Even the tiny vertical accents of trees, steeples, and human figures are located in such a way that two horizontal lines could be drawn across their tops. The strong contrast in darks and lights keeps the work from being monotonous and at the same time provides a sense of distance. It is the lines of the work that give it the predominant feeling of early evening quiet. Here the element of time enters in. We do not devote a separate chapter to *time,* but it must be understood as an important component of any composition, for it is time that makes possible our awareness of the various aspects of the work and our ultimate emotional reaction to it.

63
Al Held. *Noah's Focus I.* 1970. Acrylic on canvas, 11′6″ × 2′1″ (3.51 × .64 m). Courtesy André Emmerich Gallery, New York.

64
Amédée Ozenfant. *Fugue.* 1925. Pencil, 18 × 22″ (45.72 × 55.88 cm). Museum of Modern Art, New York (gift of the artist).

65
Caspar David Friedrich. *The Evening Star* (Der Abendstern). c. 1825. Oil on canvas, 12½ × 17½″ (31.75 × 44.45 cm). Freies Deutsches Hochstift, Frankfurter Goethe-Museum.

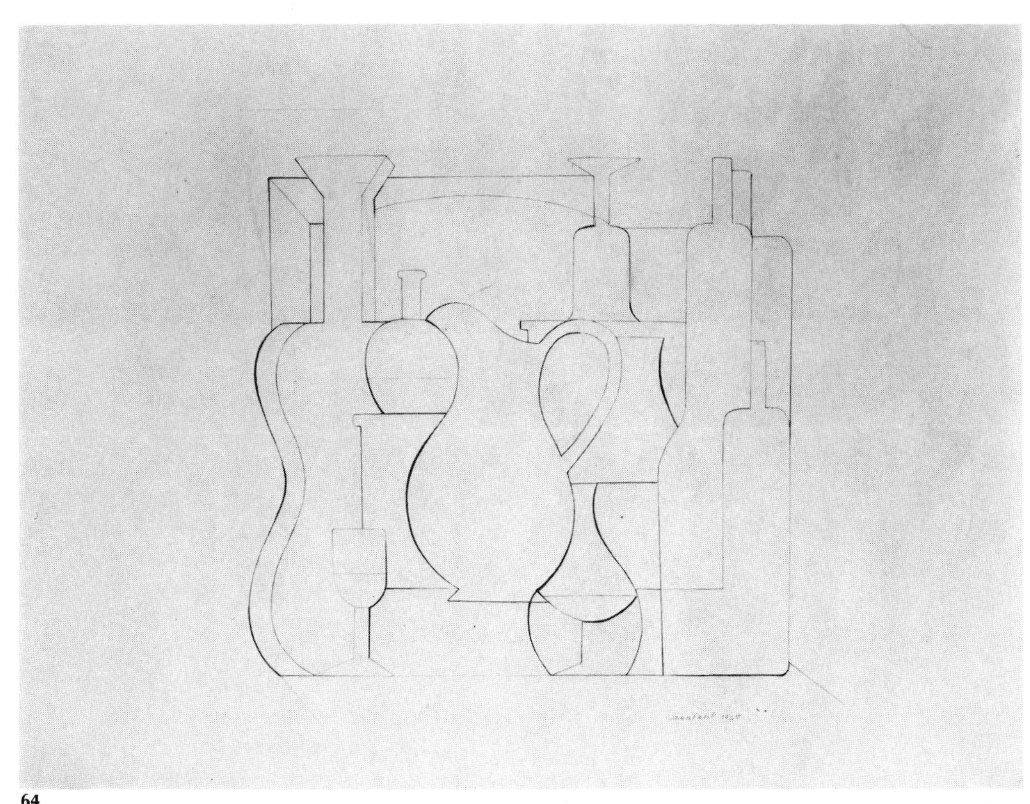

64

65

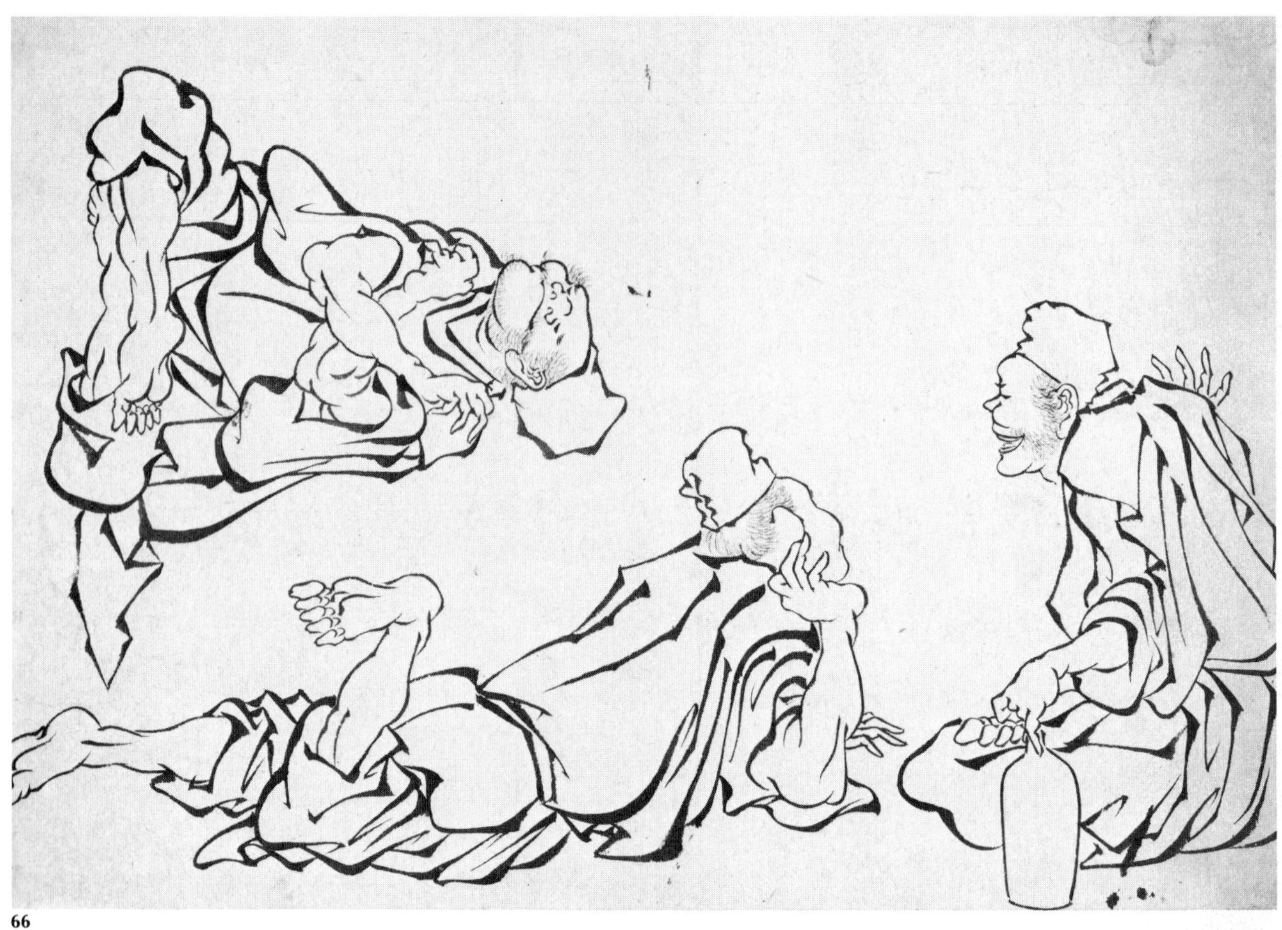

66

The Quality of Line

We have discussed a variety of lines—thin and thick, dark and light, straight and swirling. In the works by Held and Ozenfant (Figs. 63 and 64) the lines were deliberately varied to suggest contour, form, swelling, and shadow. This is what we mean by the *quality* of line.

One of the masters in the use of line was Katsushika Hokusai, a Japanese artist who lived in the late eighteenth and early nineteenth century. Known widely for his color woodcuts, Hokusai also produced an impressive group of drawings in which he used line in a dramatic manner reminiscent of the woodcut technique. In Figure 66, for example, his line, though it is always strong, varies in width from a fine line, which gives a humorous twist to a foot, to a broad, angular line, which depicts descriptively the fold of a garment. These folds and shadows delineate the figures within, transmitting, through the careless disarray of clothing, the state of utter relaxation.

Dramatic use of line is not limited to drawing. The painting by Bridget Riley in Figure 67 depends entirely upon the quality of line for its effect. The variations in width of line produce an undulating surface and a strong

66
Hokusai. *A Sake Bout.* Late 18th or early 19th century. Ink on paper, 10½ × 15" (26 × 38 cm). Freer Gallery of Art, Smithsonian Institution, Washington, D.C.

67
Bridget Riley. *Drift No. 2.* 1966. Acrylic on canvas, 7'7½" × 7'5½" (2.32 × 2.27 m). Albright-Knox Art Gallery, Buffalo (gift of Seymour H. Knox).

67

sense of form and movement. This is Op Art, relying for its effect upon optical illusions resulting from the exploitation of afterimages and retinal response. In this particular case, the illusions are created entirely by lines—light lines alternating with dark lines and with a shaded area at either edge. The quality of the lines creates a vibrant continuum, of which we seem to be seeing only a segment as it billows past us.

68

Vigorous, ragged, curving lines may imply terror or turbulent emotions in general, as in a drawing by Honoré Daumier (Fig. 68). For this work the artist has used line in a compelling manner to create a tremulous form that seems to be shrinking back in fear.

Another strong effect is communicated by Ronaldo de Juan's menacing drawing entitled *Gate # 6* (Fig. 69). The heavy charcoal lines at the center of the composition seem to loom threateningly, while the curving lines at the bottom suggest whiplash strokes.

In demonstrating the powerful use of line, we have used many examples of art rather than of design specifically. This will be true in our discussion of all the elements and principles, for, as we noted earlier, all works of art have a strong basis in design, and the impact of specific elements is sometimes particularly obvious in a drawing or painting. The importance of such examples is to emphasize the special quality of an element or principle of design, a quality that can be translated into specific designs once it is fully appreciated. The importance of line lies in its ability not only to convey shape but also, by its very quality, to express or arouse a mood, a strong emotion, or an impression.

68
Honoré Daumier. *Fright* (*L'Epouvante*). Charcoal over pencil on paper, 8¼ × 9⅜" (20.96 × 24.13 cm). Art Institute of Chicago (gift of Robert Allerton).

69
Ronaldo de Juan. *Gate #6*. 1976. Charcoal, 6'3" × 3'10" (1.9 × 1.16 m). Lerner-Heller Gallery, New York.

69

4 Shape and Mass

Shape is created by closed line. The three-dimensional extension of shape is called *mass.* The terms *volume* and *form* are synonymous with mass in common usage, but since we have already noted the meaning of form as a design term, we will use mass in our discussion of the three-dimensional aspect of shape.

We can see the difference between *shape* and *mass* by referring to geometry, which distinguishes the plane geometric figures (shapes) of square, circle, and triangle from the solid geometric figures (masses) of cube, sphere, and pyramid. Just as solid geometry is a more complicated system of mathematics than plane geometry, the designer may find greater difficulty in working with three-dimensional masses than with flat shapes. This is because the lines multiply, appearing in several planes, making more involved spaces.

Perception of Shape and Mass

In perception, shape and mass are closely related. When we look at the moon we actually *see* a flat circle against a dark sky, yet we *perceive* a round mass. The same could be said for an orange or a tennis ball. Psychologists have concluded that the brain plays a large part in shape perception, in other words, that there is a conceptual element involved. What this means is that the stimulus that acts upon the eye is broken up into discontinuous parts, which are rearranged by the brain into a pattern that can be recognized. There are various theories about how this recognition takes place. One is that the brain fits the stimulus material into templates of relatively simple shape, providing the new material with structural features that have a general kind of familiarity. It is believed that actual perception involves not unique shapes but a kind of pattern to which any given shape can be fitted.

A shape becomes a mass when the eye changes position, taking in more surfaces or aspects than were originally perceived (Fig. 70). When the image of an object changes, it is necessary to understand whether the change is in the object itself or in the context in which it is seen, or in both. In our discussion of mass we will explore the ways in which artists convey three-dimensional masses on a flat surface. First, however, we will consider the possibilities of shape as an element of design.

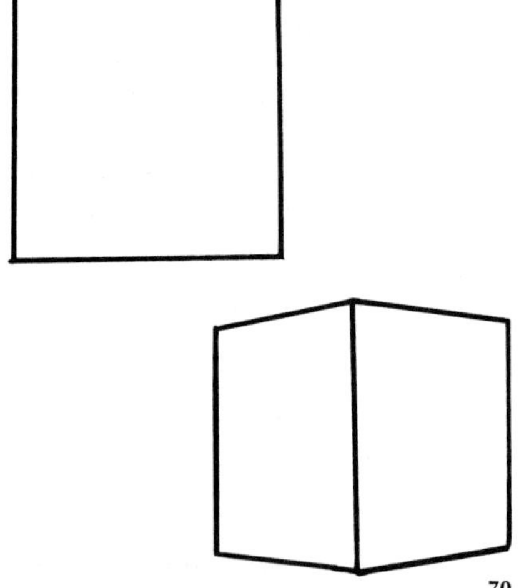

70

71

70
A square can become a cube when the viewpoint is changed.

71
Stonehenge. 1800–1400 B.C. Height of stones above ground 13′6″ (4.1 m). Salisbury Plain, Wiltshire, England.

72
Chambered nautilus (*Nautilus pompilius*) from Polynesia.

73
A microscopic view shows that cells from the cornea of an insect's eye are hexagonal.

Shape

Shapes can be divided into four broad categories: *geometric, natural, abstract,* and *nonobjective.* These are not rigid divisions but allow for some overlapping.

Geometric shapes dominate the constructed environment. They appear in buildings, bridges, furniture, and machines of all kinds. Basic *post-and-lintel construction,* which sets a horizontal crosspiece over two separated uprights to create a square shape, has been fundamental since prehistoric times. The solidity of the square has permitted the huge structures at Stonehenge to remain in position for 3500 years, despite the fact that they were erected by primitive means, with no mortar of any kind to hold them together (Fig. 71). Of course, in viewing Stonehenge in silhouette, we must realize that it is fundamentally mass, as is the case in nearly any construction. Though the stability of Stonehenge depended on the shape of the blocks of stone, its basic durability depended on their massiveness.

Industrial design depends heavily on geometric shapes, simply because they are so regular. Machines and shaping equipment can be easily adapted to these precise outlines. Besides this, many considerations of function and storage demand geometric shape. A record must be round to revolve on a turntable, but the record-album cover, being square, allows for convenient storage. Gears must be round, whether in automobiles or watches, since their function depends upon the ability to turn. We could give hundreds of such examples.

We often think of geometric shapes as having been invented by humans, but of course many geometric shapes exist in nature. We can find the square in mineral crystals, the triangle in certain leaf shapes, the circle developed to a spiral in a shell formation (Fig. 72). Microscopic views often reveal nearly perfect geometric shapes in unexpected places; Figure 73 shows row upon row of hexagons—complex geometric shapes—in an insect's eye.

72

73

74

74
Harijan patchwork quilt. Embroidered and pieced cotton, 6′9¼″ (2.06 m). From Kutch district of India. UCLA Museum of Cultural History. Gift of Mr. and Mrs. Richard B. Rogers.

75
Frank Stella. *Moultonville III.* 1965–66. Enamel on canvas, 10′4″ × 7′2″ (3.15 × 2.18 m). Nelson Gallery, Atkins Museum, Kansas City (gift of Friends of Art).

76
Japanese stencil used to decorate silk. c. 1680–1750, Tokugawa period. Slater Memorial Museum, Norwich Free Academy, Norwich, Conn., Vanderpoel Collection.

Designs from early periods of civilization or from remote areas of the world frequently have a predominantly geometric theme. American Indian designs on pottery, baskets, and rugs are almost always geometric symbols of natural forces. The quilt in Figure 74, composed entirely of squares and variations on the triangle, is from the dowry of a woman in Kutch, a region on the west coast of India.

Many twentieth-century artists have felt that geometric shapes and masses are appropriate expressions of a highly mechanized and technical civilization. Richard Anuszkiewicz executed a series of prints based on designs created from the rectangle. Although the elements are simple—concentric rectangles and straight lines—the results have a dynamic quality. In Plate 3 (p. 22) there is warmth and movement, the result of careful variation in the placement of the lines and of subtle gradations of color in the rectangular bands.

Frank Stella carried geometry even further. The canvases for a series of paintings were stretched on geometric frames that are, instead of conventional rectangles, circles, tilted rectangles, pentagons, and other more intricate shapes. By emphasizing the irregular shape of the canvas, the painting in Figure 75 manages to make the flat surface look three-dimensional through a *trompe l'oeil* (fool-the-eye) effect.

As noted above (Figs. 72 and 73), many shapes found in nature are geometric. *Natural shapes* are generally understood to include human, animal, and plant shapes, and the scope of their interpretation is immense. The Japanese silk design in Figure 76 could have been derived from either flowers or snowflakes or both; its charm lies in the originality that brings both basic forms together into a new and decorative design. The design of

75

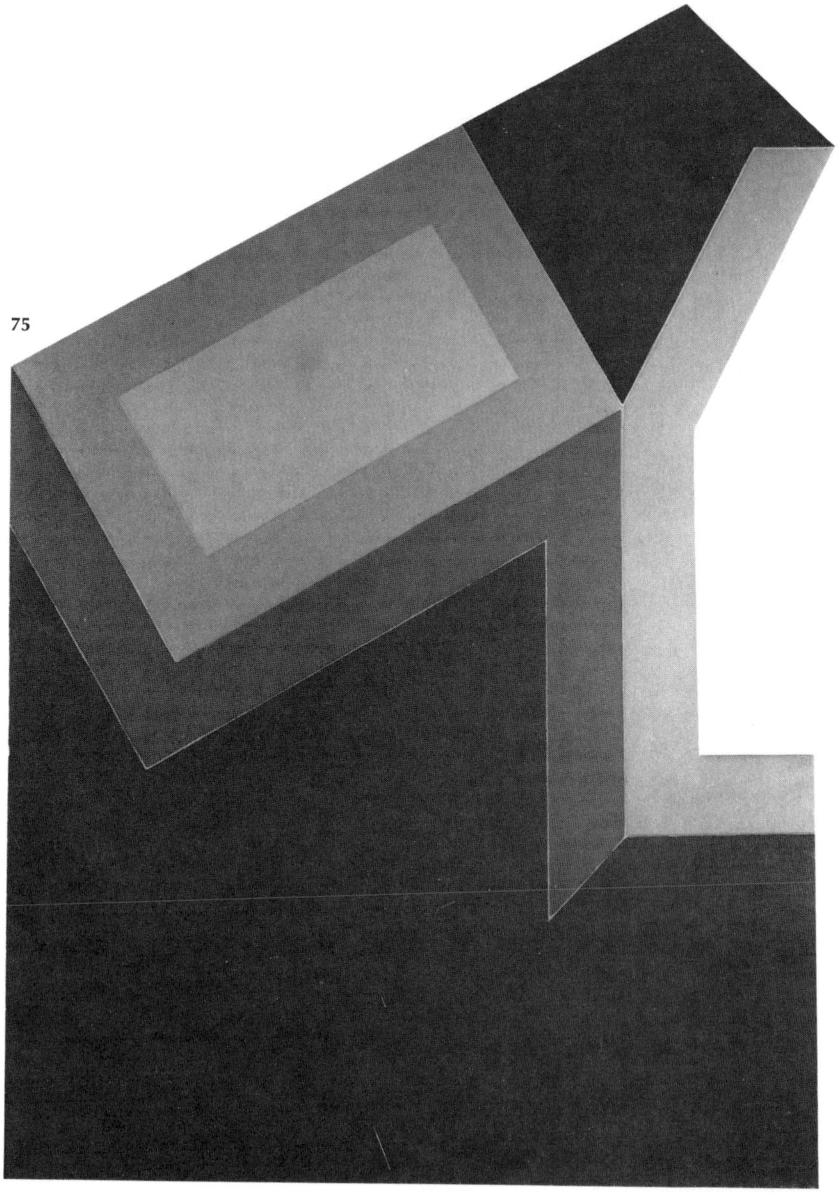

76

77

77
Medusa. Screened cotton print by Maija Isola for Marimekko, Helsinki.

78
Tak Kwong Chan. *The Horse—Away He Goes.* 1980. Brush and ink, 24 × 40″ (.61 × 1.02 m). Collection of the artist.

the cotton print from Finland (Fig. 77) looks like a huge flower form, yet its title suggests that the artist had something else in mind. In either case, the inspiration is from nature and the interpretation original and dramatic.

The sinuous forms found in nature were one of the inspirations for an art movement that flourished around the turn of this century. Now generally known by its French name, *Art Nouveau,* it had various names in Europe and took many forms. One of the most original proponents of this movement was the Spanish architect Antoni Gaudí, who designed buildings to look like organic botanical entities that grow and proliferate before our eyes. His cathedral of the *Sagrada Familia* in Barcelona is still under construction (Plate 4, p. 55).

While plant shapes lend themselves to a variety of interpretations, animal shapes are often used with a touch of whimsy. Many centuries before Christ, artists were painting or carving on walls the images of animals—bulls, cats, deer, and many varieties of birds—with almost modern stylization and often with a touch of humor. Contemporary artist Tak Kwong Chan, with a few masterful brush strokes, creates horses that are full of action and beauty. Like so many works by Chinese artists, his paintings are striking designs as well as forceful paintings (Fig. 78).

When a natural shape is distorted in such a way as to reduce it to its essence, we say that it has been *abstracted.* This means that, though the source of the shape is recognizable, the shape has been transformed into something different. Usually, this is done by simplification, by omitting all nonessential elements. A series of lithographs by Picasso, taken from an edition of eighteen, will illustrate the principle of abstract shapes.

78

The fifth print (Fig. 79) shows a fairly "natural" representation of two female nudes. Except for some distortion of the eyes and nose on the figure at left, the drawing seems lifelike, with normal shapes and volumes. By the tenth state (Fig. 80) Picasso has begun to abstract many of the elements in the drawing. Both figures are flattened, particularly the one at left, and the face at left has been drastically simplified into a circle with angular features. The left background form, which in the earlier print was a conventional suggestion of architectural space, has become a geometric screen.

By the seventeenth state (Fig. 81), the composition has been highly abstracted. Both figures are transformed into flat collections of shapes. The face at left is a primitive mask, while the one at right has all but disappeared. Breasts are circles or simple curves. Fingers and toes now resemble oversize flattened cylinders. If we had only this print to look at, we would identify it as two female nudes, but we could not see how Picasso arrived at this particular interpretation. By comparing the three states we can follow his investigation of certain shapes, planes, and outlines that fascinated him. The abstraction is not arbitrary but a systematic development from the representational drawing.

79

80

81

79
Pablo Picasso. *Les Deux Femmes Nues* (Two Nude Women). 1945–46. Lithographs, eighteen states, each c. $10\frac{1}{8} \times 13\frac{5}{16}''$ (25.65 × 34.04 cm). Cleveland Museum of Art (J. H. Wade Fund). State V.

80
State X.

81
State XVII.

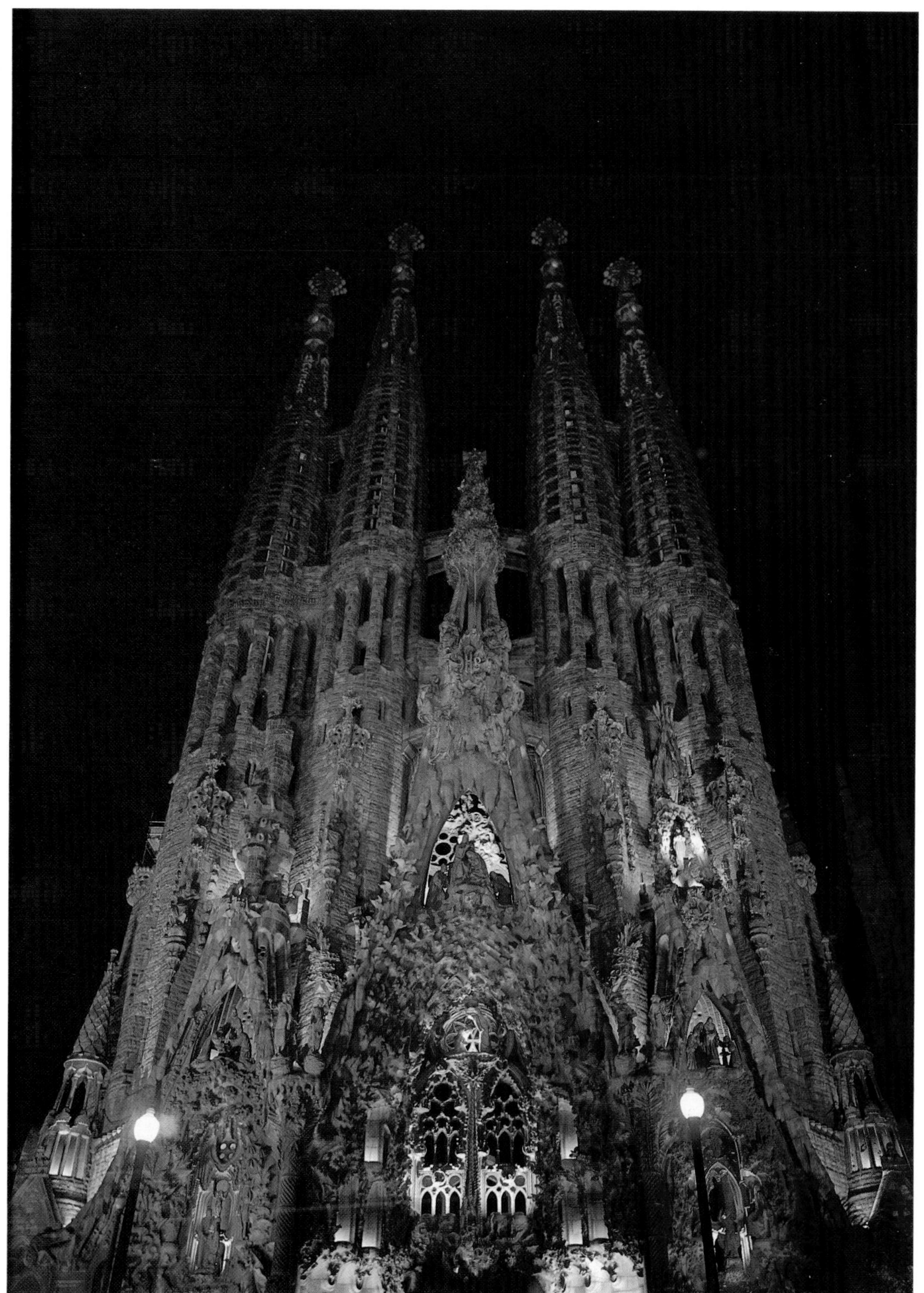

Plate 4
Antoni Gaudí. *La Sagrada Familia,* Barcelona. Begun 1903; work terminated 1926 and resumed 1952; still under construction.

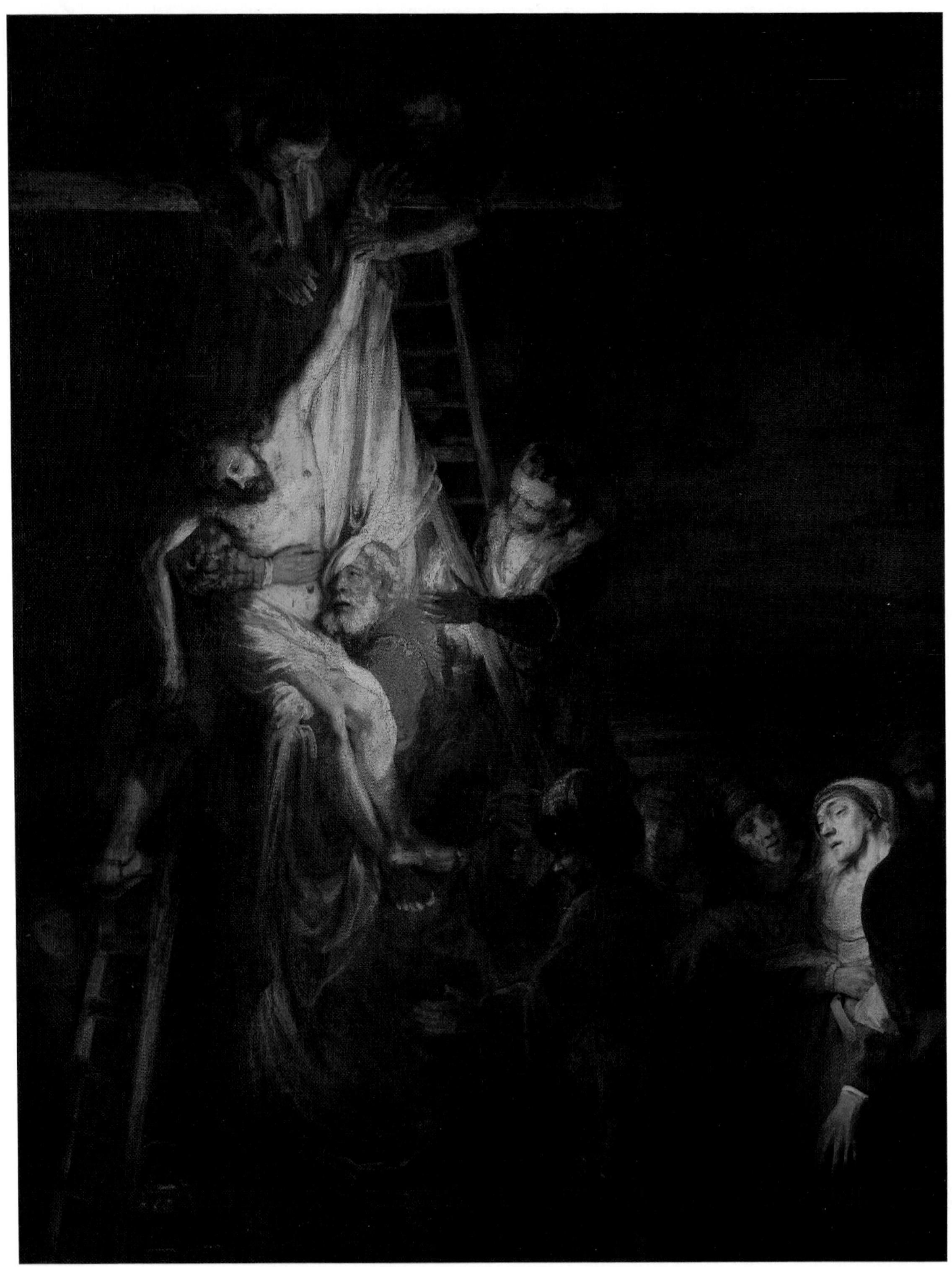

Plate 5
Rembrandt. *The Descent from the Cross.* 1651. Oil on canvas, 4′8½″ × 3′7¾″ (1.43 × 1.11 m). National Gallery of Art. Washington, D. C. (Widener Collection).

82

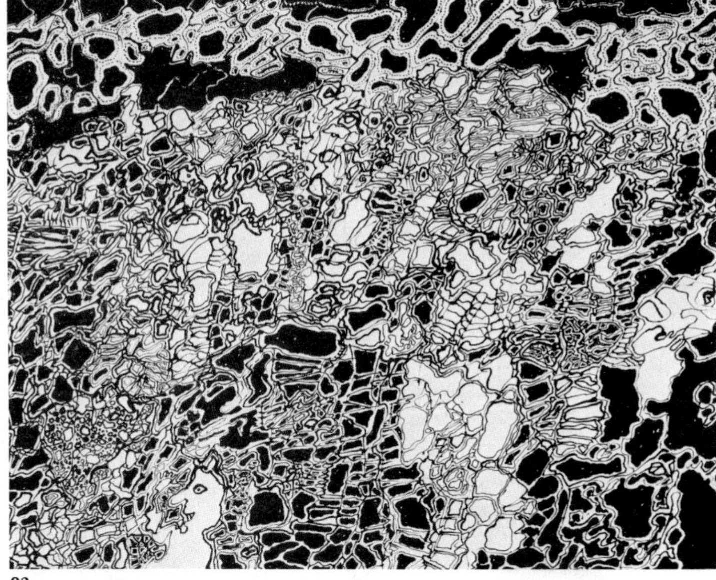

83

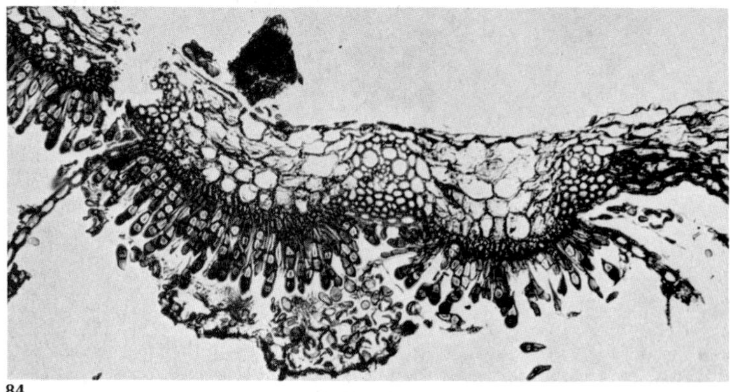

84

82
West German traffic sign.

83
Jean Dubuffet. *Radieux Météore,* from *Ferres Radieuses.* 1952. Brush and pen drawing, 19¾ × 25½" (50 × 65 cm). Courtesy Pierre Matisse Gallery, New York.

84
Microscope photograph showing cellular structure of black stem wheat rust. Photograph by Carolina Biological Supply Company.

Abstraction has long been one of the most effective means of communication, as we mentioned in connection with the symbolism of written characters (p. 35). The United States is now adopting some of the abstract highway signs that have long provided a common language for motorists in Europe. Despite the different languages spoken in European countries, drivers are able to interpret directions and warnings with no difficulty. Although American drivers speak and read a common language, the abstract pictures are more eloquent and easier to grasp than printed words, especially when seen from a moving vehicle (Fig. 82).

Shapes that do not relate to anything in the natural world are termed *nonobjective.* This is really a comparative term, because it is virtually impossible to create shapes that no one will find familiar in some way through perceptual associations. Jean Dubuffet undoubtedly was working for fantasy in his drawing *Radieux Météore* (Fig. 83) since the title (Radiant Meteor) is of a subject unseen by the human eye. It is interesting that a similar configuration can be found in nature, not in the sky but as a parasite in a wheat field (Fig. 84). Nevertheless, Dubuffet's work would be categorized as nonobjective since that was the artist's intent.

85

85
Joan Miró. *The Beautiful Bird Revealing the Unknown to a Pair of Lovers.* 1941. Gouache and oil wash, 18 × 15″ (45.72 × 38.1 cm). Museum of Modern Art, New York (Lillie P. Bliss Bequest).

86
Henri Matisse. Three panels from *The Swimming Pool,* a nine-panel mural in two parts. 1952. Gouache on cut-and-pasted paper mounted on burlap, 7′6⅝″ × 27′9½″ (2.3 × 8.47 m) and 7′6⅝″ × 26′1½″ (2.3 × 7.96 m). Museum of Modern Art, New York (Mrs. Bernard F. Gimbel Fund).

87
Josef Albers. *Homage to the Square: Silent Hall.* 1961. Oil on composition board, 40″ (1.02 m) square. Museum of Modern Art, New York (Dr. and Mrs. Frank Stanton Fund).

A painting by Joan Miró in Figure 85 demonstrates the way in which *shape relationships* interact. Miró has combined highly abstracted shapes of human heads and features with a network of geometric and nonobjective shapes. Unity in the composition is achieved by the general similarity among the various types of shapes. The dark circle that is an eye in one place becomes elsewhere just a circle or is distorted into a blob. Pattern is created by a rhythm of outlined and filled-in shapes, of light and dark. In other words, Miró has built his composition from shape relationships.

In *The Swimming Pool,* Henri Matisse abstracts human figures to interact with the water in which they are moving (Fig. 86). The figures have become so abstract, in fact, that, in many cases, they lose their original similarity to the human body. Matisse's purpose was not so much to represent swimmers as to show the pool and the shapes within it as a single entity, moving, diving, and surfacing.

Another important relationship is that between shapes within a composition and the shape of the *field* or *ground*—that is, the canvas, page, or external outline. Many of the works of Josef Albers are a series of squares related to a square field (Fig. 87). As we will see in Chapter 7, Albers was greatly concerned with the interaction of color, and his compositions with their sensitively proportioned squares provide ideal vehicles for experiments with variations in color combinations.

86

87

88

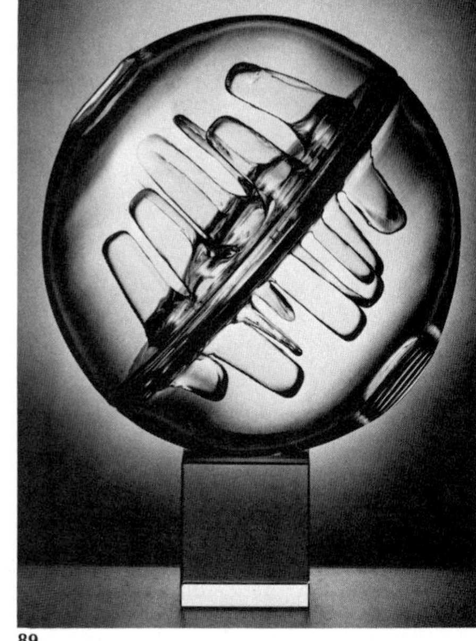

89

Mass

The categories that we identified in shape apply to mass as well. On a flat surface, shape becomes mass through illusion as a result of various devices of the artist, such as shading or the use of perspective. *Actual mass* is one of the most important elements of design.

Geometric masses—the cube, sphere, and pyramid—are the three-dimensional equivalents of the square, circle, and triangle. To these we must add the cone (a triangle rotated on its axis) and the cylinder (a rectangle rotated on its bisector).

A cube may be the most visually stable of all forms. However, it need not always be so. The sculptor Isamu Noguchi sets us on our ears, so to speak, by tipping his cube up on one corner (Fig. 88). The lines of this work, which would otherwise have been placid verticals and horizontals, now become energetic diagonals thrusting upward. This cube makes an effective counterpoint to the conventional cube of the skyscraper behind it.

Just as a cube is normally a restful mass, the sphere is somehow a *satisfying* mass. Globes, rubber balls, and the earth itself—all are spheres. Most people, when they pick up a lump of clay or dough, automatically form it into a sphere. The glass sculpture in Figure 89, shimmering with light, is made in the form of an "earth satellite." Even while it rests on its pedestal, we can imagine this airy form beginning to lift upward and hover in the air, gently spinning as it goes. This idea expresses one of the most intriguing characteristics of the sphere. It seems ever mobile, always turning, never static. There are no sharp edges to bring motion to a halt, as there are in a cube. A sphere nearly always implies movement and time.

88
Isamu Noguchi. *Cube.* 1969. Steel and aluminum, painted and welded, height 28′ (8.53 m). Located in front of 140 Broadway, New York.

89
Pavel Hlava (in cooperation with the workshop of Miroslav Lenc, Czechoslavakia). *Satellite.* 1972. Blown crystal hemispheres joined by welding, diameter 13¾″ (34.93 cm). Courtesy the artist.

90
Magician's Pyramid, Uxmal, Yucatán, Mexico.

91
Mount St. Helens, Washington. May 18, 1981.

With the pyramid form, we again return solidly to earth. The pharaohs of Egypt built their burial pyramids to last for all time, and indeed they have withstood more than four thousand years of climate, wars, pillage, and geological upheaval. Many early civilizations constructed pyramids, from the first known residents of the Middle East and Southeast Asia to the Indians of pre-Columbian America (Fig. 90). While the cube is the most visually solid mass, the pyramid is immensely stable from an engineering point of view. Stresses beginning at the tip spread out in all directions to the broad base. It is no accident that these structures have outlasted all the other wonders of the ancient world.

The cone appears by nature to be a *thrusting* mass, as in the nose cone of a spaceship or the cone of a volcano. While the form of a cone may be just as firmly rooted in earth, we somehow expect something to be coming *out* of it. A volcano, even a dormant one, remains mysterious. At any time it could erupt, spewing smoke and ash and lava over the countryside (Fig. 91). Similarly, the Indian tepee, one of the most portable habitations ever invented, was planned with a hole in the center to permit the escape of smoke from the cooking fire.

90

91

92

Finally, the cylinder is a generally utilitarian mass. Cans, tubes, vases, cooking pots, cups, and many machine parts take the form of cylinders (Fig. 92). In purely practical terms the cylinder functions well because it can contain a great deal yet has no corners or crevices. We can even visualize the human body as a collection of rough cylinders, one for the trunk and one each for the limbs. The painter Fernand Léger developed this idea during the early twentieth century (Fig. 93). At the beginning of the modern industrial age, many artists celebrated the coming of machine technology. Léger abstracted portions of the human anatomy—legs, arms, fingers, toes—into precision-formed cylinders, thus emphasizing the merger between human intellect and mechanical power.

Perhaps the most obvious use of natural masses in art is sculpture of the human form, an area of design that has flourished for four thousand years. Beginning with stiff symbolic representations among primitive people, the art of figurative sculpture reached a height in the hands of the Greeks of the fourth century B.C. and their works have inspired sculptors ever since (Fig. 94). Throughout the ages, sculptures of animals have also played an important part in human expression.

92
Silver-plated flower vases designed by Lino Sabattini for Argenteria Sabattini, Italy. 1974. Heights 14 and 10½″ (35.56 and 26.67 cm).

93
Fernand Léger. *Soldiers Playing at Cards.* 1917. Oil on canvas, 4′2¾″ × 6′4¾″. (1.29 × 1.93 m). Rijksmuseum Kröller-Müller, Otterlo, The Netherlands.

94
Aphrodite. Hellenistic (probably) copy. The Metropolitan Museum of Art, (Fletcher Fund, 1952).

93

94

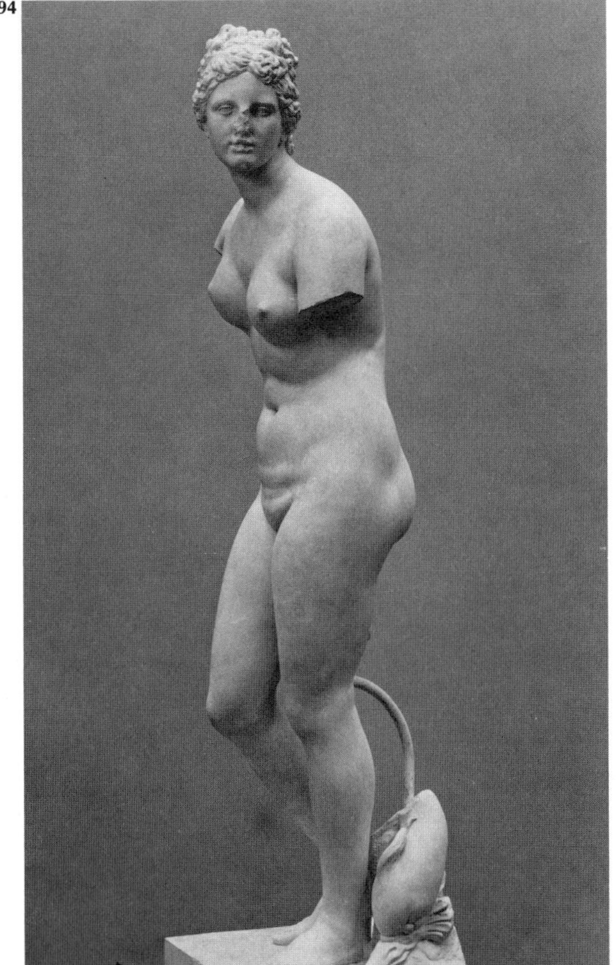

95

The abstract masses in the series of heads by Matisse shown in Figure 95 recall the progressive abstraction in the Picasso prints. Here we can see that the *actual,* rather than the pictorial, planes of the face and head have been abstracted increasingly as the artist's insight progressed. The first bust, at far left, probably shows most precisely the "real" appearance of the subject. But the last interpretation, at right, may in fact express the *character* of the sitter more accurately. The last bust is not pretty but in many ways is the most interesting view. As the states progress, Matisse gradually selects particular features for intensification, while others diminish in importance. By the third state the hair has collected into three lumps, and by the fifth it has receded to the back of the head. The nose gradually becomes bigger, stronger, and more prominent, while the eyes deepen and take on a hooded quality. Perhaps Matisse sought to capture the essence of this woman, or of Woman personified. Perhaps he was fascinated by the new relationships of mass (features) on the mass of the head. At its best, abstraction evokes the basic quality of a form, while distorting its contours. By definition the *abstract* concerns the *essence* of something.

Nonobjective masses do not refer to any specific recognizable form. When they *seem* organic, as though they might be part of some living thing, they are termed *biomorphic.* The glass form in Figure 96 could be some prehistoric sea creature or a resident of an undiscovered planet. It does not resemble anything known, and yet it seems alive. The power of

95
Henri Matisse. *Heads of Jeannette.* 1910–13. Bronze, heights 10⅜ to 24⅛" (26.42 to 61.2 cm). Los Angeles County Museum of Art (gift of the Art Museum Council in memory of Penelope Rigby, 1968).

96
Marvin Lipofsky. *California Storm Series.* 1942. Blown glass, 11½ × 13" (27 × 33.02 cm). Collection of Samuel Budwig, Jr., Chicago.

nonobjective masses lies in their ability to evoke response in the viewer, perhaps a hundred different responses in a hundred viewers. Each person who looks at such a form brings to it special associations and experiences, which will help to give the form a personal interpretation. The artist who works in nonobjective mass invites the participation of the spectator.

96

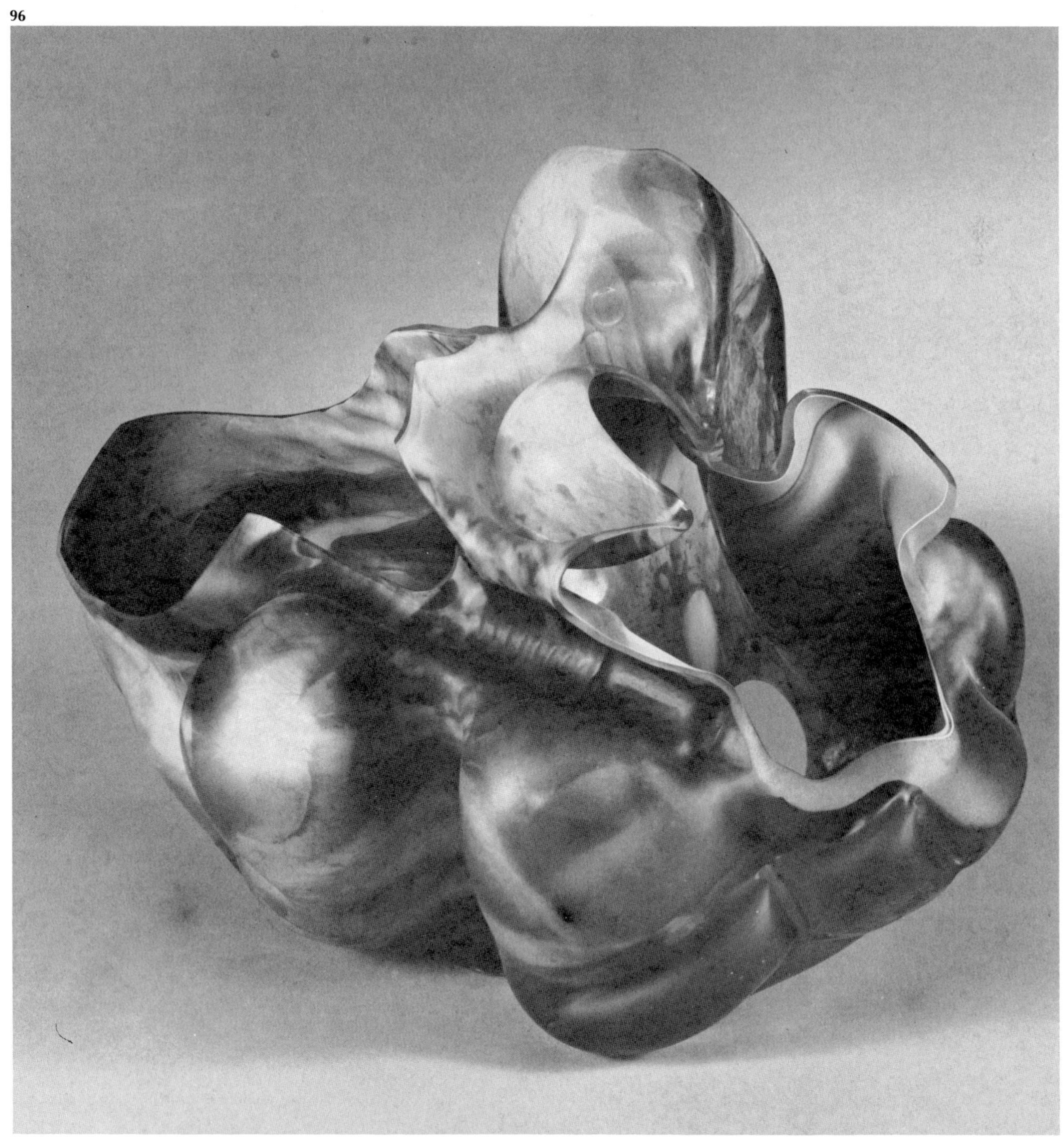

97

98

97
Russell Dixon Lamb.
Rising Wave. Photograph.
98
Pilobolus Dancers in *Monkshood Farewell.*
99
A simple line drawing of a circle when shaded can become a solid sphere.
100
A simple line drawing when shaded can become a solid geometric form.

The picture in Figure 97 shows a *moving* mass—a wave. The wave is a definite mass, yet a second after this image was captured, no single molecule of water in the wave would still have been in place, and the wave would have changed its outlines. We could point to numerous examples of this phenomenon—waterfalls, avalanches, clouds, tornadoes.

The performing arts are also concerned with mass and movement. In the dance, for instance, each dancer's body can be considered a mass—one that changes its outlines with each movement. As two or more dancers come together, they form another mass capable of transforming itself or breaking apart (Fig. 98). Each movement creates new mass and space relationships. These factors are present in a drama or a rock concert as well.

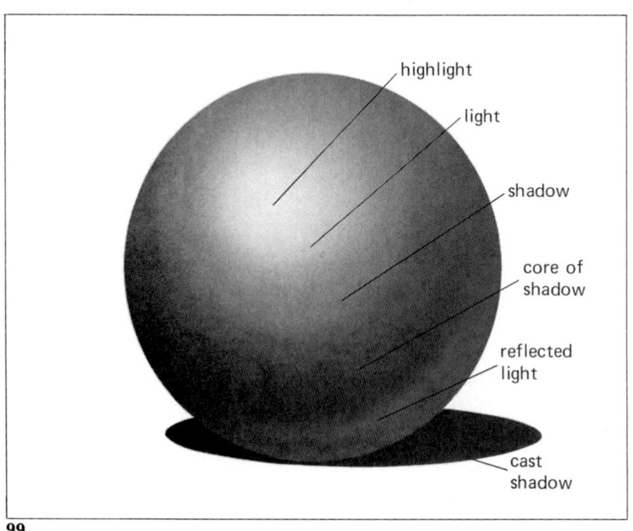

99

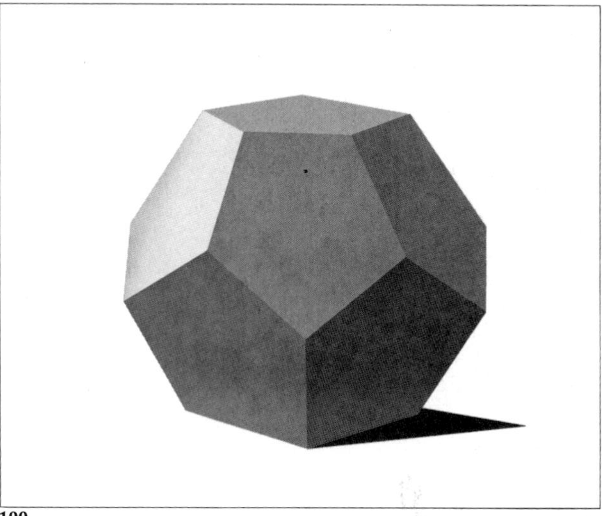

100

Converting Shape to Mass

We have implied that, generally speaking, shape is two-dimensional and mass exists in space in three dimensions. The artist also depicts three-dimensional masses on flat canvas or paper.

There are several means of achieving this phenomenon. The principal method is by shading or tonality. A circle becomes a sphere when it is shaded in a certain way (Fig. 99). A rectangle becomes a cylinder when it is shaded along the edges. A square cannot become a cube through shading alone but must be extended by means of perspective, in the same way that one's vision is extended by moving position. When a side is added to a square and shaded, a solid cube emerges. This principle can be used on any geometric mass with facets, or angular sides (Fig. 100).

Shading and tonality are basic drawing techniques. Painters use variations of these techniques by employing color and light. Grayed colors recede, so the nearest portion of a mass is made lighter. A surface catching the light emphasizes solidity and form. Darkened surfaces not only recede but turn away or under, telling the viewer the exact extent of a depicted mass. We will see examples of these devices for converting shape into mass as we study the media in which artists work. Next, however, we will explore another element that is closely associated with both shape and mass, the element of space.

5 Space

We think of space as a vast expanse in which spaceships travel millions of miles past stars and whirling planets, yet space is a vital part of even the smallest design or work of art. In creating form of any kind, one must manipulate space. The cut-paper design in Figure 101 illustrates this idea, since it can readily be seen that the design depends as much on the spaces left as on the shapes cut from the paper. In fact, if we stare at the spaces steadily, they assume a pattern of their own. In this situation, the paper pattern is known as *positive space* or pattern; the pattern left by its creation is *negative.* Continued staring may make it difficult to distinguish between the two. This phenomenon is known as *figure-ground ambiguity:* the cut paper is referred to as the *figure* and the space behind it as the *ground.* Twentieth-century painters have found this relationship especially intriguing and have made use of it in many of their works. In Figure 102, for instance, we see with one glance a classically proportioned vase. We blink our eyes and now we are looking at two profiles of Pablo Picasso, facing each other nose to nose. If we look at this work long enough, the two images (or perceptions of the image) will keep reversing, so that we alternately see one and then the other.

Psychology of Space Perception

Only a narrow range of what we see is in focus at any particular moment. When we look out over a city we feel we are seeing a panoramic view, but really our eye is capable of seeing one building at a time; the rest of the landscape is only a blur. We know the rest is there but we cannot see the details until we move our eyes. The same is true of closer range, within a room, for instance. The crystalline lens of the eye makes it necessary to select a target, a piece of furniture, a book, or a person's face, on which to concentrate our attention. This limitation is a protection rather than a handicap. The brain reacts immediately to sensory response, and if we were to be assaulted simultaneously by the details of everything around us, our intelligence would be incapable of handling all the information bombarding it. It would be like being surrounded by a crowd of people all

101

101
C. Schwizgebel. Cut-paper silhouette from Switzerland. c. 1950. 11½ × 7⅔" (29 × 19.5 cm). Schweizerisches Museum für Volkskunde, Basel.

102
Jasper Johns. *Cups 4 Picasso.* 1972. Lithograph, 22 × 32". (56 × 81 cm) Universal Limited Art Editions. Courtesy Leo Castelli Gallery, New York.

103–104
The same subject photographed with different lens settings becomes entirely different in character.

shouting at once. To bring any order out of such clamor, it is necessary to listen to one voice at a time. The need for the intelligence to sort out a point of interest is evident in our tendency to see familiar shapes in large areas over which the eye roams aimlessly. We see dragons in a bank of clouds or imagine a face in a pattern.

This principle of selective vision can be demonstrated by the camera. Standing in the same position, we have only to change the distance setting on the lens, in other words to change *focus,* to receive two entirely different images (Figs. 103–104).

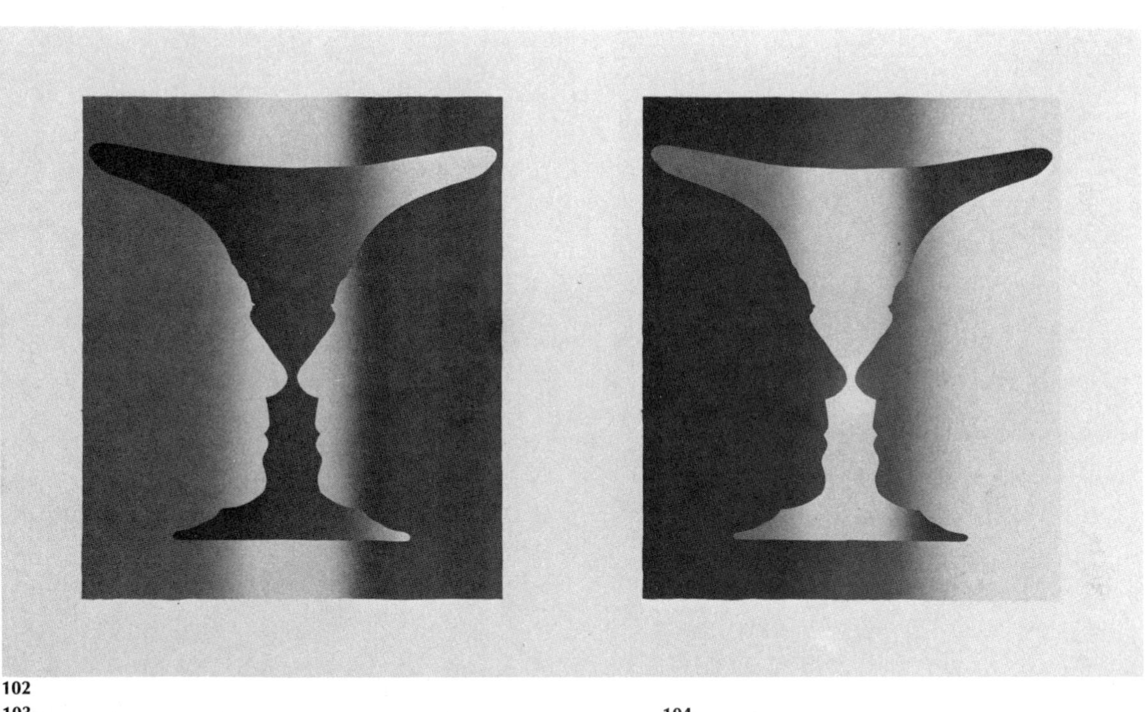

102

103

104

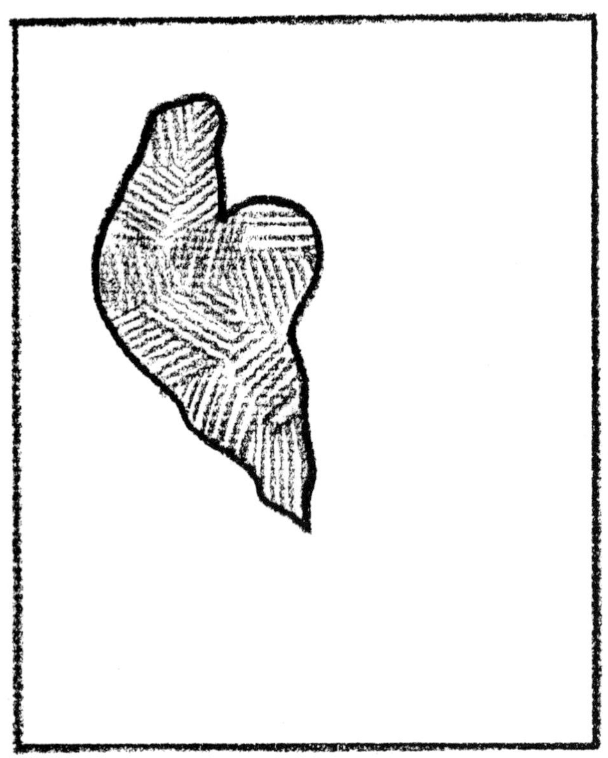
105

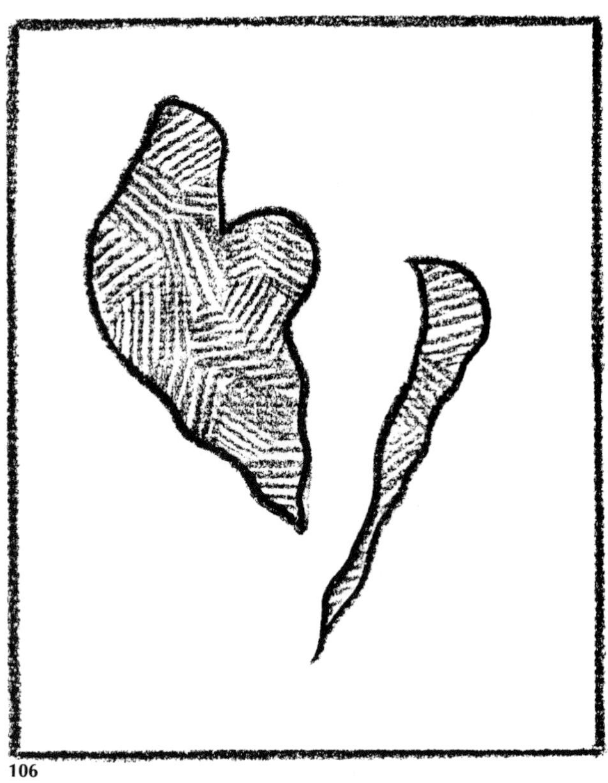
106

Early thinkers assumed that the object perceived actually entered the eye bodily, and they wondered how a large object could shrink to a size that could be accommodated by the small hole in the pupil of the eye. We know now that the eye receives not a part of the object itself but only an equivalent of it and the size of the image received depends upon the distance of the object from the eye. By choosing the proper distance, the viewer can make objects as big or as small as is necessary to comprehend them. A mountain does not become a mere bump because it is seen from a distance. The long range of vision reduces it to a form that can be comprehended in relationship to the vaster landscape in which it is perceived. The larger the object seen, the less of its environment will be visible. This principle is frequently used in cinematic photography. On a television or movie screen, a long-range shot is used to give the flavor of a setting or to portray people traveling over long distances. When the emphasis is on a personal reaction, however, the camera moves in to show only the person's face, excluding the setting entirely. In this way the mind of the viewer focuses the emotional response of the actor. The attention of the audience is controlled by the photographer's manipulation of space. Each scene becomes a composition by which the photographer and director elicit a response.

The importance of space in design can be more clearly understood if we distinguish two kinds. *Actual space* is that in which a work exists. It may be the space on the two-dimensional surface of a canvas, the space occupied by a stereo component, or the three-dimensional spaces inside and around a sculpture or a building. *Pictorial space* is the illusionary space that the artist creates in a two-dimensional work, such as a drawing or a painting. This can range from a perfectly flat, patterned surface to the illusion of

105
One nonobjective shape positioned in a space.

106
Two nonobjective shapes positioned in relation to one another in a space.

107
In graphic design, blocks of type become shapes to be arranged within the space of a page.

deep space, as in a landscape that seems to recede into infinity. In depicting pictorial space, the artist is influenced by the psychology of space perception.

Actual Space

Anyone who works on a *two-dimensional* surface is creating an illusion. A circle becomes a ball or an apple, but it remains in reality a drawn circle. An artist or designer who is about to make the first mark on a blank canvas or piece of paper has several important decisions to make. These include not only the shape of the mark, its size, perhaps its color, but also *where the mark will be* on the canvas or paper. It may be centered, off to one side, or set high or low in the white field. Assuming for the moment a rectangular piece of paper with a *nonobjective* shape on it—a shape that does not resemble any natural form—we can see that the artist has established a *spatial relationship* between the shape and the page (Fig. 105). The shape relates to the space on all sides of it and to the rectangular field itself. This idea may seem very basic, but anyone who has ever tried to locate a shape on a blank piece of paper knows that it is not easy to find the "best" solution.

If the artist then introduces another nonobjective shape into the composition, the spatial relationships become more complicated (Fig. 106). Not only does each shape relate to the space of the paper, but the two shapes are related to each other in space as well. An example from graphic design may help to clarify this concept.

Let us suppose that the designer of this book, faced with a page 8¼ by 11 inches, wants to position the title of the book on that page. The words *Design Through Discovery,* set into type, constitute a black shape. The designer has almost endless choices in placing that shape, some of which are shown in Figure 107. In the end, the placement that seems most satisfying, most effective, will be the one that creates the best spatial rela-

107

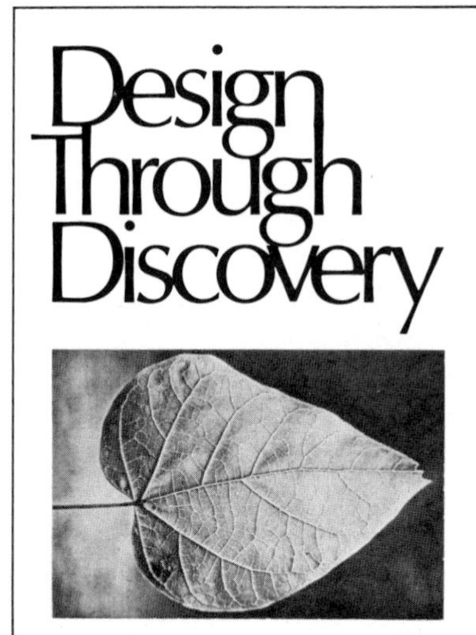

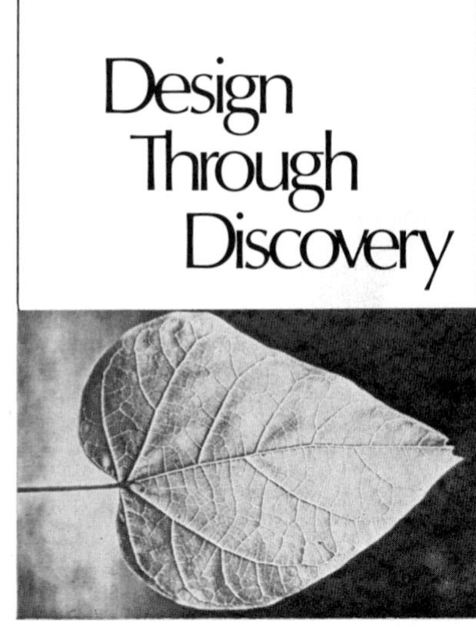

108

108
Type and illustrations combine to form the composition of a page.
Their placement in space can affect the sense of horizontality or verticality.

109
Henri Matisse.
The Parakeet and the Mermaid. 1952–53.
Paper cutout with gouache, 11¾″ × 25′4¼″ (3.37 × 7.73 m). Six parts.
Stedelijk Museum, Amsterdam.

110
David Smith. *Voltri Bolton VII.* 1962.
Steel, height 7′2″ (2.18 m).
Private collection.

111
Diagram of the negative spaces in David Smith's *Voltri Bolton VII.*

tionship between the shape of the words and the space of the page. When another shape, perhaps a photograph, must be included (Fig. 108), the relationships multiply. The page can be made to seem more vertical or more horizontal according to the placement of the elements, even though all four elements are the same size.

Spatial relationships provide never-ending fascination. When, at the end of a long and successful career as a painter, Henri Matisse became too ill to stand before an easel, he devoted himself to cutting out abstract shapes and experimenting with their possibilities. After having sheets of paper painted in the colors he wanted to use, he cut, arranged, and finally pasted the varied shapes on colored backgrounds, rearranging them endlessly until the spatial relationships were exactly as he wanted them. The result was a series of striking designs (Fig. 109). Matisse referred to this method of experimenting with shape and color and learning about them as

109

"sculpting with color." He cut away the paper in the way a sculptor chisels away stone, studying the possibilities of space and form and disposing positive and negative shapes to produce a unified result.

110

Sculpture and other *three-dimensional* works have always had as much to do with space as with material substance. When we look at the work in Figure 110, we see not only an assembly of forms but also a complex of spaces of different shapes. Of course, we are more aware of the positive forms than of the negative ones (or spaces), but we also cannot help taking note, perhaps unconsciously, of the latter. If we were to put a sheet of tracing paper over this photograph and fill in the spaces only, the result would look something like Figure 111—another interesting composition.

111

112

Moreover, because we are looking at a photograph, our position is fixed. If we were actually standing next to this sculpture, we would be free to move around it, and every time our viewpoint changed even slightly, the forms—*and the spaces*—would alter in shape. Clearly the sculptor must keep in mind not only the forms being created but the spaces as well, designing them from every potential vantage point.

We can experience such sculptural spaces in our parks and plazas. As spectators we can walk around such works and also under and through them, perhaps even climb upon them. This idea brings us again to the concept of *time.* It takes time to walk around and through a monumental sculpture. It also takes time to pass through a building and gradually experience its spaces. Public buildings illustrate this most clearly.

Anyone who has visited a European cathedral must recognize that a full realization of its many facets takes a great deal of time, but even the most businesslike buildings require time, to walk through halls and to find the appointed shop or office. Perhaps the most exciting experience in a public building occurs when one attends a concert or dramatic performance. The Metropolitan Opera House at Lincoln Center, like major opera houses all

112
Staircase and foyer of Metropolitan Opera House, Lincoln Center, New York City.
113
Augustin Hernandez. Hernandez House, Mexico City.
114
Trumpet shell from the Philippine Islands.

113

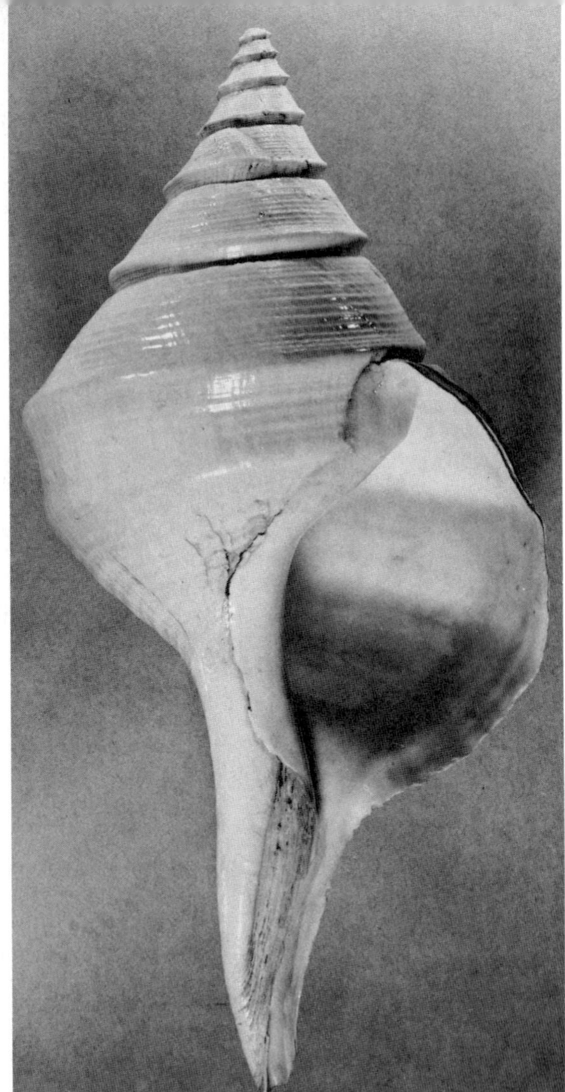

114

over the world, was designed to heighten the sense of anticipation by providing glamor and a sense of luxury from the moment one enters (Fig. 112). Especially at night, with the crystal chandeliers sparkling on the rich carpet and the lighted fountains shimmering outside the high windows, one lingers, climbing the staircase slowly, looking around to absorb this eloquent stage setting for the performance yet to come.

Smaller-scale architecture can also stimulate anticipation. The house in Figure 113 seems to have been sculpted rather than built, and there is a feeling of curiosity as to what the inside shapes will reveal. Its complex of shapes, curves, spaces, hollows, and projections would offer a fascinating adventure to anyone walking through. Looking at this photograph, we can see that if the photographer had stood just a few feet to either side of the present vantage point, the spaces would have changed. This house was designed for a woman who collects shells as a hobby, and its swooping curves and intersecting arcs seem to echo the configuration of a shell (Fig. 114). The element of time is essential in appreciating such a house. The viewer must linger and *experience* the spaces, feeling their flow and rhythm rather than merely viewing them.

115

115
Harold Swearing Oath, detail of *Bayeux Tapestry.* c. 1073–88. Wool embroidery on linen; height 20″ (51 cm), overall length 231′ (70.4 m). Former Palace of the Bishops, Bayeux.

116
Denison Cash Stockman. Cover design from *Urban Spaces,* by D. K. Specter (New York Graphic Society Books, 1974).

Pictorial or Illusionistic Space

Pictorial space begins, and sometimes ends, with the *picture plane*—a flat surface that is synonymous with the surface of the canvas or paper being drawn upon. Artists throughout history have tried to create the illusion of "real" or three-dimensional space on this surface. When we look at a landscape in the natural world, our eyes automatically make a judgment and inform our brains that certain things are farther away than other things. Pictorial space attempts to mimic this effect. In a landscape painting, for convenience, we often refer to the *foreground, middle ground,* and *background.* A few paintings actually do show this triple division of planes in space, but in a competent representation of space the various degrees of depth (or distance from the viewer) recede gradually to infinity, with no sharp divisions.

Figure 115 shows a portion of the *Bayeux Tapestry,* an embroidered cloth banner depicting the Norman invasion of England and the events leading up to the Battle of Hastings in 1066. In all, the tapestry is 231 feet (70 meters) long. It shows many different episodes, which are arranged *sequentially,* so that the viewer reads them from left to right like a book. Very little attempt has been made here to create pictorial space. In fact, the space is almost totally flat. Ships in the water seem to be in the same plane as a man sitting on a throne or a knight storming a castle. Rather than being "realistic," the effect is decorative and charming. The *Bayeux Tapestry* also recalls our discussion of time in relation to actual space, since the whole banner cannot possibly be read from any vantage point. The viewer must walk along in front of it, gradually following the episodes.

One simple device prevents the *Bayeux Tapestry* from having absolutely flat pictorial space, and that is the technique of overlapping. Occasionally, as the narrative unfolds, we will come upon a group of figures whose bodies are partially overlapped. Here the designer has made a cautious effort to place one figure behind another, to create pictorial space. For the most part, though, the action remains on the surface.

Denison Cash Stockman has used overlapping in a highly sophisticated manner for his cover design in Figure 116. The vantage point above the crowd adds considerably to the effect of three-dimensional space, as does

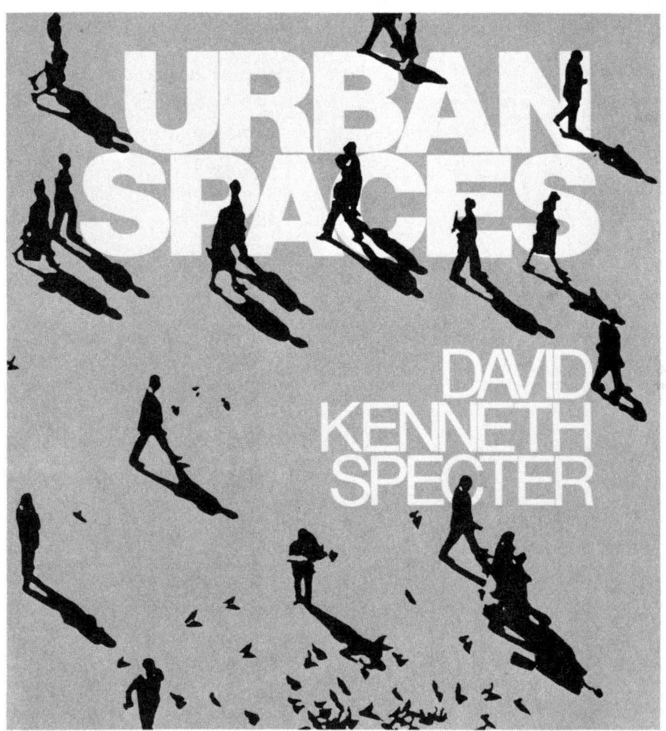

116

the way the figures seem to move across the cover in front of the type, a device that has dramatic impact as well.

Stockman makes use of another device for indicating space by placing his figures in layers or *tiers* of distance. Those at the bottom of the design seem to be directly under us, since we are practically looking at the tops of their heads. As the eye moves toward the upper edge of the composition, the figures move farther away simply because we see them from the side, in greater length. This again is a sophisticated approach involving *foreshortening,* the manner in which objects or planes diminish in length when they are tipped toward the observer.

A more basic use of tiers is found in some of the earliest drawings on record—cave paintings and the paintings and wall carvings of the ancient Egyptians and Mesopotamians. Children have always used this device quite naturally (Fig. 117). Primitive painters even today find tiers a basic tool for depicting distance, as in the painting by Eskimo painter Nauja in Figure 118. The landscape here is divided into well-defined horizontal strips that almost have to be viewed separately. The succession of strips along which the eye must move evokes the feeling of endless space characteristic of the Arctic landscape.

In the arts of the East, the use of layers is more deliberate. There is nothing primitive about the Persian miniature in Figure 119. The figures are beautifully executed, and the many areas of ornamentation are rich in their intricate patterns. The design sense here is sophisticated. If there is no feeling of distance as the Western eye perceives it, the reason lies in the fact that Western conceptions of space are an outgrowth of the Renaissance in fifteenth-century Europe. Prior to that time, European as well as Byzantine, Oriental, and Islamic artists worked from conceptual imagery in which spatial relationships were shown in ways entirely satisfactory to them but different from the perceptual imagery to which the Western world has become accustomed. The Islamic artist who painted the miniature in Figure 119 worked from these older concepts. The paving blocks do not recede into the distance but are vertical, and the rug upon which the upper figures sit is parallel to the picture plane. Still, we know that the lower figures are in front of the Turquoise Palace, while the higher ones sit in a recess within it. The use of tiers tells us exactly what the artist wants us to know about spatial relationships.

117

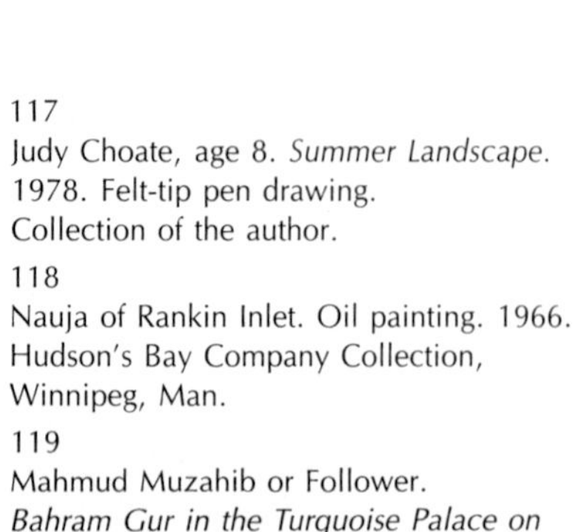

117
Judy Choate, age 8. *Summer Landscape.* 1978. Felt-tip pen drawing. Collection of the author.

118
Nauja of Rankin Inlet. Oil painting. 1966. Hudson's Bay Company Collection, Winnipeg, Man.

119
Mahmud Muzahib or Follower. *Bahram Gur in the Turquoise Palace on Wednesday,* page from the *Khamsa of Nizami.* 16th century. Illuminated manuscript. Metropolitan Museum of Art, New York (gift of Alexander Smith Cochran, 1913).

118

119

Nauja's work (Fig. 118) and the *Bayeux Tapestry* (Fig. 115) employ still another means of suggesting distance, *variation in size.* In the portion of the "tapestry" that we show here (it is not really a tapestry, since the designs in tapestry are woven into the fabric and the banner is embroidered), the men in the boat are smaller than those on land, with the waves indicated before the boat also helping to create the appearance of distance. In other parts of the work, men building the boats are as large as the other figures shown on land. In Nauja's painting, the figures on the sled are smaller than the ones before the igloo. The dogs, however, are the same size, and the higher igloo is larger than the lower one. Still, the mountains become lower as they recede toward the top. The very inconsistency of the varying sizes is characteristic of primitive artists, who do not use formulas but who work instinctively to express what they have in mind.

120

Perspective

One of the reasons the devices discussed above are interesting to us is that they are alternatives to *perspective,* the accepted method of Western artists for depicting distance.

In perceptual perspective, which strives for visual reality, there are several possible approaches. One is *aerial* or *atmospheric* perspective. Stated most simply, aerial perspective is based on the fact that objects seen from a distance seem less clear, their colors more muted than objects that are close. This effect is caused by two factors: the softening quality of the air between the viewer and the subject, and the inability of the human eye to distinguish clearly forms and colors at a distance. Aerial perspective tries to duplicate this reality by a progressive graying and blurring as the composition goes back into space.

The most painstaking and self-conscious search for "true" representation of space on a flat surface took place during the Renaissance. Artists of the fourteenth century had attempted to place their figures in a shallow space, frequently in little buildings, to create an architectural setting (Fig. 120). The progression into space ends right behind the figures, and the result often looks like a stage set.

By the fifteenth century artists had formulated the principles of *linear perspective* into an exact science. As practiced then, it is extremely complicated, but the basic assumptions are simple. First, as had long been realized, objects in the distance appear to be smaller than those close to the viewer. Second, parallel lines or planes receding into the distance seem to meet at some point, which is known as the *vanishing point.* We have all noticed this phenomenon in rows of telephone poles or in looking down an expanse of railroad track, for instance. The Renaissance painters sharpened their mastery of linear perspective by actually constructing lines and vanishing points in their pictures. In theory, once the lines were removed, we would have the same visual experience in looking at the painting as in viewing the actual scene (Figs. 121, 122).

120
Giotto. *Annunciation to Anna.* c. 1305–10. Fresco. Arena Chapel, Padua.

121
Piero della Francesca and Luciano Laurana. *View of an Ideal City* (detail). c. 1460. Tempera on panel, 1′11″ × 6′6¾″ (.58 × 2 m). Galleria Nazionale delle Marche, Palazzo Ducale, Urbino.

122
Perspective drawing based on *View of an Ideal City.*

123
Auguste Renoir. *La Première Sortie* (The First Outing). c. 1875–76. Oil on canvas, 25½ × 19¾″ (65 × 50 cm). The National Gallery, London.

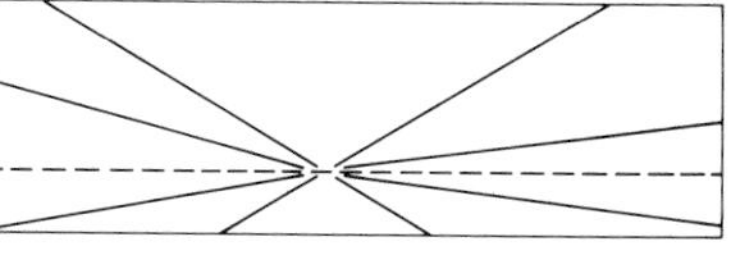

2

123

Implied Space

Until the late nineteenth century, paintings were composed within the four edges of a canvas. In figure compositions, the figures were usually grouped toward the center of the composition in order to draw the eye toward a focal point, and frequently the lines of the architecture and furnishings and even of the figures themselves would be carefully planned to lead toward the predominant character.

The nineteenth-century Impressionist painters broke with tradition in many ways. Most notable was their use of color to imply the diffraction of light (see p. 102). Equally unconventional was their interpretation of space. In paintings like the one by Renoir in Figure 123, the action is not contained within four margins. Instead, the composition is a vignette of a world that flows beyond, a part of the larger space that is *implied.* Our

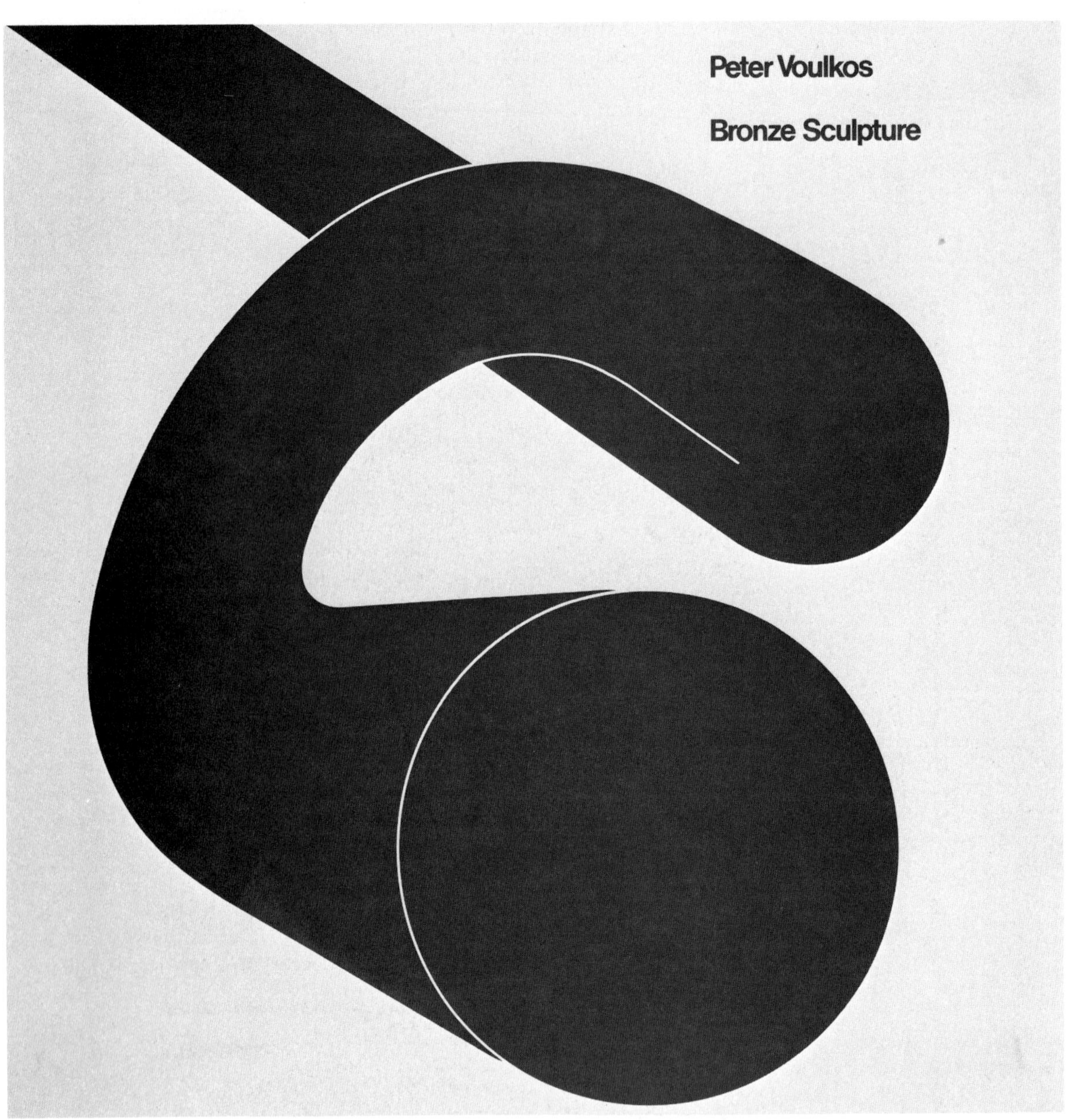

124

124
Harry Murphy. Catalog cover for
Peter Voulkos Sculpture Exhibition at the
San Francisco Museum of Modern Art. 1973.
Printed graphics, 10 × 10″ (25.4 × 25.4 cm).

125
Victor Vasarely. *Sir-Ris.* 1952–62.
Oil on canvas, 6′6″ × 3′3″ (1.98 × .99 m).
Courtesy Vasarely Center, New York.

attention is focused on a central character, to be sure, but she is watching something we cannot see, and she thus becomes a part of the greater audience. It is interesting to note that Renoir has utilized his knowledge of perception to indicate this audience. The young lady with her violets is in focus, but the other figures are intentionally blurred, as they would naturally be when our eye is focused on the foreground.

Graphic artists find the device of implied space an effective kind of symbolism, a means of suggesting much by simple means. In the museum catalog cover in Figure 124 we are tantalized by the fact that we are being shown only *part* of a form since the sculpture recedes beyond the confines of the border. Instinctively we want to know how far the form goes and what its total shape must be. A complete work could have made an effective image, but by cutting it off at the edge of the catalog, the designer arouses our curiosity. At the same time, he lets us know that there is much more to be seen, in fact, a whole exhibit of interesting works.

The optical or "Op" artists of the mid-twentieth century investigated spatial perceptions of a different sort. Through careful manipulation of lines and shapes, the Op artist creates the impression of bulges, undulations, or actual movement in space (Fig. 125). This type of visual illusion is purely sensory. It relates to the *optical* reaction of the human eye to light and color.

125

126

127

126
Jean Baptiste Corot.
Woman Gathering Faggots. 28⅜ × 22½″ (72.14 × 57.15 cm). Metropolitan Museum of Art, The Mr. and Mrs. Isaac D. Fletcher Collection (bequest of Isaac D. Fletcher, 1917).

127
Alexander Calder. *Red Petals.* 1942. Mobile-stabile. Painted iron and aluminum; height 8′6″ (2.59 m). Collection of The Arts Club of Chicago.

Light and Tonality in Depicting Space

In mentioning aerial perspective, we noted that space or distance is depicted by a softening of color as objects recede. The softening is actually a lightening of color, as well as a graying of *tone.* This quality of lightness or darkness, of brightness or grayness, is referred to as *tonality.* It is perhaps most obvious in looking at a painting that has been reproduced in black-and-white. In the work in Figure 126 the foreground is dark, with highlights striking the figure and bringing out the detail in the bark and leaves of the surrounding trees. This area is almost silhouetted against the middle ground, which appears to be flooded with light. The few trees visible in this section have little detail. Beyond is a hill that is simply a grayed form. We know by its contour that it is covered with trees, but we see no individual trunks. Tonality combines with loss of detail to suggest that this landscape stretches away into the distance.

Space can be depicted in an opposite way as well, by highlighting a center of interest and implying receding distance by surrounding areas of darkness. Rembrandt made this technique an effective means of expressing religious symbolism. In Plate 5 (p. 56) the central figures are bathed in a mystical glow while the less important figures blend into a background rich with dark color. Here great distance is not important, yet the dramatic lighting establishes a feeling of space, not only behind the figures but also above them, where the arms of the cross are barely discernible.

Light is used in many other ways. The Dutch painters flooded rooms with sunlight, giving a feeling of large airy spaces; religious painters have used beams of light to give a sense of drama; and landscape painters have worked for striking effects of light on water and on snow. We will see in Chapter 7 that there can be no color without light, but in becoming aware of the importance of space, we must realize that the depiction of space, distance, and form all depend on light as well.

Space, Motion, and Time

Space inevitably implies motion, which involves time. Meteors and satellites move through space and so do people and animals. Leaves fall, plants thrust upward, and fog drifts in response to the motion of air currents. When a painter uses tonality to depict distance there is the implication of movement—of light rays, of air, and of the human eye. When the viewer responds, not only does it require time to become aware of the illusion, but the movement and tonality within the work also indicate the passage of time, if only momentarily.

Three-dimensional design is even more obviously involved with motion and time. Any building is useless unless people move through it. Contemporary architects design buildings so indoor space and outdoor space flow back and forth, integrating the structure with its environment.

We mentioned on page 74 that sculptures of architectural scale are meant to be walked around and through and even climbed upon. Many sculptures move as well. The principle of the mobile is a careful balance of parts to facilitate continuous movement (Fig. 127). Light sculpture such as the one in Figure 60 relies heavily on movement for its effectiveness; in fact, its title includes the word *ballet.*

Light, motion, and time are among the most dynamic of the materials of the designer, materials that we will discover repeatedly in our exploration of design. They can be considered as three aspects of the enormous subject of space, a field we have only touched upon in this discussion.

6 Texture

Texture involves the tactile sense, or sense of touch. As infants, we touch before we see, and through the years the role of texture in our lives remains a vital one. Although in general a totally smooth environment could seem sterile and a totally rough one menacing, people react to textures in different ways. The variety of texture in our environment accounts for much of its interest and livability.

Texture and pattern are inevitably intertwined. A pine cone has a distinct pattern and also has a texture that feels rough to the hand. A patterned fabric gives us a *visual* sense of texture, making us feel surface variations even when none exist to the touch. An *area* of texture becomes pattern. In a design sense, pattern is created when a unit is repeated (Fig. 128). A unit thus repeated as a thematic element becomes a *motif.*

Since a strong psychological element is involved in texture and we can feel surface variations even when our eyes perceive a smooth surface, we make a distinction between *tactile* and *visual* textures. Actual changes in plane that can be felt by the fingers result in tactile textures, whereas variations in light and dark on smooth *or* unsmooth surfaces produce visual textures. A chunk of porous lava rock has definite tactile texture; if we pass our fingers over it, we can feel bumps and hollows. A smooth granite pebble also has texture, but it is visual texture resulting from flecks in the composition of the stone. Similarly, a glaze on pottery may be smooth to the touch yet be textured to the eye by fragments of chemical oxides suspended in the glaze (Fig. 129).

128

128
Tapis (ceremonial skirt), c. 1900–1925. Lampong District, Sumatra, Indonesia. Silk and cotton ground with couched metallic embroidery, 46 × 49½" (1.17 × 1.26 m). Atlantic Richfield Company Corporate Collection.

129
Kim Bruce. *Tea Set.* 1975. Stoneware. Courtesy the artist.

130
Two extremes of texture—smooth and rough.

Texture

Textures are so much a part of our environment that we generally take them for granted. The two kinds of tactile textures, rough and smooth, in Figure 130 are good examples of textures we see every day but seldom notice. The clothes we wear, the homes in which we live, and the world in which we move are all a vast collection of textures. From the rough bark of the trunk to the smooth texture of new leaves, a single tree may exhibit several different textures. The textures of different foods add immensely to the pleasure of eating, and good cooks make use of that fact, adding crisp croutons to soups and salads, smooth sauces to fibrous vegetables, and crunchy nuts as toppings for desserts.

129

130

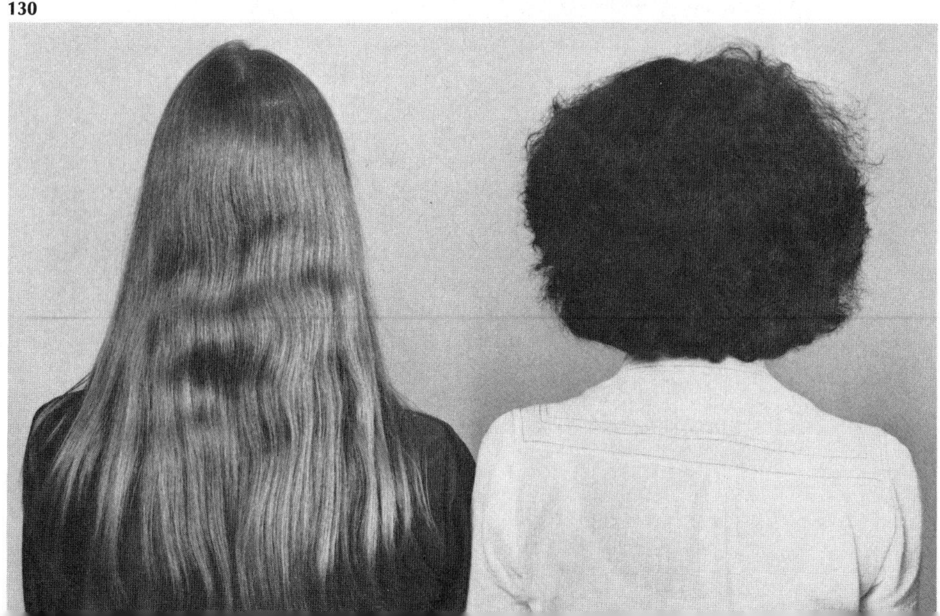

131

131
Cesar (Cesar Baldaccini).
The Yellow Buick. 1961. Compressed automobile, 4′11½″ × 2′6¾″ × 2⅞″ (1.51 × .78 × .8 m). Museum of Modern Art, New York (gift of Mr. and Mrs. John Rewald).

132
Nobuo Sekine. *Phases of Nothingness—Cone.* 1972. Black granite, height 11¾″ (30 cm). Courtesy Tokyo Gallery.

133
Philip Cornelius. Covered jar. 1981. Charcoal-glazed stoneware, height 12″ (30.48 cm). Courtesy Marcia Rodell Gallery, Los Angeles.

134
Inca feather tunic from Peru. 1100–1400. Feathers knotted on cords stitched to plain weave cotton ground 5′11″ × 2′9″ (1.81 × .84 m). Los Angeles County Museum of Art (gift of Mr. and Mrs. William T. Sesnon, Jr., 1974).

An extreme of *tactile texture* is illustrated in Figure 131. This work, which is actually an automobile compressed into a cube, has deep indentations all over its surface. It is easy to imagine how it would feel to run our hands over such a piece. However, this strong tactile texture translates visually as well, with the deep shadows within the crevices creating a powerful visual texture.

The works of Japanese sculptor Nobuo Sekine provide beautiful examples of textural *contrast.* In *Phases of Nothingness* in Figure 132, the artist has juxtaposed the perfectly smooth cone of black granite against a rough base suggestive of rock. The two sections blend and yet each acquires greater interest in contrast to the other.

One of the reasons handcrafted objects are treasured is the variety and warmth of their texture. The stoneware jar in Figure 133 has an individual quality that could not be duplicated. Its charm is partly the result of the material, but even more it is the result of the way in which the hands of the potter have worked. In addition, the glaze reminds us of geological formations after long weathering, and we feel the affinity of clay to the other materials of the earth.

Fabrics offer some of the richest textures in everyday life and assume their own symbolism. Smooth satins and lush velvets connote elegance, whereas nubby woolens make us think of the outdoors and the active life. The Incas of pre-Columbian Peru wove entire garments from feathers for an unusually lush texture (Fig. 134). Feathers were carefully sorted by color to display distinct hues as well as to show fine gradations of color.

Textures are of particular importance in interior design, since variations in texture have much to do with physical and emotional comfort. Generally speaking, smooth textures in an interior can seem cold, and when they predominate, the atmosphere may actually feel chilly. Rough textures, on the other hand, have a warmth about them that makes most people feel at ease—the kinds of textures found in brick and stone, uneven wall sur-

132

133

134

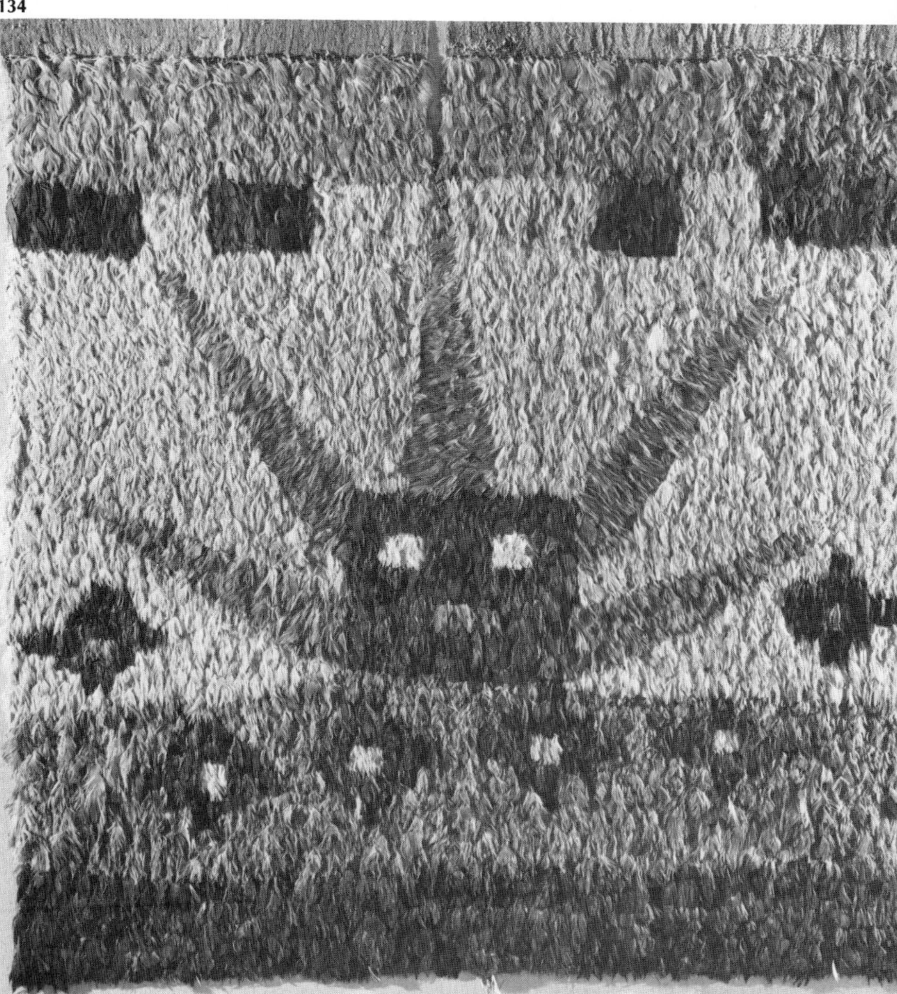

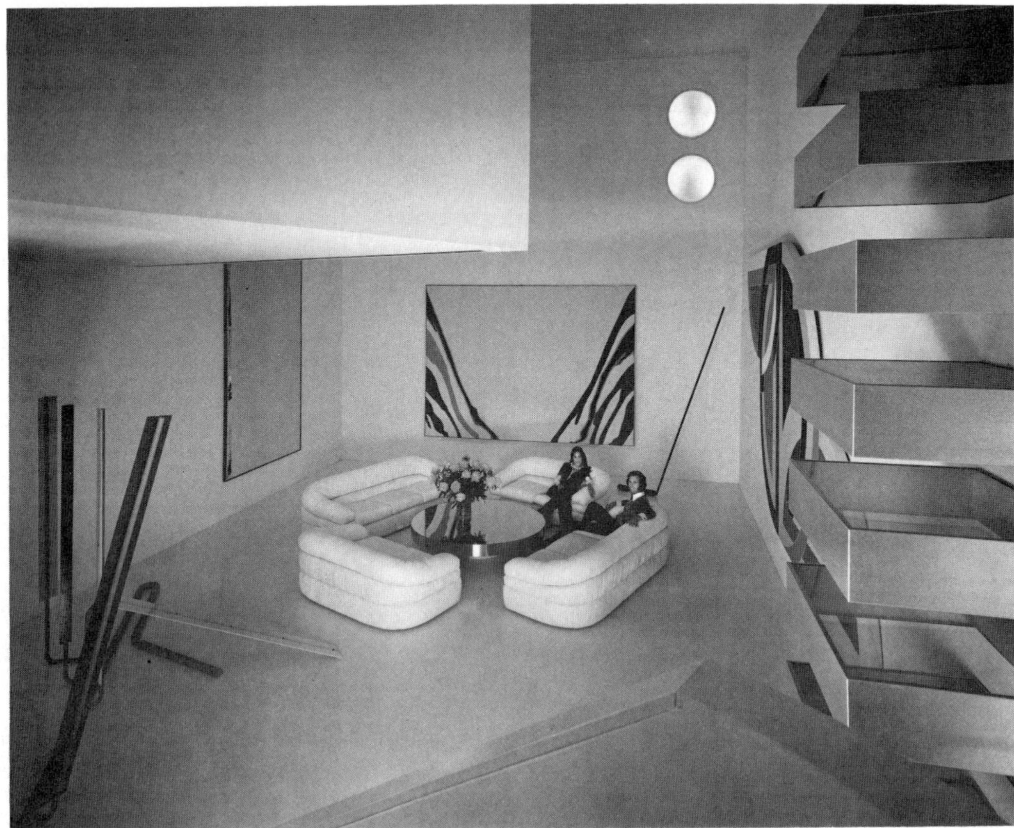

135

135
A "Minimal" all-white living room designed by Bill Ehrlich is nearly all smooth in texture except for one visual accent.

136
Hugh Hardy, designer. Both visual and tactile textures contribute to a feeling of warmth and informality in this New York City living room.

137
Vincent van Gogh. *Cypresses* (detail). 1889. Oil on canvas, 36¾ × 29⅛" (1.01 × .74 m). Metropolitan Museum of Art, New York (Rogers Fund, 1949).

138
Romare Bearden. *Carolina Shout,* from "Of the Blues" series. 1974. Collage with acrylic and lacquer, 37½ × 51" (.93 × 1.28 m). Mint Museum, Charlotte, N.C. (funds provided by National Endowment for the Arts and the Charlotte Debutante Club).

faces, and in thick carpets and nubby draperies. The rooms in Figures 135 and 136 show extremes of textural treatment. In the first room everything is smooth. In the second, what could be a bare loftlike room has been made warm and personal almost entirely by the tactile textures of the brick wall, rattan chairs, and plants, and the visual textures of bare wood and textiles, brought to a focal point in a striking painting. The variety of texture is as important as any specific texture, for the environment is enhanced by the changing sensations offered to the eye and hand.

For centuries artists have depicted textures on the flat surface of canvas, but texture in painting can also be real. Certain artists, including Vincent van Gogh, developed a technique of laying oil paint on canvas in a thick, pastelike *impasto* (Fig. 137). This effect increases the illusion of reality on the flat canvas but, perhaps more important, it also lends an energetic physical texture to the work.

In this century, artists have added texture to their paintings by introducing diverse materials (Fig. 138). The Cubists, whose style is characterized by the reduction of shapes and forms to simple overlapping planes, sometimes employed actual objects for texture. Georges Braque pasted bits of newspaper and other materials onto the canvas and then integrated them with the painted portions. This type of composition is known as *collage,* from the French word for pasting. Later artists incorporated three-dimensional objects into their work, thus obscuring the dividing line between painting and sculpture. Such works are often referred to as *constructions,* and they represent the textural element carried to the extreme.

136

137

138

The two fabrics shown in Figures 139 and 140 illustrate the difference between tactile and *visual textures.* The tapestry from Quebec is immensely varied in surface interest, yet there is no contrast in color and all the shapes are based on the rectangle. The entire composition is a study in tactile texture. The batik in Figure 140, on the other hand, is done on smooth cotton. The tremendous interest of the piece comes from the diverse shapes and the lively visual texture of light against dark, and from the veined quality that is characteristic of *batik,* a dying process in which wax is used to block out portions of the fabric.

Visual texture has always been a predominant feature of two-dimensional design. The dense concentration of black characters on white makes the Chinese scroll in Figure 141 rich in texture. The clump of bamboo adds a dramatic texture of its own, its thick leaves balancing the delicate spacing between the calligraphic characters that form the larger portion of the composition.

139

139
Helena Barynina. Tapestry, woven cotton, flax, and plastic. Province of Quebec.

140
Detail of cotton batik by Nimba tribeswomen, Liberia.

141
Li Shan (1711–after 1754).
Bamboo and Calligraphy. Hanging scroll, ink on paper; 4′4″ × 2′5¼″ (1.32 × .74 m). Collection John M. Crawford, Jr., New York.

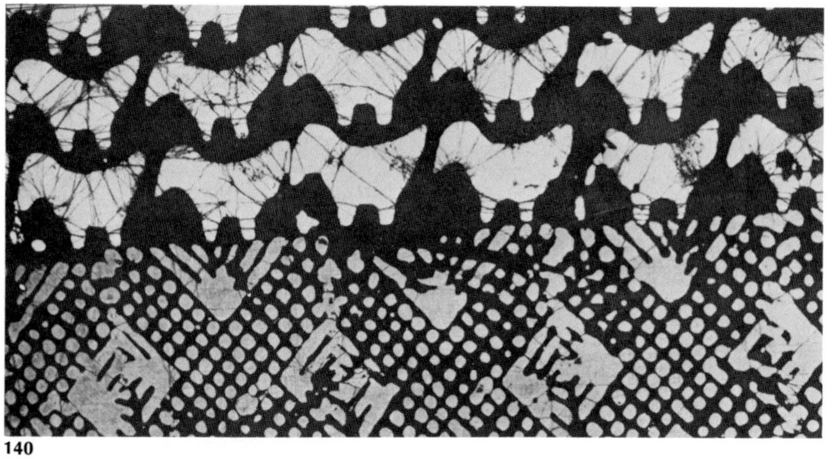

140

141

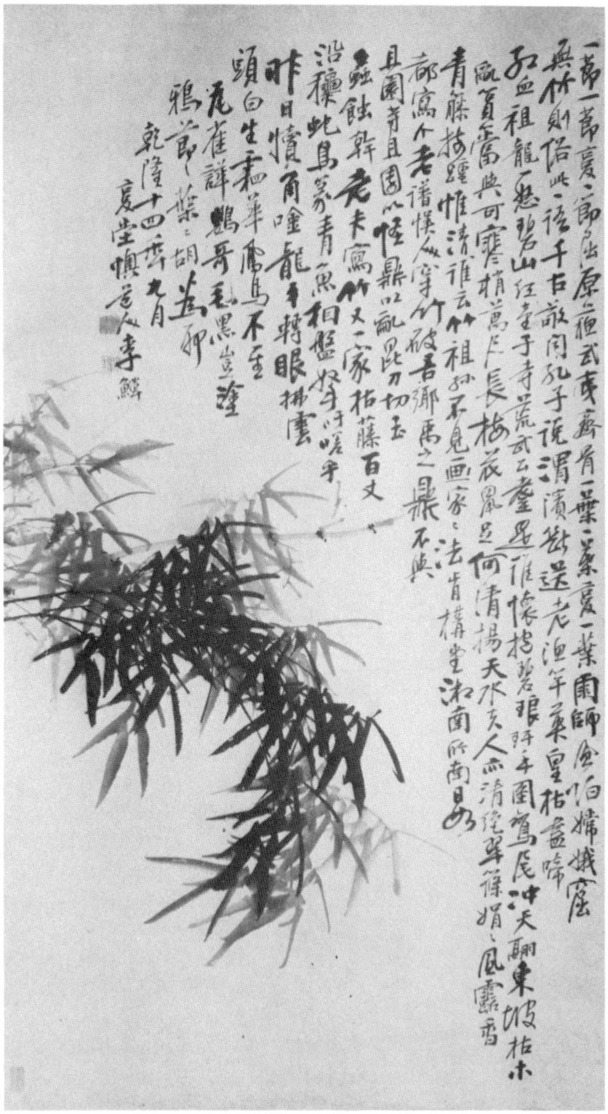

142

Similarly, the chalk drawing in Figure 142 presents such a rich, velvety visual texture that the sensory experience is almost tactile. It is interesting that the areas of darkness do not have the same textural quality as the lighter portions. The same subtle use of light and dark that has modeled the figure into the appearance of three dimensions has provided the textural surface of the drawing.

Texture Through Light

Both tactile and visual textures are dependent upon light. The Greeks developed this knowledge into a high skill, enriching their temples with carefully designed borders and molding so the brilliant sunlight would cause a texture of light and shadow (Fig. 143).

The architects of the Middle Ages used light in a dramatic way by installing magnificent stained-glass windows, whose many-colored panes poured a mosaic of light into the vast interiors of cathedrals. The light emphasized the tactile textures of stone, tapestries, and wood carving and created as well a visual texture of color.

A twentieth-century adaptation of these techniques was used by Le Corbusier when he designed his chapel of Notre-Dame-du-Haut at Ronchamp (Fig. 144). Both exterior and interior walls are rich in tactile texture, but even more interesting is the visual texture provided by the light admitted through windows of varying size, shape, and placement. The windows themselves add texture to the walls, and throughout the day, as the sun moves, the light coming through them textures the entire interior. Some of the windows are painted with scattered designs and inscriptions in red and blue, hinting at the effect of stained glass.

142
Pierre Paul Prud'hon. *La Source.* c. 1801. Black and white chalk on blue-gray paper, 21$\frac{3}{16}$ × 15$\frac{5}{16}$" (54 × 39 cm). Sterling and Francine Clark Art Institute, Williamstown, Mass.

143
Triglyphs and metope on the Parthenon, Athens. 448–432 B.C. Metope, 4'8" × 4'2" (1.42 × 1.27 m).

144
Le Corbusier. *Notre-Dame-du-Haut.* 1950–55. Interior view of the south wall. Ronchamp, France.

143

144

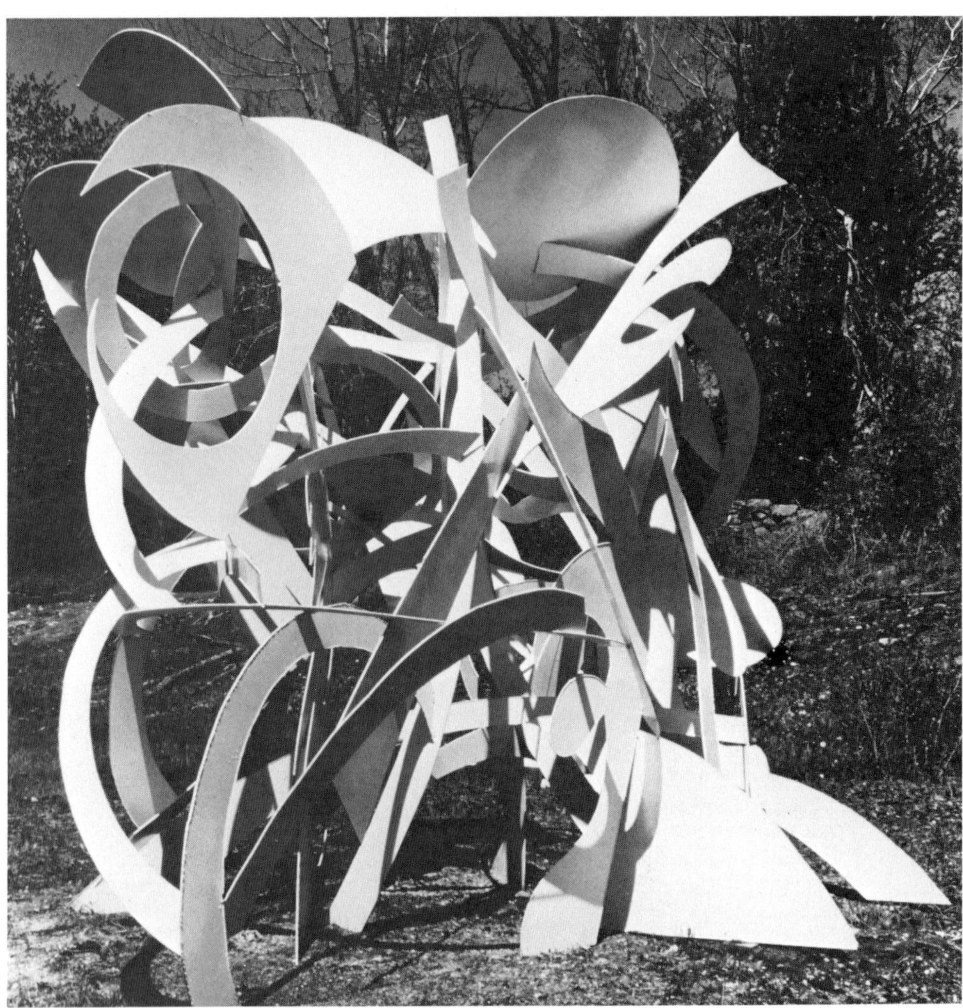

145

Light molds the forms of realistic sculpture, providing shading similar to what we have seen in the drawing in Figure 142. In Alexander Liberman's *Sabine Women II* (Fig. 145), however, it performs a different function. This work is composed of bands and shapes of steel painted and interlaced to create a sense of the chaos that must have prevailed when Roman soldiers carried off the women of the Sabines, a colony in northeast Italy conquered by the Romans. Light weaves among the layers of steel, highlighting and casting shadows. The result is one of tremendous activity. The work does not have texture; it *is* texture. We are not aware of individual surfaces or of surface quality generally but of a mass of churning texture.

145
Alexander Liberman. *Sabine Women II.* 1981. Painted steel, 8′6″ × 10′ × 11′ (2.59 × 3.05 × 3.35 m). Courtesy André Emmerich Gallery, New York.

146
Detail drawing of Ahir skirt. Embroidered cotton, mirrors; 33″ (83.3 cm). Kutch region of India. UCLA Museum of Cultural History, Los Angeles.

147
Ahir skirt. Embroidered cotton, mirrors; 33″ (83.3 cm). Kutch region of India. Gift of William Lloyd Davis and Mr. and Mrs. Richard B. Rogers.

Pattern

We implied earlier that the difference between texture and pattern is one of degree. A single brick is textured, but a wall of textured bricks creates a pattern. If texture and pattern are not synonymous, there is certainly considerable overlapping. Any pattern has visual texture but not all texture embodies a pattern. The Liberian batik in Figure 140 is patterned, and the windows of Notre-Dame-du-Haut (Fig. 144) form both a patterned wall and a pattern of light within the interior. For purposes of differentiation, we will assume that pattern is an extension of texture.

Pattern as Repetition of Design

The design motif in Figure 146 has been embroidered by Ahir women in northern India and displays diverse shapes and symbols. Alone it makes an interesting design. When it is repeated around the border of a skirt, however, it becomes an entirely different entity, a border pattern (Fig. 147).

146

147

148

149

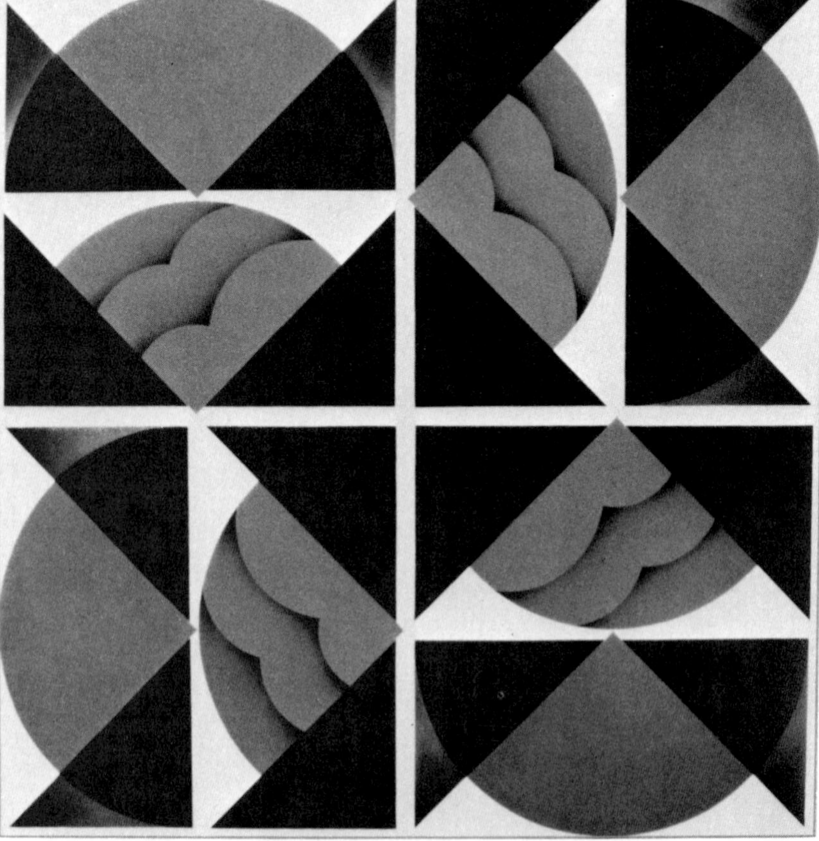

148
Packages for automotive and brake products for Wagner Division of McGraw Edison. Red and blue on a white background; measurements vary. Design: Ko Noda.

149
Shuji Asada. *Form-B.* 1980. Stencil dying (cotton), 7′2½″ × 7′2½″ (2.2 × 2.2 m).

150
Jane Hamilton-Merritt. *Norway Street.* 1976. Photograph.

151
Constantino Nivola. Mural façade of Covenant Mutual Insurance Building, Hartford, Conn. 1958. Sand-cast concrete relief, 30 × 110′ (9.14 × 33.53 m).

It is the repetitive quality of pattern that makes it distinctive; in an allover design no single feature predominates. Pattern lends itself well to backgrounds—wallpaper, carpets, and fabrics. Pattern is a feature of gift-wrapping paper and can be effective in package design. Using simply the name of a product in type that has been carefully chosen and placed, a pattern can fulfill two requirements of package design: improving the appearance of the merchandise and impressing the name of the product on the mind of the buyer (Fig. 148).

An allover pattern gains interest when the motif is varied. In Figure 149 a strong geometric unit is placed at 90-degree angles, going clockwise. There is a basic consistency of pattern but there is also a vitality in its conception that prevents the allover pattern from being monotonous.

Pattern as Surface Design

A surface can be patterned without the use of repetition. Many of the streets in Europe are patterned with cobblestones, carefully chosen as to size, shape, and color, to produce intriguing patterns (Fig. 150). Drainage gulleys may be outlined in one size and shape of stone, and sewer covers lie like the center of a flower in a radiating pattern. The basic units, the stones, are similar, it is true, yet they do not constitute a deliberate motif. Rather, they form a texture that translates into the larger areas of pattern.

Although twentieth-century cities seldom put such decorative efforts into their busy thoroughfares, texture and pattern are used to relieve the stark walls of concrete and glass buildings. In Figure 151, panels of relief sculpture (sculpture that is attached to a background) have been cast by pouring wet concrete into molds formed of sand. The play of light over the textured surface, casting accents of shadow, suggests a relationship to the natural environment that is more pleasing than would be the sterility of cold, smooth walls.

150

151

Interacting Patterns

Frequently there is an element of surprise in pattern. Units placed in repetition or in combination with other units over a large area inevitably create new units that even the designer may not have foreseen. Often these are the result of *negative space,* the space *around* the designed units, or playing *through* them. The wrought-iron screen in Figure 152 is composed of identical units fastened on vertical iron poles. The shapes themselves are interesting. However, within the allover pattern, new shapes become apparent, between the units, and flow through into ovoid shapes that change with the viewpoint. Seen as it is in the illustration, against white paper, the pattern seems almost dominated by the light shapes, in other words, the spaces.

The pattern on the Ahir skirt (Fig. 147) is quite different from the motif that composes it, for the motif is placed continuously to form a flowing band. Similarly, in Figure 149 there are diagonals that carry from square to square, creating a new design different from elements within any separate square. In designing an allover pattern, the artist is in fact making two designs: the individual motif, and the design that results when the motif is repeated. Often the placement of the motifs in relation to one another is a major decision of the designer. Any of the allover patterns shown would change character if the motifs were placed at different angles or different distances from one another.

We have discussed texture and pattern as two aspects of a single design element, exploring ways in which they can be used as tools of the designer. In Chapter 14 we will pursue the subject further under the heading "Decorative Design" as we look at the innumerable ways in which the basic human need to decorate the environment has been satisfied.

152

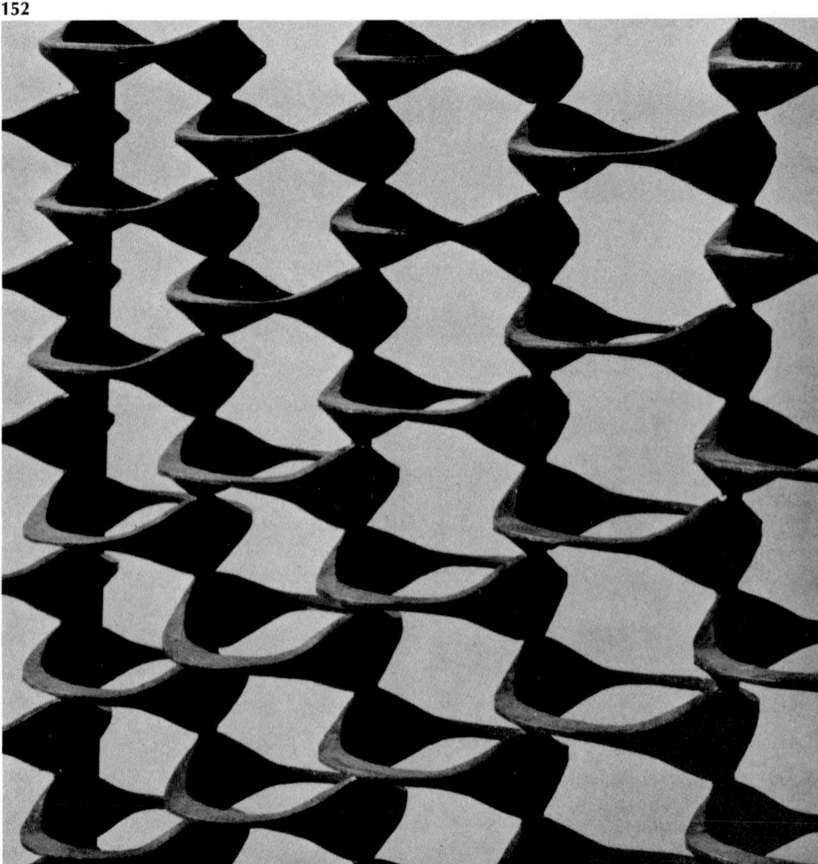

152
Wrought-iron lattice.
Werkkunstschule, Aachen, Germany.

7 Color

Of all the design elements, color undoubtedly awakens the greatest emotional response. Although it is not necessary for the creation of a great work of art, it suggests a mood and depth of experience that cannot be achieved in any other way. We speak of the color wheel in the visual arts in much the way that we speak of the tonal scale in music. Like the basic notes of the musical scale that can be expanded into symphonies, colors can be combined in an unlimited number of ways and have an enormous capacity to manipulate our emotions. Undoubtedly, color is one of the most powerful tools of the designer.

Color is both an art and a science. Physicists explain the abstract theories of color and its relationship to light, as well as the optical principles involved in color sensation. Chemists formulate rules for mixing and applying colors. Psychologists study emotional responses to specific colors. The artist needs to understand all these factors before developing a personal color system and symbolism by which color will fulfill an individual aesthetic purpose.

Color and Light

Without light there can be no color. Things that we identify as being red, green, or orange are not innately those colors, but we perceive them as such because of the action of light upon their surface.

What we call light represents only a small portion of the electromagnetic field, the part that is visible (Fig. 153). Within that portion, variations in the wavelengths of the vibrations cause the viewer to see different colors. The longest wavelength is perceived as red, the shortest as violet or purple.

Although ancient Greek philosophers asserted that color is a matter of perception rather than a physical property, it was not until 1666 that Isaac Newton established the relationship between color and sunlight. As an experiment, he directed a beam of sunlight into a glass prism. Since glass is denser than air, the light was refracted, or bent, as it passed through. Newton expected this, but he did not expect the light to be dispersed into

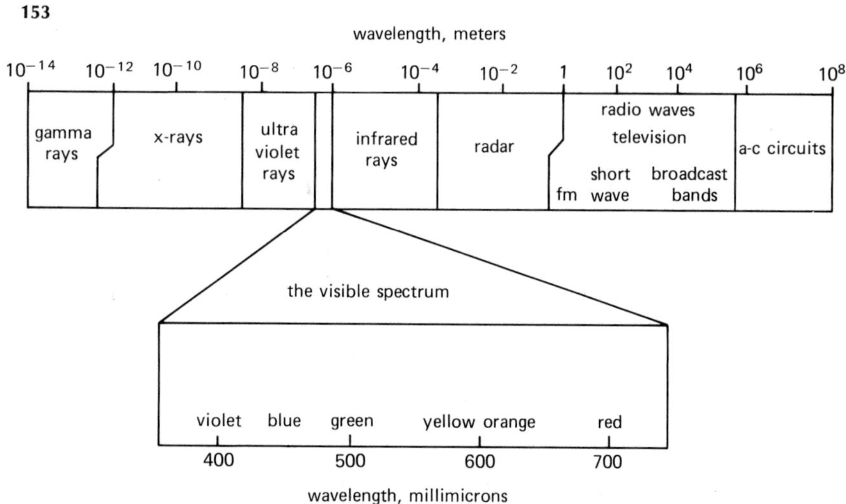

153
This diagram of the electromagnetic field shows the portion of the spectrum that is visible to the human eye—in other words, what we call "light." A millicron is one thousandth of a micron which, in turn, is one millionth of a meter.

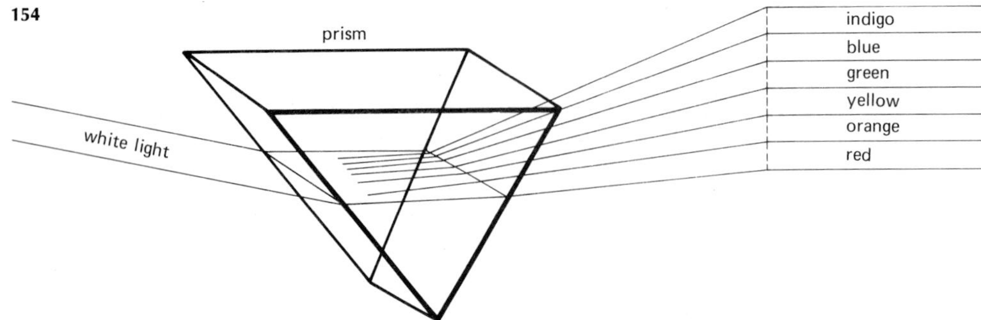

colors as it left the prism. The short waves in the light were refracted more and the long waves less, and as they emerged from the prism they arranged themselves systematically into the colors of the rainbow: indigo, blue, green, yellow, orange, and red (Fig. 154). There is no purple in the natural spectrum of color, but where the first and last colors, red and indigo, combine or overlap, the result is purple or violet. This fact gave Newton the idea of joining the colors into a circle or color wheel so the flow from tone to tone would be continuous. After separating sunlight into its color components with the first prism, he used a second prism to reverse the action, combining the colors back into sunlight. This established the fact that color is basically white light and further, that *in light,* all colors mixed together result in white.

The mechanism by which surfaces produce color is not thoroughly understood, but it apparently is related to the molecular structure of the surface, as inorganic compounds are generally colorless in solution and the hue of organic compounds can be changed by altering them chemically. Most colors seen in everyday life are caused by the partial absorption of white light. A surface that we call red will absorb all the rays *except* those from the wavelength that produces red, so we perceive red. When light is totally absorbed by a surface, the result is black. Many factors influence the way in which light is absorbed or reflected. The colors in a raindrop or a soap bubble are caused by *diffraction,* the phenomenon in which a wave of light, after passing the edge of a solid or opaque object, spreads out instead of continuing in a straight line. The blue of the sky is the result of the scattering of short-wavelength blue components of sunlight by tiny particles suspended in the atmosphere. A tree in the sunlight will seem one color on its shaded side and another on its side in the direct light, and its leaves can show tremendous variation in color, depending upon the way the light strikes them. The Impressionist painters of the later nineteenth century exploited this phenomenon to a high degree.

Impressionism sought to divorce art from intellectual interpretations, to paint what we actually see rather than what we *think* we see. If we know a house to be red, we may be tempted to paint it the same red all over, when in fact the light striking it would produce many different reds and other colors as well. The Impressionists, then, tried to see forms in terms of shimmering light and color, breaking up visual images into tiny dabs of colored paint (Plate 6, p. 105). They abandoned hard edges and lines, because they felt that these do not really exist in nature but are supplied by our reasoning process. The aim was to bypass our thought processes, to translate visual impressions directly into sensory experience.

154
A ray of white light
projected through a prism separates into the hues of the rainbow.

Perception of Color

The Greek philosophers assumed that color was not a quality of the object but a product of the mind that interprets the image striking the retina. Since the nineteenth century it has been apparent that the retina of the eye does not record each variation or even every shade of color that comes within its range. Instead, it limits itself to a few basic colors from which all the others are derived. This means that the photochemical processes of vision are selective, allowing us on the level of conscious perception to see colors as variations and combinations of the few that register on the retina. The discovery that the perception of the object differs from the object itself laid the foundation for the concept of modern art. A close look at Pissarro's painting in Plate 6 makes it clear that the artist was not painting grass or trees or a human figure realistically. He simply applied brushstrokes to the canvas in such a way that we could interpret them to be objects within our experience. The grass is not an ordinary expanse of green but a rich texture of small strokes of yellow and blue and, when they overlap, of green. If they did not overlap in a physical or *partitive* mixture, the eye would perceive an average of the wavelengths of the two colors, in other words, gray. The result of the intermixture is vibrant and alive, but it is our perception that tells us it is green and our intelligence that makes us know that it is grass.

There are numerous theories of color perception, many of which are highly technical. Of more immediate importance to us are the experiments that successful artists have made in the field of color perception. The Op (optical) painters are of particular interest. Although they did not always work in color (Figs. 67, p. 45, and 125, p. 83), their experiments have had a major impact on both painting and design.

Victor Vasarely carried out extensive experimentation in color, exploring its *architectonic* (structural) qualities, its possibilities for three-dimensional illusion, and its interrelationships through gradations of tone. His work in Plate 7 (p. 105) is based on red, blue, and yellow as is Pissarro's composition in Plate 6. By grading the colors from light to dark in squares and circles, however, Vasarely has revealed possibilities far beyond those usually associated with these three colors: a vibration emanates from the juxtaposition of variations of color, and the sense of depth fluctuates as we gaze at the surface of the painting. Each unit influences its surroundings in such a way that the shapes become reflectors and vibrators, each one changing and moving as a result of the others. One senses that the artist must have worked in a state of both curiosity and excitement, for it seems unlikely that such vibrancy could be the result of careful planning.

Color Theory

From the tremendous field of color experimentation, certain theories have evolved concerning the origins of colors and their interaction. Most of these are based on the color wheel and on a group of specific basic or *primary* colors from which all other colors can be mixed.

For many years, students learned color theory on the basis of studies begun in the eighteenth century and culminating in the work of Herbert E. Ives. Ives devised a color wheel based on red, yellow, and blue as the

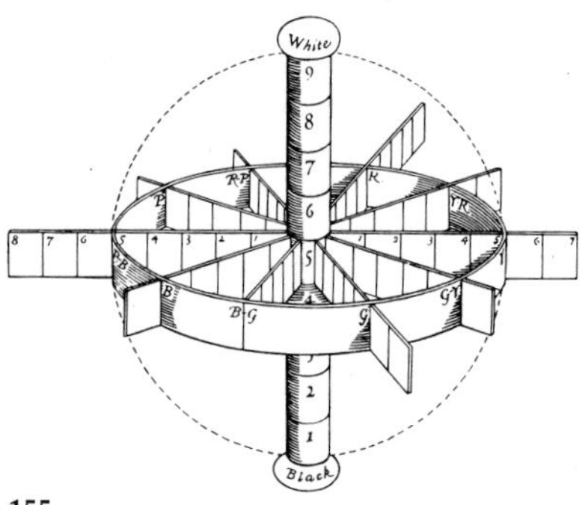

155

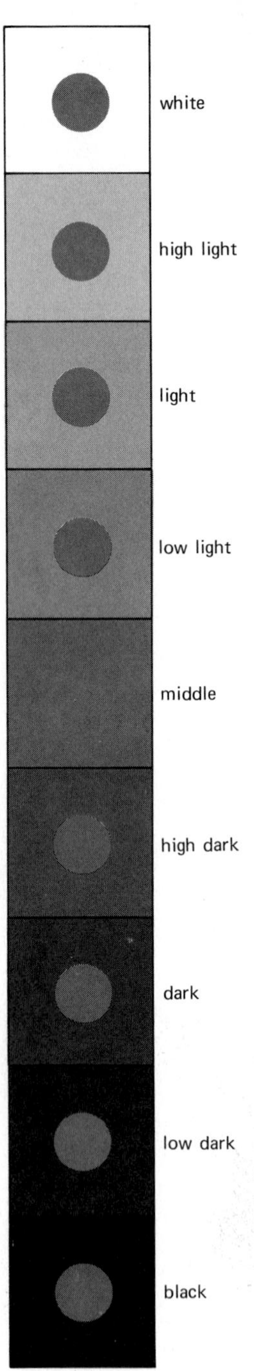

156

155
The properties of color can be demonstrated by a spherical diagram.

156
The gray scale shows variations in value from white to black. The circles in the centers are all middle value, although they seem different against lighter or darker backgrounds.

primary colors (Pl. 8, p. 106). By mixing any two primaries together, one obtains a *secondary* color: green from yellow and blue, orange from yellow and red, violet from blue and red. Going a step further, one can mix a primary and a secondary color to produce a third group, known as *tertiary* colors: yellow-orange, orange-red, red-violet, violet-blue, blue-green, and yellow-green. When all of these colors are placed in such a way that they seem to flow naturally, or to *modulate,* into one another, the basic color wheel results.

Any color wheel is to some extent arbitrary. Ives designed another wheel for use in mixing dyes and pigments, and physicists who work with light use still another. There are wheels that concern themselves with human vision and the sequence in which we see colors. Wheels vary in number of colors shown from eight to a hundred or more. They also vary in the names given the same color. What Ives calls orange, Albert H. Munsell calls yellow-red, and Ives' violet becomes purple in Munsell's designation. Such variation is not limited to color theorists, of course. Anyone who reads newspaper and magazine advertising is exposed to originality in color naming carried to the extreme. In an effort at enticing associations, firms offer plum sofas or melon-colored coats, leaving the reader to puzzle over which variety of plum or melon is being referred to.

In the hope of avoiding confusion, we will limit our discussion to the most scientific of the color systems, the one devised in 1912 by Albert Munsell. In this system, color is described in terms of three attributes: *hue, value,* and *chroma* (or intensity). There are five key hues: red, yellow, green, blue, and purple (Pl. 9, p. 106). Secondary hues thus become yellow-red, green-yellow, blue-green, purple-blue, and red-purple. Munsell used a numerical scale to designate variations in *value* or lightness, and *intensity* or brightness, of hues so any given color could be defined with precision. For this reason the Munsell system has become a standard method of designating color for government agencies such as the National Bureau of Standards, as well as for systems of standards in Japan, Great Britain, and Germany.

Color Properties

The diagram in Figure 155 demonstrates visually the properties of color: hue, value, and intensity, as Munsell understood them, and their interrelationships. *Hue* is the name by which we identify a color. It refers to the pure state of the color, unmixed and unmodified. The hue red means pure red with no white, black, or other colors added. Hue is the basis for the other color properties.

Value refers to the relative lightness or darkness of a color. It can best be understood by a study of the *gray scale* (Fig. 156). We show the scale with

Plate 6
Camille Pissarro.
Woman in a Field.
1887. Oil on canvas,
21 × 25½″ (54 × 65 cm).
Louvre, Paris.

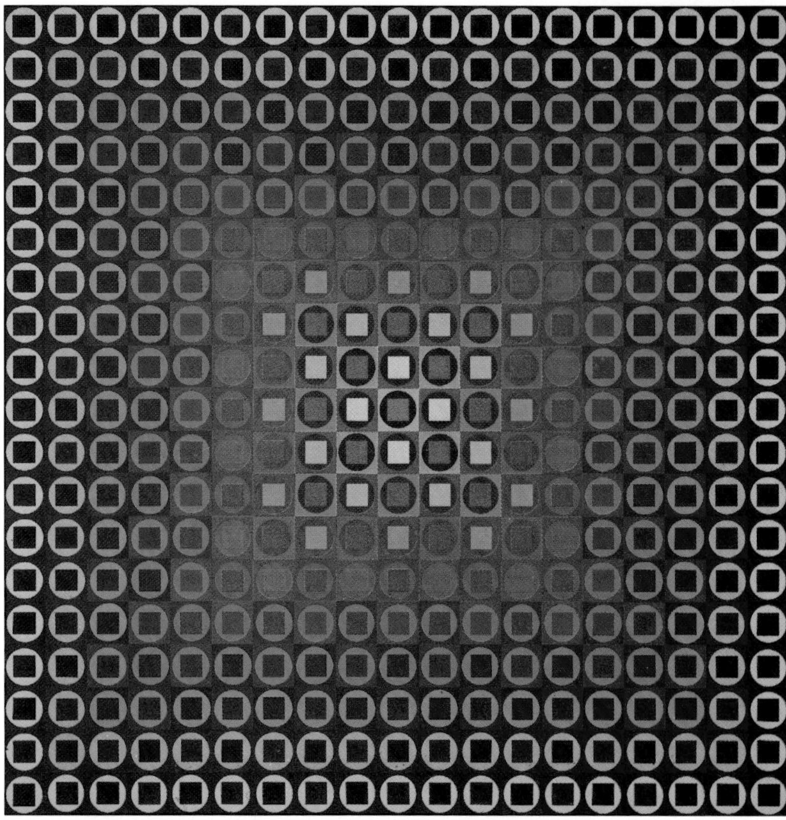

Plate 7
Victor Vasarely. *KEZDI-III.* 1966. 33 × 33″
(84 × 84 cm).

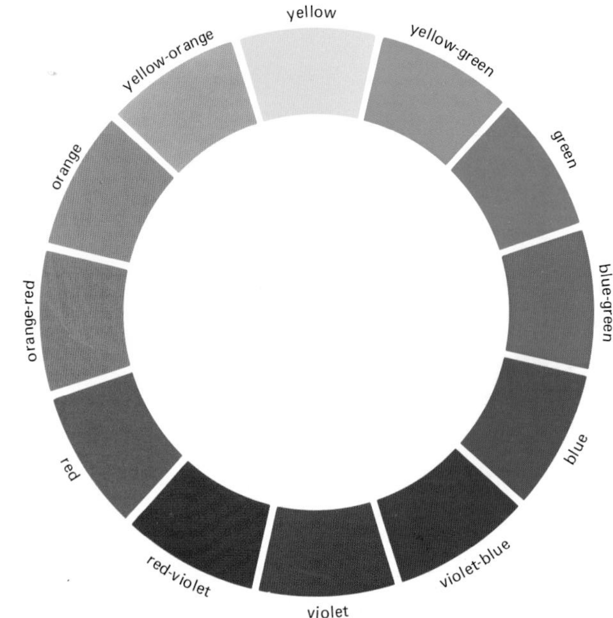

Plate 8
The traditional color wheel by Herbert Ives begins with primary colors of red, yellow, and blue. From these three hues are formed the secondary colors orange, green, and violet. Tertiary colors result from combining a primary with a secondary.

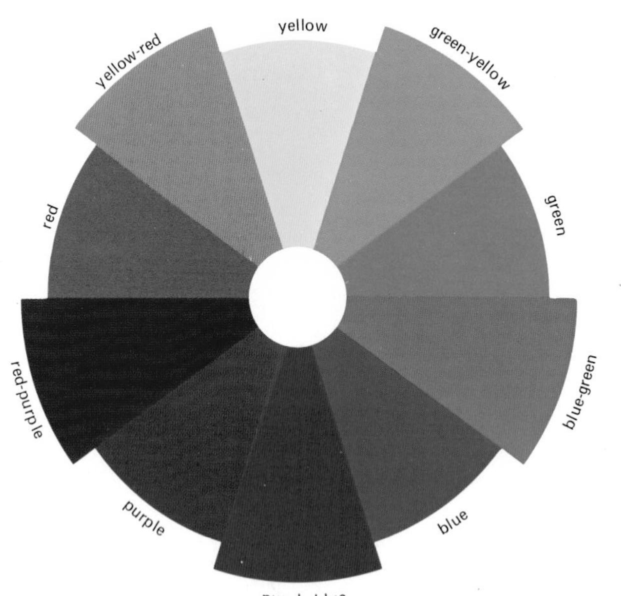

Plate 9
The Munsell color wheel is based on five key hues: red, yellow, blue, green, and purple. From these primaries are formed secondaries of yellow-red, green-yellow blue-green, purple-blue, and red-purple. Although the terminology differs slightly and the Munsell wheel has ten colors to Ives' twelve, the colors themselves are essentially the same.

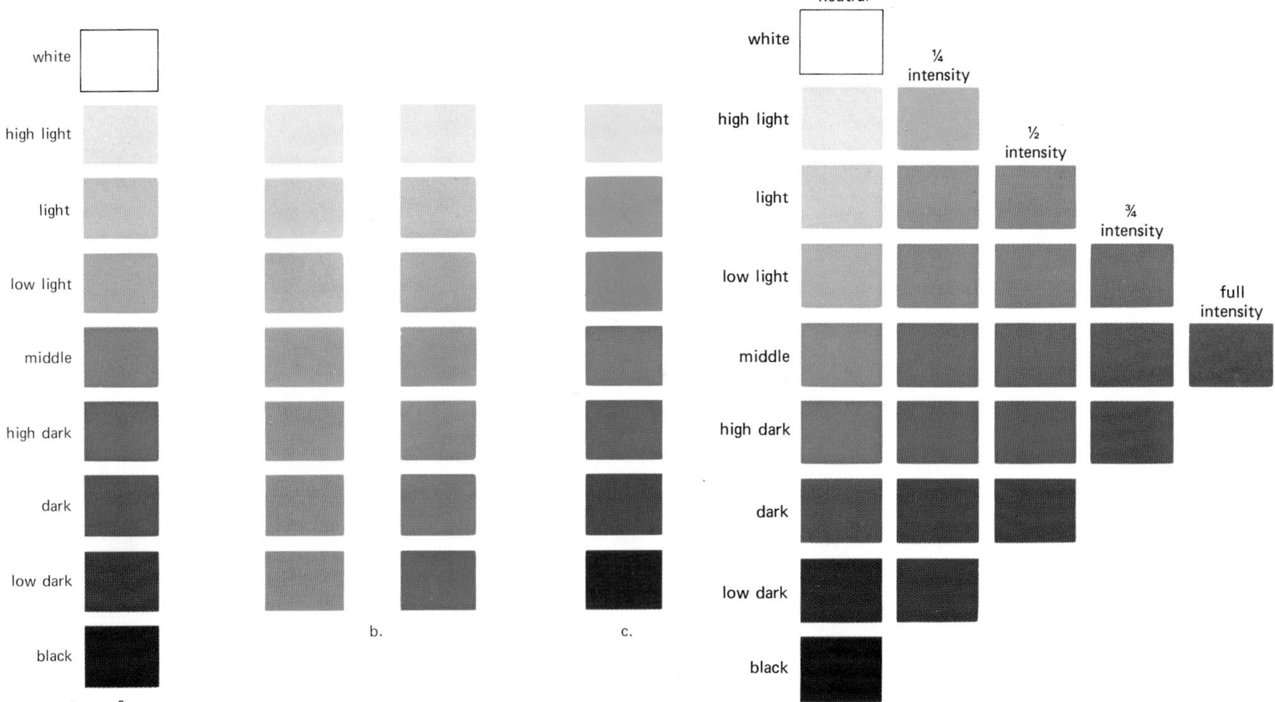

Plate 10
The value scale indicates shades of gray between pure white and absolute black (a). Hues in the color wheel can also be arranged in such a value scale, as with yellow-red and blue (b). At normal value, all the hues forming the color wheel can also be arranged in a vertical scale of lightness and darkness, with gradations from yellow to purple or violet (c).

Plate 11
The intensity or chroma scale shows the full range of brightness of which a hue is capable; from pure color at full intensity to the varied tones made possible by successive degrees of graying.

Plate 12a
According to the additive principle in light, the three primary colors, red, blue, and green, when overlapped, create the secondary colors of yellow, cyan, and magenta. When combined, they add up to white light.

Plate 12b
In the subtractive principle, the process is reversed. Yellow, cyan, and magenta are considered the primary colors and when they are overlapped, they produce red, blue, and green. When combined, they add up to black.

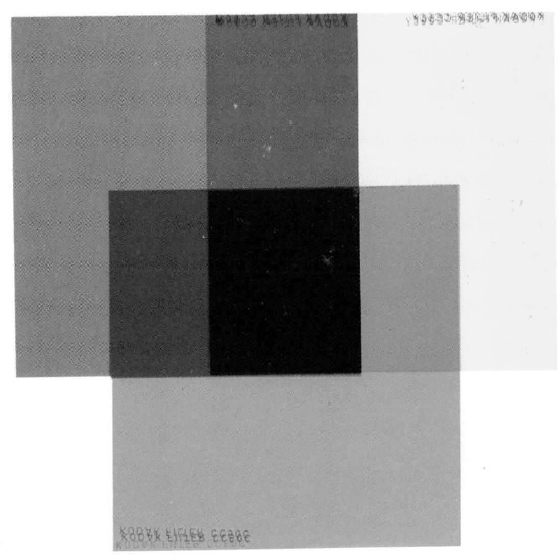

Plate 13
Experiment in *after-image.* If you stare at the red circle for half a minute, then switch to the white one, you will see not white but blue-green, the complement of red.

Plate 14
Experiment in *reversed after-image.* Stare at the yellow circles for half a minute, then switch to the white square below the circles. You will see not circles but the curved diamond shapes between circles and squares, and they will be not white but yellow.

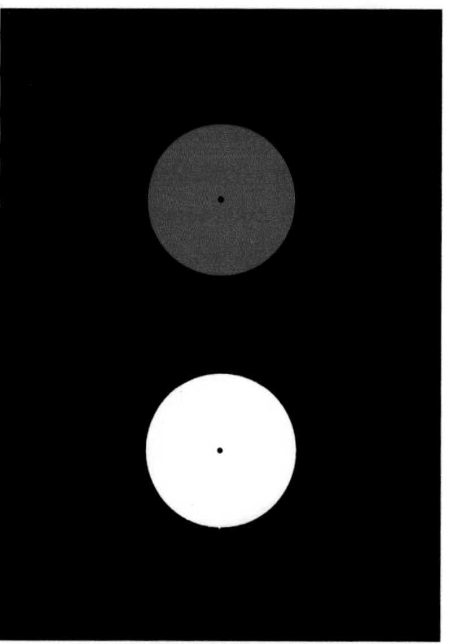

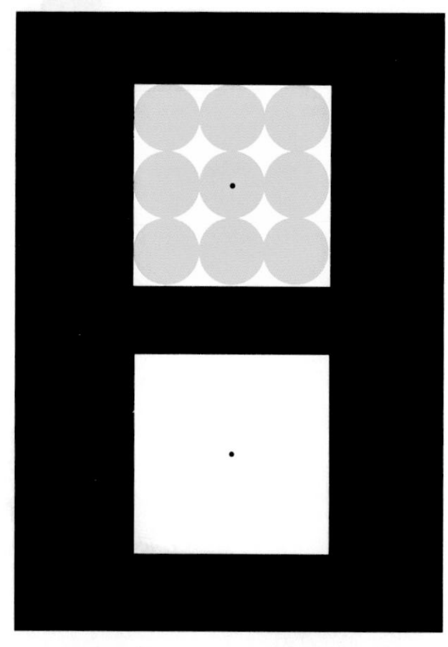

Plate 15
Albert Bierstadt. *Rocky Mountains.* 1863. 6′1¼″ × 10′¾″ (1.86 × 3.07 m). Metropolitan Museum of Art, Rogers Fund, 1907.

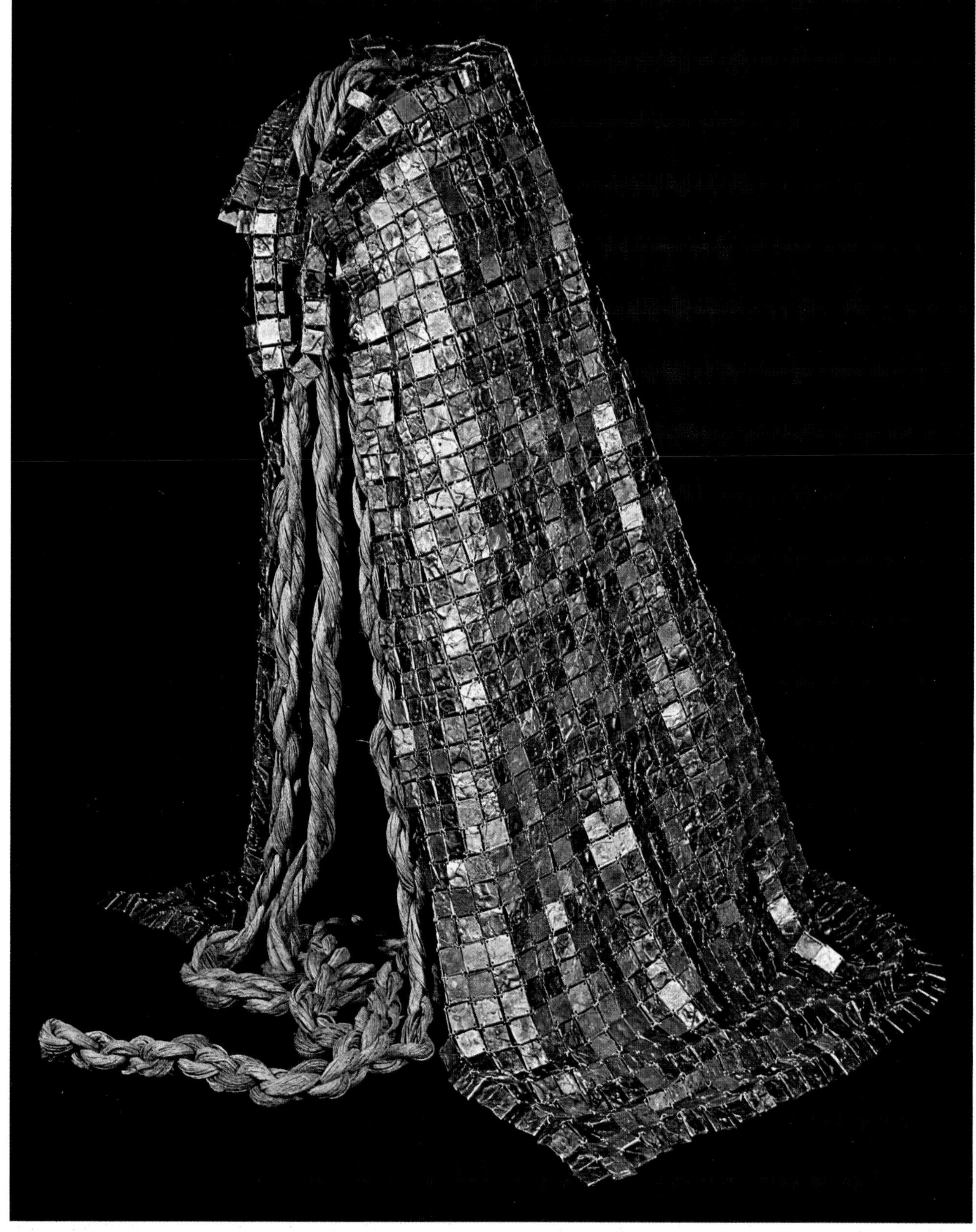

Plate 16
Barbara Chase-Riboud. *The Cape.* 1973. Multicolored bronze, hemp, and copper; 8′1½″ × 4′10½″ × 4′10½″. (2.48 × 1.49 × 1.49 m). The Lannan Foundation, Palm Springs, Florida.

Plate 17
Page from the beginning of the Christmas story in St. Matthew. *Lindesfarne Gospels*. Folio 29. Late 7th century. Courtesy Trustees of the British Museum.

Plate 18
El Greco. *The Resurrection of Christ.*
1600–05. Oil on canvas, 9′¼″ × 4′5″ (2.75 × 1.35 m).
Prado, Madrid.

Plate 19
Barnett Newman. *Dionysius.* 1949. Oil on canvas, 5′9″ × 4′ (1.75 × 1.21 m). Collection Annalee Newman, New York.

157

157
Albert Gleizes. *Port.* 1912. Pencil, 6 × 7⅝" (15.24 × 19.3 cm). The Solomon R. Guggenheim Museum, New York.

a center circle of the same middle value in each of nine blocks ranging from white to black. Compare the changes in the circles and squares in Vasarely's work in Plate 7 (p. 105). In both cases, the changes are the result of the background or adjacent value. The average person can distinguish perhaps 30 or 40 gradations between white and black, although a person with high acuity (visual sharpness) might be able to see as many as 150 gradations. The colors on the gray scale have no hue and are therefore termed *achromatic.*

Since most drawings are achromatic, the variations that give mass and accent are achieved by value alone. The use of value, like the use of color, can be a personal earmark, and frequently is expressed by the artist's choice of medium, with ink and charcoal usually the choices for strong contrasts in value. The individuality possible through use of value can best be shown in two drawings in the same medium. Let us consider pencil, for example. The heavy dark lines in the drawing in Figure 157 give it strong linear quality. Few portions are left white; diverse cross-hatching tech-

158

158
Jean Auguste Dominique Ingres.
Family of Lucien Bonaparte. 1815.
Graphite on white wove paper, 16¼ × 20¼″ (41 × 51 cm). Fogg Art Museum, Harvard University, Cambridge, Mass. (Grenville L. Winthrop Bequest).

159
Hudson (Gordon Jackson) and Rose (Jean Marsh) in a scene from the television production *Upstairs, Downstairs.*

niques are used to indicate mass and shadow. In the Ingres drawing (Fig. 158) the pencil is used to depict an immensely complex subject with the least possible means. Darks are held to a few crisp accents, and modeling is achieved by sharp lines and a suggestion of shading. The result is one of delicacy, gaiety, and fragile charm.

The gray scale (Pl. 10a, p. 107) is the basis for value in color, for the gradations can be translated into any hue (Pl. 10b, p. 107). The reverse process—a conversion of colors into values of gray—occurs in black-and-white photography (Fig. 159). Values that are not noticeable in a color painting become much more important in a black-and-white photograph of the work.

Every color has what is termed a *normal* value. This has to do with the inherent lightness and brightness of the hue; for instance, yellow is lighter and brighter than purple and will therefore have a lighter normal value. The term *normal* refers generally to the value in the middle of the value scale. This value of a hue is what is represented on a color wheel. Hues at their normal value can themselves be arranged in gradations of value corresponding to the gray scale (Pl. 10c, p. 107). Color values that are lighter than normal value are called *tints,* those darker than normal value *shades.* Thus, pink is a tint of red, and maroon is a shade of red. In mixing paints, the addition of white will lighten value and black will darken it.

Intensity, also known as *chroma* or *saturation,* indicates the relative purity of a color. Colors that are not grayed, which are at their ultimate degree of vividness, are said to exhibit *full intensity,* as shown in Plate 11 (p. 107). It is often difficult for students to comprehend intensity. One way of visualizing the meaning is to imagine a jar of powdered pigment in any hue and a saucer of oil into which the pigment will be ground with a mortar and pestle to form paint. When the first portion of pigment is added, the color is weak and diluted, but as the amount of pigment increases, the hue becomes more intense; the oil becomes saturated with pigment and, therefore, with color. The term *low intensity* means that the pigment has been grayed by addition of another color or of black or white. Low-intensity colors are often referred to as *tones,* and they include one of the most useful and subtle ranges of color.

Many dark colors are not only low in value but low in intensity. Maroon, in addition to being a shade of red, is also a low-intensity version of it. Browns are generally low-intensity, low-value yellow-red. Tan is a low-intensity, high-value yellow-red.

A knowledge of how to mix colors is fundamental to the artist. This, again, is both an art and a science and requires a thorough knowledge of the interaction of color.

159

Color Interactions

In all color wheels it is assumed that the two colors directly opposite each other are as different in character as possible. These pairs are called *complementary,* and their special relationship is an important element in creating color harmonies. On the Munsell color wheel, for instance, we note that blue and yellow-red are opposite each other. In Plate 6 (p. 105) we see that Camille Pissarro has used blue extensively for the shadows on grass and trees as well as in depicting the sky. He has balanced the variations of blue with accents of yellow-red in roofs, chimneys, and the capping on the wall. Complementary color harmonies have long been fundamental to the work of painters and interior designers.

In studying color in light rather than in pigment, we find that complements contain the hues known to compose white light. Photographers and printers working in color make use of this fact in formulating the principles of additive and subtractive primaries. The additive primaries are green, red, and blue: this principle is demonstrated in Plate 12a (p. 107). Here white light has been projected simultaneously through gelatin filters, one in each of the three colors. A red filter transmits the color red because the gelatinous film of the filter has absorbed the waves of all other colors. Similarly, a green filter will cast a green light, a blue filter a blue light. When red and green are focused on the same area, the light will be yellow. When green and blue are overlapped, the result is called cyan, or turquoise, and a combination of red and blue is known as magenta. In the area where all three colors overlap, we see white, or *all light,* derived from the three *additive primaries.*

Reversing the process produces *subtractive primaries,* as shown in Plate 12b. Suppose the light were projected through three more filters in magenta, yellow, and cyan. Wherever two areas of light overlapped, we would see an additive primary: green from cyan and yellow, red from magenta and yellow, and blue from magenta and cyan. Where all three overlap there would be not white, but black. When subtractive primaries interact, color is *subtracted* from light.

These principles have a relationship to color in pigment, which we will discuss in more detail later in the chapter. In exploring the interaction of color it is necessary to consider pigment as well as light. For instance, two complements mixed in equal parts in paint do not produce white but a neutral color, usually a variation of gray. However, when the same two complements are placed side by side, they become not grayer, but more intense. This phenomenon is known as *simultaneous contrast.*

The quickest way to understand this term is to take part in one of the experiments of Josef Albers, who made a career of the study of color. If you will turn to Plate 13 (p. 108) you will see two circles, a red one and a white one, each with a small black dot in the center. Fix your eyes on the dot in the center of the red circle and stare at it steadily for perhaps half a minute. Moon-sickle shapes may appear around the periphery, but do not be distracted; continue staring. Now, when your eyes have become thoroughly used to the red circle, quickly switch them to the white one, focusing once more on the little black dot. If you have the usual reaction, you will see a circle that is not white but blue-green, the complement of red.

Albers explained that this reaction is due to the fact that the human eye is tuned to receive any one of the three primary colors of red, yellow, and blue. Staring at red will fatigue the nerve ends in the retina so that a sudden switch to white (which consists of red, yellow, and blue) will register only the mixture of yellow and blue. Thus the eye perceives blue-green, the complement of red. The complement thus seen is called the *after-image.*

Albers' explanation of simultaneous contrast could apply to the increased intensity of adjacent complements. Since we know that mixing colors grays them, we can assume that overlapping them might cause us to see gray. However, when we separate them, looking first at one and then the other, the nerve ends tire of each in turn. Thus, whenever the eye changes, it sees the color it has focused upon without any of the components of its complement. To be specific, if red and blue-green are placed side by side and the eye is concentrated on the red until the nerve ends tire, when the eye is moved to blue-green it will perceive only blue and yellow mixed with no modifying color. The blue-green will therefore be of maximum intensity.

It must be stressed that no one really knows the reasons for the various aspects of color perception. Albers stated unequivocally that color is the most relative medium in art.

Related to simultaneous contrast is another phenomenon known as *successive contrast.* If we were to look at the red circle in Plate 13 (p. 108) and then look at a red circle instead of a white one, we would not see blue-green; instead we would see black. The possible explanation of this is that the fatigued retinal nerve ends see the complement of red (blue-green) but there is no white light to reflect it, so instead they superimpose the blue-green over the red surface, eliminating all light and resulting in black. In successive contrast, then, the afterimage is added to the perceived color instead of reacting to white light. Here again the explanation is purely theoretical.

Still another experiment reinforces the illusory quality of color by demonstrating the *reversed after-image.* This time look at the yellow circles in Plate 14 (p. 108). Once again, fixing your eyes upon the circles, stare fixedly for half a minute or so. Now shift focus suddenly to the white square below the circles. One might logically expect to see purple or blue circles (the complement), but this is not the case. One does not even see circles, but the curved diamond shapes resulting from the difference between the circles and the squares. These are not in the complement but are yellow. Albers characterized this as a double illusion and gave it the name *reversed after-image* or *contrast reversal.*

Objects change color for one of three reasons: a change in the chemical composition of the object, a change in the position of the object in relation to other colored objects, or a change in the source of light. It is this last change that we will now examine.

Lighting and Color

The color of any surface depends to some degree upon its ability to reflect light. The effect of the sun as it progresses across a varied and often moving landscape is one of almost magic complexity. Painters for centuries have tried to capture their impressions of light on land and water and the drama of atmospheric conditions under diverse light. One group of nineteenth-century Americans even called themselves Luminists, making these effects their primary objective (Pl. 15, p. 108).

160

160
Turk's cap shell (*Turbo sarmaticus*), from Capetown, South Africa.

161
Deborah Remington. *Capra.* 1974. Oil on canvas, 6′4″ × 5′7″ (1.92 × 1.7 m). (© Deborah Remington)

If we responded to every change of color in our surroundings as the result of daylight, we would soon find ourselves exhausted visually and psychologically. We therefore screen out much that happens around us visually, just as we ignore many smells, sounds, and tactile experiences. The artist cultivates these sensations as the materials of creative work and thus acquires a reputation for being unusually sensitive. A painter learns to notice the change in color that occurs when a cloud passes over the sun, or the totally different colors of field and water on a stormy day and on a sunny one, and the variations of green in a blade of grass from its tip to its base.

Artificial lighting has expanded our color experiences into a full-time adventure. At night our world is bathed in yellow or blue light that gives familiar outlines an eerie look. We are no longer startled by spotlighted landmarks rising mysteriously from the darkness with unreal colors accentuating their contours. Most dramatic, of course, is the use of light in the theater. In the circus, a drama, a concert, or an athletic event, light becomes a full-scale medium controlling our attention and pleasure through the use of colored filters, changing spotlights, and alternating beams.

The use of light and chemistry can achieve intriguing *expansion of color,* providing diversity through such illusory qualities as iridescence, luminosity, luster, and transparency. *Iridescence* is the rainbow effect evident in a raindrop or a seashell (Fig. 160), wherein the play of light on the surface color appears to produce all the hues of the spectrum. Iridescence can be difficult to achieve with paint, but many sculptures and constructions, especially in plastic, are iridescent.

Luminosity implies an actual or illusionary glow of light. We can see this effect in a work by Deborah Remington (Fig. 161), in which a subtle modulation of value from white to electric gray brings an aura of mystery to the painting. Remington manipulates oil paint in such a way that light seems to be coming from behind the canvas, casting a glow outward.

Luster in a work of art is the quality of shine or brilliance, the glow of reflected light. Specially formulated luster glazes are common in ceramics, and contemporary metal sculptures often display a high degree of luster (Pl. 16, p. 109). The painter achieves luster effects through the use of glazes of thinned paint built up in successive layers. Touches of gold add to the illusion of luster.

Finally, *transparency* is the appearance of being able to see through a

161

surface to what lies underneath. Albers conducted experiments to achieve this effect through the interaction of colors, but most painters rely on thin layers of paint that reveal masses and shapes underneath. Of course, in other media transparency is implicit in the material, as in Steven Weiss' table in Figure 61 (p. 41).

Color and Pigment

Pigments are substances of various kinds that have been ground into a fine powder to color paints and dyes. Paints are classified not by their pigments but by their *binders*—the substances used to hold them together. Thus, the same pigment that is added to linseed oil to make oil paint can be bound in gum arabic for watercolor, or in acrylic.

Originally pigments came from the earth or from other natural sources. The so-called earth tones got their names during the Renaissance, when they were dug from the soil around the city of Sienna or in the region of Umbria. These pigments retain today the names of raw sienna and raw umber in their natural state or, when baked to give a deeper hue, of burnt sienna and burnt umber. Other colors were taken from plants, sea creatures, or insects. Most pigments today are produced by chemical means; this increases their supply and also improves their durability and intensity.

The designer's approach to color depends upon the medium involved. The absorptive and reflective qualities of pigments can be affected by the binder, so it is necessary to become familiar with a medium by experimentation before definite results can be predicted. Mixing two colors of oil paint, for instance, may yield a result different from that of mixing similar colors in acrylic. Made from chemical components different from those in the traditional media, acrylics frequently have color names such as dioxazine purple or quinacridone red, which are not found in other media. Such innovations require their own rules for mixing.

Whenever pigments are mixed, a certain amount of light is lost. The amount of this loss depends upon both the reflective capacity of the individual pigments and their relationships to one another. The most unified color harmony is *monochromatic,* resulting from variations on a single hue. A computer, dealing with the possible variations of value and intensity, could come up with unlimited combinations within the range of one hue. As we saw in the Albers experiments, pigments most closely related in hue—next to each other on the color wheel—lose the least reflective light and therefore retain most of their brightness or intensity when used next to each other. Since complementary hues are the least chromatically similar of all possible combinations, being opposite each other on the wheel—red and green, for instance—a mixture of two complementaries drastically reduces their intensity so that the result is neutral, usually gray.

In mixing gray itself, awareness of the complements makes possible a whole range of vibrant shades. Black and white may be mixed to produce grays of various values, depending upon the proportions used, but all will be totally neutral. By mixing complements, however, we may produce a neutral that has slight reflective qualities and therefore some intensity—for example, a warm gray resulting from yellow dominating purple or a cool gray from blue and yellow-red, with the blue predominant.

Similar diversity is possible in the range of browns. Any three colors that are equidistant on the color wheel will form a triangle if we draw lines joining them; such colors are known as *triads*. The mixture of three colors in any triad will usually result in brown. This explains why some complements mixed together produce a hue closer to brown than gray, if either has components of the hues next to it on the color wheel. These interactions are inherent in specific media, and the only way to be certain of results is to experiment with the medium to be used.

Psychological Aspects of Color

Psychologists have long known that certain colors have the power to evoke specific emotional responses in the viewer. Among other qualities, colors seem to have a psychological temperature. Red, yellow, and their variations are referred to as warm colors, perhaps because we instinctively associate them with sunlight and fire. Conversely, blue and green—related to forests, water, and sky—are considered cool colors.

Human response to color has become of sufficient importance that people now make careers of color styling, which involves various activities such as designing color schemes for subways or factories and offering counseling services to industrial concerns and small businesses. Color stylists base their services on a thorough knowledge of the relationship of color to human reaction.

In general, warm colors stimulate and cool colors relax. A room with green walls can actually make people feel cold, and office workers have been known to have chills when working in blue surroundings. With the room temperature held constant, the chills lessened when the walls were repainted in yellow or the chairs slipcovered in orange. Employers have also found that their workers produce at higher levels when they are stimulated by bright colors.

The famed Notre Dame football coach Knute Rockne had the locker rooms for his own team painted red and those of the visiting teams painted blue. When halftime came, the visitors instinctively relaxed in their soothing quarters, while the home team remained keyed up and ready for a winning second half. Similar psychology has been adopted in painting the stalls of racehorses, proving that color psychology is not limited to human reaction. Although cats and dogs are color blind, insects react emphatically to color. Mosquitos avoid orange but approach red, black, and blue. Beekeepers wear white to avoid being stung, for they have found that if they wear dark colors, they are besieged. The knowledge that flies dislike blue has helped the meat-packing industry.

Warm colors tend to make objects look closer than cool colors do. For instance, a red chair seems closer than a blue one placed at the same distance from the observer. This knowledge can be useful to the interior designer who needs to alter the apparent size of a room. Painters make use of such knowledge in rendering both landscape and interiors.

Beyond these general, shared responses to color, each individual may react in a special way to particular colors. Each of us brings to the perception of visual stimuli a collection of experiences, associations, and memories that may be triggered by a given color. This could be the color of one's room as a child, or the color of the sky on a special well-remembered day. Color can evoke strong responses, pleasant or unpleasant, and even the viewer does not always understand the reason for the response.

Color Throughout History

The most important fact we need to know about color, whether using it in everyday life or in the profession of designer or painter, is that there are no rules. Even the most scientifically formulated color systems are not infallible, and the full orchestration of color goes much further than any system—its limitless variations and combinations can, like a great symphony, have profound effects upon the human spirit.

Perhaps the best way to comprehend the immense possibilities of color would be to explore its use throughout history. Primitive peoples used earth tones, of course, since the earth was their only source of color. As more sophisticated sources were found, such as marine life and exotic plants, the choices became more arbitrary. Finally, the use of chemistry made selection of color virtually limitless.

In Plates 17 (p. 110) and 18 (p. 111) we see a design and a painting using the same basic hues. Both works are religious in character. Plate 17 is a page from a gospel book done in calligraphy and decorated painstakingly by a monk in a seventh-century monastery on a stony island off the northeast coast of Scotland. It is a part of one of the masterpieces of manuscript *illumination* (decoration), and its beauty lies not only in the tremendous intricacy of the design but also in the subtle use of color to express profound and quiet devotion. Plate 18 is one of the masterpieces of the Spanish painter known as El Greco, who lived and worked in Toledo during the Inquisition in the seventeenth century. Here the forms are writhing human figures, produced by El Greco's unique expression of intense religious fervor. Just as the same musical tones are used in ancient plainsong and in a Bach mass, the same hues have produced these very different visual works created ten centuries apart. However, the Lindesfarne Gospel page employs a red verging on magenta, whereas El Greco uses a deep, luminous red, which radiates from the figure of Christ, the focal point of the painting. The blue of the gospel page is touched with green, like the softness of the sea at evening. El Greco's blue is a regal shade approaching purple. The golds differ as well: the gospel page shines as though touched by sunlight; the painting glows with passion. The closest the two works come to a common interpretation of hue is in the copper color, interspersed throughout the initial letter of the gospel and used, as well, in the figure at the left-hand side of the painting. Throughout the gospel page, the colors are a serene, highly decorative expression. In the painting, El Greco has used them dramatically, their rich tones heightened by dark shadows.

Throughout art history, the use of color has undergone specific changes according to the period and location of designers and artists. In the Renaissance, the painters of Florence, working in a warm, sunny climate, used clear bright colors. At the same time, the painters of Venice on its 120 islands painted with a kind of golden haze typical of the sunlight reflected off the sea and its lagoons. We have discussed the Impressionists' use of color to flood their canvasses with light and give a shimmering surface to their work (Pl. 6, p. 105). One of the most interesting developments in twentieth-century use of color was Color Field painting, which emerged during the late 1940s. With these works we are meant to experience colors directly, since color and form are indistinguishable. There need be no psychological or emotional content in the color, and the artist has deliberately omitted any shape reference that could distract from the purely sensory response (Pl. 19, p. 112). A little later the Op artists emerged as a movement based on the science of optics. Both groups are interested in color not as a means of depicting scenes or objects but as an endless source, in and of itself, of aesthetic possibilities.

Art historians often identify paintings as to period, and even to their painter, by the use of color. In the twentieth century, however, painters are exploring color for its own limitless, and often still inexplicable, qualities. Physicists can tell us about its composition, and psychologists can tell us something about how the eye perceives it. Color stylists tell us how color may affect us physically and emotionally. It is the realm of the artist to reveal perhaps the most important of the many aspects of color, its effect upon the human spirit.

8 Unity and Variety

Having examined the elements of design, we now consider the principles, those guidelines by which the elements are combined into a successful composition. We will consider seven principles governing the organization of any design or work of art. Of these seven, unity and variety are basic and overriding, for no work can function aesthetically without them.

A work devoid of a unifying element is liable to seem haphazard and chaotic. A work that is totally unified, with no variety, can seem boring. These two principles are interlocked. Unity represents the *control* of variety, whereas variety provides the *interest* within unity. In most cases, the ideal objective in a composition is a balance between the two qualities—diverse elements held together by some unifying device. The design in Figure 162 is an excellent example. The thirteen fish and thirteen fowl are all headed in the same direction: this is the first device toward unification. Furthermore, the artist has placed both shapes so the negative shapes resemble the shapes of the opposite species; the spaces between the fowl are similar to the shapes of the fish, and the fish are held together by shapes resembling the fowl. A third unifying device is the diamond shape within which the figures are composed, a variation of the square ground. A fourth is the border of lines that pulls the entire composition together.

Variety also is skillfully handled. Beginning with the shapes at top and bottom, the top goose and the bottom fish are rendered realistically through a detailed depiction of surface texture. Working toward the center,

162

162
M. C. Escher. *Lucht en water I* (Sky and Water I). 1938. Woodcut, $17\frac{3}{8} \times 17\frac{3}{8}''$ (44 × 44 cm). Haags Gemeentemuseum, The Hague.

163
Great variety can be found in the types of starfish.

each line of figures becomes more abstract until realism disappears completely and both fish and fowl become intermingling shapes forming an abstract design. The reversal of background—black geese against a white ground and white fish against a black ground—is a means of achieving both unity and variety, since in each case the background flows into the figures in the opposing area. Indeed this example shows us why it is impossible to consider unity and variety separately. Even in as unified a pattern as evenly spaced polka dots, there must be variety, or *contrast* between the color of the dots and their background, for the dots to be clearly visible.

Unity

Examples of underlying unity surround us in the natural world. All people, for instance, look somewhat different from one another, but we have no difficulty in identifying them as people. A collection of starfish (Fig 163) might exhibit different characteristics of color, texture, and even number of points, yet a unity of design—in this case, points radiating from a central body—marks them all as starfish. In creating unity within a composition, the designer may use various techniques, as we have seen. Among the most fundamental is *repetition*.

163

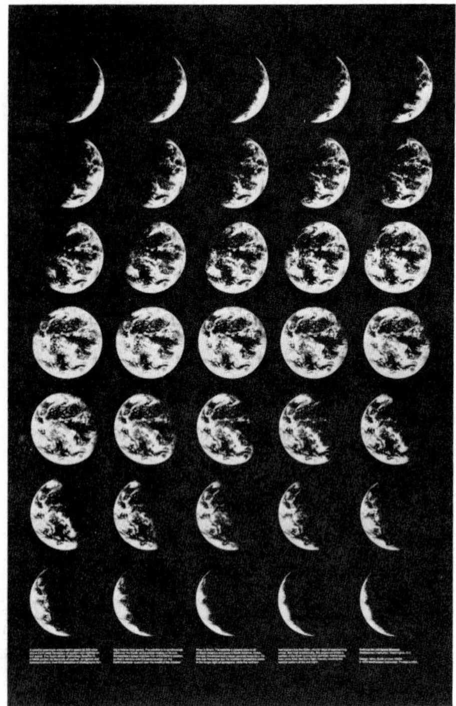
164

Repetition of motif, shape, pattern, size, or color can create an underlying unity. Repetition of motif, shape, and size are all obvious in the satellite poster in Figure 164. Actually, only the five shapes in the middle row are identical, yet through *closure,* the perceptual completion of a shape, our mind tells us that all the shapes in the poster are the same. The gradual modification of the circular shape, working in from the upper left-hand corner and out again at the lower right, provides not only variety in shape but also a flow of action as the shadow moves across the surface of the planet, yet the variety is secondary to the basic unity of the composition.

A more subtle repetition of shape is used in Renoir's *Le Moulin de la Galette* (Pl. 20, p. 129). Our first impression of this composition is that the canvas seems filled with a colorful *mass* that moves and changes constantly. Upon closer analysis, however, we find that the artist has carefully composed the crowd into a series of triangles. A dancing couple forms a natural triangle, and this motif has been expanded to include the predominant group of large figures in the foreground so that the smaller shapes seem to radiate backward from it. In counterpoint to the triangles are the circular shapes of heads and hats, beginning large in the foreground and shrinking to dots in the background, then repeated with emphasis in the globes of the lighting fixtures overhead. These lights serve an additional function. They repeat the light blue throughout the composition, providing unity through repetition of color.

Unity can be established by harmony of color, texture, or material. The stitchery in Plate 21 (p. 130) exhibits all three. The color is a full range of browns, from beige to orange to deep shades that blend readily into accents of black. The black in turn is lightened into small areas of gray, reaching highlights in white shapes that play throughout the composition. The brown and the black tonal scales thus play in harmony over the surface. Textures are repeated with equal skill, some of them visual, as in the shapes cut from printed fabric and *appliquéd* (stitched onto the background), and some of them tactile, with the interest supplied by tiny stitches. The fabrics are repeated in carefully balanced shapes and intervals, but particular interest lies in the way in which stitches and fabrics echo one another, carrying a theme throughout the composition but with infinite variation.

This type of harmony can be achieved in various media. The great Chinese landscape painters were masters at blending diverse topographical elements (Fig. 165). Their technique was not so much a matter of obvious brushstrokes as of an appreciation of the unity of nature, of Tao, which seeks harmony in all things. In *Buddhist Temple amid Clearing Mountain Peaks,* Li Ch'eng conveys the mysterious unity behind all the elements of the landscape—hills and trees in foreground, the cluster of temple buildings, and the tall, craggy mountains in the background—harmonized by the enveloping softness.

Harmony of *material* can be a unifying device. Sculptor Louise Nevelson concentrated for many years on assemblages of "found" objects—bits of wood, wheels, old newel posts, and other miscellaneous oddments. The fact that they were all of wood contributed unity even to such diverse collections, but the artist used further unifying techniques (Fig. 166). First, she sorted her materials into similar sizes and shapes and then *enclosed* them in boxlike shelves. You will note that some boxes contain thin vertical shapes, others are horizontal in feeling, while others have curved shapes or a combination of shapes. Then she placed each box with great care so the different categories are balanced throughout. Finally, she

164
Poster for National Air and Space Museum. Design: Miho. Earth photos: NASA. (© 1976 Smithsonian Institution)

165
Attributed to Li Ch'eng (Ying-ch'iu). *Buddhist Temple amid Clearing Mountain Peaks.* 10th century. Ink and color on silk, 44 × 22" (1.12 × .56 m). The Nelson-Atkins Museum of Art, Kansas City, Mo. (Nelson Fund).

166
Louise Nevelson. *Sky Cathedral.* 1958. Wood construction painted black, 11'3½" × 10'¼" × 1'6" (3.44 × 3 × .46 m). Museum of Modern Art, New York (gift of Mr. and Mrs. Ben Mildwoff).

165

166

painted the entire composition the same color. The result is one of dynamic texture. The Nevelson constructions thus assemble widely varied objects into an intriguing harmony of material, color, and texture.

Variety

The continual change and variety in nature provide the artist with the greatest possible material for design. From the vast storehouse of nature the designer chooses and combines different elements establishing the principle of variety within the context of an original design.

Variations in flowers, rocks, butterflies, animals, and seashells offer such enchantment that people travel the world in search of specimens for their collections. Near at hand, rocks, soil, and dirt roads all have their range of colors and textures derived from mineral deposits, and there is variety in the shape and size of puddles, which glint from changing lights.

167

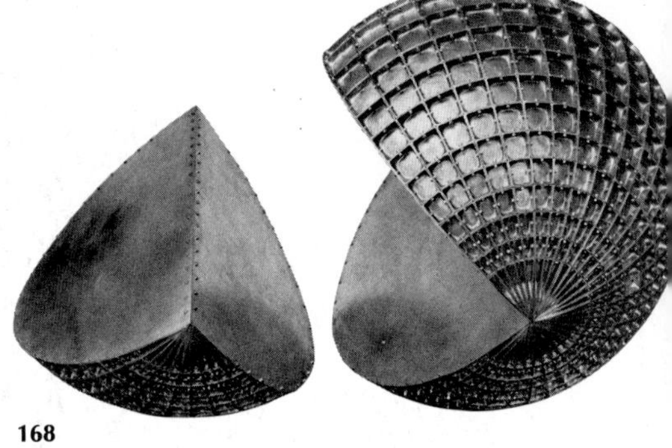

168

Although variety can be very subtle, the essence of variety is *contrast*—rough against smooth, light against dark, large against small. In Figure 167, the photographer used dramatic lighting to emphasize these contrasts. The result is a fascinating interplay of shapes and textures whose relationships seem to shift as we watch. The intense lights and darks flow throughout, unifying the rugged surface into a harmonious composition. This is an excellent example of what we mean by choosing and combining natural elements to establish the principle of variety within unity.

An eloquent expression of both unity and variety through the use of a single material can be seen in the cast aluminum sphere in Figure 168. A simple metal sphere would be unified but would not be interesting; therefore Robert Bart has covered the surface with a fretwork that radiates and expands with the curvature of the mass, the frets being small at the two poles and increasing in size toward the center. What arrests our attention, however, is the slicing open of the sphere, revealing perfectly smooth surfaces within. These now lie exposed and in startling contrast to the patterned exterior, though the use of rivets along the inside edges serves as a transition from the smoothness to the extreme roughness.

167
Minor White. *Capitol Reef, Utah.* 1962. Photograph. Gelatin-silver print, 12⅛" × 9¼" (30.73 × 23.5 cm). Courtesy Minor White Archive, Princeton University, N. J.

168
Robert Bart. *Untitled.* 1965. Cast aluminum, 12¾ × 17¾ × 17½" (32 × 45 × 44 cm). Courtesy Leo Castelli Gallery, New York.

Plate 20
Auguste Renoir.
Le Moulin de la Galette. 1876.
Oil on canvas, 4′3½″ × 5′9″.
(1.31 × 1.75 m). Louvre, Paris.

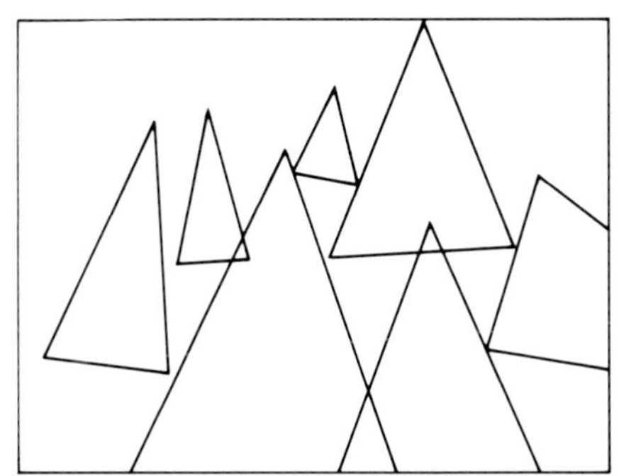

Diagram of Renoir's
Le Moulin de la Gallette.

Plate 21
Martha Mood. *America's First Families.* Post-1967.
Stitchery, 36 × 60" (80 × 150 cm).

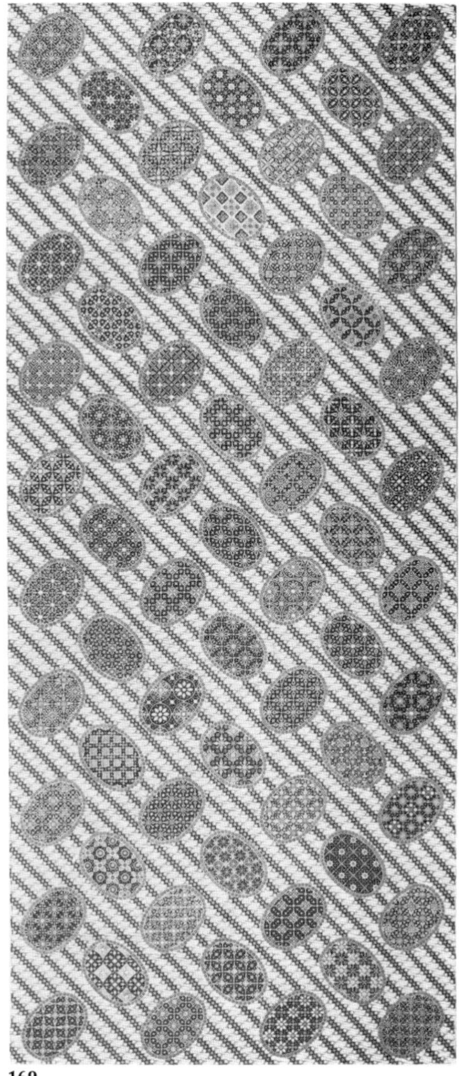

169

In quite another medium, the same principles were an obvious consideration. The textile in Figure 169 was woven and then decorated by the batik method, which has long been a skilled art among the people of Indonesia. This example from Java is done on the diagonal, a form of design considered to be more interesting when worn than designs on the horizontal or vertical axis, and therefore of superior merit. There are two unifying devices here: the allover consistency of the background pattern, and the repetition of identical ovals over the entire surface. As always, the interesting part is the handling of such unified elements to give variety. Every other oval is turned at right angles: this immediately varies the visual pace. Even more important, perhaps, is the fact that each oval is unique, with an individual design unlike that of any of the other ovals on the fabric. This is variety carried to a superlative degree, yet there is nothing chaotic about it, for the regularity of the ovals and their skillful placement guarantee a unified pattern. These careful design considerations have made this particular textile a superb example of the art of batik.

169
Kain panjang. Java, Jogjakarta region. Batik, cotton; warp 8′ (2.45 m), weft 3′4″ (1.04 m). The Sylvia Bishop Collection, Palm Beach, Florida.

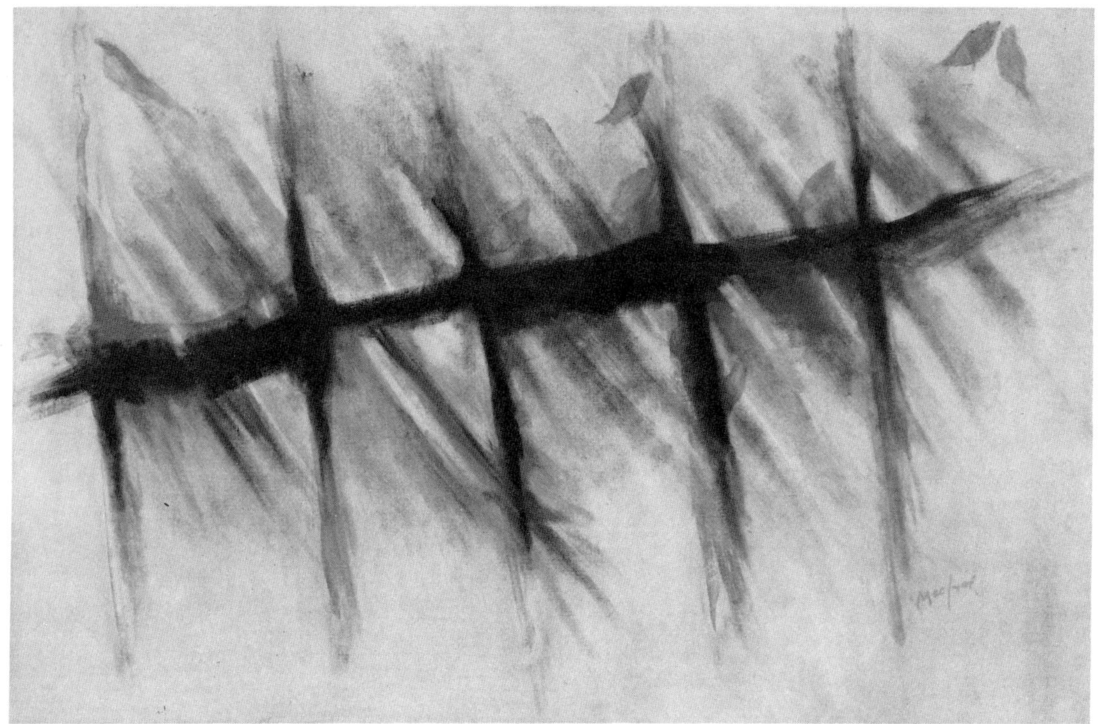

170

In contrast to this complex design is Loren McIver's painting in Figure 170. Here the basic lines are strong and simple, consisting of a slightly slanted line with other lines at right angles to it, which suggest window frames through which light and patterns are revealed. The unity again is obvious, but the variety is achieved by the placement of background lines in an opposing direction. This immediately sets up a tension that is dynamic, implying movement. The addition of a few leaf forms contributes to the reaction of the viewer, tossing out symbols from which to visualize our own concept of how it would seem if we were looking through a skylight. We sense wind, light, and movement—the result of a few strong elements skillfully used.

Variety of form in architecture has appeared in many styles through the centuries, from medieval castles to Victorian homes. The Russian church in Figure 171 displays what may well be the extreme limits of variety in a wooden structure. The series of onion domes reaching upward, the curved niches behind them, and the curved and serrated shingles all represent ways in which wood can be formed and bent with careful skill. Behind this skill, however, lies more than the desire for tremendous variety, for there is an obvious unity in the repetition of the dome shape throughout the structure, and the continuation of the textural richness on both domes and gable. Moreover, the series of crosses on the domes provides not only a symbolic unity but a very real visual thread that unifies the diverse structural masses.

These, then, are some of the ways in which variety and unity can be achieved. With the importance of these two principles in mind, we now move on to other principles we will find closely related and frequently intertwined with those we have just considered.

170
Loren MacIver. *Sky Light.* 1980. Oil on canvas, 26 × 41" (.66 × 1.04 m). Courtesy Pierre Matisse Gallery, New York.

171
Church of the Transfiguration, Kizhi, USSR. 1714.

171

9 Balance, Emphasis, and Rhythm

The three principles to be discussed in this chapter are so basic a part of the world around us that they necessarily influence the work of any sensitive designer. Not only are they intrinsic to the environment in which we live, but they are vital to human life itself. As a principle of design, each plays a major role in the achievement of unity.

A particular type of *balance* causes human beings to walk erect, in contrast to most other creatures on the earth. In all forms of life, balance is necessary for survival. For every intake of breath, one must exhale, and periods of activity must be balanced by periods of rest. Science and mathematics are founded on the principle of balance. In an algebraic equation, for example, the two sides must balance. Politicians seek a "balance of power," with political parties balancing one another in order to represent as nearly as possible the will of all the people. We find balance everywhere in the natural world. The cycle of the seasons, the distribution of day and night, and the landscape in which bright sunlight is softened by the blues and greens of field, forest, and water—all display a fundamental balance.

The achievement of a goal, a moment of deep happiness, a visual element that attracts our attention by being spectacular: these provide *emphasis,* being high points that stand out from everything around them. In nature, a violent storm (Fig. 172), a mesa jutting out from the flat landscape, and a mountain peak against the sky are all examples of emphasis. Composers and writers guide their works through a series of emphatic incidents, usually culminating in one great climax from which the rest of the composition takes its significance. Our individual lives are a series of climaxes that stand out in memory because of their influence on the rest of our experience.

Another basic component of the universe we inhabit is *rhythm.* Planets in our solar system have a rhythm of revolution around the sun, as does our moon around the earth. The seasons follow regular rhythms, resulting in a rhythm of sowing and harvesting. Animals, birds, and fish in their migration and breeding habits follow precise rhythms human beings find astounding. Tiny hummingbirds fly from the Canadian border to South Amer-

172

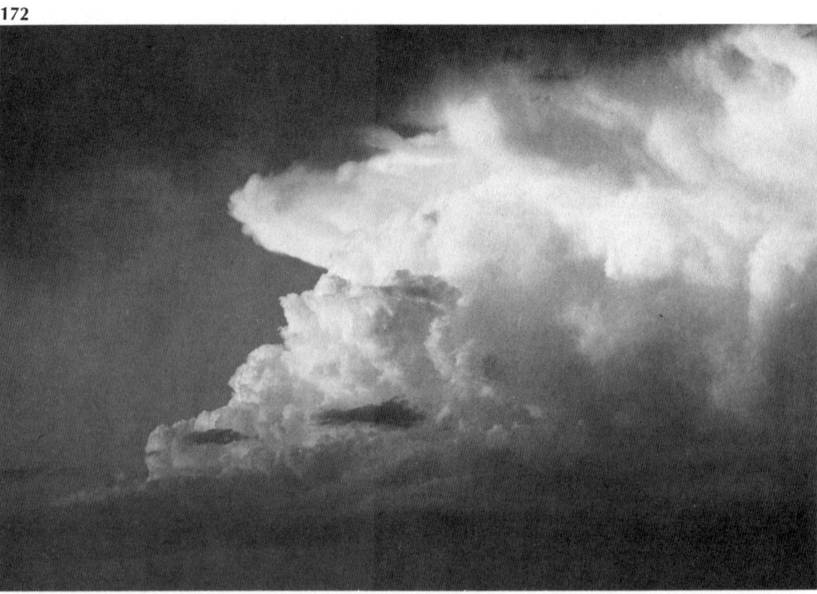

172
Myron Wood. *Plains storm east of Pueblo, Colorado.* 1975. Photograph.

173
Diagrams of three types of balance.

174
Logo for International Harvester. 1973. Design: DeMartin Marona Cranstoun Downes, Inc., New York.

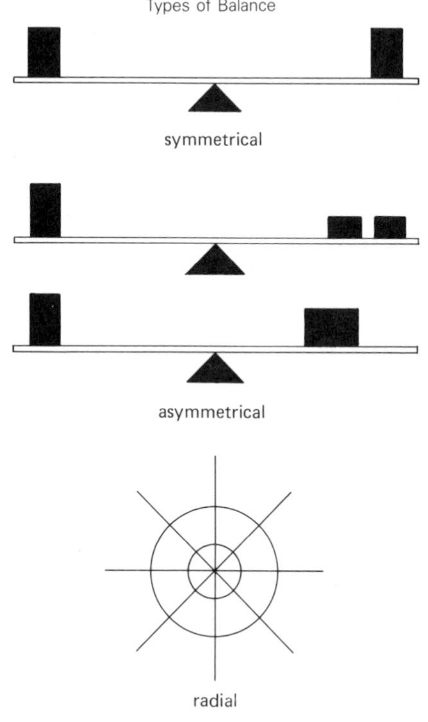

173

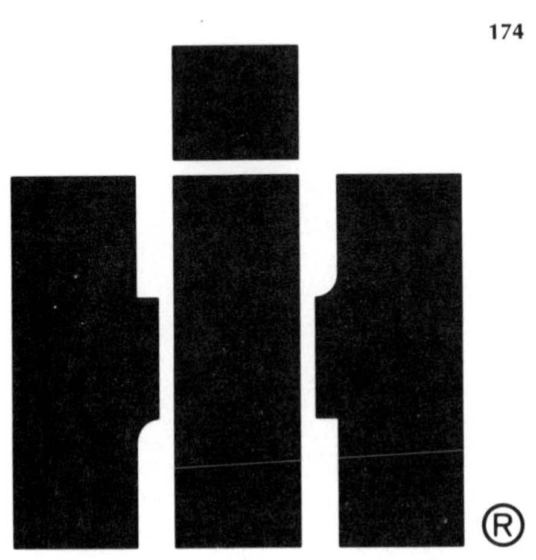

174

ica each winter, yet arrive back at almost the same moment each year, and each autumn the salmon from deep northern waters fight a heroic struggle through shallow and tumultuous streams to get up to their spawning grounds. When travelers suffer "jet lag" it is because the natural rhythms of the body are upset by flying long distances in a short period of time. Every aspect of our being depends upon such rhythms. The heartbeat and throb of pulse and the regularity of breathing are known as "vital signs" because their rhythms are essential to survival. We can assume that rhythmic movements of the body as expressed in music and the dance are satisfying to us because they respond to a rhythm deep within us.

Since these three principles of balance, emphasis, and rhythm are such a fundamental part of us, it follows that they will be among the most important qualities of any successful design. We will find that they are closely interwoven in the visual arts, for rhythm provides balance, and emphasis is a component of rhythm. We will discuss each one of these principles individually, but we will find that in nearly every case the other two are hovering nearby.

Balance

The absence of balance is usually noticeable and its removal can be catastrophic. If we remove the lowest card in a house of cards or topple the first domino in a line, the structure collapses. Lack of balance in a composition is equally unsettling, making us feel vaguely uneasy. For this reason, artists sometimes deliberately upset our sense of balance in an effort to create a startling effect. For the most part, however, balance is a basic characteristic of a work of art. *Balance of shape and mass* is traditionally divided into three categories: symmetrical, asymmetrical, and radial (Fig. 173).

In *symmetrical* balance, we can draw an imaginary dividing line through the center of a composition so the two resulting halves will form a mirror image of each other (Fig. 174). Another term for this is *bilateral symmetry.* Although we are told that no human body is exactly the same on each side, most human bodies are visually symmetrical, and therefore most things associated with them, such as furniture and clothing, are designed symmetrically. Symmetrical balance comes naturally to most designers. Certainly it is the easiest type of balance to achieve.

A composition that is balanced symmetrically tends to seem stable, dignified, and calm, creating a sense of repose. Most architecture, and especially public architecture, is symmetrical. Colonial and Federal period houses in the United States characteristically had a door set directly in the middle of the façade, with windows evenly arranged on either side and a chimney at each end. It is interesting that young children usually draw their houses in this fashion, as though the inclination toward symmetrical balance were a basic human instinct.

In *asymmetrical* balance, the two imaginary halves of a composition will have equal visual weight, but the forms will be disposed unevenly, as in the second and third drawings in Figure 173. As anyone who has ever played on a seesaw knows, balance can be established by moving backward and forward from the center or fulcrum. It can also be established by distribution of weight. In other words, two small people will balance one large one. Stated mathematically, 2 plus 2 equals 4, but so does 1 plus 3.

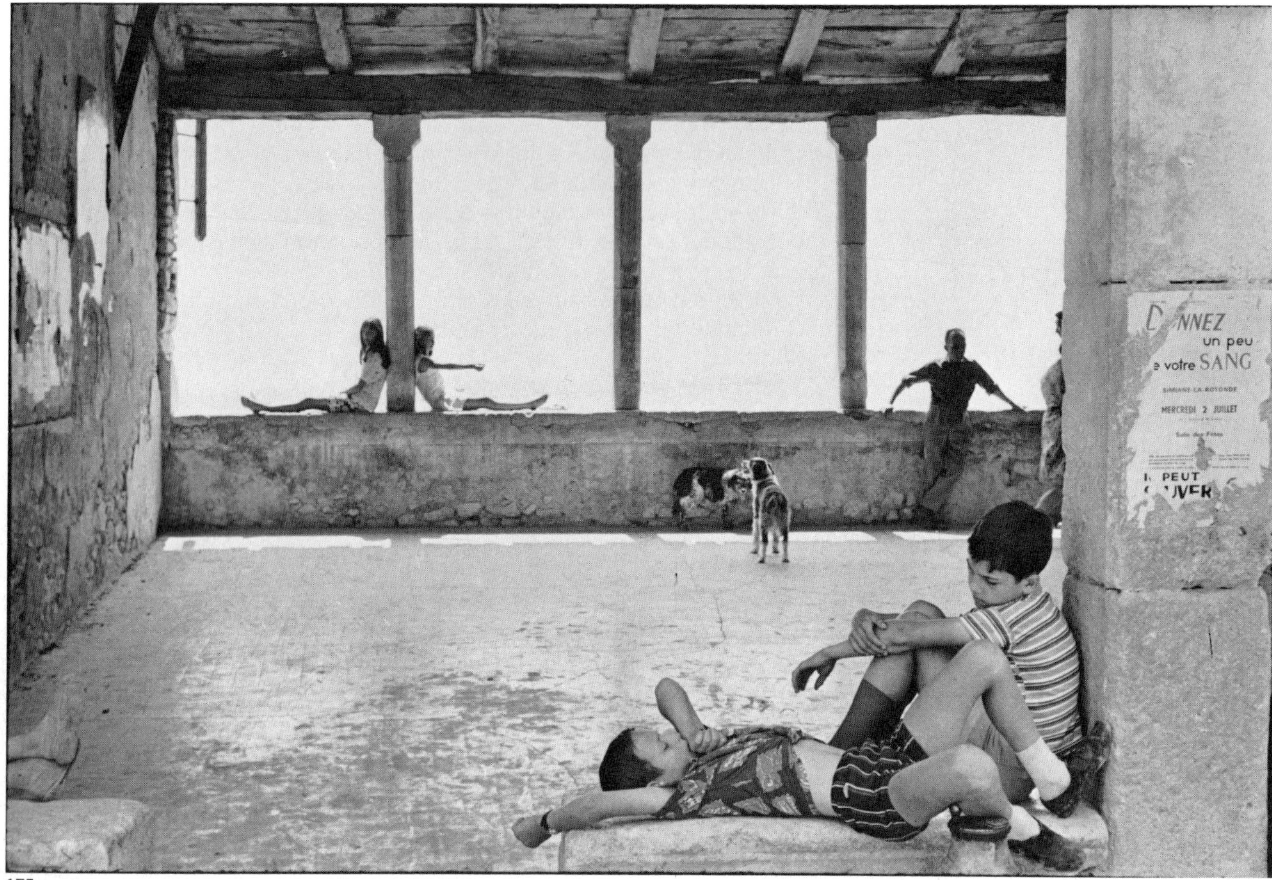

175

175
Henri Cartier-Bresson. *Simiane la Rotonde.* 1970. Photograph.

176
John Makepeace, FSIAD FRSA. Storage unit in birch, acrylic, and stainless steel. 1972. Pillar of birch plywood and acrylic drawers cantilevered on a stainless steel column, height 4′10″ (1.48 m). Courtesy the artist.

177
Aequorea, a species of marine life. Carolina Biological Supply Company.

178
Pier Luigi Nervi and Annibale Vitellozzi. Cupola and dome, Palazzo dello Sport, Rome. 1957.

Translated into visual terms, this kind of symmetry can produce a composition like the one in Figure 175. Perhaps the most remarkable thing about this photograph is not so much the superb balance as the fact that no one posed for it. No doubt dozens of people walked by without seeing anything unusual about the scene, but Henri Cartier-Bresson, with his artist's eye, immediately recognized the unique elements and recorded them. The center of interest, of course, is the two small boys in the foreground, but they are balanced by the two little girls in their book-end pose *plus* the textural interest of the peeling wall at the left. Only a trained eye would have realized the necessity for the expanse of wall. The light patches balance the light panel at the right, pulling the composition together and complementing the figures of the girls. The arms of the man echo the triangular shapes of the boys' legs, which are repeated in the letters on the disintegrating poster.

The storage unit in Figure 176 illustrates both symmetrical and asymmetrical balance. When it is closed, its balance is symmetrical, but the open position reveals an exciting asymmetry. If symmetry tends to suggest repose, asymmetry is characteristically active and dynamic. Interior designers use asymmetry to create a more interesting effect in a room, by balancing two chairs against a sofa, for instance, or a group of small paintings against one large one. This kind of balance involves not just shape and size but color and texture. An area of rough or interesting texture can balance a larger area of smooth surfaces.

Radial balance results when a number of elements point outward from a central core, like the spokes of a wheel. It is found abundantly in nature—in rays emanating from the sun, an age-old symbol of the sun god; in the structure of flowers whose petals follow a radiating pattern; and in the seed structures of such plants as dandelions and milkweed. Many species of zoological life also develop in a radiating pattern (Fig. 177). In architecture, radial symmetry is used widely, in the dome and other circular forms (Fig. 178). It is perhaps the most dynamic type of balance, for it connotes explosive action, like the sparks from a skyrocket that shoot into a breathtaking circular pattern, filling the sky. It further has a connotation of infinity, as do the ripples of water spreading in a pond.

176

177

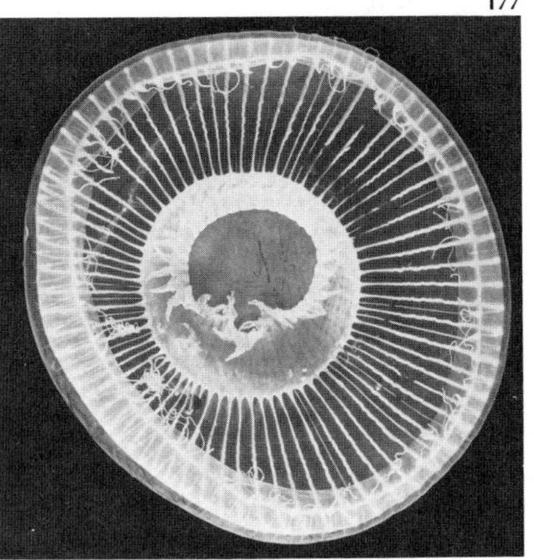

178

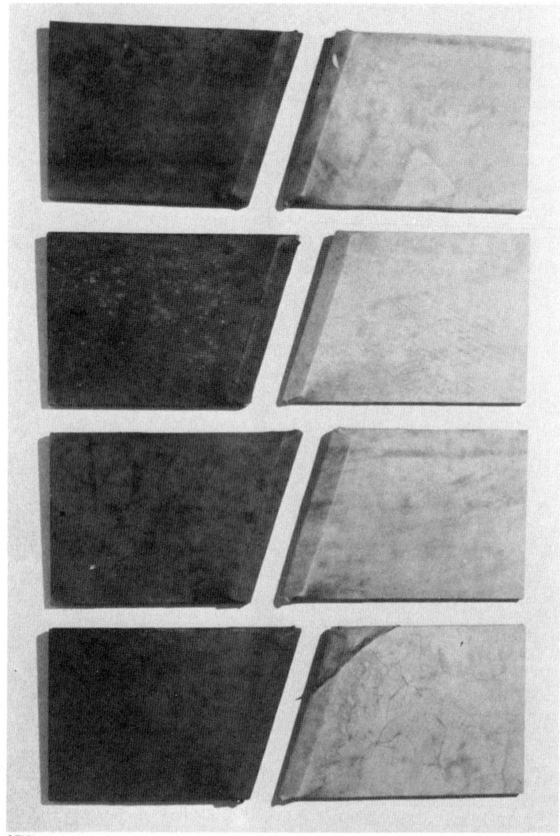

179

180

179
Joe Atteberry. *Zig Zag.* 1980.
Rawhide, tea-stained wall piece,
4′9″ × 3′ (1.45 × .91 m). Private collection.

180
Robert Rauschenberg. *Summer Rental.* 1960.
Oil and paper on canvas, "combine" painting.
5′10¼″ × 4′6″ (1.78 × 1.37 m).
Private collection, New York.

181
Residence, on the Gulf of California,
of James T. Flynn, architect AIA.

182
This Japanese garden stresses the
interplay of many natural textures. From
House & Garden Garden Guide;
copyright © 1968 by The
Condé Nast Publications, Inc.

Balance of value simply means a balance between lights and darks in a composition. In the wall piece by Joe Atteberry in Figure 179, the balance is perfectly symmetrical but on a horizontal axis instead of the more usual vertical one. This could be a mechanical division of space and of value except for the texture of the leather, which carries echoes of the light value into the dark areas and marks the light bands with a mottled darkness throughout. Thus the balance is more subtle than is obvious at first glance. In the canvas in Figure 180, the balance is even less clearly defined. Blocks of dark balance blocks of light, but the shapes are quite different and the distribution is not at all symmetrical. An interesting aspect of this composition is the fact that although we usually think of dark as being heavier than light, the darks seem to hang from the top of the canvas, suspended over the large portion of light toward the bottom.

Architects work with values in balance when they design the projections and openings in a building. Any projection from the exterior will create dark values of shadows, which can be balanced against light values where sunlight hits the smooth façade (Fig. 181).

Japanese gardeners have a deep appreciation for *balance of texture.* With twelve centuries of gardening tradition behind them, nearly every family has its garden in Japan, often tiny plots carefully cultivated to express an inborn veneration for nature, which is interpreted in moss, wood, and stones as well as in shrubs and other plantings. The textures of stones and plants are meticulously balanced, as are the varied textures possible through the use of different kinds and sizes of stones (Fig. 182).

181

182

183

Texture is handled in a rhythmic way to provide balance in the work in Figure 183. By laminating thin pieces of wood, the artist has built up a flowing work that almost seems to tie itself in a knot, yet stands firmly in balance on its pedestal. The textures supplied by the varying colors of wood are balanced by four smooth areas and by the dark spots placed in careful balance to one another.

The *balance of color* in design or painting takes its cue directly from nature. Warm, advancing colors—red, yellow, and orange—tend to have more visual weight than the cooler blues, greens, and purples. A painter who is trying to balance a composition in many colors may find that a very small amount of red will be equal to a large field of blue and green. To some extent, we are undoubtedly conditioned to this response because of nature's example. The overwhelming proportion of our landscape is composed of cool colors: the blue of sky and water, the green of grass and trees. Bright, warm colors appear primarily as accents, in birds and flowers. We expect red, for instance, to be either isolated (in a clump of flowers) or transitory (in the flush of sunrise or sunset or the brief glory of fall colors). This may be why we attach more visual weight to bright hues; we notice them more because they are not our customary background.

A composition of predominantly cool colors can, of course, be in perfect balance, as can one of all warm colors. In such cases, the balance is achieved by variety of hue and value, of texture and shape. The relative emphasis of warm and cool is dramatically demonstrated in Barnett Newman's painting in Plate 19 (p. 112), however. Here a field of green is broken by two simple lines, one a clear yellow and the other, wider line a yellow-orange. The lines vibrate against the cool background, drawing our attention not only because of the contrast in color but also because they are the only variations in a field of solid green. The interest they arouse and their strong contrast to the background make for perfect balance.

183
H. C. Westermann. *The Big Change.* 1963. Laminated pine plywood, 56 × 12 × 12″ (142.2 × 30.5 × 30.5 cm). Private collection, New York.

184
Jacques Louis David. *The Death of Socrates.* 1787. Oil on canvas, 4′3″ × 6′5¼″ (1.3 × 1.96 m). Metropolitan Museum of Art, New York (Wolfe Fund, 1931).

Emphasis

Certain types of design have no special point of emphasis. These are repetitive and decorative by nature, and we are more interested in the allover effect than in focusing on one part of the composition. Textiles and wallpaper are good examples of this. However, many works of visual art benefit from having a *focal point* or points, some element that attracts the eye and acts as a climax for other sections of the composition, providing the kind of emphasis that is supplied, for example, by the climax in a play. Without such points, our eye is apt to move restlessly through the work, unconsciously searching for something on which to focus. It may be helpful to explore the means by which emphasis is achieved in two very different paintings.

In Jacques Louis David's *Death of Socrates* (Fig. 184), the focal point is obvious: the figure of Socrates himself. Here the artist makes striking use of light and tonality to achieve both emphasis and drama. The body of Socrates is also rigidly vertical, whereas all nine of the men surrounding him lean toward him. The upraised finger is the highest point in the foreground, creating a focal point within a focal point. Furthermore, David has positioned Socrates alone almost at the center of the canvas, whereas all the others are grouped at the sides. Finally, a color reproduction of this painting would show that Socrates alone is dressed in white, whereas his followers are all garbed in cool tones of red, blue, and orange.

184

185

Since David's style was a thoroughly *classical,* intellectual one, his aim was utmost clarity. Francisco Goya could be considered as almost an opposite to David, for his work is characteristically dark, brooding, and strongly emotional, or in other words, *romantic.* Even so, the same emphatic devices operate in his *Executions of the Third of May, 1808* in Figure 185. The figure of the man about to be shot is spotlighted this time, isolated from his fellows by a brilliant glare. He is also dressed in a light color in contrast to the dark garments of the others. His arms are raised in a crucifixion pose, an automatic center of attention. The soldiers' rifles, with fixed bayonets, point directly to him, and the angle of their bodies further directs the viewer's eye in his direction. Perhaps the placement of the figure in the total composition exemplifies as much as anything the difference between the two styles. As a classicist, David has used a formal, almost symmetrical structure for his composition, with the arched doorway and lighted distant figures balancing the weight of the heavier cluster of figures at the right. Goya's composition is spectacularly *asymmetrical,* depending upon the heavy group of figures at the right, interspersed with light accents, to balance the high drama of the central figure to the far left.

185
Francisco Goya.
Executions of the Third of May, 1808.
1814–1815. Oil on canvas,
8′9″ × 13′4″ (2.67 × 4.05 m). Prado, Madrid.

186
Athanase Papavgeris. Low relief panel.
Terra cotta with polychrome glaze
decoration, height 29″ (73.66 cm).

In both works five devices were used to achieve dramatic emphasis—light, direction, height, position, and color.

In the design in Figure 186, in contrast, emphasis is achieved primarily through texture. In this terra cotta panel reminiscent of a terraced Greek village, the band of pebbled surface running vertically just left of center becomes the cobbled street. The primary focal point is the textural interest of the pebbles. The appearance of the element of texture in textured clay throughout the composition underscores the textural emphasis of the pebbled band, contributing at the same time a sense of balance.

186

Rhythm

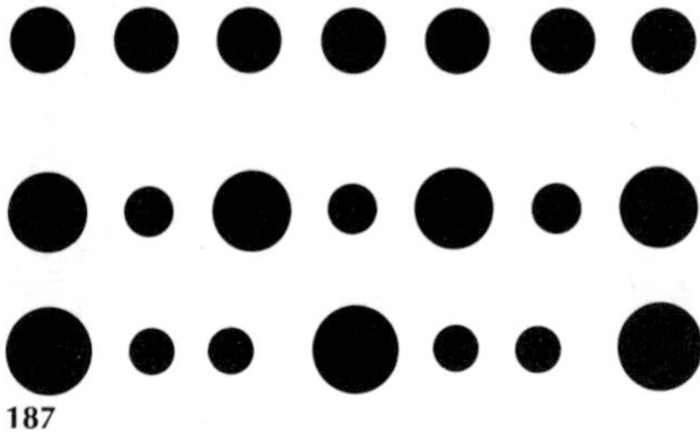
187

Rhythm is a regular pulsation, like the beating of the heart or a drum beat. Figure 187 shows a visual translation of three rhythmic patterns, the first consisting of regular pulsations, the other two having evenly spaced points of emphasis. One could tap out these patterns with a drumstick or a pencil, giving more intensity to the stronger beats, shown by the larger dots.

Some artists work to the accompaniment of music in order to transmute rhythmic sounds into their work. Others express a natural sense of rhythm without conscious effort, much as rhythm is expressed naturally by a dancer. All expressive processes can set up rhythms, and all works can convey them. In creating a visual design the artist may lend a *physical* rhythm to the application of brushstrokes, the impact of hammer on chisel, the thudding of the shuttle on the loom, or the humming of the potter's wheel. The rhythmic leg motion in working the pedals of a potter's wheel is vitally important to the smooth turning of the pot; in fact, the entire body is engaged in rhythmic motion when a potter or a weaver is at work. On the other hand, in painting or sculpture the rhythms may be purely *visual,* deliberately introduced into the composition to provide the impression of flow and unity.

A textile often combines both kinds of rhythm. The person who wove the twined border in Figure 188 undoubtedly experienced the physical rhythms of weaving. In addition, she has created two varieties of rhythm within her design. The center panel is a geometric version of a *flowing* rhythm, such as we find in waves beating upon the shore or rippling endlessly in a rushing stream. The points provide a continuous series of climaxes balanced by their counterparts as the lines dip downward. The designs at the edges, on the other hand, are beats like the ones in the diagram; only these are chevron shapes, repeated with regularity as though they were marching in carefully paced accompaniment to the flowing rhythm in the center.

Swirling curved rhythms are particularly dynamic, as we associate them with something whirling into a vortex, often beyond human control. We see such rhythms in whirlpools and tornadoes, and experience them in reverse in the music of a symphony or opera when the music builds to a resounding climax. In the filament hanging in Figure 189 we experience these rhythms in a subtler form. In the fine mesh of twisting, turning threads that works downward to the sturdier strands curling at the bottom, there is a sense of continual movement and of culmination.

Like unity and variety, the principles of balance, emphasis, and rhythm cannot be considered separately. In every example in which we have cited one of these principles, at least one of the others is present. The wall piece in Figure 179 with its balance of values is a classic example of a beating rhythm. The Flynn house in Figure 181 shows balance of light and dark but also has a dynamic swirling rhythm, with strong emphasis laid on the light cylindrical shapes. It would be a good exercise to carry this analysis through all the illustrations in the chapter, for in this way it would become clear how closely the principles and elements of design are intertwined. We now come to two more principles that are present in all of the designs we have considered: the principles of proportion and scale.

187
The rhythm of a drumbeat can be interpreted visually as a series of dots. Dots of different sizes indicate variations in rhythm and points of emphasis.

188
Twined border using hooked diamond in rhythmic pattern. Sumba, Indonesia.

189
Kay Sekimachi. Hanging.
Multilayer nylon multifilament weave; length 40" (1.02 m).

188

189

10 Proportion and Scale

Both proportion and scale deal with relative size. *Proportion* usually refers to size relationships within a composition, whereas *scale* indicates size in comparison to some constant, often the size of the human body or the size that we expect something to be. One illustration may help to clarify this difference.

The leather chair in Figure 190 is in *proportion* to the room it occupies. Since the room itself is big, two stories tall, and largely open to the outdoors, the oversize piece appears in fitting proportion to the expansive surroundings. However, as a receptacle for the human body, it expands to a very *large scale.* Seen as a baseball glove, its scale becomes enormous!

Since size is a factor in both proportion and scale, the two often overlap. Something that is too large to be in satisfying proportion to its surroundings could be large in scale as well. Realizing that the two are often inseparable in design, we will nevertheless separate them for individual analysis.

Proportion

It is differences in proportion that make people look different from one another. The proportion of leg length to torso, of waist to height, of shoulder width to length of body—all of these differ widely in human beings. Proportions within our faces give us individuality in appearance also. One person will have a short nose, another big eyes, another high cheek-

190

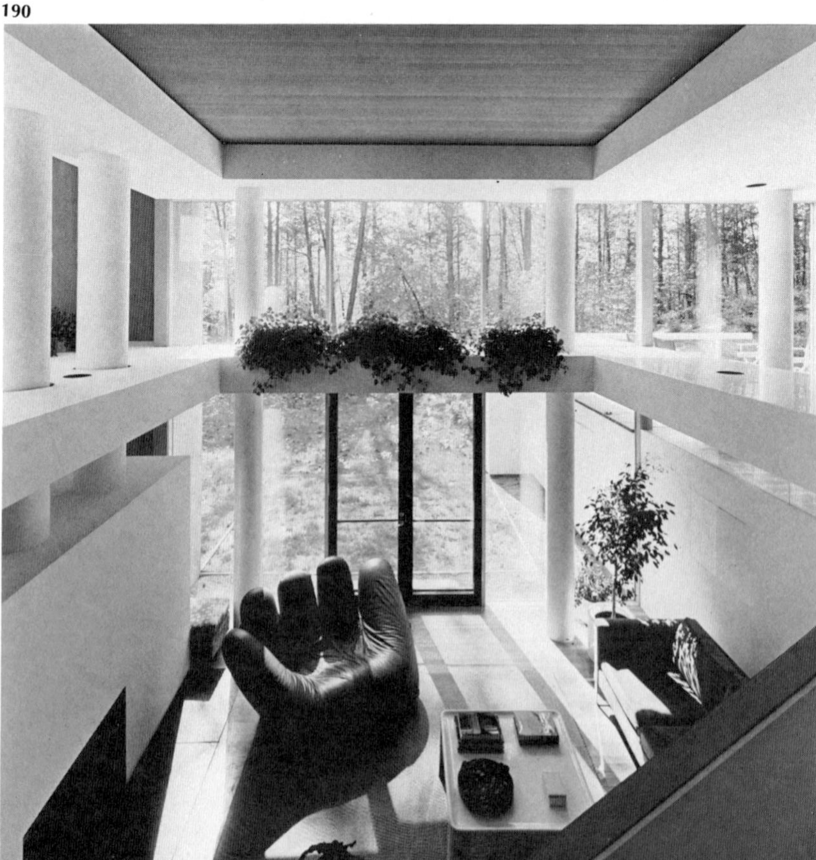

190
An enormous baseball-glove chair was selected by interior designer Ann Hartman for a home in the suburbs of Washington, D.C. (designed by architectural firm of Hartman-Cox).

191
René Magritte. *La Folie des Grandeurs.* 1961. Oil on canvas, 39½ × 32" (100 × 81 cm). (© Private Collection, USA)

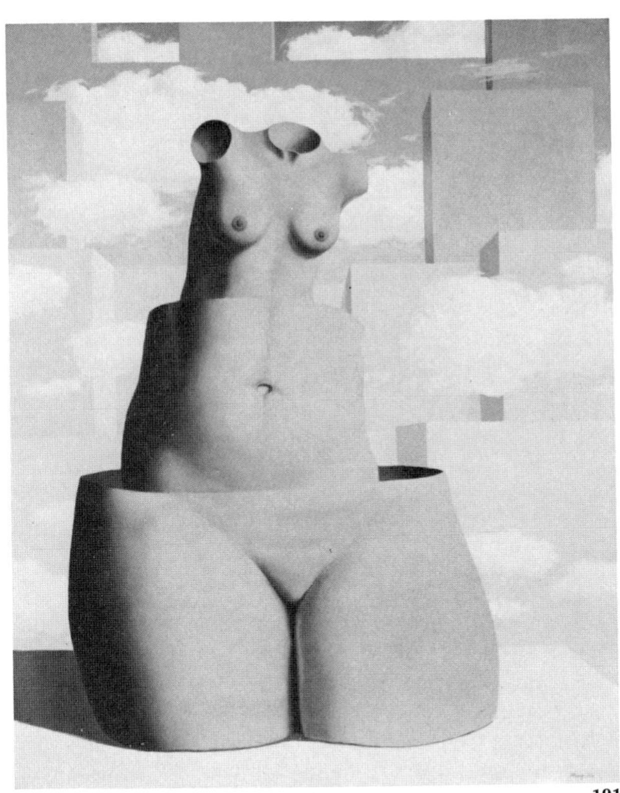

191

bones—all of these are a matter of proportion. Many people would feel quite different if they were two inches taller or shorter, or if they had a different nose or chin. Our proportions become an integral part of our appearance to the world and so, to some degree, determine our personality.

Proportion is usually based on an ideal or a norm. Different cultures have different ideals of what is beautiful, and these ideals are frequently a matter of proportion. Things that are unduly out of proportion jar to some degree, whether we are speaking of a giant, a small painting hung on a vast expanse of wall, a huge pattern in a dress on a diminutive woman, or an overreaction to an imagined verbal insult. This is not to say that disproportion is necessarily bad. Sometimes it is unique and interesting. For this reason, artists frequently and deliberately vary the proportions in a composition to attract attention or create impact (Fig. 191).

Perception of size bears a definite relationship to the distance from which we view it. The size of an object is not the size that projects on the retina of our eye but is supplied by the mind, which works from experience and preconceived judgment. An automobile seen at a distance is smaller than the fire hydrant beside us, yet our subconscious mind establishes the automobile as being big enough to dwarf the hydrant if they were side by side. People visiting New York City for the first time are often surprised that the skyscrapers seem so high, just as we are impressed by the great size of Niagara Falls or a European cathedral when we first see them in person. We are familiar with these sights through pictures, which place them in proportion to a small rectangle we can encompass with a glance. Standing before them, our perception can grasp only a small area at a time; consequently the total picture seems enormous.

192

This distortion of proportion can be a matter of position as well as distance. The pyramids of Egypt were built to overwhelm, to show the greatness of the pharaohs buried within them and to stand as monuments for all time. Even the individual stones are of such scale that human beings climbing upon them look like flies. Their proportion, however, can be a matter of viewpoint. In Figure 192 the great pyramid of Chephren looks so small that the figure in the foreground could reach up and touch the top of it. The reason is that he is standing on the neighboring pyramid of Cheops. Both pyramids are roughly the same height—about 450 feet (137 meters). Because of the unusual angle and the telescoping properties of the camera, the mighty Chephren looks almost like a toy.

The camera does this to us repeatedly on the television or movie screen. Tiny insects loom as giants, and even the cells seen under a microscope are shown in immense size and clarity. Such devices can be instructional and artistically effective. We rely on our perception and its subconscious adjustments to assure us that our world still has its normal proportions.

192
Pyramid of Chephren. c. 2570 B.C. Height c. 447′ (136.2 m). Photographed from the pyramid of Cheops.

193
The golden section. a:b = b:(a + b). The proportion of side *a* to side *b* is the same as the proportion of side *b* to side *a* plus side *b*. The smaller rectangle and the larger one are therefore in the same proportion. In the resulting 1:1.618 ratio, 1 represents the square and .618 the rectangle.

194
Ictinus and Callicrates. The Parthenon, Athens. 447–438 B.C.

The Golden Mean

For centuries, the shells of snails have fascinated mathematicians because of their orderly growth pattern. This pattern follows the logarithmic spiral and can be reduced to the same mathematical formula that the ancient Greeks followed in planning their temples, sculpture, and vases. It was included in Euclid's writings and gives explicit form to the Greek belief in the importance of mathematics as a governing force in the universe. This precept was expressed philosophically by Aristotle as the *golden mean,* the virtue that is the median between two vices, as courage is the mean between cowardice and foolhardiness.

Mathematically, the precept is known as the *golden section.* The formula for it would read as follows: $a:b = b:(a + b)$. In referring to the plan for a Greek temple, for instance, if *a* is the width of the floor plan and *b* is the length, the proportion of side *a* to side *b* would be the same as the proportion of side *b* to side *a* plus side *b* (Fig. 193). The ratio works out as 1:1.618. It has been noted that such a relationship avoids the obvious mechanical unity of a 1:2 relationship, in which a rectangle would be composed of two squares. The golden section is more subtle, and classical scholars have spent years exploring the many uses to which the ancient Greeks put it—in spaces within temples, as rectangles within which sculpture was composed, as the invisible rectangle encompassing Greek vases.

The outstanding example of beautiful proportion in the history of art is the Parthenon (Fig. 194). In its design flexible units known as modules were used to ensure a unified relationship of each part to the whole building. These modules were not units of measurement as such but variable units, such as the diameter of a column, which would be different for different buildings. Built of blocks of Pentelic marble with no mortar, the Parthenon is a supreme example of Greek subtlety. What appears to be a rectangular building is actually a study in harmonious curves that give the various parts a fluid yet substantial harmony. Sculpture positioned above eye level slopes slightly outward toward the top to compensate for the position of the viewer on the ground. The columns are thicker and closer together at the corners because they are seen against the sky and would otherwise appear to be slimmer than the rest. Individual columns curve outward slightly toward the center because if they were straight the weight of the upper part of the building would make them appear to buckle. Numerous other refinements contribute to the graceful proportions that are still evident even in the temple's present deteriorated state.

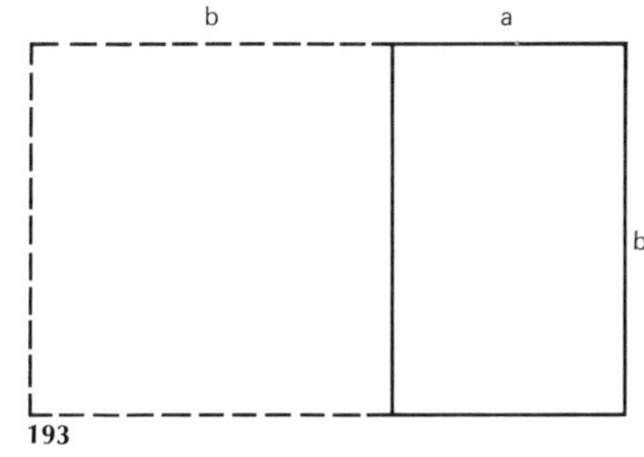

193

194

195

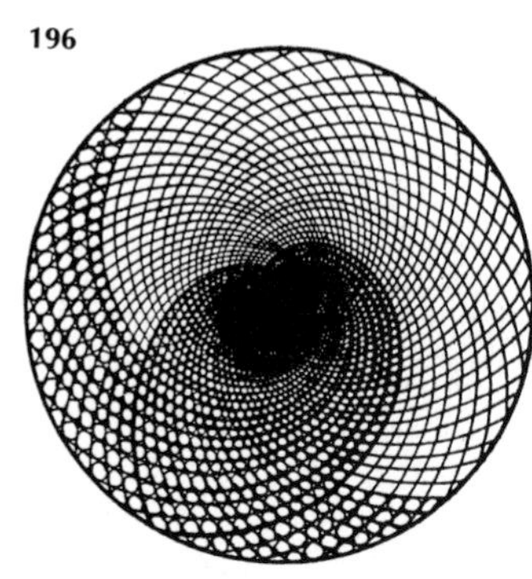

196

195
Paul Caponigro. *Sunflower.* 1965. Photograph. Private collection.

196
Seed structure of a sunflower.

197
The logarithmic spiral is based on arcs of circles, which in turn, are based on squares of graduating size.

198
Radiograph of a nautilus shell.

The Fibonacci Series

We have continually stressed the design inspiration to be found in nature, but none is more exciting than the discoveries related to the snail shell and the logarithmic spiral upon which the golden mean is based. This ratio was the subject of intensive study during the Renaissance and was no doubt an influence on Leonardo da Pisa (Leonardo Fibonacci), medieval Europe's greatest mathematician, who in the early thirteenth century developed the so-called Fibonacci series. This is a progression of numbers that has been found to reveal the secret of much of nature's structural design, particularly in the field of botany. The progression runs as follows: 1, 1, 2, 3, 5, 8, 13, 21, 34, 55, 89, 144, and so on, with each number being the sum of the two numbers preceding it. It has been found that pine cones have 5 and 8 rows of seeds, pineapples have 8 and 13, dandelions 13 and 21, daisies 21 and 34, and sunflowers 55 and 89 (Figs. 195, 196). Count the leaves on a stem, starting at the bottom; when you reach one that is directly over the one you started with, it will be one of Fibonacci's numbers.

To understand what is meant by the logarithmic spiral, one must draw a rectangle that has the relationship of 0.618 on one side to 1 on the other. By drawing a diagonal line from one corner, you will arrive at a perfect square. This is not unusual, but there is a unique feature: the remaining rectangle will be in exactly the same proportions as the original one. If one continues this process with increasingly smaller rectangles, the space eventually becomes too small to draw in. Now, if a curve is swung through each square from the inside out, the result (Fig. 197) will be exactly the shape of the chambered nautilus (Fig. 198). Nautilus and snail shells increase on the outward edge so that they grow in size but do not change shape. Many other natural forms grow in size but do not change proportion—the tusks of an elephant, the horns of a ram, and the claws of a cat, for instance. All of these reflect the logarithmic spiral in their final form. It is easy to see how one might become fascinated by such research, finding that so much in nature is based on a single law of proportion.

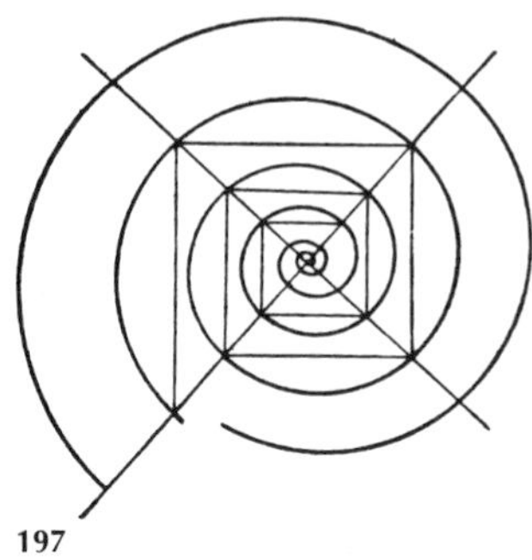

197

Few contemporary designers work consciously with a formula such as the golden section, yet many painters have done studies based on the square. Josef Albers' painting in Figure 87 is based entirely on the pleasing proportional relationships between squares of various sizes and their rela-

198

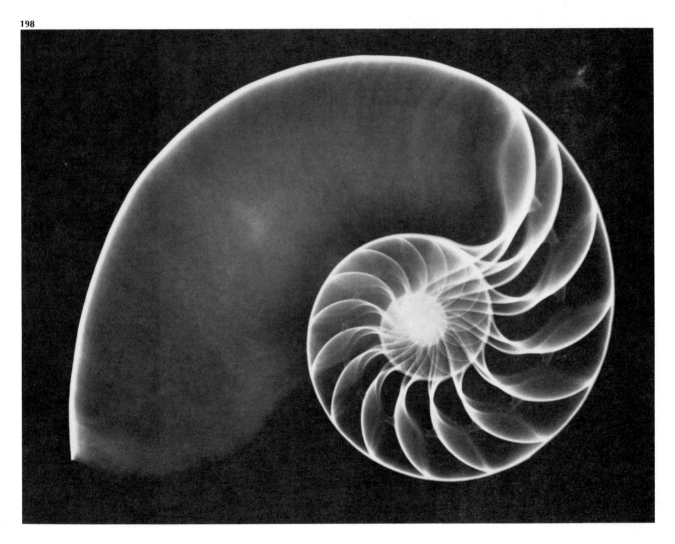

tionship to the canvas. Other painters have used the square and circle together in a variety of proportional relationships. In Jasper Johns' *Target with Four Faces* (Fig. 199) one circular motif dominates the field, but with bands of color repeated within it, so that the whole establishes a satisfying relationship with the square.

In Plate 22 (p. 163) Cleve Gray does not create paintings to hang on a wall. The paintings *are* the wall. Gray states that he has sought to return to "that early moment when man's experience of totality preceded his experience of the particular." To accomplish this, he has filled the four walls of the room with a continuous color, joining fourteen figures in a dance of death and life around the room. Gray sees the room as an environment for meditation where one can enter and possess one's own thoughts, as in a cathedral. In such a context, there can be no question of the appropriateness of the proportions.

The matter of proportions within a composition is a kind of *hierarchy,*

199

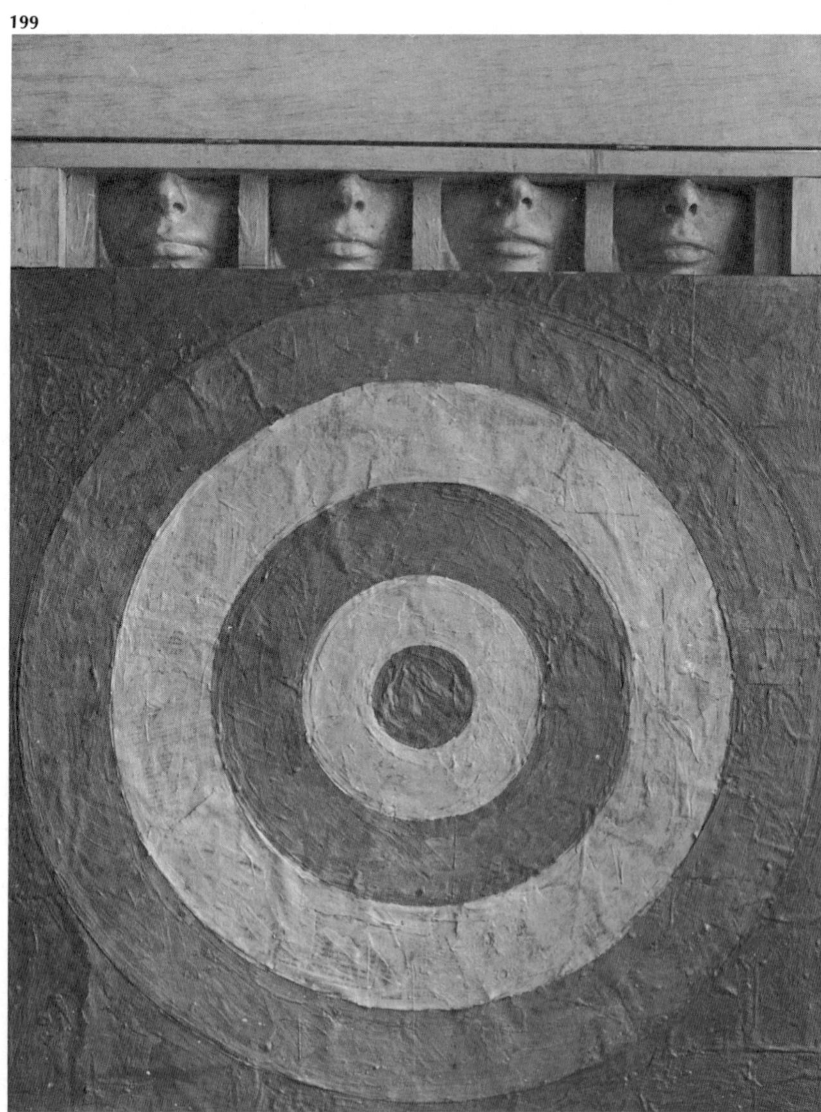

199
Jasper Johns. *Target with Four Faces.* 1955. Encaustic on newspaper over canvas, 26″ (66 cm) square, surmounted by four tinted plaster faces in wood box with hinged front, overall dimensions, 33⅝ × 26 × 3″ (85 × 66 × 8 cm). Museum of Modern Art, New York (gift of Mr. and Mrs. Robert C. Scull).

200
Last Judgment. 12th century. Mosaic, west wall, Cathedral at Torcella, Venice.

200

like the star system in the theater. One element frequently is the most important and all others are subordinate to it, in varying degrees of importance. In the Johns painting (Fig. 199) the targetlike circle dominates, with the faces as supporting actors, so to speak. The title calls our attention to them and we are pleasantly surprised because we didn't really notice them at first.

An even more obvious use of hierarchical proportion characterizes the mosaic in Figure 200. Here proportion is a function of *symbolism.* The figures of Christ and two angels are disproportionately large, their exaggerated size being an indication of their importance. Their size also balances the composition, since the angels are placed at either corner, echoing the dominant figure of Christ in the center.

201

Scale

In discussing large or small *shapes* on a two-dimensional surface, we have spoken of proportion, since the shapes are in *proportion* to the size of the area—paper, canvas, or wall—on which they appear. *Masses* are seen in *scale* with their surroundings or with human beings viewing them, for this is a matter of *comparison* rather than of relationships inherent in the work.

The heads shown in Figure 201 are among thousands found on Easter Island in the South Pacific, all similar in size and style. First discovered in 1722, these statues were described in detail by Captain James Cook when he visited the island in 1774. Centuries of drifting silt have buried many of them up to their necks, but they are actually full figures—some over 30 feet (9.1 meters) high. Who carved the megaliths and when and why are questions that remain unanswered. Perhaps the most baffling question is how a tribe with only primitive stone tools managed to erect such heavy structures. One romantic theory suggests a tribe of giants who planned the images in their own likeness—in other words, what to them was natural scale. A more likely explanation assumes that these are ancestor images, elevated to superhuman scale by death. At the time of Captain Cook's voyage, most of the figures were standing upright, but later the inhabitants of the island toppled all those that were not buried. Again, the reasons for this are not clear. In any event, it is the mammoth scale that makes these Easter Island carvings remarkable.

Contemporary uses of scale can have the same goal—to make a work remarkable. The composition in Figure 202 was created for an advertising

201
Stone images. 17th century or earlier. Height 30′ (9.14 m). Located outside crater of Rano Raraku, Easter Island.

202
Photo created by Brand Advertising as part of a campaign for Safety-Kleen, a company that specializes in recycling waste industrial products. © 1981, Denise R. Tegtman.

campaign by a company that specializes in recycling industrial solvents. Although the Statue of Liberty is depicted by a live model standing in a 55-gallon drum in the middle of a plastic-lined pool, the photographers manipulated the scene to produce the compelling picture of the statue gradually sinking beneath a New York harbor filling up with sludge. Even though the actual monumental statue is impressive, this picture showing the upper part of her body at huge scale sends out a message that is difficult to ignore.

202

Clean up your act, America.

203

204

203
Stephen Lowe. *The Hermit.* 1972.
Chinese watercolor on rice paper,
37 × 23″ (94 × 58 cm).
Private collection.

204
Rockwell Kent. *Voyaging.* 1924.
Chiaroscuro wood engraving on maple in black, white, and olive green; 6″ (15 cm) square. National Gallery of Art, Washington, D.C. (Rosenwald Collection).

205
John Tenniel.
Alice after Taking the Magic Potion, illustration from *Alice's Adventures in Wonderland* by Lewis Carroll, written in 1865.

206
Big Bird, Susan (Loretta Long), and Bob (Bob McGrath) in front of the brownstone set for "Sesame Street." Courtesy Children's Television Workshop.

Just as the Venetian mosaic in Figure 200 expresses Christian faith by depicting Christ in larger proportions than the other figures, the Chinese characteristically express a veneration for nature by showing the human figure as a minute entity amid the awesome beauty of a natural setting. In the painting in Figure 203, the single figure moves through the landscape like a tiny speck, compared to which even the bark of the pine tree looks enormous. A contrast can be made with a Western treatment of the human wanderer in Rockwell Kent's *Voyaging* (Fig. 204). Here it is the man who is important, the conqueror of mountains. Nature awaits his conquest.

Many people are fascinated by miniature scale. At one time, there was a craze for engraving documents on the head of a pin—the Lord's Prayer or the Gettysburg Address, for instance. To read the words, one needed a strong magnifying glass. A less drastic devotion to the miniature is shared by people who collect dollhouses and their furnishings or who make a hobby of model railroads. Few people can resist the charm of an object that is perfect in every way yet tiny in scale.

Four generations of children have been intrigued by Lewis Carroll's story of *Alice's Adventures in Wonderland,* which centers around her changing scale from very small to very large (Fig. 205). The possibilities that arise from changing scale in relation to one's environment are tantalizing. Carroll explores the advantages and disadvantages with whimsical humor.

Another contemporary figure whose role depends on scale is Big Bird, the genial character around whom much of the action in "Sesame Street" revolves (Fig. 206). The fact that he is out of scale with the rest of his species gives him the special quality needed for his unique function.

205

206

207

207
Scene from Act I of Richard Wagner's *Parsifal.* Produced by Wieland Wagner. Bayreuth Festival, Germany. 1968. Collection: Bildarchiv Bayreuther Festspiele.

208
Thomas Cole. *The Course of Empire: Destruction.* 1836. Oil on canvas, $39\frac{1}{4} \times 63\frac{1}{2}''$ (99.7 × 161.3 cm). The New-York Historical Society, New York.

The use of scale in theater is legendary, since drama can be heightened by the use of immense scale in a setting, which can dwarf the actors as Chinese paintings do. In Wieland Wagner's production of *Parsifal,* this use of scale is particularly striking. The manipulation of both lighting and scale convey the solemnity and sense of the supernatural in the quest for the Holy Grail (Fig. 207).

Just as lighting enhances the scale in the Wagnerian production, lighting and tonality can be allied to scale in painting. Look again at the Stephen Lowe painting in Figure 203. The entire composition is wrapped in white, which seems to drift through the trees and surround the figure. We feel that the hermit is moving through a mysterious world filled with mist, totally alone in a vast universe. This sense of the supernatural is partly a matter of scale, as we stated, but it is also in large part the result of the artist's skilled use of tonality. It is the sharp darks of the trees standing out from the misty whites that make us feel the infinite spaces and the aloneness of the figure.

In the painting by Thomas Cole in Figure 208, both large and small scale are used effectively. The subject itself is immense: the Roman Empire being destroyed by fire and battle. In order to depict such a catastrophe, it was necessary to use comprehensive symbols of an entire nation, next to which any individual element in the painting would be proportionately small. The exception is the statue in the right foreground, which is used to throw the rest of the composition into scale. There can be no doubt that the effectiveness of the work relies heavily upon tonality, the manner in which the artist has dramatized the inferno, highlighting certain spots, plunging others into darkness. The tonality of the statue is particularly eloquent. The back toward the viewer is struck with light, but the side facing the destruction is partially obscured by darkness.

As we have seen, the elements and principles of visual design interweave and flow together, becoming interdependent components of the total composition. Not all of them will necessarily appear in any one composition, but they form a body from which the designer can choose; they are the tools with which one works to create a successful design. In Part II we will explore other tools and materials and the ways in which they, too, affect the designer and the design.

208

e Designer: Ma terials, Proce
sses, and Ex pressive Fo
rms T he Tools of t
he Desig ner: Mate
rials, Pro cesses, and
Expressi ve Forms T
he Tools of the Designer:
Materials, Processes, and
Expressive Forms The T
ools of the Designer: Mat
erials, Processes, and Expressi
ve Forms The Tools of the De
signer: Materials, Processes, and Ex
pressive Forms The Tools of the Des

Part Two

igner: Materials, Processes, an
d Expressive Forms The To
f the Designer: Materials, Processes, and Ex
ive Forms The Tools of the Designer: Ma
s, Processes, and Expressive Forms The T
of the Designer: Materials, Processes, and
essive Forms The Tools of the Designer:
Materials, Processes, and Expressive
Forms The Tools of the Desig
ner: Materials, Processes, and E
xpressive Forms The Tools of th
e Designer: Materials, Processes, a
nd Expressive Forms The Tools of th
e Designer: Materials, Processes, and Exp
ressive Forms

The Tools of the Designer: Materials, Processes, and Expressive Forms

Plate 22
Cleve Gray. *Threnody*. 1972–73. Acrylic polymer on canvas, filling perimeter of gallery;
96 × 68 × 22′ (29.26 × 20.73 × 6.7 m). Neuberger Museum, State University of New York at Purchase.
Courtesy the artist.

Plate 23
Toshiko Horiuchi. *Atmosphere of the Forest.*
1975. Linen, gold, silver, Mylar, knitting.

Plate 24
Cuna Indian *mola.* c. 1950–70. Appliqué
fabric. Courtesy Michèle Herling.

11 The Influence of Materials on Design

Different materials have different qualities—of appearance, of durability, of the manner in which they respond to manipulation. Much of the success of any creative work results from the "feel" that the artist has for the material involved. In our exploration of the ways in which designers work, it will be helpful to look at some of the materials available and at the qualities that make them respond to the hands of the artist. First, we will consider the *characteristics* that make materials workable.

Characteristics of Materials

Plasticity is the predominant trait of clay. It is also a quality of glass, although glass, to be plastic, must be in a hot molten state. This is true as well of the large body of contemporary design materials designated by the term *plastics,* a term arising from their extreme ease of shaping. Plasticity is a characteristic of artist's paints and is the quality that makes it possible to manipulate them with a brush or palette knife.

Malleability derives from the Latin word for mallet, and refers primarily to manipulation through the use of various tools. The malleability of metals makes it possible for them to be hammered, melted down and cast, or shaped by any number of industrial processes. The term can be applied to wood or to clay, but in general it refers to the capacity of metal to be extended or shaped under great pressure. Gold, the most malleable of metals, can be hammered into gold leaf—sheets thinner than the finest tissue paper.

Related to malleability is the quality of *tensile strength,* by virtue of which a material resists breakage under pulling or bending forces. It is tensile strength that allows metal to span great distances without underlying support at the center, as in much contemporary architecture and especially in suspension bridges (Fig. 209). Still another related characteristic to be found specifically in metal is *ductility,* a quality that permits it to be drawn out into fine wires.

209

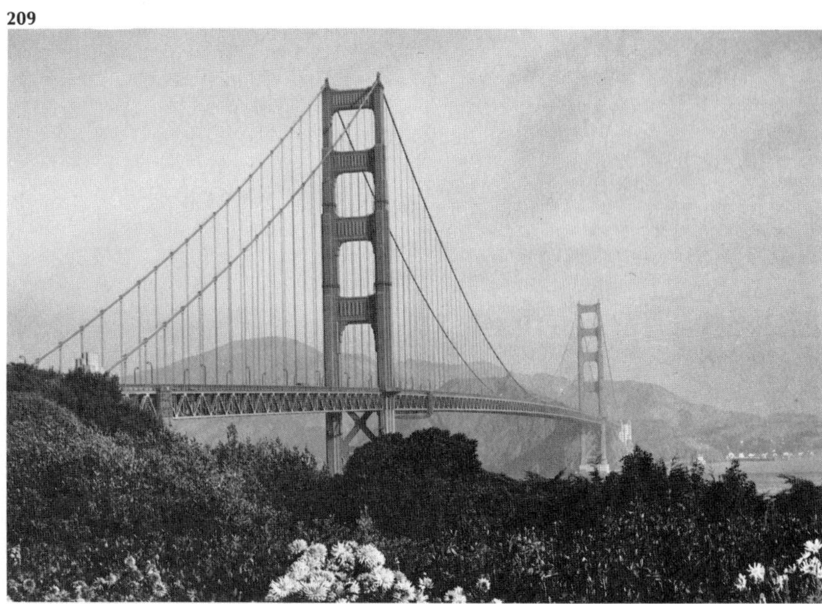

209
Golden Gate Bridge, San Francisco.

210

211

210
David N. Ebner. Sculptural writing chair. 1978. Bubinga, 30 × 18 × 18″ (76.2 × 45.72 × 45.72 cm). Collection of Mr. and Mrs. Mohlmann.

211
Killoanig. *Carving of a Man.* Spence Bay, North West Territory. c. 1978. Soapstone, 12 × 7 × 5″ (30.48 × 17.78 × 12.7 cm).

212
Henry Moore. *Reclining Figure.* 1945–46. Elmwood, length 6′3″ (19.05 m). Private collection, USA.

213
Most wood is cut in one of three ways, each presenting a distinctive grain pattern.

214
Retable of carved and painted wood. Liebfrauenkirche, Oberwesel. Rhenish, c. 1340.

Flexibility refers to the capacity of a material to be bent, twisted, or turned without breaking. Most obvious among flexible materials for the artist's use are textiles, fabrics, and leather. Wood can be made flexible in several ways. It can be *laminated* by cutting it into thin sheets and gluing them together. Laminated wood can be molded freely to achieve shapes not possible with a straight plank. It can be shaped into *bentwood* by application of steam. Many designers shape it into sculptural forms, using a combination of bending and carving (Fig. 210).

The *rigidity* of a material can be exploited by the designer. The sculptor and carver work *against* a rigid mass, pitting human hands and strength against a substance that yields but does not bend. Metal, wood, and stone all provide such rigidity. The sculptor welds or rivets rigid metal, or carves from resistant plastic, wood, or stone (Fig. 211). Many of the materials of architecture and furniture design are necessarily rigid, since they must support weight and provide permanent shape. Landscape designers use rigid materials in walls and fountains to supply accent to the softness of plantings and splashing water.

Solidity combines rigidity with mass. It is a quality that is found more often in sculpture than in the other arts, since the sculptor carves from a solid block, usually of wood or stone. Solidity makes possible the carving out of positive and negative masses to form a unified design (Fig. 212).

Materials as Components of Design

Wood

The growth pattern of trees determines the grain of wood. Each year, in temperate zones, trees produce two rings of growth. The early or spring wood is lighter in color than the late or summer wood, so the rings alternate between light and dark to form a definite grain pattern. Grain is also affected by the branching characteristics of a tree. Knots form where a branch begins, so a tree with many branches, such as pine, will produce knotty lumber.

The method of sawing lumber has a great deal to do with the way in which the grain shows (Fig. 213). Even so, each type of tree presents its special grain pattern.

212

Wood is classified in two ways. *Hardwood* comes from deciduous trees, which generally have broad leaves that are shed annually. Hardwoods (maple, oak, walnut, mahogany, and the fruitwoods such as cherry and pear) are difficult to carve but take fine detail without splintering. They are widely used for furniture and have provided exquisite carvings through many centuries (Fig. 214).

Softwoods generally come from coniferous trees. The terms *hard* and *soft* refer to the cellular structure rather than to actual hardness, although the so-called softwoods are usually not so difficult to work as the hardwoods. Wood can be painted, stained, or simply waxed or oiled and buffed to a soft *patina,* the term for a mellowing of surface texture and color.

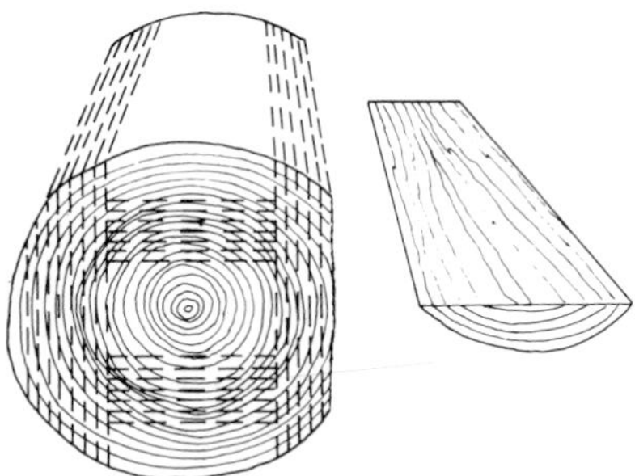

Plain (flat) sawed
(cut tangent to annual rings)

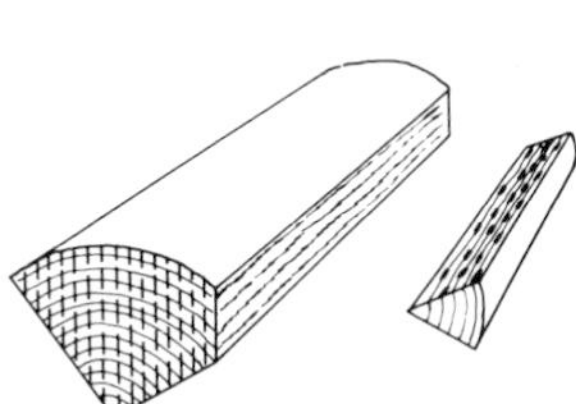

Quarter sawed
(showing figure)

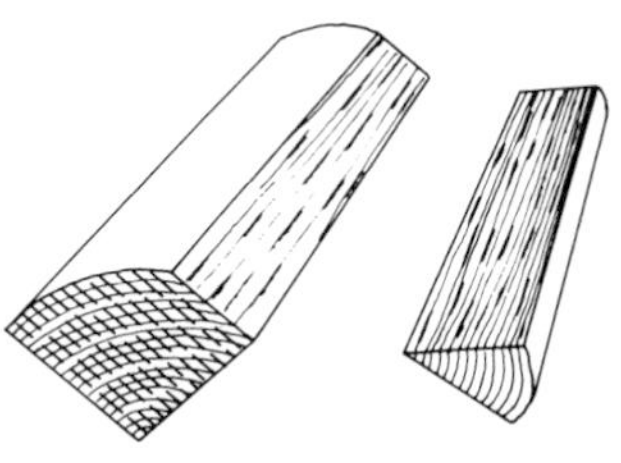

Rift sawed
(showing a pencil line grain)

213

214

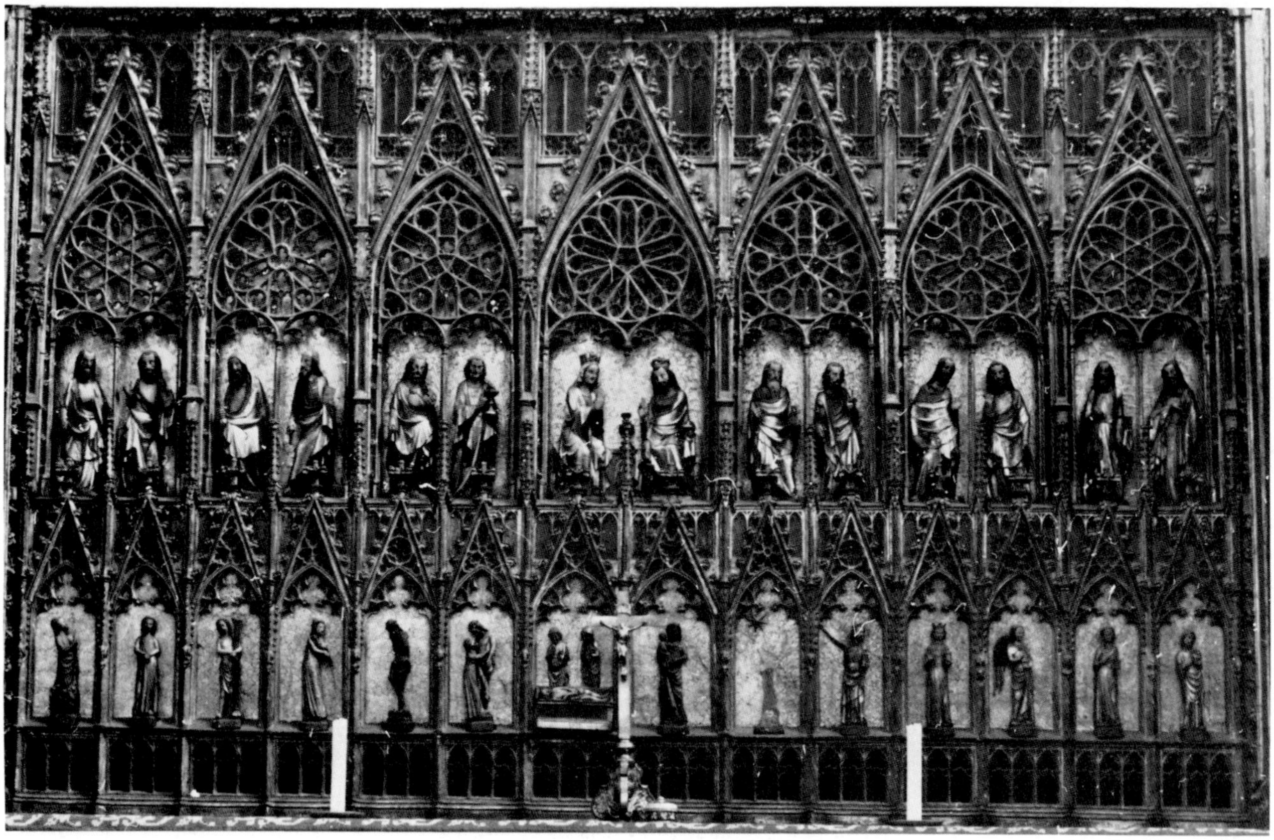

215

Carved wooden figures have often been *polychromed,* or painted in many colors (Fig. 215). The ancient art of *inlay* calls for small pieces of wood, shaped and usually in different colors, to be set in a framework according to a particular pattern. *Parquetry* is seen in flooring, in which wood is laid in geometric designs (Fig. 216). *Marquetry* is also a form of inlay, but combines other materials such as ivory with wood, and is used primarily in the decorative design of furniture.

We have mentioned the use of laminated wood and bentwood (p. 166). *Plywood* is a form of laminated wood but with the layers alternating at right angles to one another. There are usually three or five layers, resulting in greater strength than could be found in a board of the same thickness. When the outer or visible layer is of finer wood than the others, this layer is known as *veneer.* Veneer, a thin layer of decorative wood used to enhance strong structures, is widely used in furniture design.

As a design material, wood offers infinite variety in grain and texture, ease of workability, and an innate warmth and glow not to be found in any other material.

216

215
Erasmus Grasser. *A Morris Dancer.* 1480. Painted wood, height c. 25″ (63 cm). München Stadtmuseum, Germany.

216
Parquet flooring in the waiting room of the new addition to The Frick Collection, New York. Harry Van Dyke, architect; John Barrington Bayley, designer. Courtesy The Frick Collection.

217
Rhyton. Persian, 5th century B.C. Gold; height c. $6\frac{3}{4}$″ (17 cm), diameter at mouth $5\frac{1}{2}$″ (14 cm). Metropolitan Museum of Art, New York (Harris Brisbane Dick Fund, 1954).

218
Chunghi Choo. *Decanter.* 1980. Silver plate on copper, 8 × 6 × 5″ (20.32 × 15.24 × 12.7 cm).

Metal

The value of metal to the designer lies in its potential for being formed. Because of its tensile strength, metal can be hammered, stretched, and shaped in many ways. The diverse visual qualities of the various metals are also of tremendous value in design. *Gold,* considered the most precious of metals throughout recorded history, has long been shaped into many forms, both decorative and practical (Fig. 217). Both gold and *silver* are too soft to be worked in their pure state so they are *alloyed*—combined in a fluid state with another metal. Silver is usually alloyed with copper, whereas gold may be alloyed with both copper and silver.

Another way of combining metals is to *plate* a layer of metal on top of another metal, in much the same way as veneer is applied to wood. The flowing form of the decanter in Figure 218 has been given a rich gleaming surface by the use of silver plating.

217

218

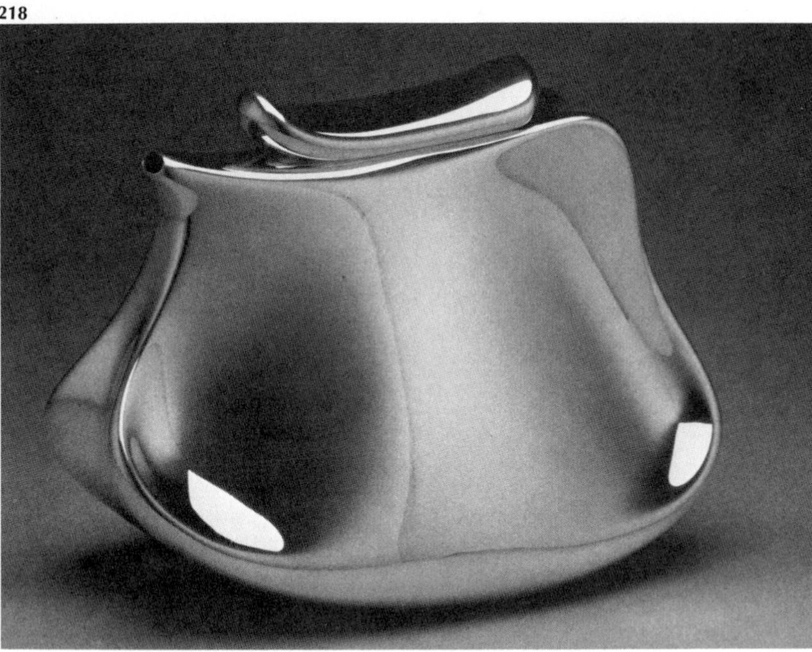

219

219
Augustus Saint-Gaudens.
William Tecumseh Sherman. 1903. Bronze. Over lifesize. Grand Army Plaza, New York.

220
Dorothy Gillespie.
Conjured Image of a Past Presence. 1980. Enamel on aluminum, 8 × 5 × 5″ (20.32 × 12.7 × 12.7 cm). Courtesy Birmingham Museum of Art (gift of Silvia Pizitz).

Pewter, an alloy of tin with varying amounts of antimony, copper, and lead, has been used since the days of the Roman Empire and possibly before. Both pewter and silver frequently bear *hallmarks,* tiny stamped insignia that identify a work by maker and place of origin and that testify to the purity of the metal. These marks are indications of excellence and are invaluable guides for collectors of old pewter and silver.

Other alloys that are used by designers are *brass* and *bronze.* An alloy of copper and zinc, *brass* has a long history, especially in the Orient and the Middle East, where brass objects have been manufactured for centuries. Typically, these works are incised with elaborate designs, and they may be inlaid with enamel or other contrasting materials. Brass has a yellower color than copper and it takes a high polish. Among its uses are musical instruments, ceremonial pieces for churches, and decorative door hardware. Bronze is darker, harder, and longer lasting than brass. Its rich brownish-red color makes it popular for desk accessories, medals, and commemorative plaques. Most bells are cast from bronze, since the metal provides not only durability but the potential for a rich tone. In addition, bronze is the primary metal for cast sculptures, including the large statues that dominate parks and plazas around the world (Fig. 219).

Aluminum is noteworthy for being among the lightest and most plentiful of metals. It neither tarnishes nor rusts, and it can be treated in a variety of ways—chasing, etching, and hammering—to produce practical and relatively inexpensive bowls, trays, and kitchen utensils. It is also used by contemporary sculptors (Fig. 220). Mexican designers have shown delightful originality in adapting *tin* to a whole range of fanciful forms, often

220

221 222

painting portions of them or setting them with colorful stones. Practical items are sometimes backed with wood for solidity, but the metal used by itself finds shape in lighting fixtures, wastebaskets, and ornamental frames (Fig. 221).

Iron has a long history of both decorative and practical uses. Iron tools more than five thousand years old have been found in Egypt, and the first farmers used tools forged from iron. Medieval blacksmiths created architectural accessories whose beauty still embellishes old churches and castles (Fig. 222).

Steel, like iron, is a structural material of enormous importance in the contemporary cityscape, with its high-rise buildings and steel bridges. It is also widely used by contemporary sculptors (Fig. 223).

223

221
Mexican tinsmiths are skilled in adapting the metal to whimsical designs, as seen in this contemporary mirror and candle holder.

222
Doorhinge. German, 15th century. Wrought and incised iron. Metropolitan Museum of Art, New York (gift of Henry G. Marquand, 1887).

223
Kenneth Snelson. *Free Ride Home.* 1974. Aluminum and stainless steel, 30 × 60 × 60′ (9.14 × 18.29 × 18.29 m). Collection Storm King Art Center, Mountainville, New York. Installation Waterside Plaza, New York City, 1974.

224
Façade of Saint Wulfran, Abbeville, France. Begun 1488.

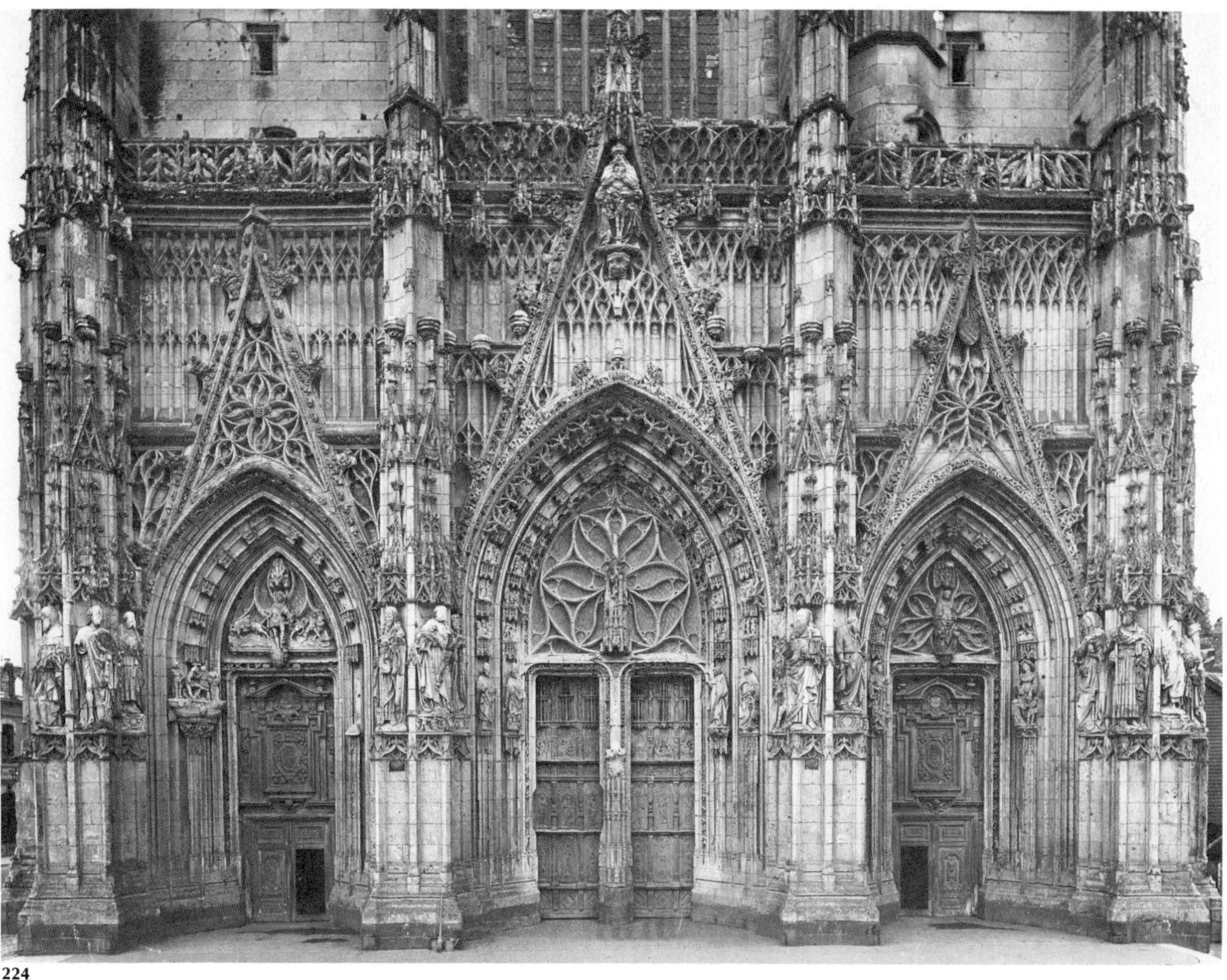

224

Effective design in metal depends upon the designer's knowledge of the potential of the many metals available. A thorough grounding in the processes by which metal can be formed is also necessary. We will discuss these processes in Chapter 12.

Stone

Our oldest known buildings and monuments were erected of stone. Among the earliest known designs are those carved on the stone tools and structures of primitive peoples. The Egyptian pyramids, built of limestone quarried from the cliffs along the Nile, and the Parthenon, erected from Pentelic marble from the mountains of Greece, have survived through the centuries to tell us of the customs, beliefs, and especially the artistry of ancient peoples. Most of the medieval cathedrals were built of granite or sandstone, the hard and enduring varieties of stone that nevertheless yielded to the hands of sculptors to produce amazingly intricate forms (Fig. 224). For a contemporary use of granite, look again at Figure 132 (p. 89). Buildings today make use of a variety of stone, from marble to "fieldstone," which gives a warmth to interiors when used in walls and fireplaces.

225

Type of stone and type of design in stone are related to the vicinity in which the artist works. The Eskimos of northern Canada carve in soapstone, which comes in a range of grays. The people of the Orient and Central and South America have created symbolic works in jade for many centuries. Being extremely hard, jade is not carved with chisels but is worked with blasts of wet sand or crushed stone, or with drills of carborundum. It comes in a gamut of greens and a creamy white with an elegant translucence (Fig. 225).

There are, in addition, the many precious stones used as jewelry and as symbols of wealth, royalty, or religious devotion. Semiprecious stones are used in jewelry by many contemporary designers.

Concrete

Concrete is a mixture of cement, sand, stone, and water. The cement is carefully standardized by manufacturers and is termed Portland cement, a name given to it in 1824 by an English cement maker, who saw a strong resemblance between hardened cement and the so-called Portland stone that was much used for building in England at that time. Ancient Egypt and Rome both used concrete for construction. Today concrete is cast in decorative building blocks and in panels such as we saw in Figure 151.

A dramatic development in the use of concrete was made in the mid-twentieth century by Italian architect Pier Luigi Nervi with his invention of *ferrocement.* Ferrocement is composed of layers of steel mesh sprayed with cement mortar so that the total thickness of the material is only slightly greater than that of the mesh itself. The result is superior strength coupled with elasticity, a combination that stands great strains without cracking yet can be used in amazingly thin shells and intricate designs (Fig. 226).

Clay

Clay is composed of alumina, silica, and various other elements, frequently including minerals that give it color. Geologically, there are two types: *residual clay,* which has remained in the place where it was formed, and *sedimentary clay,* which has been carried by the action of water and wind to be deposited in new locations. The sedimentary clay picks up impurities as it moves, and it also breaks down in particle size. The impurities contribute color, and the finer particle size means the clay will be more plastic.

Rarely does one natural clay offer all the characteristics desirable for ceramic design. Most often clays are mixed to yield a *clay body,* and these can be classified into three basic types according to the temperature at which they are fired.

Earthenware fires in the lowest temperature range, at around 2000 degrees Farenheit. A rather coarse, porous ware, it is usually reddish in color and is never completely waterproof except when glazed. Unglazed earthenware pots are ideal for plants because the water can "sweat" through the walls. The Italian "terra cotta" (baked earth) refers to this ware, which is also used for sculpture and red-clay tiles.

Stoneware fires in the middle range of temperatures. The clay is usually light gray or tan, is relatively durable, and has a warm earthy quality that makes the ware a popular choice for decorative bowls and vases and for dinnerware (Fig. 227).

The highest-fired ware of all is *porcelain,* made from a very pure and

225
Regardant Feline with Bifid Tail.
Chinese, 6th–10th century A.D.
Light grey-green jade with white and black markings; $3\frac{1}{4} \times 4\frac{1}{8}''$ (8.26 × 10.41 cm).
Asian Art Museum of San Francisco.
(The Avery Brundage Collection)

226
Pier Luigi Nervi. Interior of dome, Baths at Chianciano. 1952.

227
Ray Finch. Selection of functional stoneware pots.

228
Jars. Crete, 1600–1500 B.C.
Buff-colored earthenware with red-and-black slip. Herakleion Museum, Crete.

usually white clay. In firing, porcelain becomes extremely hard and glossy; therefore it can be molded into thin and translucent forms. The term *china* refers to a white ware similar to porcelain but firing at a lower temperature.

Clay is the very substance of the earth, and as such it has played a long and vital role in civilization. Every ancient culture developed ceramic techniques (Fig. 228).

226

227

228

229

Glass

Glass is among the most naturally beautiful of all materials. Simply molded, colorless, and unadorned, it provides for fascinating study in transparency, fluidity, and sparkle. We think of it as fragile, but many types are as hard and durable as steel.

Like clay, glass is based in the earth, although it is also formed on the moon by volcanic action and the bombardment of meteorites. Its chief ingredient is silica sand in its purest possible state. Most glass is manufactured, but *obsidian,* a shiny black substance created by volcanic action, is an example of glass that has formed naturally. As long ago as 75,000 B.C. primitive peoples carved it into flints, arrowheads, and simple tools.

Chemically, glass consists of silicon dioxide fused with metallic oxides; when cooled, this substance becomes a brittle solid. There are literally thousands of types of glass, but they fall generally into six broad categories.

Lead glass is the aristocrat of glasses. A complex of potassium-lead silicate, lead glass, often known as crystal, is the most important to the designer. Its high refraction makes it useful for lenses and prisms, and because of its brilliance when cut, it serves for fine table crystal, decorative cut glass, and reflective chandeliers (Fig. 229).

Windows, lighting fixtures, table glasses, bottles, and other common glass products are made from *soda-lime glass,* which is inexpensive and easy to form.

Borosilicate glass has the special property of being highly resistant to heat and temperature changes. It therefore goes into such hardworking products as cooking utensils, laboratory equipment, and aircraft windows.

Fused silica, 96-percent silica glass, and alumino-silicate glass are all remarkably tough materials that have been developed for scientific and industrial applications. They function in such demanding places as missile nose cones, laser beam reflectors, and space vehicle windows.

Various compounds are added to molten glass to improve its appearance. Iron oxides, often present as impurities, give glass an undesirable greenish or brownish cast, so decolorizers must be used. Coloring agents, on the other hand, give the jeweled tones that distinguish stained-glass mosaics, as well as the various hues that can be seen in tableware.

Perhaps the most important element in glass design is space, since transparency provides an added dimension. When glass is backed to form a mirror, this quality becomes almost infinite. In Lucas Samaras' *Room #2* (Fig. 230), a construction of wood and mirrors, an area 10 feet deep becomes a never-ending landscape of shimmering planes and angles. This work might be considered the very embodiment of those almost ethereal qualities that make glass a particularly exciting material for design.

Fiber

By definition, a fiber is a thread, or something capable of being spun into a thread. Until this century, fibers were limited to organic materials—the products of plants (cotton, jute, sisal, linen, and others) or of animals (wools, silk, and specialty furs). The introduction of nylon in 1940 vastly increased the vocabulary of fibers, and today different fibers are made from such ingredients as wood pulp, chemicals, and petroleum.

Fibers are another of the ancient materials of design. Clothing, baskets, and even shelters have been constructed from fibers since earliest times. Weaving, of course, has a long history in most parts of the world. Today fibers in themselves are an important medium of design (Pl. 23, p. 164).

229
Cut-crystal chandelier. 1969.
21″ (53 cm).
Designed by Carl Fagerlund,
Orrefors, Sweden.

230
Lucas Samaras. *Mirrored Room.* 1966.
Wood and mirrors, 8 × 8 × 10′
(2.44 × 2.44 × 3.05 m). Albright-Knox
Art Gallery, Buffalo, N. Y.
(gift of Seymour H. Knox, 1966).

Plastics

The most contemporary of all design materials are the versatile substances we categorize as plastics. All plastics share one basic trait: they are composed principally of carbon compounds in long molecular chains. Each type of plastic on the market today has been developed by polymer chemists to have a specific molecular structure, which in turn offers a definite combination of properties. The process of developing plastics began in the middle of the nineteenth century with the invention of celluloid to replace the ivory lost because the elephant herds were being decimated. A hundred years later plastics became a major material in industrial design.

230

There are two main divisions in the field of plastics. *Thermoplastic* substances can be softened and resoftened indefinitely by the application of heat and pressure, provided there is not enough heat to cause decomposition. While changing their shape, the materials do not lose their molecular cohesion. *Thermosetting* plastics, on the other hand, undergo a chemical change during the curing process; after that change takes place, the shape becomes set and cannot usefully be modified again when exposed to heat and/or pressure.

Although plastic materials now number in the hundreds, they can be categorized into several general "families." *Acrylics* are thermoplastic materials with outstanding brilliance and transparency (Fig. 231). Because they can be molded into large, unshatterable shapes, are readily carved, withstand weather and hard use, and accept a high polish, acrylics have become popular with sculptors and jewelers. Acrylic-based paints are among the most popular artists' media today.

Polyester is a thermoset plastic commonly used by designers. Several different chemical types are available. In fabric form, polyester can make a huge unbroken sheet. When reenforced with fiberglass, laminating polyester offers the artist a highly expressive working medium, which can be saturated with intense colors. Clear polyester works well for casting or embedding.

Epoxy, another thermoset plastic that is popular with designers, resembles polyester in many ways. It costs more, but it does not have the shrinkage factor associated with polyester castings. When combined with metal powders, epoxy can yield a cold-cast metal very similar in appearance to

231

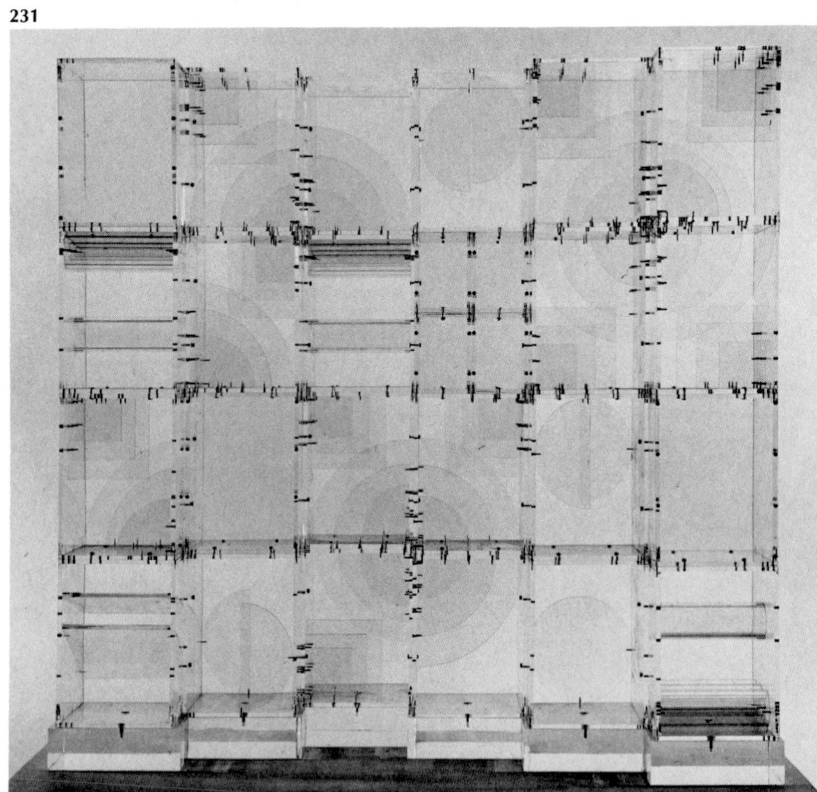

231
Louise Nevelson. *Model for Atmosphere and Environment: Ice Palace I.* 1967. Clear Lucite, 24 × 26 × 12″ (61 × 66 × 30 cm). Private collection.

232
Duane Hanson. *Artist with Ladder.* 1972. Polyester and fiberglass, lifesize. Private collection.

foundry-cast metal. Epoxy can be cast in the design studio without elaborate equipment, because it will cure at room temperature after the components have been mixed.

FRP, or fiberglass-reinforced plastic, is literally a plastic with which fiberglass has been combined for added strength. It appears in molded and laminated furniture, boat hulls, and automobile bodies. These plastics are weather-resistant and can be colored as desired. Artists use polyester reinforced with fiberglass as a sculpture medium because of the great freedom it provides in modeling. When applied to figural sculpture, this material can be amazingly lifelike (Fig. 232).

232

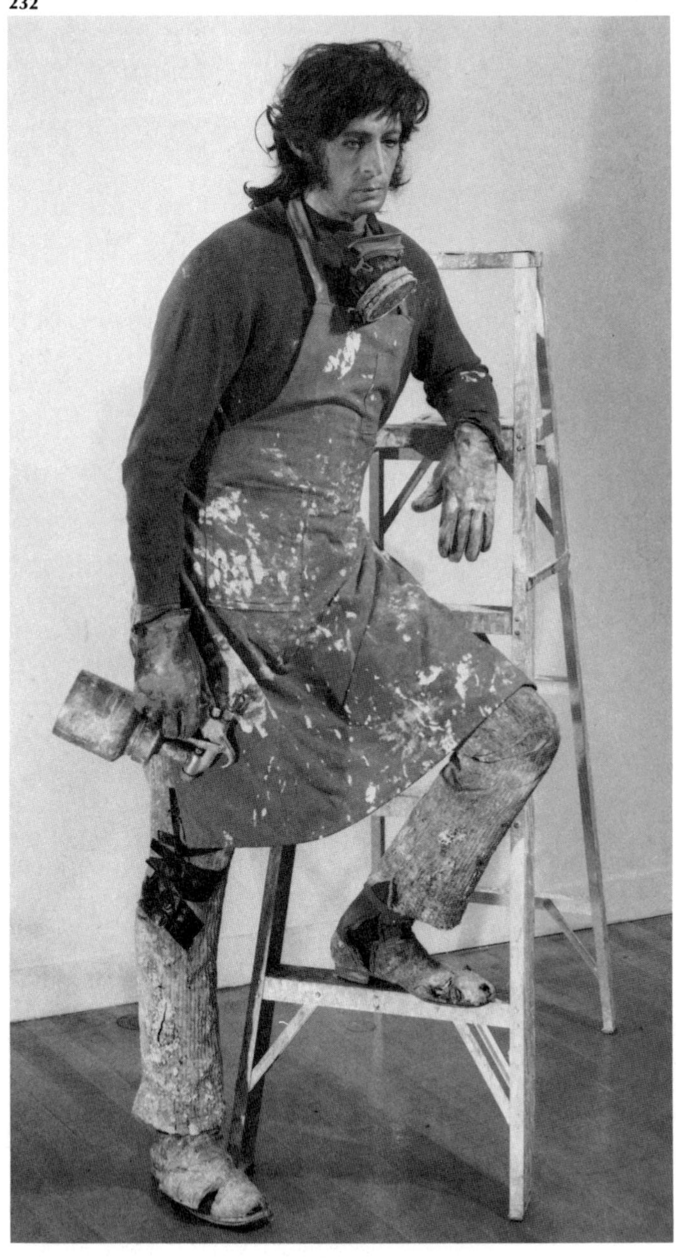

233

234

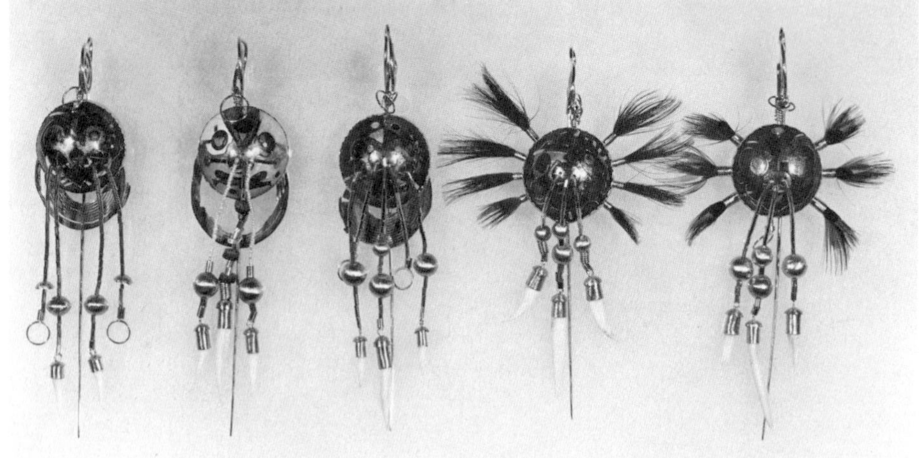

Melamines are exceptionally hard and durable plastics that have become a staple in kitchen countertops and casual dinnerware. Depending upon composition, these plastics can be transparent, translucent, or opaque, and they are available in many colors.

Polyethylenes may be flexible, semirigid, or rigid in form. A waxy surface identifies them in such products as squeeze bottles and freezer containers. Polyethylenes are resistant to breakage, weather, and extremes of temperature; this makes them practical for outdoor sculpture.

Urethanes are especially valued by artists and architects because of their ability to foam. This permits them to be sprayed onto a limitless variety of forms, whereupon they become rigid or semirigid (Fig. 233). Sculptors, too, make use of this exceptional flexibility of form. It should be noted, however, that the ingredients for urethane foam are highly toxic, and the foam itself is dangerously flammable.

Vinyls are tough, lightweight plastics best known for their applications to fabrics, floors, and walls. Designs can be printed onto vinyl fabric, and the shiny "wet" look of vinyl appeals to many contemporary sculptors.

A complete list of materials available to the designer would encompass materials from all parts of the world. The stickpins in Figure 234, which combine silver, gold, enamel, pig's teeth, and feathers, give an idea of the endless variety possible. Materials, in all their diversity, stimulate creativity. In Chapter 12 we will look into the ways in which designers convert these materials into works of art.

233
Stan Nord Connolly, AIA-Architect. "Igloo" house. Built 1969. Plastic foam sprayed over balloons. Each dome 36′ (10.97 m) diameter and 16′ (4.88 m) rises.

234
William Harper. *Kabuki Boogie I-V.* 1980. Stickpins, gold cloisonné enamel on fine silver, 14K gold, sterling silver and pig's teeth; IV and V, also feathers. II, also glass and seed pearls. Largest $5\frac{1}{4} \times 1\frac{3}{4}''$ (14 × 5 cm). Courtesy Kennedy Galleries, Inc. New York.

12 Forming Techniques

From earliest times people have molded clay and whittled wood to create objects of original design. These acts represent two basic techniques for forming materials into designed objects: the *additive* method and the *subtractive* method.

The Additive Method

In the additive method, material is built up or joined together to form a shape or mass. This is usually considered a sculptural technique, but it applies to many other areas as well. We will begin, however, by considering the additive method in sculpture.

In working with metal, the sculptor may rivet or weld. *Riveting* consists of cutting holes in two pieces of metal, inserting a metal bolt or pin, and then hammering the plain end down to form a second head. Often these heads form an integral part of the design (Fig. 235).

Welding is a twentieth-century technique for fusing metals, which is based on the fact that acetylene and oxygen will produce a flame hot enough to fuse most kinds. Originally restricted to industrial uses, welding has become an effective method for contemporary sculptors. Most use bronze or fusion welding, in which an acetylene torch is applied to the metals to be joined as well as to a welding rod that melts and fuses with them: the resultant joining is of tremendous strength and durability. Immense welded sculptures may seem to be an outgrowth of the industrial world around them, but they are even more an expression of the mind and soul of the contemporary artist (Fig. 236).

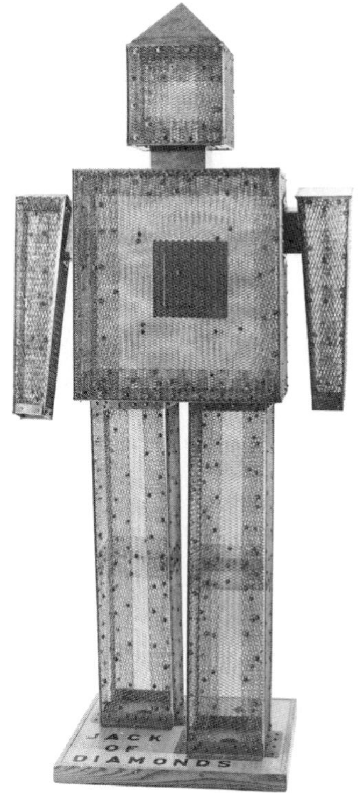

235

236

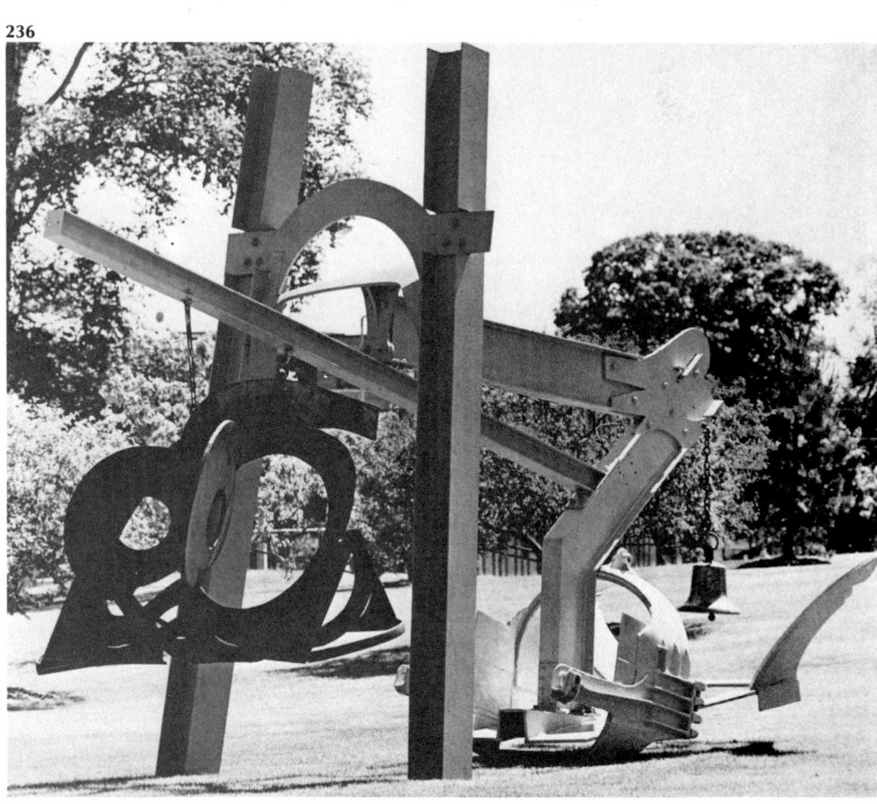

235
H. C. Westermann. *Jack of Diamonds.* 1981. Galvanized wire lath and corner beading with brass bolts and washers. Wooden base. 6′8″ × 3′3″ × 1′11″ (2.02 × .97 × .59). Collection of Mr. and Mrs. Alan Press, Chicago.

236
Mark di Suvero. *Gorky's Pillow.* 1969–1980. Painted steel, 15′6″ × 9′6″ × 23′4″ (4.72 × 2.9 × 7.11 m). Collection of the artist and ConStruct.

237

Building sculptures from materials other than metals usually comes under the heading of *modeling*. This process enables the artist to build up, tear down, change, and modify as the work progresses. Materials such as clay, wax, or plaster are often built on an *armature,* or framework, of metal, cardboard, wood, or other fairly rigid material, which supports the work much as the skeletal structure supports the human body. Sculptors use this method for making models of works they will later cast in metal or carve in stone (Fig. 237).

Wooden constructions can be built up by various methods of *joining,* such as gluing, nailing, bolting, or pegging.

The additive method can be applied to *clay* by modeling or by other methods that fall into two general categories: *hand-building* and *throwing*. Hand-building breaks down into several different methods, which include pinching, coiling, and slab construction.

Pinching is a simple process of pressing the clay between the fingers to produce a form. No doubt the earliest clay objects were formed in this way, and today the "pinch pot" is usually the first project undertaken by a beginning potter. Pinching requires no tools—just the lump of clay and the potter's hands. It has distinct limitations as to size and shape.

Coiling affords possibilities for all kinds of shapes. The potter begins with a flat slab of clay for a base, then gradually builds walls by coiling ropes of clay upon one another (Fig. 238). The walls can be smoothed or left to show the ridges of the coils. This is the method used by Indian potters of the American Southwest and, while it is time-consuming, it is among the most versatile of hand methods. There are no limitations of shape or size. Ceramic sculptor Bruno La Verdiere has used the coil method to build structures more than seven feet high (Fig. 239).

Slab construction consists of rolling out flat sheets of clay, cutting them to size, and joining the slabs. Box shapes are the most obvious application for the slab technique (Fig. 240). However, slabs can be joined, curved, bent, and distorted in any number of ways. Marilyn Levine's *Knapsack* (Fig. 241) was built with slab construction.

238

237
Honoré Daumier. *Le Fardeau* (The Burden). Before 1852. Terra cotta, height 13⅜" (34.04 cm). Walters Art Gallery, Baltimore.

238
Coils of clay are wound one upon the other and the form shaped with a curved piece of wood and a paddle.

239
Bruno LaVerdiere. *Arch.* 1975. Clay with sawdust and grog, coil-built; 7'3" × 4' (2.21 × 1.22 m). Courtesy the artist.

240
In the slab method, sides and base are formed separately and then joined by the use of a wooden tool.

241
Marilyn Levine. *Knapsack.* 1970. Slab-constructed stoneware with leather laces, 15 × 19 × 13" (38 × 48 × 33 cm). Courtesy the artist.

239

240

241

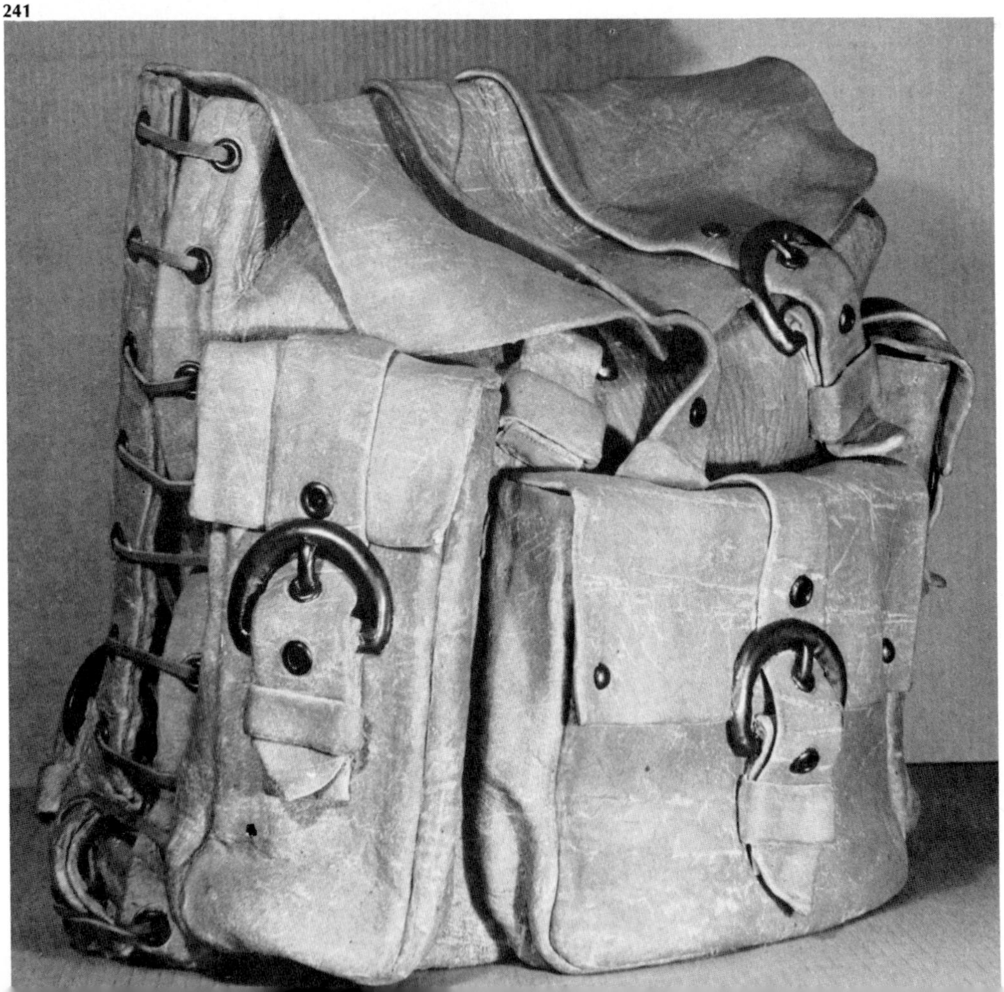

242

243

244

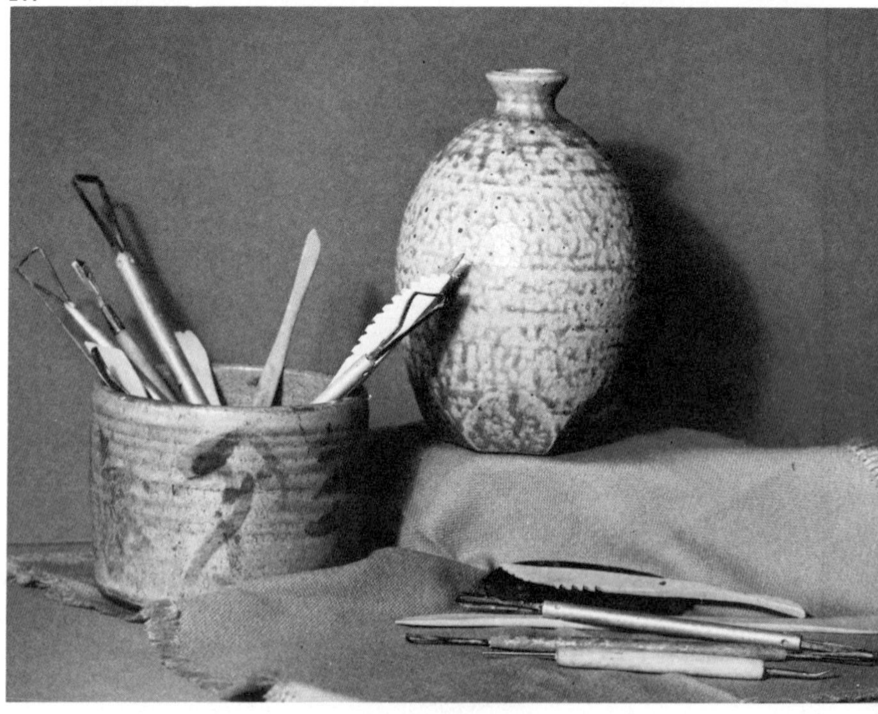

242
Denton Vars side-treadle potter's wheel, designed by Bernard Leach. Hardwood frame, weighted flywheel, fiberglass pan; 13" (33.02 cm) aluminum wheel head.

243
Throwing on the potter's wheel.

244
Hand tools used in making pottery.

245
Kenneth Green. Lidded vessel. Slab-built stoneware with stamped and carved decoration. Barnard slip under a mat dolomite glaze, height 13½" (34.29 cm). State University of New York, College at New Paltz, New Paltz, New York.

Throwing on the potter's wheel is the most efficient means of creating round, symmetrical objects such as bowls, plates, mugs, and vases. Potters' wheels may be powered by kicking (Fig. 242) or by electric motor. In either case, the potter works upon a flat disc that turns at varying speeds as the ball of clay centered upon it emerges into the desired form. This is a highly skilled technique requiring months—perhaps years—of practice to achieve complete control (Fig. 243). During the throwing process, various devices can be employed to provide texture, ranging from a comb or fork to the potter's fingertips. Wheel-thrown pieces display an absolute symmetry that, for many designers, brings one of the greatest satisfactions in working with clay. Also, there is a rhythm in working on the wheel that unites artist and material as a creative unit.

Regardless of the forming method, pottery, while in the plastic state, responds readily to manipulation. The potter uses hand tools for trimming, blending edges of coils, and providing surface texture (Fig. 244). This is best done at the *leather-hard* stage, when the clay is dry enough to be handled without marring the surface but still contains enough moisture to make it malleable. The means for providing texture are limited only by the potter's imagination. The jar in Figure 245 was carved and stamped with a metal object.

245

Greenware is clay that is thoroughly dry and ready to be fired in the kiln (Fig. 246). Kilns can be heated by gas, electricity, wood, coal, or oil and are frequently built by the potter, using fire brick and other materials. The heat of the kiln is measured by pyrometric devices, the most usual of which is the pyrometric cone. The cone is placed before a peephole in the kiln, and when it bends, the kiln is turned off and allowed to cool for eight or more hours before being opened. The greenware has now become *bisque*.

If a *glaze* is desired, a second firing takes place. The glaze (a powder containing silica, alumina, and flux, plus metallic oxides to provide color) is mixed with water and applied to the bisque ware by brushing, spraying, or dipping. When the pot is placed inside the kiln for the glaze firing, it is usually chalky white or gray, but after firing it may have brilliant color and/or visual texture, depending upon the composition of the glaze. During the firing, the chemicals in the glaze fuse with the clay, and surface quality and structure become permanently allied.

In addition to sculpture and ceramics, the additive method applies in principle to the *construction of furniture and buildings* and to much of *industrial design*.

The Subtractive Method

The subtractive processes include *carving, sawing,* and *turning*. Generally speaking, the subtractive method is more demanding than the additive one, for material once carved away cannot readily be replaced. This explains the practice of constructing preliminary models of clay, which can be altered without permanent effect. When the designer has achieved exactly what is desired in the clay model, which is often at a reduced scale, the full-size work in the desired material can be undertaken.

As in the work of Michelangelo (see p. 11), the subtractive method is often used to reveal a form the artist visualizes in a block of wood or stone. This cannot be said of metal. *Sculptural* methods in metal are primarily additive, yet there are processes for converting metal into designed objects that cannot be placed in either category. We will consider these under a separate heading.

246

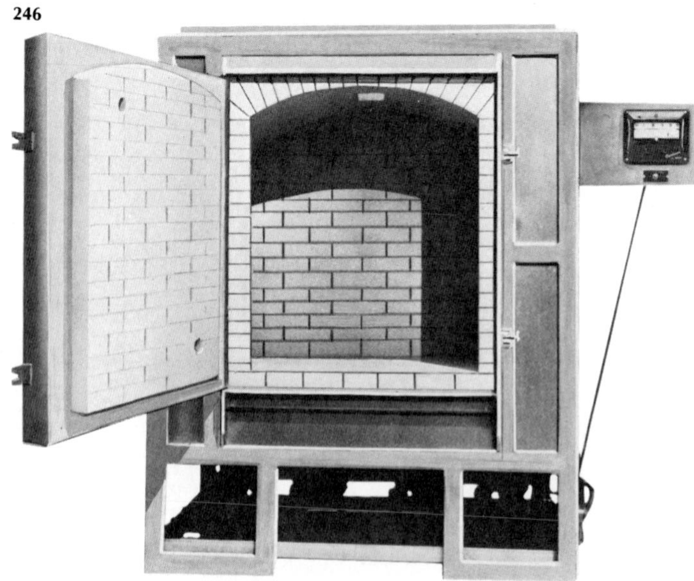

246
Alpine updraft gas kiln for temperatures to cone 14. Chamber 24 cubic feet (0.7 cubic meters).

247
L. Brent Kington. *Weathervane #27.* 1980. Forged mild steel, 47 × 14 × 51″ (1.19 × .36 × 1.3 m). Collection of the artist.

Forming Techniques for Metal

Hammering, one of the oldest ways of treating metal, is still much used. The softer metals, such as gold or tin, can be hammered cold. There are several variations of this method, of which *raising* is the most usual. The metalworker repeatedly strikes the flat sheet with hammers, working from the back and sometimes over a rounded form of wood or metal, until the sheet "rises" into a curved or hollowed shape, such as a bowl or saucer. *Beating down* reverses the process of raising. In this technique the metalworker places the flat sheet over a recessed area and then hammers the metal into the depression.

Harder metals such as iron must be hot-hammered, or *forged.* A hundred years ago the blacksmith and the ironmonger were as prevalent as the corner grocer, serving the needs of an agricultural society by making and mending farm equipment as well as the harnesses and horseshoes that were a vital part of transportation. Today blacksmithing is experiencing a rebirth, both as a way of making tools and as a medium of design (Fig. 247). In simplest terms, forging calls for a piece of metal to be heated in a furnace until it is red hot (sometimes white hot), then held on an anvil with tongs and pounded with hammers.

247

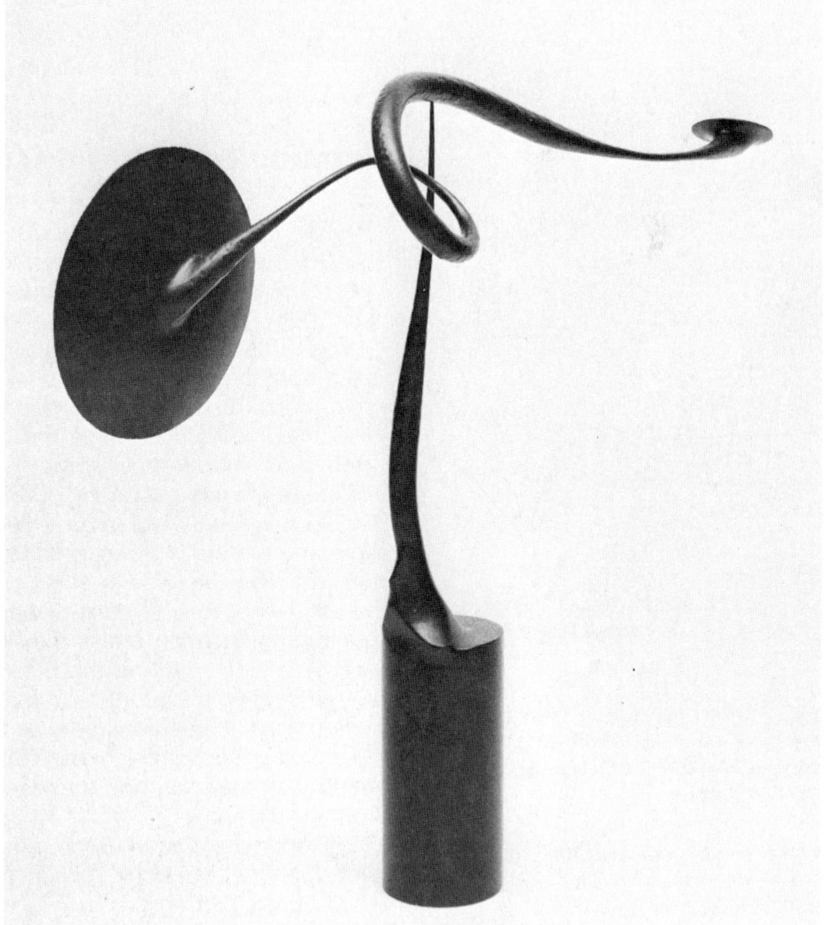

248

Spinning is the method by which round objects are formed on a revolving *lathe,* a process similar to turning wood. Flat sheets of soft metal are pressed over wooden forms that turn on the lathe to create the round shapes of pitchers, goblets, vases, and sometimes jewelry.

Because metal is so widely used in industrial design, other methods have been developed for forming metal objects on a large scale. We will discuss these in Chapter 23.

Forming Techniques for Glass

Glass is one of the few materials that must nearly always be worked in a state too hot to handle. Furthermore, the molten glass cools and hardens very quickly, so the forming must be done in a short time, and with great skill. There are five basic methods of forming glass.

The oldest forming technique is *pressing,* in which semifluid glass is taken from the melting pot and worked into shape by means of paddles or other tools. In large-scale production, machine-operated presses force the glass into molds that shape the outsides of objects, while plungers are inserted to smooth the insides.

One of the most dramatic of all forming techniques is the ancient art of *glassblowing,* believed to have been invented in the first century B.C. The blowpipe is a hollow metal rod about four feet long with a mouthpiece at one end. The glassblower dips up a small amount of molten material with the other end, rolls or presses it against a paddle or metal plate to form a rough cylinder, then blows into the mouthpiece, producing a bubble of glass (Fig. 248). During the blowing, form is controlled by twisting the pipe, rolling with a paddle, cutting, shaping with a caliper, or adding more molten glass. Glassblowing is an exciting process to watch. The glow of the furnace, the slashing of the shears, the sizzling vats of fluid, the crash of abandoned material, and the ever-present threat of disaster are all highly dramatic.

Glassblowing can be done in molds; however, in the last two decades there has been a strong revival of free-hand glassblowing. Wonderfully novel effects can emerge from the blowpipe in the hands of a designer. Frequently the blown form is cut and polished (Fig. 249).

248
Bob Held and Marvin Lipofsky blowing glass at the World Crafts Council Conference, Toronto, 1974.

249
John Nickerson. *Bowl Form.* 1981. Blown clear glass, cut and polished; 10″ (25.4 cm) diameter, height 9″ (22.86 cm). Collection of Robert Collard.

250
Břetislav Novák, Jr. *Totem.* 1980. Plate glass in five parts, cut on both sides, metal base; height 7′1″ (2.16 m). Corning Museum of Glass.

Rods and cylinders, glass fibers, and some window glass are made by a process known as *drawing*. This method calls for the molten glass to be pulled from the furnace by some device that controls its shape, such as a core to form tubes or a long, narrow trough to form sheets. Drawing can also be done by hand. Affixed between two blowpipes, a glob of hot glass is drawn as the blowers gradually move apart.

Rolling produces uniform sheets of glass, such as those needed for plate-glass windows or mirrors. Rolling is a factory technique, but some artists have explored its potential in sheet-glass constructions (Fig. 250).

The fifth method of forming glass is *casting*. As this is a basic technique applied to several materials, it will be under a separate heading.

250

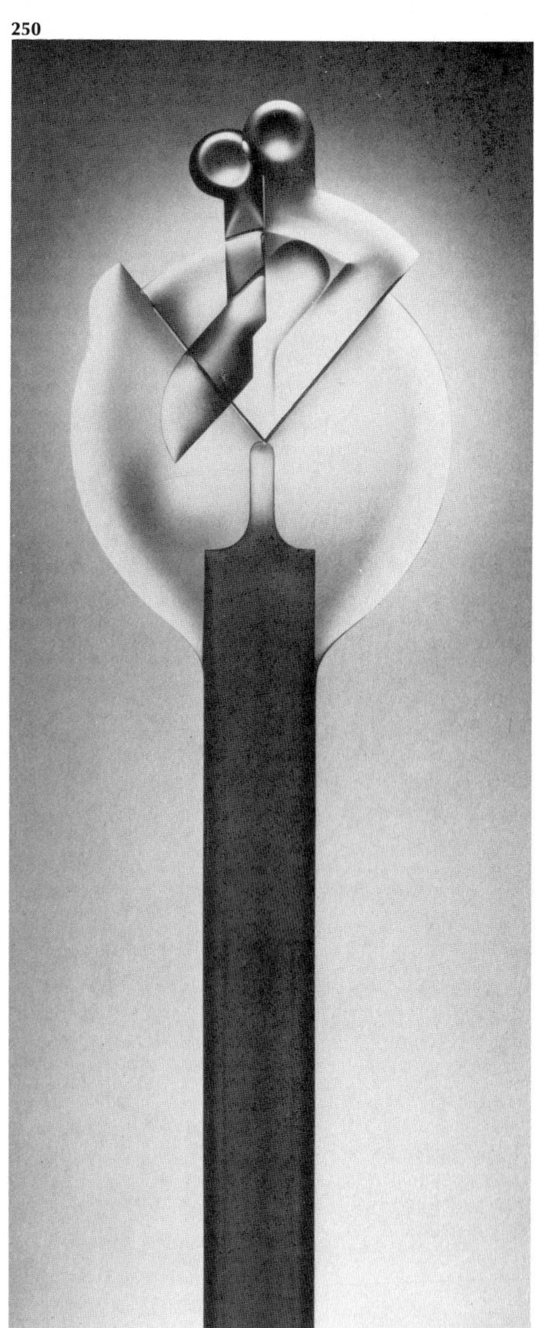

249

Casting

Casting is the process of forming a liquid or plastic substance into a specific shape by pouring it into a mold and allowing it to harden. Since the method is similar regardless of the material used, the creative process of design takes place largely in the planning and construction of the mold. As mentioned above, glass is often *blown* into a mold. It can also be poured and pressed.

Clay that is cast must be in a semiliquid state, a mixture known as *slip*. In addition to being poured into the mold, clay is sometimes *press-formed*. This is basically an industrial technique in which a large mechanical press forces plastic clay into a predetermined shape.

Casting *metal* is a modern technique based on an ancient tradition. Again, the metal, like glass, must be heated to a molten state. Chinese craftsmen of the Shang Dynasty (the second millennium B.C.) cast remarkable bronze vessels in molds that were probably made from clay (Fig. 251). Archaeological sites near An-Yang in the central plains of China have provided a wealth of these vessels ornamented with highly *stylized,* or abstract, designs derived from parts of animal bodies.

Casting is perhaps the most common process for molding *plastics*. Thermoset plastics usually come in liquid form, hardening when mixed with certain chemicals. Thermoplastics are supplied as pellets that must be melted. The materials flow easily, will readily assume nearly any shape,

251

251
Footed vessel, from China. Shang Dynasty, 12th century B.C. Cast bronze, height 7⅞" × 7⅜" (20.07 × 18.8 cm). Courtesy of the Freer Gallery of Art, Smithsonian Institution, Washington, D.C.

252
Sheila Hicks. *White Letter.* 1962. Wool, plain weave in white yarns; 38 × 47½" (.96 × 1.20 m). Museum of Modern Art, New York (gift of Knoll Associates).

and will hold that shape without breaking or cracking. When they solidify, some plastics may be almost as hard as bronze. Plastics also make superior molds for casting other materials. The designer can purchase plastics in many forms, including liquids, pastes, pellets, foams, emulsions, rods, sheets, strips, tubes, fibers, and molding powders.

Forming Techniques for Fiber

Fibers are usually used to create fabrics, by means of two types of techniques: *interlacing* and *pressure*. Chief among the interlacing techniques is weaving, an elaboration of basketry, a process by which reeds or grasses are interlaced by working them in and out to form a solid surface. Fibers that are used must first be spun. Many fibers come from natural sources: cotton, linen, and wool. *Spinning* is a process by which fibers are twisted together into a long, unbroken strand, a *yarn,* which can then be used in interlacing. Today spinning is practiced by enterprising weavers, who often raise their own sheep, card their own wool, and follow the fiber to its culmination in beautiful handwoven fabrics. Hand spinning greatly expands the possibilities of weaving, offering a new range of textural and color effects. Using a plain weave and no color, Sheila Hicks has created a subtly elegant design by varying the thickness of her yarns (Fig. 252).

252

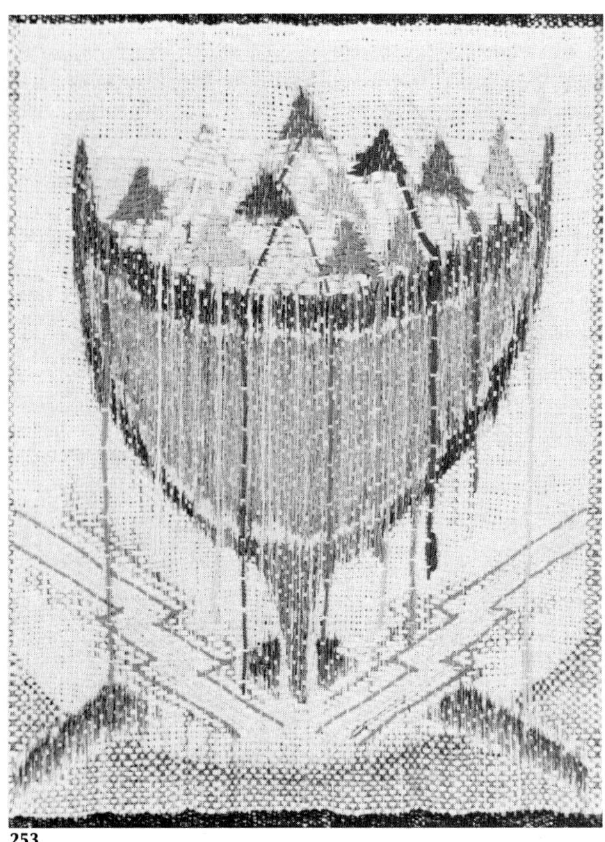

253

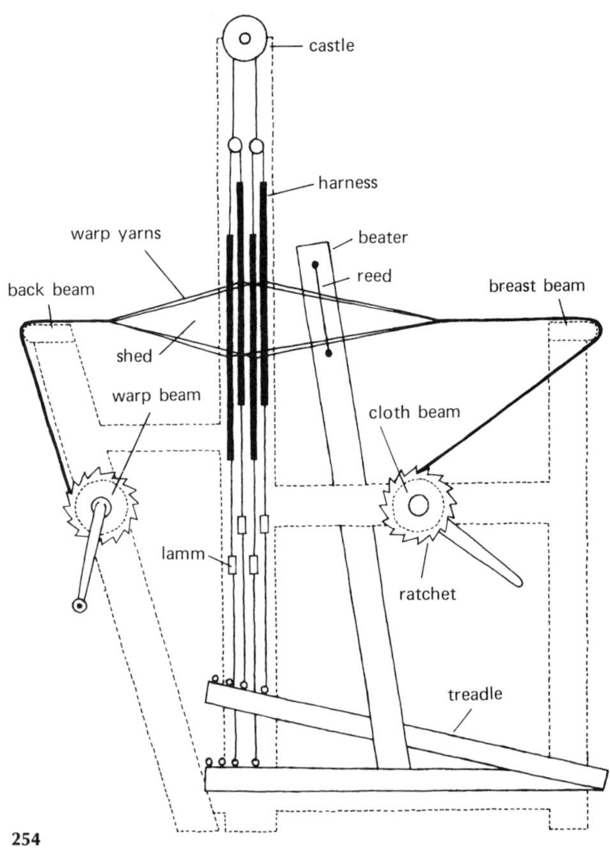

254

In weaving, two sets of yarns, arranged at right angles to each other, are interlaced. Ted Hallman's *Reverberations* (Fig. 253) shows this relationship clearly. The basic instrument for weaving is the *loom,* on which the lengthwise yarns (the warp) are held rigid, while the intersecting crosswise yarns (the *weft,* or *woof,* or *filling*) move back and forth to create a *web,* or fabric. Modern looms look tremendously complicated, but they all depend on a few simple principles (Fig. 254). First of all, the warp must be kept under tension. Second, there must be some device to raise selective warp yarns, to create a *shed* for the weft to move through. In *plain weave,* for example, the weft is supposed to move over one yarn and under the next, evenly across the fabric, so the shed would be one-up-and-one-down

253
Ted Hallman. *Reverberations.* 1982.
Warp painted, twill satin, embroidery wool; 26½" × 33½" (67.31 × 85.09 cm).

254
Diagram of a counterbalance loom, showing the basic parts common to all modern floor looms.

255
The beater of the loom showing a reed in position.

256
Theo Moorman. Sketch for tapestry, establishing lines and rhythms.

257
Theo Moorman. Working drawing for tapestry, showing shapes and values.

258
Theo Moorman. *Trees in the Wind.* Tapestry.

255

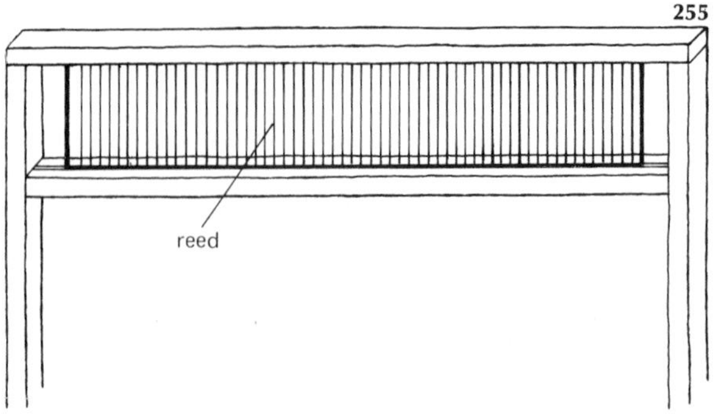

throughout. Third, it is necessary to secure each weft yarn into position in the cloth, a task that is accomplished by a beating mechanism. This device has two parts: the *reed,* whose function is to keep the warp yarns perfectly aligned, and the *beater,* a framework that holds the reed (Fig. 255). After each passing of weft yarn through the reed, the beater is pulled against the web so that the reed places the new weft securely against the previous one. Further refinements to the loom are convenient but not essential.

In creating a painting, the artist first makes a sketch, gradually refining it until it reaches the stage at which the work can be translated into paint. The illustrations in Figures 256, 257, and 258 show how the weaver proceeds in precisely this way, working first with lines and rhythms, next with shapes and values, and finally, in the medium itself, refines these original studies into areas of emphasis and gradations of color that translate into an eloquent expression of the art of weaving.

256

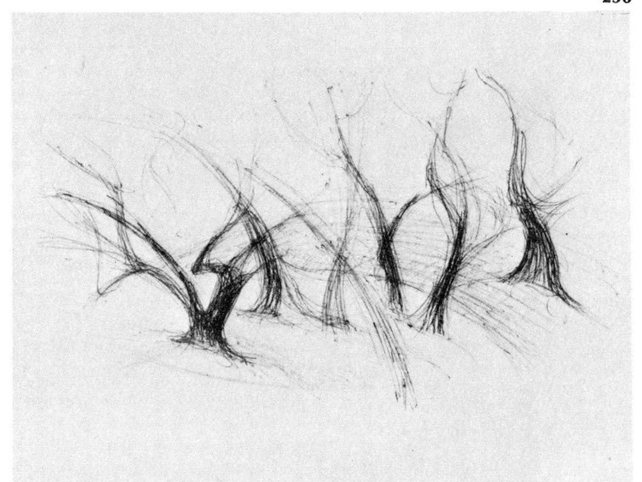

257

258

Tapestry is a specialized form of weaving in which weft yarns are hand controlled. Rarely does a single weft yarn move completely across the fabric. Instead, yarns of a particular color or texture appear and disappear on the surface of the web as the pattern demands. Tapestries have been created for centuries in many parts of the world. Perhaps the most famous is a series called *The Hunt of the Unicorn,* woven about 1500, probably in Flanders (Fig. 259).

To the standard warp and weft of flat weaving, pile weaves add another dimension, a depth resulting from a stand-up yarn called a pile. This type of yarn is evident in velvets, carpets, and terry cloth. Shag rugs are the result of an unusually long pile.

In *knotting* techniques, the yarns are not merely interlaced but are tied—together or to each other. Most knotting methods involve only a single set of yarns oriented in the same direction, rather than the crossing yarns of weaving. This is the method used in *macramé,* which employs combinations of knots.

259

259
The Unicorn in Captivity, from *The Hunt of the Unicorn.* Franco-Flemish, c. 1500. Tapestry weave, 12′ × 8′3″ (3.66 × 2.51 m). Metropolitan Museum of Art, New York (gift of John D. Rockefeller, Jr., 1937).

260
David H. Kaye. *Bound Linen and Loops.* 1972. Linen blocking cord, knotted and sewn; 22 × 16″ (56 × 40.5 cm). Collection Mr. and Mrs. Lee Howard, Willowdale, Ontario.

261
Fragment of *salalua,* tapa-cloth skirt from the Futuna Islands. Bark cloth, paper mulberry. 7′11″ × 4′10″ (2.42 × 1.48 m). Collected by E. G. Burrows, 1932. Bishop Museum (Division of Ethnology), Honolulu.

The art of *wrapping* yarns around one another emerged as a design medium in the late 1960s and early 1970s. This technique is not really involved with interlacing but achieves novel effects through working yarns together in unusual ways (Fig. 260).

Knitting and *crocheting* both rely upon a method of pulling successive loops of yarn through one another to construct a fabric.

One of the oldest methods for making fabrics is by *pressure,* compressing or pounding fibrous materials. In the cold regions of the world early cultures developed *felting,* in which loose fibers are bonded together by a combination of heat, moisture, and pressure. In warmer climates fabric was made by pounding the bark of paper mulberry trees. The result was tapa cloth, a brittle, warm-hued material often decorated with geometric designs (Fig. 261). Color variations result from dyeing the bark with natural dyes or from pressing in dried leaves and flowers. We find examples of tapa in South America, Africa, and Southeast Asia, but the material is most closely associated with Hawaii and the South Sea Islands.

260

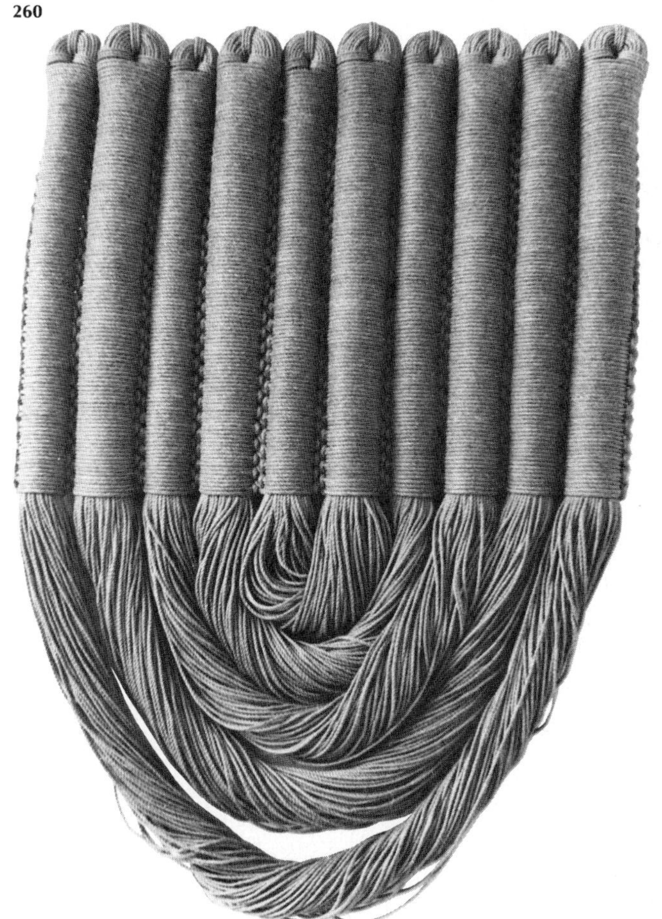

261

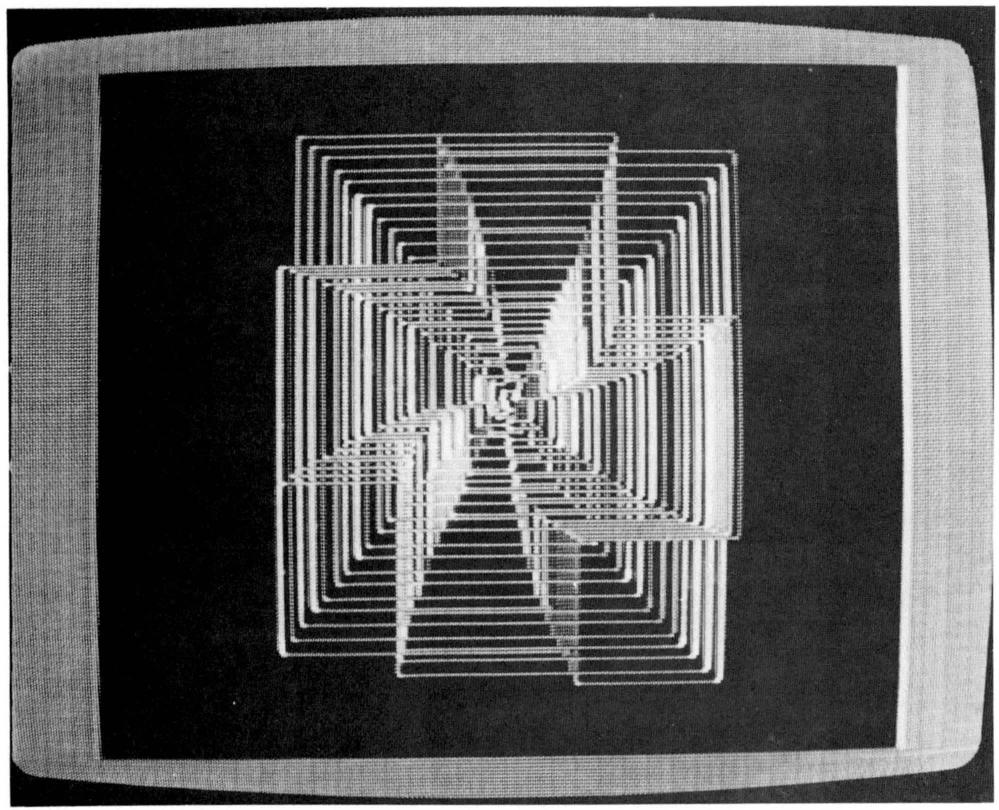

262

Computer Techniques

When the computer first came into general use, contests were held to determine the most interesting drawing that could be programmed by a computer artist (Fig. 262). In those days the results were considered interesting because of their novelty. Sixteen years later, the computer is playing a substantial role in many areas of design.

The weaver uses a computer to explore the possibilities of color and weave structure as elements of design, letting it generate all the possible color permutations of a given pattern and thus eliminating hours of experimentation on graph paper or the loom. Computer-aided drafting has become a production tool for architectural designers and will no doubt be widely used by industrial designers and interior designers as well. The computer stores standard details of plan drawing and applies them to the drawing board with a "puck," modifying alterations in a split second so that design alternatives can be considered instantly without laborious drawing. Once a design has been established, the time-consuming process of making working drawings is transformed through the use of a computer system, for shapes are permanently recorded once they are drawn and their scale can be changed simply by inserting the required scale on a keyboard.

Perhaps the most visible use of the computer in design has been in the art of film, where computer-generated images have opened up an entire new field. Startlingly realistic images have been produced by randomly

262
Jake Commander. Computer painting. 1982.

263
Computer-generated imagery. The opening of the *NBC Nightly News.*

263

adding curves and zigzags to smooth geometric forms to create crags, gullies, seascapes, and trees. Another technique generates flat images and then wraps them around solids, resulting in stunning effects too complicated to produce by conventional methods. The possibilities have enraptured an entire group of computer artists who have been involved in making films like *Tron,* in which 286 of the 350 backgrounds were drawn by a computer. For 15 of the film's 105 minutes, everything on the screen—settings, vehicles, and even a character—was the work of high-speed data-processing equipment. Other efforts have livened up television commercials, as well as the opening of the *NBC Nightly News* (Fig. 263).

Early in 1982 an exhibition was organized at Lehigh University in Pennsylvania at which 22 major artists exhibited works produced by computer techniques. Although the works were admittedly experimental, indications were that the artists were taking computer art seriously.

Many people have understandable reservations about the idea of the computer invading the fields of art and design. Artists compare the state of the computer with that of the camera a hundred years ago, pointing out that today we accept some photography as art of the highest order (see Chapter 20). Whether this is possible with the computer is a question whose answer will depend upon the ingenuity of those dedicated to its development as an instrument of design. Of one fact we can be certain: no machine, however sophisticated, can take the place of human emotion and creativity. If computer techniques aid in expressing these qualities, they are not denigrating the role of the human designer but simply expanding it.

13 Structural Design

Structural design refers to the way an object is built and shaped as a result of forming techniques. The structural design of a textile, for example, is the result of the fibers used and the manner in which they are woven—the particular combination of colors and sizes of threads (Fig. 264). In a mosaic, the structural design lies in the choice and placement of the *tesserae,* the individual pieces that compose the design (Fig. 265). Generally, structural design concerns the practical existence of an object. Without sound structural design a building will fall, a pot will collapse, a textile will pull apart. In this chapter we will explore certain basic considerations in structural design.

Perception of Structural Design

Our relationship to structural design is influenced by two factors: *scale* and *position.*

We experience the structure of a seashell by holding it in our hand, running our fingers over and around it. We can stay in one position and experience all aspects of the shell, since we can twist it and turn it to provide every possible viewpoint. Perceiving forms of larger scale is quite another experience. We may perceive the curves of rolling hills and valleys from a distance, but we experience them fully only as we wander through them, allowing them to unfold around *us* and to change form according to our position in space (Fig. 266). Similarly, we perceive mountains jutting in jagged angles against the sky, but we experience their structure only by moving among them, permitting their plunging canyons and steep cliffs to enter our consciousness by becoming challenges that affect our lives at that

264

264
Jack Lenor Larsen. *Labyrinth.* 1981. Upholstery fabric, Jacquard "repp," worsted wool, Kelim group.

265
Empress Theodora, detail of wall mosaic, San Vitale, Ravenna. c. 547.

266
Dewitt Jones. *Windy Hill, Portola Valley, California.* Photograph.

265

266

267

moment. Again, the surface of a body of water with its waves and currents is an entirely different entity to the viewer standing on shore and the person guiding a boat over it. To the latter, the waves, while beautiful, become the expression of a structure to be encountered and respected, with its depths and eddies carrying a possible threat.

Our reactions to human designs vary in the same way. We respond to the structure of a handmade pot as we handle it, cup it, and feel its form. The structure of a fabric becomes more obvious when we run our hands over it, fingering the varying thickness of the fibers.

Larger structures involve more complex perception, entailing an awareness of *space* and *time.* The structural design of a building, a landscape, or a city can best be appreciated through the consciousness of the space created by structure and the time we allow ourselves to feel its impact.

The Importance of Space and Time

267
Village of the Dogon tribe, cliffs of Bandiagara, Mali, west Africa.

268
John Utzon and others.
1957–1973. Main Hall, Sydney Opera House. Bennelong Point, Sydney Harbor.

269
Myron Goldfinger, architect.
Vacation house designed from angular masses. 1971. Westchester County, New York.

The understanding of *space* and its effective use has a great deal to do with successful design. We have discussed positive and negative space and figure-ground ambiguity as aspects of two-dimensional design (pp. 68–69). We have also considered positive and negative space in sculpture (p. 73). The space that exists within a ceramic bowl or a silver chalice is equally important as negative space, since it determines the structure of the object as well as its capacity for use. The importance of space to architecture becomes clear if one conceives of space as being unlimited until the architect demarcates it by erecting walls. The quality of the designed space determines the success of the building, for it is within the negative space that the inhabitants live and move, the positive space of walls and ceilings being textured and colored only after the negative spaces have been established. One could even say that the delimitation of space *is* the structural design of a building, with the walls being merely the decorative design that defines and enhances it.

The dimension of *time* is important to the appreciation of any work of art, but it plays the greatest role in architecture. Anyone who has learned to "feel" a building in all its possibilities can sense almost endless dimensions in its relationship to the human personality. It is this relationship that makes it possible for an individual to relate to a specific space in such a way that it becomes an integral part of existence. The space becomes "home," the most intimate of connections between space and the human spirit.

The *passing of time* also can affect a design or work of art. Depending upon the circumstances in which it is placed, a work in metal can achieve a rich mellow film, or *patina,* of oxidation; a tarnished surface; or a coating of rust that will eventually cause it to disintegrate. Wood mellows or decays, colors in paint or dye grow softer or dimmer with age, and industrially designed products simply wear out and can no longer function. Models become outdated in such products, as they may do in clothing design or even furniture. Time thus becomes both a positive element of appreciation and a universal instrument for change. Our personal spaces, while changing character to reflect our growth or development over a period of time, can become even more intimately a part of us and of our family, absorbing and reflecting a segment of history and all its associations.

Personal spaces are formed by a variety of influences. One reason people in Africa build round or cylindrical houses is to prevent evil spirits from lurking in the corners (Fig. 267). Cabins in northern countries are rectangular primarily as a result of building with heavy, unyielding logs. Contemporary materials have so expanded the possibilities of structural design that walking through a building can be much like wandering through a natural landscape, with rhythmic undulating spaces that seem to enfold the observer (Fig. 268), or vertical angular spaces that provide a surprise and a challenge (Fig. 269). The principal difference is that, unlike a landscape, a building circumscribes the effect, concentrating it within finite boundaries.

268

269

270

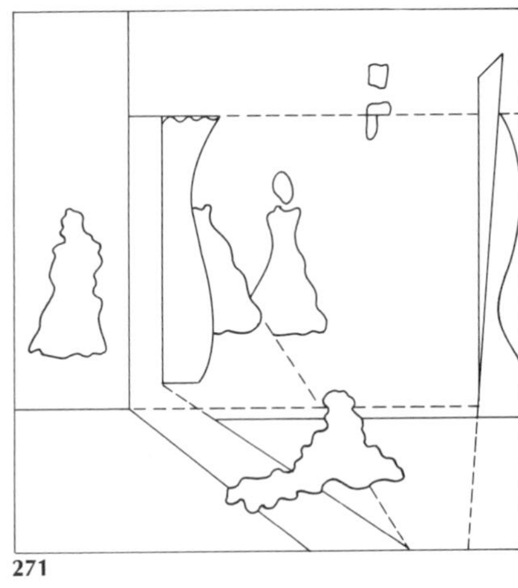

271

Composition

270
John Singer Sargent. *The Daughters of Edward Darley Boit.* 1882. Oil on canvas, 7′3″ (2.21 m) square.
Museum of Fine Arts, Boston
(gift of Mary Louise Boit, Florence D. Boit, Jane Hubbard Boit, and Julia Overing Boit, in memory of their father).

271
Diagram showing composition of painting in Figure 270.

272
Andrew Wyeth. *Ground Hog Day.* 1959.
Egg tempera on board, 31″ (78.74 cm) square.
Philadelphia Museum of Art (gift of Henry F. du Pont and Mrs. John Wintersteen).

In two-dimensional works, particularly paintings, structural design is frequently referred to as *composition.* The composition of a work is actually the total of all the elements and principles of design that compose it. This statement will become clearer if we analyze the structural design of a specific work.

In his painting *The Daughters of Edward Darley Boit* (Fig. 270), John Singer Sargent started with a rectangular canvas within which he placed certain shapes representing recognizable things—four girls, a rug, architectural elements, and two large vases. We tend to assume that when a painter undertakes a portrait, the subject is simply placed in an attractive setting and work begun. A careful analysis will reveal that this is not the case. In the first place, the girls are not placed together but are separated into two groupings, each with strong vertical lines leading to the most interesting shape in the composition, the small figure seated in the foreground. Her importance as a shape is extended by the addition of a doll that nearly doubles the size of the light area composing the shape. Our eyes are led to this focal point by the downward sweep of white aprons and by another strong element, the slender thrusting triangle at the right. This geometric shape is buttressed by the curved edge of a second vase echoing the one against which one of the figures is leaning. This leaning figure provides a diagonal line, which, if extended, would meet an extension of the triangle. Together, these lines suggest a support for the compositional structure, much as a metal armature supports a sculpture in clay. Still another arm of the support is produced by the diagonal of the rug that meets the vertical wall.

One of the most revealing ways to study structural design in painting is to lay a sheet of tracing paper over a work and draw the salient lines and shapes. This we have done in Figure 271. However, design in painting involves more than line and shape. Color plays a vital part, and by studying the work in black-and-white, we are able to see how value contributes to the structure. There are three predominant values: the darkness of the upper center section; the flashing whiteness of the children's aprons; and the transitional middle value of the floor, the vertical wall, and the triangle. All three values meet and mingle in the pattern on the vases and in the rug. Of subtle but decisive importance is the small rectilinear light implying a window high in the darkness of the wall. This unobtrusive shape breaks the expanse of darkness, tying the upper part of the composition to the light forms elsewhere by suggesting a reflection of them.

Analysis of a very different composition will serve further to illustrate the fundamental importance of structural design in a work of art. The painting by Andrew Wyeth in Figure 272 is straightforward and simple. The framework is obvious, as geometric as the canvas itself. Table, walls, and window are all composed of angles, a basic theme that culminates in the rectangular pattern of windowpanes. Against this angularity, the round shapes of plate, cup, and saucer sound as clear accents heightened by the chunks of sawed log outside, then muted by the circles of the wallpaper design. Meanwhile, there is a strong vertical in the fence post, of which the knife on the table seems almost a shadow. Trunks of trees continue the lines upward out of the picture, and since both tree trunks and fence post have been shaded to imply their roundness, they become a transitional element between straight lines and circles. Here again, value plays a vital role, as the light area of the tabletop reaches upward and disperses into the sparkling highlights of window framing, log, and molding.

272

273

274

273
Eduardo Chillida. *Abesti Gogora III.* 1962–1964. Oak, 6′9⅝″ × 11′4⅜″ (2.07 × 3.46 m). Art Institute of Chicago (Grant J. Pick Purchase Fund).

274
Henning Koppel. Sterling silver pitcher. 1951.

275
Masakazu Kobayashi. *W³W to the Third Power.* 1977. Vinylon, 7′8″ × 6′1″ × 1′11″ (2.34 × 1.85 × .58 m). Courtesy The Allrich Gallery, San Francisco.

276
Grau-Garriga. *Reprimida.* 1972. 5′10¾″ × 2′3½″ (1.8 × .7 m). Courtesy Arras Gallery, Ltd., New York.

Materials as Structural Design

Often the innate qualities of a material determine the character of a design. The work in Figure 273 is a good example. Conceivably this form could have been cast in metal or glass or molded in ceramic, but the result would have been entirely different. The charm of the piece is in its *blockiness,* the grain and cracks of the wood, the marks of nails, and the sawed openings. The interlocking forms intrigue us because they are solid and bulky, yet they seem to interweave as fibers might do. The eye seeks the key to how the pieces work together and why the total sits just as it does. Here the material *is* the structure, and the most important aspect of the design.

The pitcher in Figure 274 is just as irrevocably concerned with being made of silver. Here again, glass or clay could have formed a similar mass but the *essence* would have been lost. The elegance of this particular form lies in the simplicity of its shining surface with its sharp reflections.

Tremendous variety in structural design is possible in the fiber arts, which include techniques ranging from lacemaking to tapestry weaving. Many contemporary artists combine fibers with other materials in works of fantasy such as the construction in Figure 275. This is another example of material and structural design being inseparable. It is the particular substance of the vinylon fibers that makes possible the intriguing looping in this structure, with enough flexibility to fall in place yet sufficient body to hold a shape.

Even in more conventional weaving techniques, the nature of the yarns is essential. In Figure 276, the sizes and textures of the yarns make possible a rich textural variety that could not have been achieved otherwise.

275

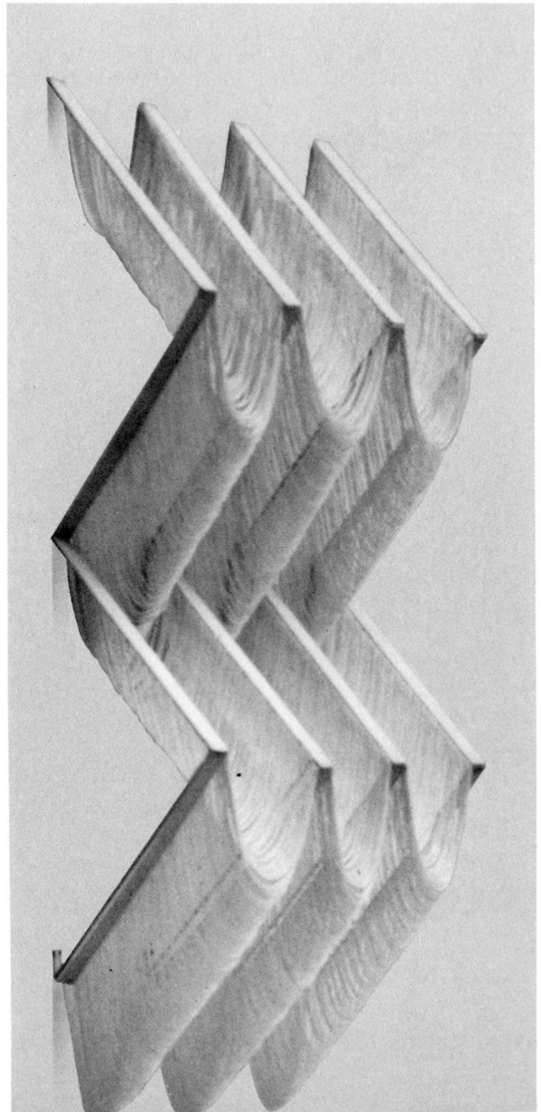

276

277

As structural design always depends upon the material used, there is inevitably some degree of exploitation of the special characteristics of the material and of the processes that form it. This is particularly true of glass, with its qualities of fluidity and transparency. The vase in Figure 277 is as essentially glass as if it had just dropped from the blowpipe, a swirl still molten, its clarity and transparency so eloquent that the shell of material itself seems almost to vanish. The structure of this piece is as dependent on the glassblowing process as it is on the material from which it was formed.

Structural design on a grand scale has been possible in glass ever since sheet glass become practical and relatively inexpensive. Modern cities are filled with soaring towers of glass built on steel frameworks, and we take them very much for granted. However, the most extraordinary glass structure of all was built on an iron framework more than a hundred years ago in London's Hyde Park—the famous *Crystal Palace* (Fig. 278). This fantasy creation was the plan of Joseph Paxton, a designer of greenhouses, to contain the Great Exhibition of 1851, which was a project of Prince Albert, consort of Queen Victoria. Its purpose was to bring together under one roof the "Works of Industry of All Nations." Today most of the exhibits have been superseded by more recent inventions, but the building conceived by Paxton has never been equaled.

By all reports Prince Albert was delighted with the structure, as were most of its visitors. In Victorian times people were accustomed to heavy, ponderous buildings crowded with heavy, ponderous furnishings, and the *Crystal Palace,* by comparison, must have seemed like a fairyland. Long, open vistas carried the eye to infinity, with no solid walls to interrupt the view to the outside. Within, live trees growing to ceiling height gave the breathtaking impression of the outdoors flowing into the indoors. Paxton

278

277
Andries D. Copier. *Unique Piece C.B.7,* blue with a green spot. 1958. Free blown, 14¾" (37.47 cm). Museum Boymans van Beuningen, Rotterdam.

278
Joseph Paxton. Interior, Crystal Palace, London. 1851. Cast iron and glass, width 1851′ (564.18 m).

279
Marian Powys. Lace. c. 1924. 6 × 9" (15.24 × 22.86 cm).

wisely left his design free of any applied ornamentation. The structure and the glass are inseparable and constitute an eminently successful design.

When we contrast the *Crystal Palace* with a piece of handmade lace (Fig. 279), we begin to understand the full scope and variety of structural design. Whatever the character of the work of art, there is a fundamental framework that determines its ultimate form. Frequently this form is influenced further by decorative design. In the next chapter we will look at some of the ways in which the human need for decorative design has found expression.

279

14 Decorative Design

The urge to decorate surfaces is as old as humanity. Through the centuries, all over the world, this inclination has produced a rich body of design.

Expressive Forms

The forms of decorative design fall into several specific categories. Simple *geometric shapes* span history from Neolithic times until the present and are now considered by many artists to be an appropriate expression of an impersonal technological society. There is no inhabited area in the world where some form of geometric design cannot be found. In the garment in Figure 280, at least six geometric designs (if we do not include the stripes) are combined in a *pilu saluf,* a headhunter's costume from the Indonesian island of Timor.

280

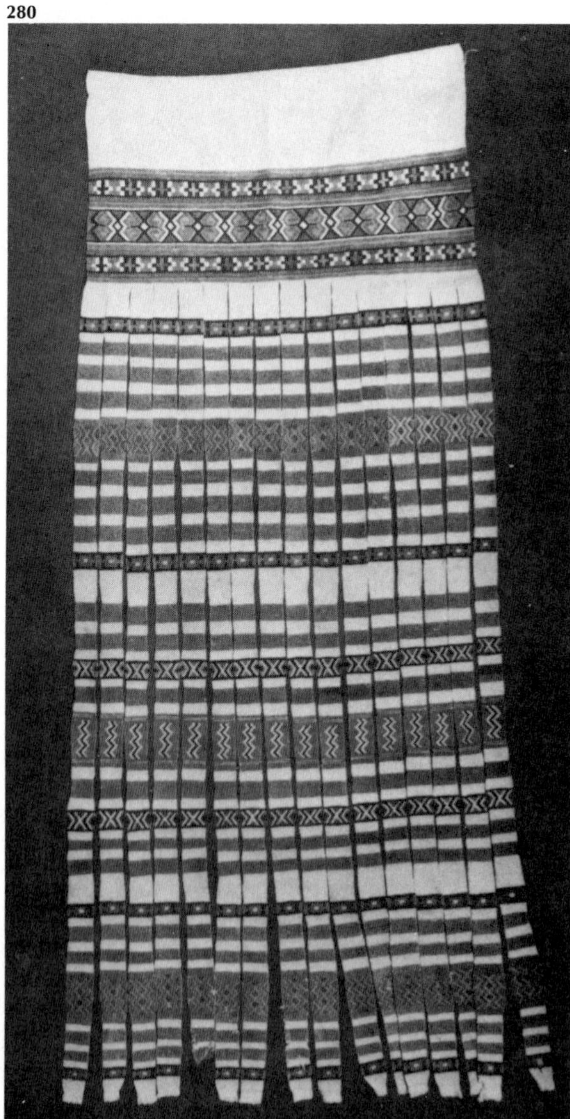

280
Pilu saluf (*meo,* or headhunter's costume piece). Timor, Indonesia. Tapestry weave, twining and plain weave, cotton; warp 32¼" (82 cm), weft 12¼" (31 cm). Rijksmuseum voor Volkenkunde, Leiden.

281
Fowler Hunting in a Marsh. Egyptian, c. 1400 B.C. Water-based mineral pigments on plaster, height 8¼" (82 cm). British Museum.

282
Chinese medallion with five-clawed dragon. 18th century. Embroidery with gold wrapped thread. Metropolitan Museum of Art (Anonymous gift).

Geometric shapes result from a simple joining of lines, which no doubt explains their widespread use by so-called primitive peoples. Far removed from civilization, many groups exhibit nevertheless a highly developed design sense, an innate characteristic that allows them to achieve elaborate expression of the forms of their natural habitat.

The *shapes of plants, birds, and fish* have inspired graceful designs since the days of the early Egyptians (Fig. 281), and animal shapes have been developed in many cultures into mythological beasts of ferocious fantasy and marvelous design. One of the most elaborate of all such developments was the dragon that blossomed in ancient China (Fig. 282).

281

282

283

283
Antoni Gaudí. *El Drac.* Entrance gate to the Güell Pavilions, Barcelona. 1885. Laminated, cast, and wrought iron with wire mesh for the dragon's wings.

284
Tsimshian clan headdress, collected by C. F. Newcombe at Kitkatla, British Columbia, 1895–1901. Painted wood with seashell teeth and bear canines; height 17" (43.18 cm), base diameter 12½" (31.75 cm). Canadian Ethnology Service, National Museum of Man, Ottawa.

285
Detail of the jamb of the Great Door, Santa Maria Novella, Florence. Executed by Giovanni Bertini from the designs of Leon Battista Alberti, 1456–1470.

The dragon has probably enjoyed the most varied coverage of any animal form in the area of design. In early mythologies the dragon was associated with evil and destruction, particularly among nations infested with venomous reptiles. The ancient Greeks and Romans, however, believed that dragons had the ability to understand and to convey to people the secrets of the earth. Consequently, the dragon was seen as a benign and protective influence and, because of its fearsome qualities, it was adopted as a military emblem by the Romans. It flourished throughout British history on coats of arms and battle standards, and sprang up in nineteenth-century Spain in a surprisingly contemporary personification for the gates of the Güell Pavilions in Barcelona (Fig. 283).

Similar to the dragon are the fabulous animals portrayed by the Indians of British Columbia. The whale, raven, and all the beasts of the northern forest achieve a highly designed stylization at the hands of tribal artists. A headdress such as the one in Figure 284 becomes decorative design for the person who wears it. Similar figures are carved or painted on chests, door lintels, and small objects for tribal use.

284

285

Plants, too, have been given extensive symbolic interpretation. The lotus denoted rebirth in ancient Egypt, and the Taoist Chinese attributed spiritual qualities to many plants and blossoms. The carvers of decorative design on the Gothic cathedrals used plants as symbols of the Christian faith. Later, during the Renaissance, the philosophy of Humanism turned attention from the world-to-come to an appreciation of humanity and earthly beauty. As a result, Renaissance churches are richly ornamented with carvings depicting plant forms in elegant designs (Fig. 285).

286

287

286
Walter B. Broderick for Schumacher. Floral screen print on cotton. Introduced 1975.

287
Ernst Haas. *Newly Fallen Snow on Stones in Bed of a Shallow River.* Photograph. 1964.

288
Façade of the Otto Heinrichsbau, Castle of Heidelberg. Begun 1556.

Contemporary artists use plant forms in many media. One of the most usual areas for the application of floral designs is printed fabrics (Fig. 286).

The *human form* is basic to nearly all art. We create in our own image, making buildings and objects on a scale capable of human perception and use, and incorporating human elements into our decorative designs. The outstanding exception is Islamic art, which forbids the use of the human figure on the basis that it invites idolatry. Most people, however, tend to see even in nature the forms of the human body (Fig. 287).

In sculptural design the human figure is frequently used in a symbolic sense—to commemorate heroes or to narrate episodes from the past. The most spectacular examples are the Gothic cathedrals, great treasure houses of sculpture presenting the history of Christianity. Three centuries later, the Renaissance swirled human figures over painted walls and ceilings or ensconced them in stone niches on the façades of palaces and churches. The Ottheinrich Wing of Heidelberg Castle (Fig. 288) is adorned with a mixture of geometric, floral, and human forms, the latter ranging from a Roman emperor to the biblical David, interspersed with such allegorical figures as Hope and Love.

288

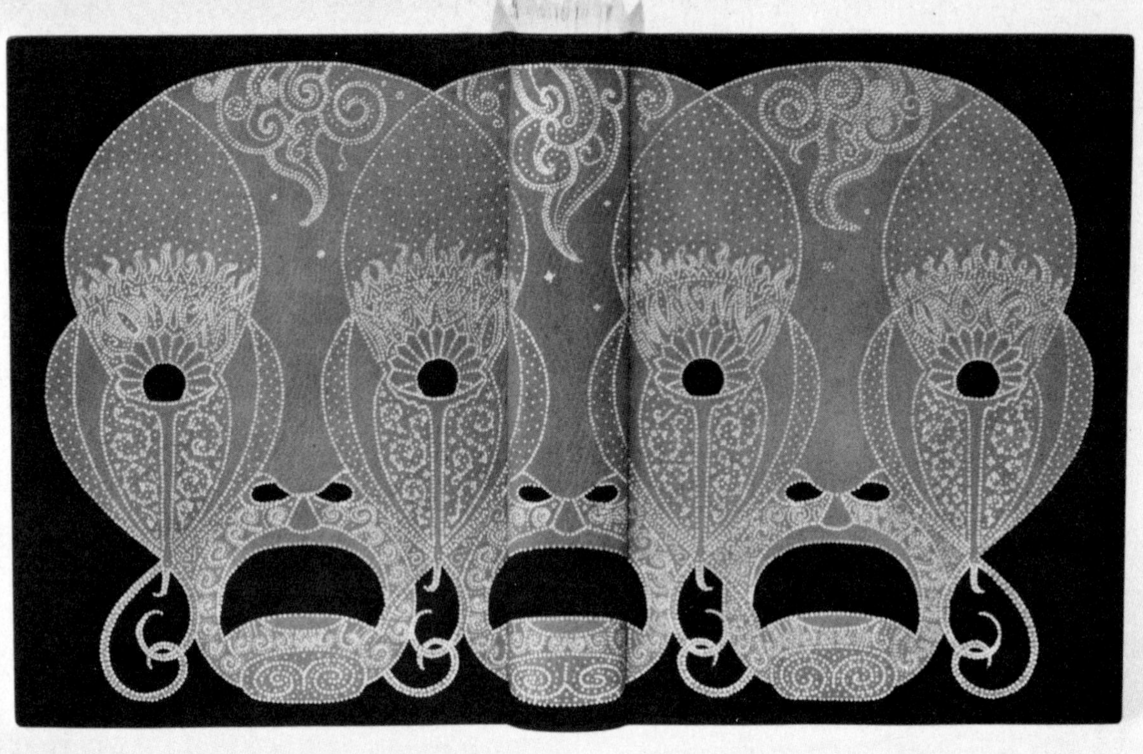

289

289
Michael Wilcox. Bookbinding for *Tales of Mystery and Imagination* by Edgar Allan Poe (pub. London, 1919). 1978. Leather, gold-tooled; 10⅞" × 8½" (27.69 × 21.59 cm). Collection Raymond M. Wapner.

290
Front of a chest. French, Valley of the Loire. c. 1535. Musée des Arts décoratifs, Paris.

291
Detail from *The Book of Kells.* Irish, late 8th century. Panel at end of genealogy of Christ according to St. Luke. Trinity College, Dublin.

The most purely decorative use of figurative forms is not related to narrative but exploits the shapes of face or body simply because they are interesting in themselves. The bookbinding in Figure 289 has a strong element of symbolism attached, yet its primary interest lies in the decorative design the artist has developed from the simple shape of a human face.

Sometimes design motifs are used in a distinctive way to form a kind of pattern, a new entity in itself. Such an entity is the *arabesque.* Used in painting, carving, mosaic, textiles, and many other arts, the arabesque combines foliage or fruit (and sometimes animal and figural) forms in involved patterns of intertwining lines. In Islamic art the arabesque is geometric and angular, whereas the Renaissance interpretation is curved and flowing. Although the name derives from Arabic design, it is more often applied to the curving style in which animal and human figures are included (Fig. 290).

A very different kind of intertwining is the distinctive decorative style developed in the monasteries of the British Isles from the seventh to eleventh centuries. This intricate straplike ornamentation was used extensively to enrich manuscripts. Painted in glowing colors touched with gold, these manuscripts have become unique treasures of decorative art (Fig. 291). (See also Pl. 17, p. 110).

Our survey of decorative design would not be complete without an introduction to a style that is overwhelmingly curvilinear and filled with movement, *the Baroque,* a term that encompasses one of the most flam-

292

293

boyant and dramatic styles of decorative design in the history of art. Originating as a counterbalance to the Reformation, when churches were stripped of all reminders of their former association with Rome, the Baroque burst forth in the Catholic churches of the sixteenth century as a dramatic reminder of everything the Protestant churches were denying. Statues of saints and angels whirled about ceilings filled with clouds and cherubs, columns of striped marble supported pulpits of gold, and chapels, medallions, and shrines were encrusted with curving moldings and exuberant decorative forms. All of this was fabricated in plaster, painted in white or gold, and touched with pastel colors or rich jewel tones. Structural design virtually disappeared as decorative design imposed a new and ethereal setting (Fig. 292).

292
Gianlorenzo Bernini. *Cathedra Petri* (Throne of St. Peter). 1657–1666. Marble, bronze (partly gilt), colored glass, and stucco. St. Peter's, Vatican, Rome.

293
Vjenceslav Richter. *Relief Meter.* Movable aluminum elements, 39 × 39 × 7″ (100 × 100 × 18 cm). Belgrade.

294
Anne Echelman. Cuff bracelets. 1975. Silver with repoussé and chased decoration.

Texture as Embellishment

In contrast to the Baroque, the arts of the twentieth century have tended to minimize ornamentation. During the first half of the century, there was a strong feeling that structural design should stand stark and unadorned, that structure *was* the essential decorative form. In the face of this philosophy, the only acceptable decorative design was the use of texture, which could be considered a part of the structural material.

Today we have begun once more to appreciate the time-honored arts of embellishment, yet we also continue to value texture as an important element in decorative design. Many contemporary artists enjoy the challenge of creating a design whose entire interest depends upon this single element. The all-white wall hanging in Figure 252 is an excellent example. The wall panel in Figure 293 translates the same emphasis on texture into aluminum cubes. In both cases there is no color, no line, no delineated shape to contribute to the design. The panel relies upon *relief,* the protrusion of the cubes at varying heights, and the shadows that result. The fact that the pattern varies according to the source of light and its intensity lends a lively quality not always found even in works with a more elaborate composition. Here, although the texture is *tactile,* it translates into strongly visual terms.

Decorative Processes

Having touched on the principal types of decorative forms, we will now look at the many ways in which artists apply these forms to the materials with which they work. Although a few processes are applicable to several materials, many are directly related to certain special qualities. We will therefore consider each material or process individually.

Metal

The bright mirrorlike surface of some metals is one form of decorative treatment. The "satin finish" on certain metals such as pewter is another. Still other metals, notably bronze, thrive on adverse natural conditions such as dampness and temperature extremes, developing over time a mellow, subtly colored patina. Metals such as gold, silver, or brass can be polished to a high gloss. However, even precious metals can gain surface interest through a variety of decorative procedures.

Chasing and *repoussé* are perhaps the most usual methods of working metal surfaces (Fig. 294). Both are accomplished with rounded tools held against the metal and struck with a hammer, so that a depression is formed.

294

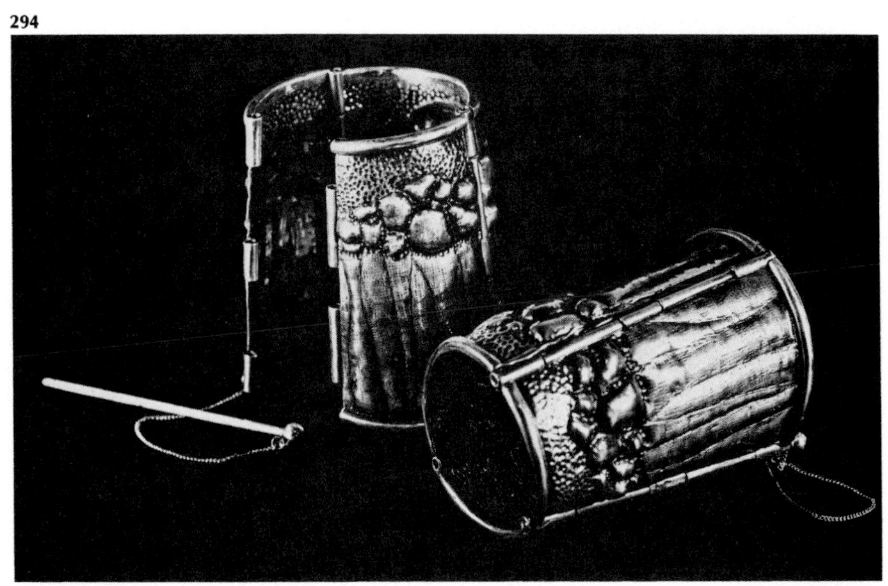

295

In chasing, the work is usually done from the face or outside; thus a *recessed* design appears on the finished piece. Repoussé, from the French verb meaning to "push back," is done from the back, and therefore the lines or images are *raised* on the surface.

Engraving and *etching,* which developed as methods of embellishing medieval armor and goldwork, involve *incising* or cutting fine lines into the surface of metal. In the case of engraving, the work is done with a sharp tool. Etching relies on the cutting action of acid. To etch metal the craftsman first covers, or *stops out,* portions of the surface that are not to be cut with an acid-resistant substance, such as wax. Then the acid is applied and allowed to eat into the metal to the desired depth, but only in the exposed areas. Sometimes incised lines are filled with a black material called *nigellum* to create color contrast. The resulting effect is known as *niello.*

Contemporary methods of giving interest to metal include *torch texturing,* in which a welder's torch is held against the metal at a certain point until the surface melts and begins to flow. Rich mottled textures can be obtained in this manner. Simple hammering on solid metal can also give textured surfaces.

Enameling is related to glass in composition and to ceramics in technique, but since it is applied to a metal base, it can be considered a decorative process for metal. The raw material of enameling consists of ground-glass particles that are applied, either dry or in a pastelike state, to a metal ground and then fired. Firing causes the particles to melt, forming a smooth lustrous coating on the metal. Any metal can serve as the ground as long as it will fuse with the enamel. Copper, silver, and gold are the most frequently used.

There are several kinds of enamel design. In *cloisonné* (French for "partitioned") enameling, the pattern is delineated by tiny flat metal wires known as *cloisons.* These are affixed to a metal base and the enamel applied between them. Firing causes the enamels to fuse with both the cloisons and the base, so the resulting design has a delicate weblike pattern running through the areas of color (Fig. 295).

Plique à jour enamel resembles stained glass, because the metal base material is removed after firing to leave only the cloisonné wires and the enamel. The result is a transparent or translucent colored shell interspersed with the fine lines of the wires.

Champlevé is a process by which the portions of metal to be enameled are engraved or cut out. Enamel paste is then applied to the depressions and the piece fired.

Wood

The natural grain of many woods is the most expressive of decorative designs. For certain purposes, however, designers may wish to enhance the surface of the wood with various decorative techniques. Perhaps the simplest method is to combine different woods to give a variety of colors, textures, and grain patterns.

Painting is a traditional means of embellishing wood, and often wood carvers of the past applied many colors (polychrome) to their figures.

Carving, of course, is a decorative process that spans all centuries, all cultures, and all parts of the world (Fig. 296). Because the tools needed for wood carving are relatively simple, even quite primitive cultures have produced ornate wood carvings.

295
Gael and Howard Silverblatt.
Cloisonné pendant. 1981.

296
Door panel from New Caledonia, Melanesia.
Carved wood, height 6′10¼″ (2.09 m).
Museum für Völkerkunde, Berlin.

297
Tom Turner. Bottle vase. 1976.
Blue porcelain with salt glaze, height 8″ (20.32 cm). Private collection.

296

Clay

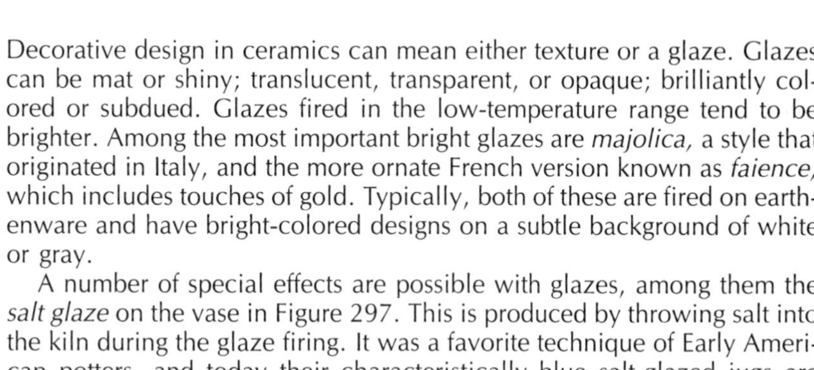

Decorative design in ceramics can mean either texture or a glaze. Glazes can be mat or shiny; translucent, transparent, or opaque; brilliantly colored or subdued. Glazes fired in the low-temperature range tend to be brighter. Among the most important bright glazes are *majolica,* a style that originated in Italy, and the more ornate French version known as *faience,* which includes touches of gold. Typically, both of these are fired on earthenware and have bright-colored designs on a subtle background of white or gray.

A number of special effects are possible with glazes, among them the *salt glaze* on the vase in Figure 297. This is produced by throwing salt into the kiln during the glaze firing. It was a favorite technique of Early American potters, and today their characteristically blue salt-glazed jugs are prized as collectors' items.

Crackle glazes result when the rate of expansion or contraction in the clay body of a piece is different from the rate in the glaze. The Chinese of the Sung Dynasty (A.D. tenth–eleventh century), perhaps the master potters of all time, calculated the effects of the crackle glaze precisely so they could predict what pattern would appear on the finished product.

Raku is a Japanese technique associated with Zen Buddhism. The glazes are low-fire and are used on bodies with a high proportion of grog (hard clay that has been ground into small particles).

297

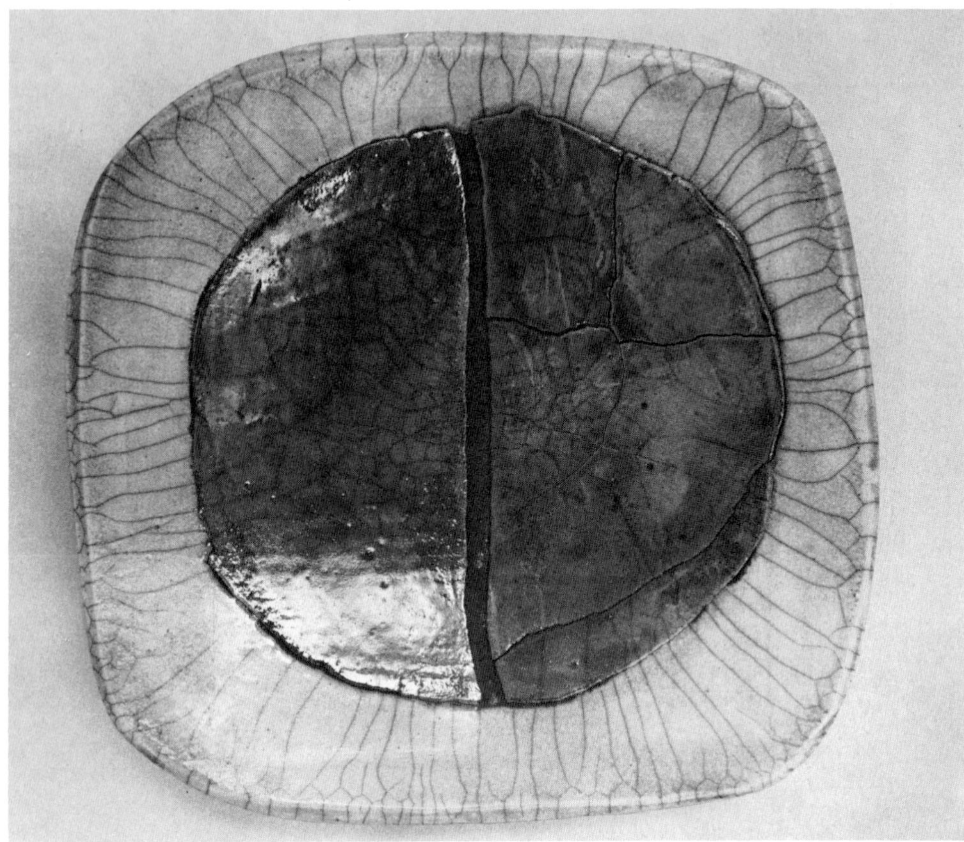

298

Barbara Segal's *Shattered Sun* (Fig. 298) combines the effects of a crackle glaze with a raku technique. This piece also makes use of a *luster glaze,* which includes gold or silver for an even richer quality. The complex decorative design is appropriate since the basic shape is extremely simple.

Glass

298
Barbara Segal. *Shattered Sun.* 1975. Raku-fired clay with amber luster and white crackle glaze, diameter 14" (35.56 cm). Private collection.

299
Ann Wärff. *Give and Get.* 1973. Sandblasted and etched plate, diameter 19½" (49.53 cm). Courtesy the artist.

300
Millefiori glass bowl. Roman, 1st century B.C. Metropolitan Museum of Art, New York (gift of Henry J. Marquand, 1881).

Surface decoration on glass seems to float on the transparent body and becomes even more attractive when light shines through it.

Laid-on designs consist of separate shapes of glass applied to the body of the object. In the past, these shapes were often of contrasting color and were sometimes gilded for luxurious effects.

Etching on glass creates a frosted texture or gives a linear quality to a design, as in the combination of sandblasting and etching used in Figure 299. Glass is etched in the same manner as metal, by using wax and acid.

Heavy crystal may be ornamented by *cutting.* Cut glass reached considerable popularity early in the twentieth century, when the designs became quite elaborate. Most cutting is done by small diamond wheels.

Engraving is used for the finest crystal since it enhances the surface without detracting from the inherent qualities of brilliance and clarity. Rapidly turning copper or diamond wheels engrave the glass, which is pressed against them, in a delicate and painstaking process.

Glassmaking reached a peak in Venice, where it is still carried on in workshops on the island of Murano, which has been a glassmaking center since 1292. One of the Venetian specialties is *millefiori* glass, based on a method devised by the ancient Romans. In millefiori glass, narrow rods of glass are bundled together, partially fused, then sliced into discs for mounting in the body of glass as it is being fired. The rings appear in the finished piece as little rings of color, giving the effect of flowers floating within the glass (Fig. 300). From the late fifteenth century through the seventeenth century Venetian glassmakers made great technical strides in introducing new colors and surface decoration. Glass vases were painted, gilded, covered with swirls of opaque white glass, and *crackled,* that is, carefully heated and cooled to create an overall pattern of fine lines.

299

300

301

301
Louis Comfort Tiffany and Tiffany Studios. *Triptych: Landscape.* c. 1910–1919. Stained glass window, 4′2″ × 7′7½″ (1.27 × 2.32 m). Art Museum, Princeton University (Gift of Norman C. Ballantine, Princeton, New Jersey).

302
Adam and Eve and King and Queen. Mid-17th century. Embroidery in silk on canvas, 19¼ × 20¾″ (48.9 × 52.71 cm). Metropolitan Museum of Art, New York (Irwin Untermeyer Collection).

Stained glass has little in common with other types of glass design, for it is closer to painting in its final results. Its unique quality lies in the effects of light shining through it, making it glow with gemlike iridescence.

Stained glass is made by coloring glass with metal oxides, molding it into sheets or blowing it into a bubble that is then split into sheets with variations in texture. When the sheets have hardened they are cut into individual pieces and joined by inserting them into U-shaped strips of metal, usually lead, which can be bent to accommodate the design. The work is then mounted with supports of metal bars.

As with sculpture, stained glass found its ultimate expression in Gothic cathedrals, whose magnificent windows were designed to illustrate the teachings of the Bible and Christian tradition for a largely illiterate population. Their glowing colors played a major role in creating the emotional atmosphere, which was heightened by the aroma of incense and the sounds of the organ. Together, these appeals to the senses transformed massive gray stone walls into a mystical ever-expanding space.

In contrast, the secular works of Louis Comfort Tiffany were designed to enhance the homes of wealthy clients in New York and other urban areas. Tiffany was associated with Art Nouveau, and his work is filled with sinuous plant forms translated into stained glass. His primary interest was in windows that made it possible for the residents of a home to retreat from the urban ugliness growing up around them into a world that was pastoral and benign (Fig. 301).

The earliest *mosaics* were composed of little colored stones, which the Romans and other ancient people laid in concrete to make streets or floors. Later, these *tesserae* were made of glazed ceramic or glass. Both are used today.

There are two methods of making mosaics, the *direct* and the *indirect.* In the direct method the tesserae are laid directly into wet mortar. The designer works with the realization that irregularities of surface will add to the interest of the finished composition, catching the light, casting shadows, and making a tapestrylike pattern. In the indirect method, the work is done from a full-scale drawing or *cartoon* that is a representation of the design in reverse. The tesserae are placed on the paper with a special paste, and much of the mosaic composition is completed before the mortar is applied to the base. When the mortar is ready, the paperbacked mosaic is set face down against it and pressed into the mortar. After the paper has dried, it is peeled off. *Grout* can be added to fill in the crevices between tesserae. Mosaics can be seen in Figures 265 (p. 199) and 5 (p. 5).

Fabrics

Decorative design is used on fabrics to impart color, texture, or pattern. The types of fabric treatment can be covered under two broad categories: *fiber techniques* and *printing techniques.*

Fiber techniques include all the methods that call for a yarn or thread to be worked through a fabric, and it is generally designated as *stitchery.*

Embroidery is a specialized form of stitchery in which the individual stitches are highly decorative. Embroidery may or may not cover the entire surface of the fabric. Its unique appeal lies in the variety of stitches and the ways in which they are combined. The eighteenth-century embroidered piece in Figure 302 shows Adam and Eve in the Garden of Eden, accompanied by the King and Queen of England. This naive transport through time and space was intended to show the maker's devoted loyalty to King Charles and his consort.

302

303

Other forms of stitchery are *crewel* and *needlepoint.* Crewel requires using a twisted ropelike thread; in needlepoint stitches are made through a relatively stiff meshlike backing.

The technique of *appliqué* concentrates less on the stitches themselves than on what they hold together. In appliqué, pieces of some material, usually fabric, are applied to a fabric background with tiny stitches that do not show as part of the finished design. The purpose is to add pattern or contrasting color in large areas. It may also have the effect of making the design seem three-dimensional. (See Pl. 21, p. 130.)

Printing techniques for fabrics include *silk screen,* a process described under *serigraphy* in Chapter 18. This is essentially a stencil technique and makes possible the printing of all types of designs, from intricate detail to bold brightly colored fabrics like the one in Figure 286.

Batik and tie-dye are both *resist printing* methods, which means some device prevents color from penetrating the fabric where it is not wanted, but the control is less specific than in the use of silk screen. In *batik,* nonprinting areas are covered with a wax coating and then the fabric is dipped in dye. Only the unwaxed areas of the cloth will accept the color, and when the wax cracks during the dipping the color seeps through, giving the cloth a characteristic visual texture of fine lines. (See Fig. 140.) When the dye has dried and *set,* the wax is melted off and reapplied in other portions of the fabric for the printing of the next color. In *tie-dye,* the nonprinting sections for a particular color are twisted and tied tightly to retard color absorption. This method is less precise, for some color will bleed around the knots so that a soft blurred quality results.

Finally, images and patterns can be *photoprinted* onto fabric using the techniques of photography. Catherine Jansen's *Blue Room* (Fig. 303) is a whole environment of stuffed and stitched forms that have been photo-printed to create, among other things, the figures on the bed, the mirror image, and the television screen. The effect of a totally soft world, with flattened people, makes us see familiar objects in a completely new light. The confusion of imagery between two and three dimensions provides an intriguing experience of space.

We have now surveyed the tools of the designer—the elements and principles of design and the materials and processes with which they are expressed. In the next two sections we will discuss the broader areas in which design is significant in human life: first, in communication between people, and finally, in the enrichment of our environment.

303
Catherine Jansen. *Blue Room.* 1972.
Photo-blueprint on cotton and vinyl, 9 × 12′ (2.74 × 3.66 m). Courtesy the artist.

Part Three

Visual Communication and Design

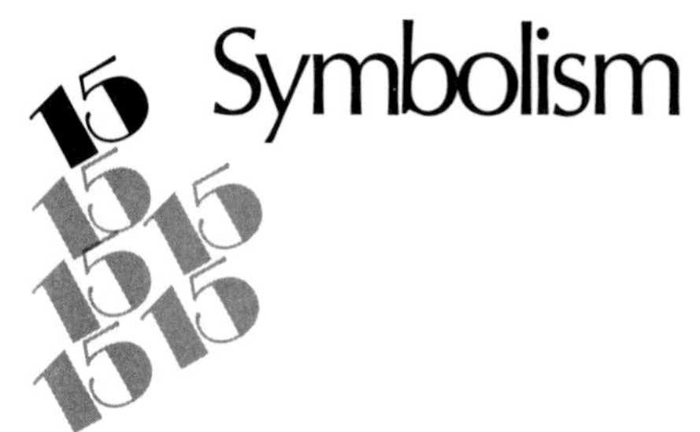

15 Symbolism

We communicate by symbols, things that stand for something else. For example, the words we speak are sounds that imply emotions, ideas, actions, descriptions—the whole gamut of human experience. Each language has its own special sounds, often quite different from sounds in other languages but able to convey the same meaning. Sounds become *symbols* when *they mean the same thing to a certain group of people.* Our written communication goes a step further, for the lines and squiggles from our pens are *visual* symbols for the spoken sounds.

The visual arts are almost entirely a matter of symbols. A drawing of a horse is not a horse but a symbol for one, and a painting or sculpture of a human being, no matter how realistically it may be done, is still a symbol for the real thing. Symbolism is a powerful tool in the arts. It permits the professional designer, for instance, to communicate ideas, often abstract and philosophical, with a few lines and shapes. Certain shapes have special meaning for us, just as certain songs become important to us because of personal memories. A design that makes use of symbols, whether they are universal, general, or intensely personal, becomes much richer in its implications.

We will consider some of the principal categories of symbols, realizing that each category could easily be the subject of an entire book.

Cosmic Symbols

No doubt the best known cosmic symbols are the signs of the Zodiac (Fig. 304). The Zodiac is an imaginary belt in the heavens, 16 degrees wide, that includes the paths of the moon and all the principal planets, with the sun's path as the center line. It was originally plotted by the

304

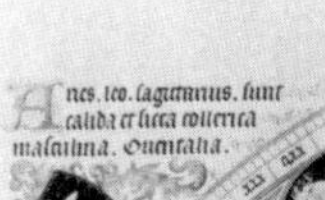

304
L'Homme Zodiacal (Zodiac Man), designed for the Duc de Berry. 1413–1416. Manuscript illumination, 10³⁄₁₆ × 7⅜″ (26 × 18.8 cm). Bibliothèque Nationale, Paris.

305

305
Albrecht Dürer. *Fall of Man.* 1504.
Engraving, 9⅞ × 7⅝" (25.15 × 19.3 cm).
Metropolitan Museum of Art, New York
(Fletcher Fund, 1919).

306
Yin-yang symbol.

307
Bison, prehistoric cave painting.
c. 10,000 B.C. Pigment on natural rock.
"Salon Noir," Niaux Cave, Ariège, France.

Chaldeans in the second century B.C. with twelve divisions, each of which was given a symbol named for a constellation within the zodiacal belt. Over the centuries these signs have represented forces believed to govern not only the movement of bodies in the heavens but, through complex systems and influences, the behavior of human beings on Earth. Found in both Oriental and Western contexts, the visual images of the Zodiac appear in numberless works of art that cut across cultural lines of all periods.

Another effort to understand human behavior inspired the European belief, during the Middle Ages and early Renaissance, that four humors within the body controlled personality. These humors consisted of gall, phlegm, choler, and blood, and behavior was believed to depend upon their balance or imbalance. All four existed within every human body, but if one dominated, the individual would develop a distorted personality and lapse into sin.

The sixteenth-century German master Albrecht Dürer has symbolized the humors in his engraving *The Fall of Man* (Fig. 305); in fact, to the viewers of his own time, Dürer's work was filled with symbolism. The elk stands for an excess of gall, which leads to melancholy, despair, and greed. The ox is extreme phlegm, causing gluttony and laziness. Excessive choler is represented by the cat, which personifies, therefore, cruelty, pride, and anger. Finally, the rabbit, the emblem of blood, indicates sensuality and sins of the flesh. Embodied in these symbols, then, are the results of Adam and Eve's fall from grace. At face value *The Fall of Man* stands as a superb work of composition and draftsmanship. The beautifully drawn bodies of Adam and Eve could provide study for generations of artists, and the details of vegetation sparkling against the depths of the forest demonstrate supreme mastery of line. Seeing the hidden meanings in the work, however, enriches our experience and appreciation of it as a whole.

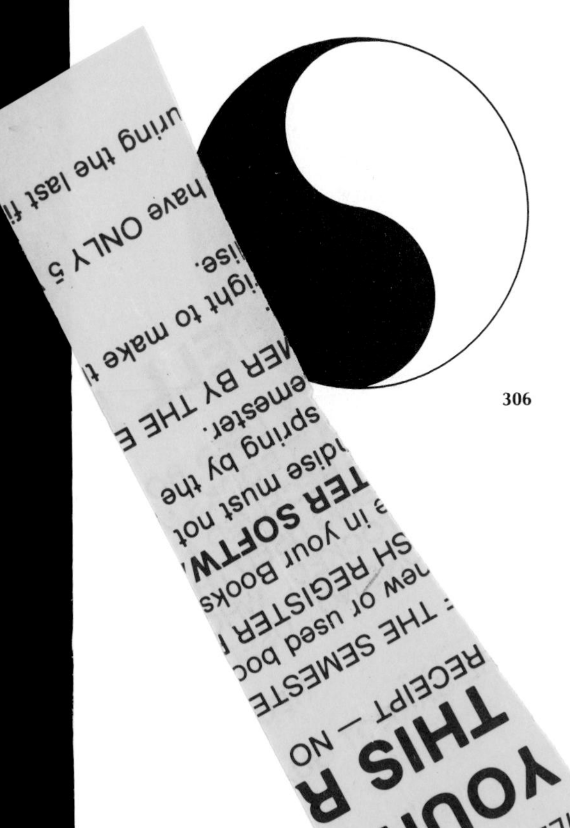

306

In the Chinese cosmic system all qualities are divided into *yang,* the masculine (light, heat, dryness), and *yin,* the feminine (dark, cold, wetness). An ideal can be achieved only when yin and yang balance to complement each other (Fig. 306). Symbols of the yang and yin principles appear throughout Chinese design and indeed Chinese life. Even without knowing the philosophy behind this image, we sense a great deal by looking at it. We see that the two halves are the reverse of each other, that they are equal, and that the two together create balance and harmony.

Magical Symbols

Magical symbols deal with the most vital aspects of life—food, shelter, procreation, and the preservation of life itself. Primitive peoples drew pictures or fashioned masks in the image of animals they hunted to ensure success in the kill (Fig. 307). They made symbols of the mighty gods who controlled climate in the hope they could thus contain the elements. For example, rain is a tremendously important force in any agricultural society. If one could personify it in a symbol (the Rain God) and hold that symbol in a tight enclosure, one could hope to control rain.

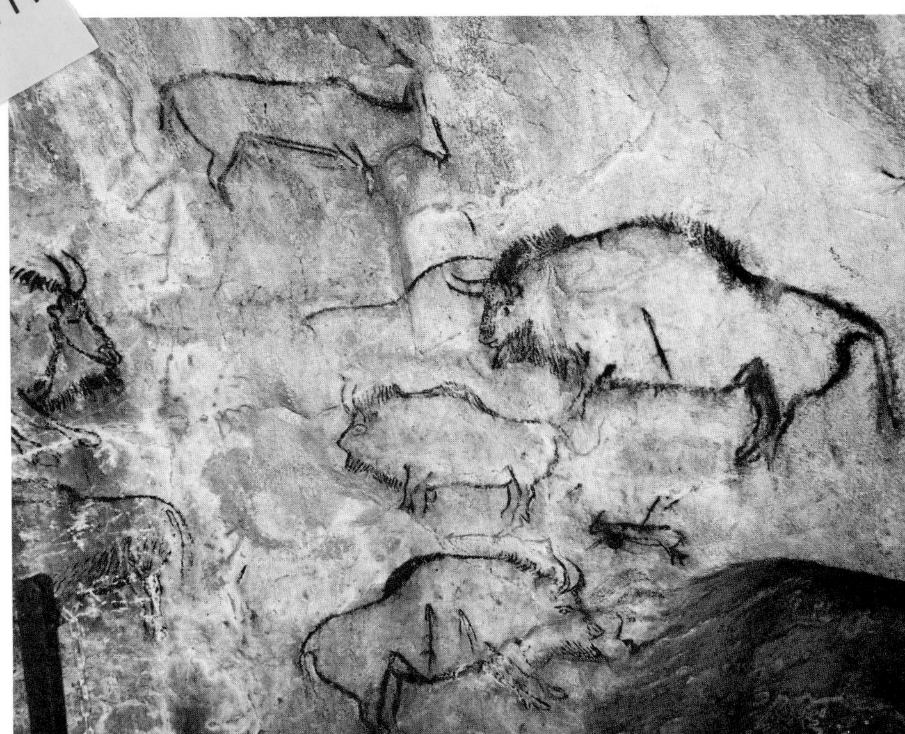

Tribal masks are among the strongest magical symbols in primitive art. Often their makers will endow them with great ferocity to frighten enemies, and such masks are worn in the dance, either to anticipate or to commemorate victory in battle. Other masks, such as the Bamileke example in Figure 308, indicate the status of the wearer. In this instance the snakes on the crown are a royal symbol; this is fitting because the mask would have been used in the dance for installation of a new chief. More generally in Africa, the snake acted as a fertility symbol, since it was considered a guardian of the waters. (It is interesting to compare this symbolism to that of Christian art, in which the snake always represents evil.)

Fertility was an overriding concern for primitive peoples, for survival required both abundance in crops and great numbers of children. Phallic symbols abound in primitive art and are often of great size to denote power in procreation. The ancestor poles in Figure 309 with their delicate openwork tracery, seem at first to be just ornate designs carved for their decorative quality until we are told that the openwork symbolizes semen and the generative powers of the sperm. Here again, the works themselves are beautifully designed, but our appreciation of them is enhanced by familiarity with the symbolism.

Many times symbols evolve and become disassociated from their original applications. This is true of the *mola,* an art form practiced by the Cuna Indians of the San Blas Islands off the coast of Panama. Until about a hundred years ago, these Indians used direct body painting as a means of making tribesmen invisible to evil spirits. For reasons that are not clear, eventually the designs were transferred to cloth, which was worn as a sort of blouse. The present mola panel consists of several layers of cloth of different colors stitched together, with designs created by cutting shapes from the upper layers to expose the colors underneath—usually red, orange, and black. On the top layer several more thicknesses of cloth are applied (or appliquéd) with a variety of stitches to lend further richness to the surface. The designs derive from flowers, trees, fruit, animals, and the native religion. The designer chooses a central theme and then, with an intuitive sense of balance and unity, covers the surrounding area with intricate harmonious detail (Pl. 24, p. 164).

Symbols can evolve not only in their outward application but also in their basic meaning. The Christmas tree is the descendant of a custom thought to have originated among the Romans of pre-Christian times. The tree in this context was a fertility symbol, both a phallic form and an emblem of plenty, with fruits and nuts decorating it. Germanic people later adapted it as a symbol of the feast surrounding the birth of Christ, associating it with the gifts brought by the Magi.

Cultural Symbols

Cultural symbols thread through the life of a people, giving form to holidays and celebrations, starting in one place as mythological or religious entities and ending up somewhere else in a different guise. The jolly American Santa Claus, for instance, is far removed from the tall, serious St. Nicholas of Asia Minor who was the original symbol of the mystery of gift-giving on Christmas Eve. Similarly, the symbols of the customs associated with him differ in various countries—the stockings hanging by the chimney in North America are the shoes waiting to be filled in Europe. In

308
Ceremonial mask made by the Bagam Chiefdom of the Bamileke people. Cameroon Grasslands, Africa. Wood, height 28″ (71.12 cm). Metropolitan Museum of Art, New York (Louis V. Bell Fund, 1971).

309
Ancestor poles, from the Asmat tribe, New Guinea. Wood, paint, and fiber; height c. 11′ (3.35 m).

Germany, shops sell little bunches of gilded twigs as symbols of what naughty children may expect instead of gifts on St. Niklaus Day.

In England and Scotland on St. Valentine's Day, each young bachelor and maid drew lots by which they received one of the opposite sex as a "valentine" for the coming year. As a result, the Western world celebrates the day with hearts, flowers, cupids, love birds, and other symbols of love.

The three-leafed shamrock, denoting the Trinity in St. Patrick's time, today graces a secular St. Patrick's Day parade and celebration in many cities. The shamrock symbolizes all things Irish to many people.

308

309

Hallowe'en, a pre-Christian celebration, apparently originated with the Druids, who believed that on Allhallows' Eve, Saman, the lord of the dead, called forth crowds of evil spirits. The Celts expected the spirits of the dead to revisit their earthly homes on that evening, and lit bonfires to greet them. The Romans added features of their November harvest festival in honor of Pomona, the goddess of the fruits from trees. From all these customs innumerable symbols have arisen—pumpkins hollowed out, carved with grotesque faces and lighted with a candle inside; witches, black cats, goblins, and ghosts. From an ominous beginning has evolved a favorite holiday for most children (Fig. 310).

Easter, one of the major Christian holidays, also had pre-Christian origins, its name probably having derived from Ēastre, the Anglo-Saxon name of a Teutonic goddess of spring and fertility, to whom was dedicated the month corresponding to April. While the religious symbolism of Easter centers around the cross and the lily as symbols of resurrection, the holiday's pagan sources are still reflected by the Easter bunny, a descendant of the rabbit that symbolized fertility, and by the bright-colored eggs, originally painted to represent the sunlight of spring.

Oriental history provides an extensive and particularly exotic source of symbolic design. The festivals and beliefs of the Far East, with dragons, kites, and fantastic figural entities, display a color and drama unique to this section of the world.

All symbols are to some extent cultural in that they result from socially transmitted behavioral patterns, arts, and institutions. Many such symbols, lively with tradition and centuries of celebration, provide a spirited counterpoint to the business of day-to-day living. Other symbols, deeply embedded in religious belief, are so rich in association that they evoke the very foundation of a civilization.

310

311

310
Amy Cole, age 5. *Hallowe'en.*
Crayon drawing.

311
Tombstone menorah. 2nd–3rd century A.D. Marble, engraved and inscribed, with traces of paint. Found in catacomb of Vigna Randanini, Rome. Jewish Museum, New York (gift of Henry and Lucy Moses Fund, Inc.).

312
Plan, Church of St. Sernin, Toulouse. c. 1120.

313
Chartres Cathedral. c. 1194–1221. View through nave, looking toward the apse. Chartres, France.

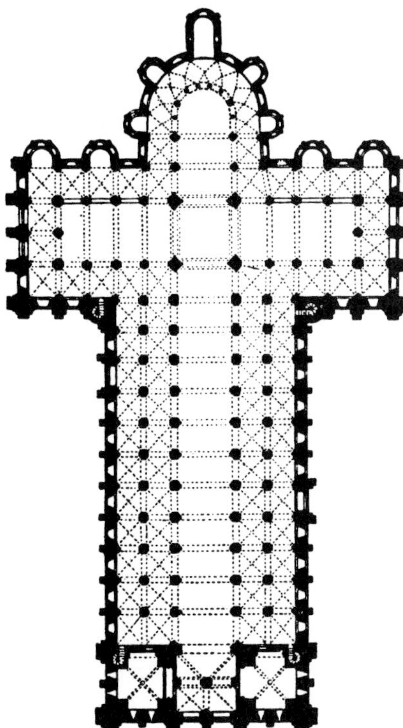

312

Religious Symbols

Because religions deal with *ideas,* they become veritable strongholds of symbolism. Faith and philosophy, hope and virtue, love and generosity—all of these are abstract concepts, more readily embodied in symbols than in descriptive words. Even when a religion deals with historical episodes, as in the Old Testament, the episodes, after centuries of veneration, become symbolic in themselves.

Both Judaism and Christianity carry an enormous weight of associations in traditions, theology, scripture, and history, and both have extensive bodies of symbolism. Nearly every plant and animal has symbolic significance in Christian art. Probably the only more inclusive symbolism is that of the ancient Chinese, who imbued every flower, tree, blade of grass, insect, and bird with specific traits. The Star of David and the menorah (Fig. 311) have a long history of significance in Judaism.

The cross permeates all areas of Christian practice. Most large churches and cathedrals are designed on a cross plan, so that the structure itself becomes an immense architectural symbol. We can see this clearly in the floor plan of the Church of St. Sernin in Toulouse (Fig. 312). The long nave or main section, terminating in the rounded apse, is cut by a transverse section, literally the "crossing." Three-dimensionally, the symbolism extends into every facet of the building. The Gothic cathedrals carried this symbolism to the ultimate in their use of interior spaces to focus attention upward by means of soaring vertical lines and vaulting articulated by pointed arches (Fig. 313). Here the sense of endless space was clearly symbolic of the infinity of God and of the human spirit rising to meet it. On the exterior, tall spires against the sky guided pilgrims from great distances, symbols of refuge, security, and peace. Even criminals were inviolate once they were within the cathedral walls.

313

Crosses appear in hundreds of different forms, from the very simple to the very elaborate in design (Fig. 314). Many of the cross forms have names—for example, the Greek cross and St. Andrew's cross; they occur in painting, sculpture, illuminated manuscripts, and as jewelry; and, of course, their most obvious use is to crown the steeple, dome, or gable of a church (see again Fig. 171, p. 133).

Contrasting specific symbolism as it is used in two great religions can be an enlightening exercise. An interesting comparison can be made between an eleventh-century image of the Amida Buddha (Fig. 315) and a Giotto painting of Christ in the Last Judgment (Fig. 316). There are many versions of the Buddha. This one, the Amida Buddha, is the kindliest and most approachable. Here he is portrayed in the *Raigo* or descent from heaven, when the Buddha comes forward to welcome a worthy dead soul into his Western paradise. A similar event takes place in the Last Judgment, which occurs after the end of the world. Christ sits in judgment and triumph, separating the faithful who will be taken into heaven from those damned to hell for eternity. The figures of both Buddha and Christ are separated from their compositional backgrounds by an ovoid aura, and each has a halo around his head. The Buddha sits in the traditional yoga meditation pose, which is one of his symbolic attributes. His hands are usually depicted in one of several *mudras,* or gestures. The one shown in this painting, with thumb and forefinger touching, signifies the Wheel of Learning. Christ's hands, by contrast, are held in positions symbolic of the Last Judgment, the right hand outstretched to welcome the faithful souls into heaven (the faithful always being on the right) and the left, palm backward, seeming to cast away the damned. The Buddha is surrounded by 25 Bodhisattvas, which are a kind of sub-Buddha, not quite deity and not quite angel. Behind and around the Bodhisattvas are angels playing musical instruments, indications of the lush pleasures to be found in the Western paradise. Christ, as is usual in Last Judgment scenes, is flanked by his twelve Apostles. Legions of angels, some playing trumpets, gather about him and help to conduct the saints into paradise. One important difference exists between these two visions. In the *Last Judgment* by Giotto we see in the lower right corner an image of hell, with Satan ready to torment the damned souls. But no suggestion of punishment mars the perfect tranquility and bliss of Amida's Western paradise.

The symbolic details we have cited in these two paintings, the story behind the work of art, are called their *iconography.* In the same way, the four humors portrayed in the Dürer engraving (Fig. 305) make up part of its iconography. To understand fully any work of religious art, it is necessary to be familiar with its underlying iconography, the meaning of the forms depicted through the religious symbolism.

Status Symbols

The term *status symbol* has been given a bad name in recent years, being used to imply the struggle to impress others with material possessions. Originally, status symbols simply indicated the exact status or station in life of their owner. Wedding rings are status symbols, for they mark the wearer's role as a married person. All military insignia are status symbols and so are special religious items, such as clerical collars and bishops' miters. The most complicated system of status imagery, however, is to be found in the field of *heraldry.*

314
Variations on the cross motif.

315
Amida Raigo Triptych. Japanese, late 11th century (Heian Period). Color on silk, height 6′11″ (2.11 m). Museum Reihōkan, Wakayama.

316
Giotto. *Last Judgment.* 1305–1306. Fresco. Arena Chapel, Padua.

315

316

317

317
Cornelis Engelbrechtsz. Detail of *Constantine* from *Constantine and St. Helena.* c. 1510–1520. Entire panel, 34½ × 22¼" (87.63 × 56.52 cm). Alte Pinakothek, Munich. Constantine is pictured wearing a tunic decorated with his arms.
318
The national flag of Canada.
319
The most generally used symbol of the Women's Movement combines the biological symbol for woman with the equal sign.
320
Mary E. Humes. Rendering of carved and gilt wood "Jenny Lind" figurehead from the ship *Nightingale* of Portsmouth, New Hampshire. Built 1848. Watercolor, 1938. Index of American Design. National Gallery of Art, Washington, D.C. The original figurehead resides in the Mariners' Museum, Newport News, Virginia.

Heraldry began with the ancient custom of certain peoples' adopting a particular symbol to identify their soldiers or citizens. The Romans took as their emblem the eagle, the Goths used the bear, the French adopted the lion and later the fleur-de-lis (white iris or sword lily). By the twelfth century, when both feudal wars and the Crusades were in progress, it became necessary for a knight to be recognized at a distance, so every family would carry a personal emblem on the shield, which, when decorated, became known as an *escutcheon.* Later, the family arms came to be embroidered on a kind of coat worn over the armor, thus giving rise to the term *coat of arms* (Fig. 317).

In time, heraldry became increasingly complex. A knight who married an heiress could incorporate her family arms into his own. When he died, only his eldest son was entitled to use the arms in their original form; other children would have to adapt them, perhaps by changing some of the *charges* or figures. Families, kingdoms, towns, abbeys, and even some corporations are entitled to display a coat of arms. Quite apart from their status value, coats of arms are beautiful and intriguing as pure design.

Patriotic and Political Symbols

The designs of many national flags have changed and developed over the centuries. A flag changes because of wars and jurisdiction or because of a new political stance. Until recently the flag of Canada had an English Union Jack in the corner, symbolic of close ties with the British Commonwealth. With the upsurge of interest in establishing a unique Canadian identity, the Union Jack was replaced by an entirely new design, the maple leaf (Fig. 318). This was an important beginning toward increased Canadian industry, an enthusiastic encouragement of Canadian culture, and an independent constitution.

In the United States we have an assortment of patriotic symbols, from the Statue of Liberty to the eagle with olive branch and arrows. The flag is

318

unique because the thirteen stripes signify the original colonies and the fifty stars the present states. More importantly, the symbolism has been composed to form a striking design, one of the principal requirements of effective visual symbolism.

Uncle Sam and the British John Bull are the work of political cartoonists, as are the Democratic donkey and the Republican elephant. Politically active groups usually create a symbol to exemplify their ideals and establish their identity in convention halls and parades. The Women's Movement uses variations based on the ancient Greek biological symbol for woman. The most common version includes the equal sign. (Fig. 319).

319

Commercial Symbols

In many parts of the world the sign of three balls is recognized as signifying a pawnbroker's shop. A red-and-white-striped revolving pole for many years denoted a barber shop, and before the era of modern dentistry, a huge tooth hanging outside a window marked the office of a "tooth extractor." These are all examples of commercial symbols; they advertise the service or product to be sold.

Symbols with a slightly different relationship to commerce were the figureheads that adorned sailing ships in their heyday. Most figureheads were women (Fig. 320), carved of wood with flowing hair and billowing skirts to suggest the speed of the ship in plying the waves. It is said that the captain of the ship was symbolically "married" to the figurehead. This would explain why, if the ship foundered, he was expected to "go down with the ship," his symbolic wife.

320

321

322

323

324

321
Man with Grapes, barroom figure or tavern sign found in Wells, Maine. 19th century. Painted wood, bone, and wire; height 15″ (38.1 cm). Guennol Collection, New York.

322
Logo for Senate of Priests, Archdiocese of Los Angeles. Design: Don Kano of Will Martin Design Associates.

323
Logo for Cotton, Inc. Design: Walter Landor.

324
Poster by Paul Smith. Collection of the Artist.

325
Marc Chagall. *I and My Village.* 1911. Oil on canvas, 6′3⅝″ × 4′11⅝″ (1.92 × 1.51 m). Museum of Modern Art, New York (Mrs. Simon Guggenheim Fund).

The little statue in Figure 321, a man holding aloft a bunch of grapes, was carved in the nineteenth century, probably as a tavern sign. In both its forthright symbolism and its stylized detail, it has a great deal of charm. Today, corporations pay thousands of dollars to have advertising agencies or public relations firms develop symbols called *logos* especially for them. This is a real design challenge, since the company logo must be read and immediately understood by the consumer, whether it is small, as on a letterhead, or large, as on the side of a factory or plane. The logo in Figure 322 tells us immediately that it is associated with religion, even before we analyze the design to recognize the cross combined with trefoils, a basic architectural element of Gothic cathedrals. The initials *SP* (for Senate of Priests) are skillfully worked in with the other motifs to establish an unmistakable symbol of identity. Equally distinctive is the logo for the American cotton industry showing a stylized cotton boll "growing" from the two central *T*'s in the word *cotton* (Fig. 323).

Posters depend upon symbolic implication to deliver a message quickly within a small space. The use of symbolic shapes in the poster by Paul Smith in Figure 324 conveys a spirit of lightness and pleasure on a musical theme.

Psychological Symbols

When Sigmund Freud wrote *The Interpretation of Dreams* in 1900, he opened a Pandora's box of psychological symbolism that has become the staple of painters, photographers, and filmmakers ever since. Many, but by no means all, of these symbols are sexual in context.

Marc Chagall's *I and My Village* (Fig. 325) represents a remembered dream vision of childhood in Russia. The images are tumbled and superimposed, with little attention to scale, just as they might be in a dream. Chagall remembers the images of cow, milkmaid, farmer, houses, and tree, but does not try to fit them into any logical order. Rather, they appear as a dreamlike patchwork of impressions.

325

326

Filmmakers such as Ingmar Bergman and Federico Fellini rely heavily on symbolism in their work. Most films use background music to manipulate our emotions to respond to the action more intensely, but visual symbols may also be used to increase a sense of mystery by suggesting the underlying significance of the action. In the scene from Fellini's *La Dolce Vita* in Figure 326 the characters are exploring an old castle. Two symbols become obvious. First, the man at right is wearing a black robe and an eyepatch—surely this figure symbolizes potential menace. Second, the candles offer the only light—this could symbolize hope or reason. In one image, Fellini has created a duality: evil versus light. Such symbolism prepares our sensibilities for the action to come.

Personal Symbols

Much of the symbolism in contemporary painting and sculpture could be described as personal, meaning that the artist creates symbols to express individual needs. This practice originated early in the twentieth century, when the German Expressionists painted to protest the cruelty and injustice of a world turned upside down by the Industrial Revolution. The Expressionists were known for their bold colors, which they used as symbols in themselves. The Belgian painter James Ensor was not an Expressionist, but he influenced many members of the group with his disillusioned art of masks and grimaces. His childhood supplied him with the symbols of his art, for he grew up among the toys and masks of his parents' curiosity shop in Ostende, where masks were a major feature of carnivals. In *Self-Portrait with Masks* (Fig. 327) we see the artist wearing a jaunty hat, surrounded by masked figures whose vacant or threatening expressions reflect what he felt to be the ugly, vacant spirits of the bourgeoisie. Though he is in the midst of them, he is totally alien to them.

326
Scene from Federico Fellini's *La Dolce Vita*. 1960.

327
James Ensor. *Self-Portrait with Masks*. 1899. Oil on canvas, 46½ × 32½" (1.18 × .8 m). Private collection.

Much contemporary sculpture is an exploration into uses of materials to achieve abstract masses or to discover the possibilities of space. In this context, sculpture cannot be considered strictly symbolic, although frequently the names given to specific pieces imply that they are (Fig. 223). The true use of symbolism in sculpture can be summed up in Rodin's *Monument to Balzac,* which we discussed in Chapter 1. This is not a representation of a man but the expression of a mind and spirit beyond realistic human representation. In such a work symbolism becomes an art form in itself, conveying the essence of something by the configuration of something related to it.

We have now discovered the relationship of the elements and principles of design to various forms of expression, and we have laid the groundwork for exploring visual communication through our awareness of the uses of symbolism. In the chapters to follow, we will be delving further into *art* forms and *design* forms, showing how the elements and principles are common to them both.

327

Painting

The importance of design in painting is basic. As recently as the nineteenth century a painter, regardless of any other attributes, could not hope to be successful without a strong sense of design. The twentieth century has brought revolutionary changes in painting styles and in the criteria for judging them. At one point, it was considered derogatory for a critic to say of a painting that it *was* a design, implying that there was nothing in the work beyond its visual interest. With the advent of color field painting, in which entire canvases were sometimes covered with subtle gradations of a single color, viewers often wondered if the painter had used any of the elements and principles of design at all. In this chapter we will explore the traditional requisites of painting: *subject, form,* and *content;* we will look into some of the ways in which twentieth-century painters have worked; and we will discover how, in paintings today as in the past, the art of painting is indeed a form of design.

The Materials of Painting

The material for any work of art is called its *medium.* Paintings can be done in a variety of media, a term which has become confusing because of its association with mass communication. In painting, a medium is a spe-

328

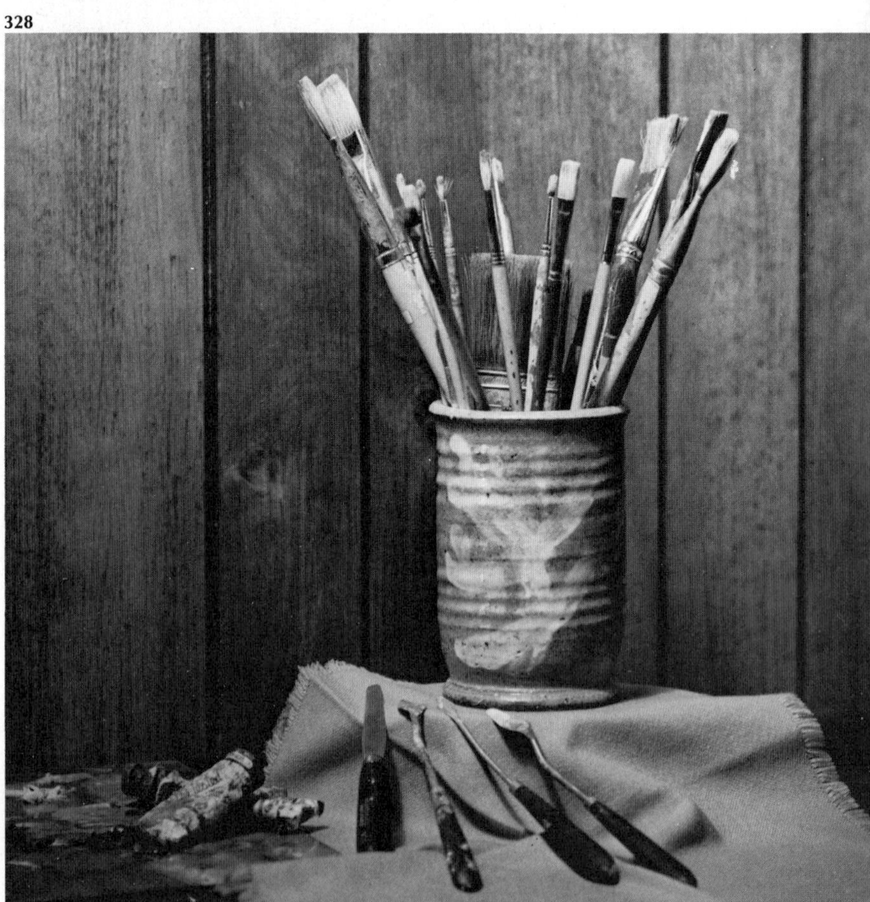

328
Assortment of brushes and palette knives used in oil painting.

329
Jasper Johns. *Between the Clock and the Bed.* 1981. Encaustic on canvas, 6′ × 10′6¼″ (1.83 × 3.21 m). Museum of Modern Art, New York.

329

cific category, based on the composition of the paint. We will discuss various media shortly.

In creating a painting, the painter must first have a *support,* something on which to paint. This may be a wall, a wooden panel, a piece of masonite, a sheet of paper, or, most traditionally, a piece of canvas tightly tacked to a rigid frame, which provides a taut, drumlike, slightly resilient surface that responds to brushstrokes. Frequently a *ground* is applied to wood or canvas, first a coating of glue to seal the pores and then a coat of paint, usually white, to provide a smooth working surface.

The artist applies paint with a brush or a painting knife. These are available in a wide range of widths, lengths, and shapes (Fig. 328). Most painters have an assortment, using different brushes according to the needs of the painting.

The painting medium is determined by the *binder,* the vehicle that holds the particles of pigment in suspension and makes possible the spreading of the paint upon the support.

The oldest known painting medium, and the most permanent, appears to be *encaustic,* a mixture of hot beeswax and pigment perfected by the ancient Greeks. The mixture is applied to wood with a brush or a metal instrument known as a *cauterium.* As the wax cools, the cauterium is heated and successive layers are applied, making possible considerable plasticity and modeling. After centuries of neglect, encaustic has been revived by contemporary artists (Fig. 329).

Tempera generally has egg yolk as a binder, although animal and vegetable glues can also be used. It is most often applied to a ground of *gesso*

330

331

330
Andrew Wyeth. *Anna Kuerner* (detail). 1971. Tempera on panel, 13½ × 19½″ (34.29 × 49.53 cm). Private collection. Photograph Courtesy of the Brandywine River Museum.

331
Vincent van Gogh. *Cypresses.* 1889. Oil on canvas, 36¾ × 29⅛″ (1.01 × .74 m). Metropolitan Museum of Art, New York (Rogers Fund, 1949).

(plaster or gypsum mixed in glue) built up on wood panels, but it can also be worked on canvas. It has an opaque quality and is often built up with small brushstrokes for meticulously modeled effects (Fig. 330).

Casein, with a binder of milk curd, is water soluble and can be applied to gesso panels, cardboard, paper, and other surfaces. For both tempera and casein, water serves as the thinning agent. Casein, too, is opaque.

Oil paint came into general use in the fifteenth century. Pigment is ground and mixed with a binder of linseed oil, which dries slowly but permits precise manipulation. Oil paint allows the application of either an opaque or translucent film, so it is possible for an artist to paint over areas that need to be changed. It can be applied in one thick coating or built up in successive transparent layers or *glazes.* The latter technique accounts for much of the subtle modeling found in the works of old masters. In contrast, *impasto* is a technique in which paint is applied so thickly, often with a palette knife, that its texture assumes an expressive role all its own (Fig. 331; compare Fig. 137, p. 91).

Watercolor is bound by gum arabic. *Gouache,* an opaque watercolor, contains in addition a paste of zinc oxide. Both dissolve in water and lend themselves to rapid painting. Used on specially prepared paper, transparent watercolor has a unique clarity and sparkle.

Acrylic polymer emulsion is a twentieth-century medium (Pl. 25, p. 245). Acrylic paints are favored for their durability and quick drying properties. Most dissolve in water or stronger solvents, so they can be used for painting in thin washes, as in watercolor, or for impasto, as in oil. One can add glaze upon glaze in immediate succession, to create a paint film of extraordinary inner glow and brilliance. On the other hand, it is possible to build up thick layers at once without danger of peeling, since the film created is porous and allows moisture to pass through to the surface without cracking the paint.

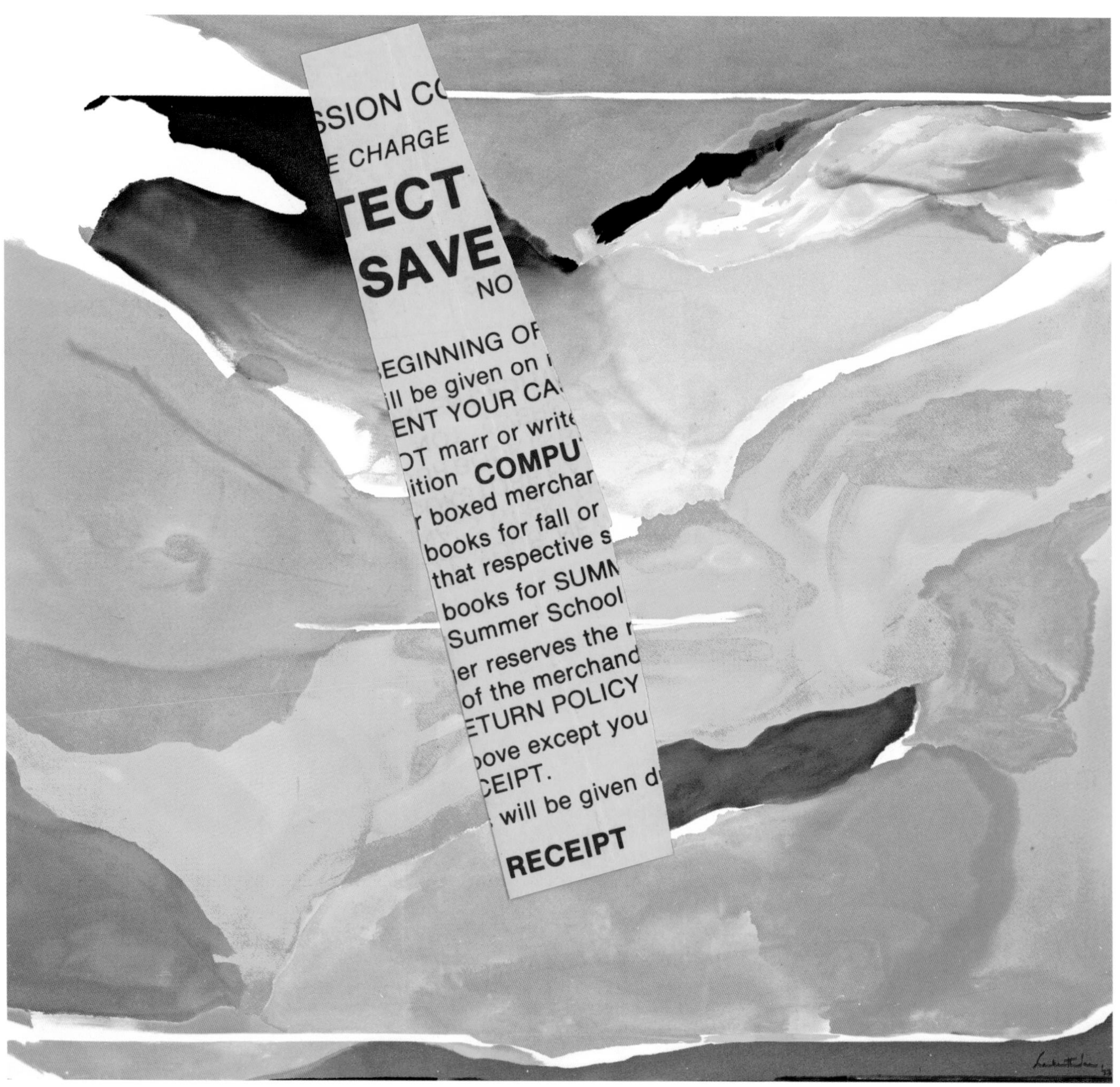

Plate 25
Helen Frankenthaler. *Nature Abhors a Vacuum.* 1973. Acrylic on canvas, 8′7½″ × 9′4½″ (2.63 × 2.86 m).
Courtesy André Emmerich Gallery, New York.

Plate 26
Paul Cézanne. *Mont Ste. Victoire.*
1904–06. Oil on canvas,
2′4⅞″ × 3′¼″
(73.34 × 92.08 cm).
Philadelphia Museum of Art
(George W. Elkins Collection).

Plate 27
Wassily Kandinsky.
Improvisation No. 30 (on a Warlike Theme). 1913. Oil on canvas, 3′7¼″ (1.10 m) square. Art Institute of Chicago (Arthur Jerome Eddy Memorial).

332

333

332
Arman. *Frozen Civilization #2.* 1971. Compressed garbage in Plexiglas, 4′ × 3′ × 4¾″ (1.22 × .91 × .12 m). Courtesy Andrew Crispo Gallery, Inc., New York.

333
Terence LaNoue. *Sepik.* 1975. Acrylic, fiber, latex, rubber, tobacco cloth, and metallic powder; 5′ × 9′4″ (1.52 × 2.84 m). Courtesy Nancy Hoffman Gallery, New York.

A thick paste of acrvlic or polymer applied to a ground can provide an adhesive and durable surface for a collage. Artists today press assorted materials into this kind of medium to achieve unique effects (Fig. 332).

Mixed media is a term that has become increasingly comprehensive in meaning. Originally used to describe any combination of media—such as oil with charcoal and collage with pen-and-ink—it has become the encompassing term for much of the experimentation characteristic of contemporary artists. Figure 333 is a typical example, with its combination of acrylic and at least five other materials.

Wall painting can be done in several media. Many of the famous works of the Renaissance were done on lime plaster while the plaster was wet, with the pigment being applied with a brush and then forming a molecular bond with the wall as it dried. Such works are called *fresco*. When the paint is applied to dry plaster, the work is known as *secco*. Today, canvas is frequently mounted on a wall with glue and the painting done on the canvas in oil, tempera, casein, or acrylic. Such paintings are grouped under the term *mural,* from the Latin meaning "of the wall."

334

Attributes of Painting

334
Paul Cézanne. *Mont Sainte-Victoire as Seen from Bibemus Quarry.* c. 1898–1900. 25½ × 32″ (64.77 × 81.28 cm). Baltimore Museum of Art (The Cone Collection, formed by Dr. Claribel Cone and Miss Etta Cone of Baltimore, Maryland).

The three traditional attributes of painting are *subject, form,* and *content.* The relative importance of the three varies from painting to painting. When all three exist in a work, they are interlocked and it is difficult to isolate them for analysis, in the same way that it is difficult to arrive at the quality of "green" by analyzing blue and yellow. We will, for the sake of understanding, separate the three attributes for consideration, using one painting that obviously has all three.

The *subject* in Figure 334 and in Plate 26 (p. 246) is a mountain near the home of Paul Cézanne. Cézanne purposely chose the subjects for his paintings with the intention of showing them as solid objects sitting firmly in space. He used still life, landscape, and people as subjects, but none interested him more than the mountain that towered over his village of Aix-en-Provence.

In a series of paintings of Mont Sainte-Victoire, Cézanne depicted the mountain in entirely different guises, yet in each it has solid *form*. Figure 334 is a relatively early depiction, showing it from a stone quarry, with every aspect of the landscape simplified into geometric masses. All details have been excluded, with the exception of a few tree trunks and branches that provide a counterpoint to the large areas of light and dark. In Plate 26 (p. 246) done six years later, the severity of the earlier work has been relieved by the texture of broad brushstrokes. Instead of segregating the large areas of light and dark, Cézanne allows the darks to disperse upward from a wide band at the bottom of the painting, causing the lights to sparkle throughout in lively contrast. This is a particularly interesting example of Cézanne's work, for he has arrived at his goal of depicting solid form and at the same time captured scintillating light and color.

Because our concern in this text is primarily with visual design, the subject of form requires special attention. We will consider two different but related aspects: the arrangement of forms on a two-dimensional surface and the forms of *illusionistic space*.

We have previously analyzed the Renaissance concept of space in terms of linear perspective (Chapter 5). Form was conceived in a highly intellectual way as an orderly progression backward that was intended to mimic depth perception of the natural world (Figs. 121, 122). The boundaries were clear, often reinforced with black.

The first group of painters to challenge seriously the traditional ideas of form were the Impressionists (see p. 102). Cézanne and others felt that in achieving a shimmer of light and color, the Impressionists had lost the feeling of solid form. Recapturing this solidity became Cézanne's primary goal, and his early works all but rejected light and color in favor of solid, almost monochromatic masses. In his amalgamation of light and color with form, then, he achieved a personal victory, one toward which he worked throughout his life. Plate 26 sparkles yet gives an almost tangible sense of depth and volume: the brushstrokes carry us into the distance through a succession of overlapping planes, and the three-dimensional form is unmistakable—the cone of the mountain, the cubes of buildings, and the cylinders of trees.

Much of what we have said about subject and form is involved with *content,* the feelings and ideas the artist hopes to share with the viewer. It is always presumptuous to try to explain what an artist had in mind when working, except when a general statement will aid in comprehension of the work. In his paintings of Mont Sainte-Victoire, however, Cézanne tells us clearly of his enchantment by this mountain. One of his works shows it as a volcanically restless mass, heaving up into the sky, another depicts it as clear and almost jewel-like, standing as an inspiration to those who live in its shadow. Still another version is stately, with a kind of grandeur that looks down on everything below. In Plate 26 the mountain is a vibrant beacon, related to the world around it, but again, rising like a fortress, to give protection. From these varying personalities with which Cézanne imbued his mountain, we can assume that it was a strong influence on his life, something that he regarded with fondness and joy, probably the first thing he looked for when he viewed the landscape every morning. This, then, is what we mean by content.

335

Some contemporary paintings seem to have no subject, such as the one in Figure 335. In giving a number for a title, the artist seems to tell us that this is just one in a series of studies and that we are not to look for anything that fits a name. Here form, while unmistakable, is quite different from the solid three-dimensional form of Cézanne. In the work by Pollock, the form develops from layers of paint dribbled over the canvas, emerging in intricate allover patterns and from shapes and depths that vary according to individual perception. The form becomes dynamic, changing, charged with energy. This energy is a dominant force in the content as well. We know that Pollock painted his canvases by laying them flat on the floor and then striding about, dribbling the paint from a bucket in his hand. We can assume that the act of painting was strongly physical and that he was releasing feelings and emotions as he worked: the act of painting becomes the content.

Both the painting by Cézanne and the one by Pollock reveal more as they are studied. We have spoken of the element of *time* in architecture and of moving through space in order to experience a three-dimensional design. Time is equally important in appreciating a work on a two-dimensional surface. The artist spends hours creating the work, and the viewer cannot expect to absorb the content in a brief glance. It is important to approach works of art with an open mind and a relaxed viewpoint, allowing subject, form, and content to reveal themselves through careful observation.

335
Jackson Pollock. *Number 17.* c. 1951. Duco on canvas, 4′9⅞″ × 4′10⅝″ (1.47 × 1.49 m). Collection Mr. and Mrs. S. I. Newhouse, Jr., New York.

336
Marcel Duchamp. *Nude Descending a Staircase, No. 2.* 1912. Oil on canvas, 4′10″ × 2′11″ (1.47 × .89 m). Philadelphia Museum of Art (Louise and Walter Arensberg Collection).

Directions in Contemporary Painting

The twentieth century has been a proving ground for much that is experimental in the arts, and a comprehensive treatment of its developments in painting has filled books and provided material for entire college courses. It has been a time of *-isms,* movements away from traditional styles, sometimes identified by scoffing critics, sometimes by young rebels more involved in heated discussion than in actual work. Many *-isms* have flared briefly and disappeared; others, practiced by a group devoted to a certain doctrine and developing within its framework, have become currents influencing the development of contemporary painting.

Since our purpose is to explore the role of painting in the field of design, we will confine our discussion to the ways in which certain movements have provided a unique expression of the elements and principles of design.

We have mentioned *Impressionism* in its primary aspects, the imbuing of canvas with light and color and the innovative use of space to imply a larger world beyond the boundaries of the canvas (p. 81). The practice of Impressionism necessarily involved the painter with texture, since the scintillation of light was the result of small brushstrokes creating a visually textured surface.

In reaction to Impressionism, the *Cubists* stressed sharply outlined geometric shapes, working in neutral tones. Subject matter is barely recognizable and the planes seem to slip and slide over one another in a kind of static rhythm (Fig. 336). Shape and space are of primary concern, with balance achieved through distribution of values and shapes.

336

337

Closely related to Cubism is *Abstraction,* which emerged at about the same time, preceding World War I. In a period of restlessness and experimentation, both movements reduced subject to a point of departure for innovations in line, space, shape, and texture. The guiding force in Abstraction was Russian-born Wassily Kandinsky, one of the most significant figures in the history of painting. In an interview quoted in a book published in 1917, Kandinsky described his work entitled *Improvisation No. 30,* which had often been designated *Cannons* (Pl. 27, p. 246). He begins by declaring that the presence of cannons is in no way to be construed as the content of the painting. The content is "what the spectator lives or feels while under the effect of the form and color combinations of the picture. This picture is nearly in the shape of a cross. The center . . . is formed by a large irregular blue plane."[1] He goes on to say that the presence of the cannons could probably be explained by the constant war talk that had been going on throughout the year. "But I did not intend to give a representation of war; to do so would have required different pictorial means; besides, such tasks do not interest me—at least not just now. This entire description is chiefly an analysis of the picture which I have painted rather subconsciously in a state of strong inner tension."[2] Finally, he states: "Whatever I might say about myself or my pictures can touch the pure artistic meaning only superficially. The observer must learn to look at the picture as a graphic representation of a *mood* and not as a representation of *objects.*"[3] In these last words, Kandinsky gives us the key to much that

337
Wassily Kandinsky. *Composition 8, No. 260.* 1923. Oil on canvas, 4′7″ × 6′7″ (1.41 × 2.0 m). Solomon R. Guggenheim Museum, New York.

338
Franz Marc. *Kämpfende Formen.* (Forms in Combat). 1914. München, Staatsgalerie Moderner Kunst.

[1] Bernard S. Myers, The German Expressionists (New York: Praeger, 1917), p. 214.
[2] Ibid.
[3] Ibid.

followed, not only in his own work but also in subsequent twentieth-century movements. *Improvisation No. 30* was painted in 1913; ten years later, Kandinsky's work was strongly linear and geometric (Fig. 337). It has been said that he removed the impediments of naturalism to reach the real meaning of things and ideas.

Kandinsky's intellect and a childhood grounded in the rich emotional images of his native Russia made him the unique figure that he became. He is often associated with the *German Expressionists,* however, as he went through periods in which his work could readily be classified under that heading. Like him, the Expressionists emphasized painting *mood* rather than objects and they worked at depicting the inner nature of things, employing a highly personal imagery that often evolved into grotesqueness. During this chaotic period under the cloud of war, there was much distortion of form in painting and an expression of inner turmoil and rebellion. There was also vibrant color and a striking sense of design. A work such as Franz Marc's painting in Figure 338 exemplifies design quality at its best, with great swirling rhythms and a spectacular balance of light and dark.

The end of the war brought a new influence into the world of art. With the popularization of the teachings of Sigmund Freud, many artists in the late 1920s gravitated to the realm of dreams and the subconscious, and

338

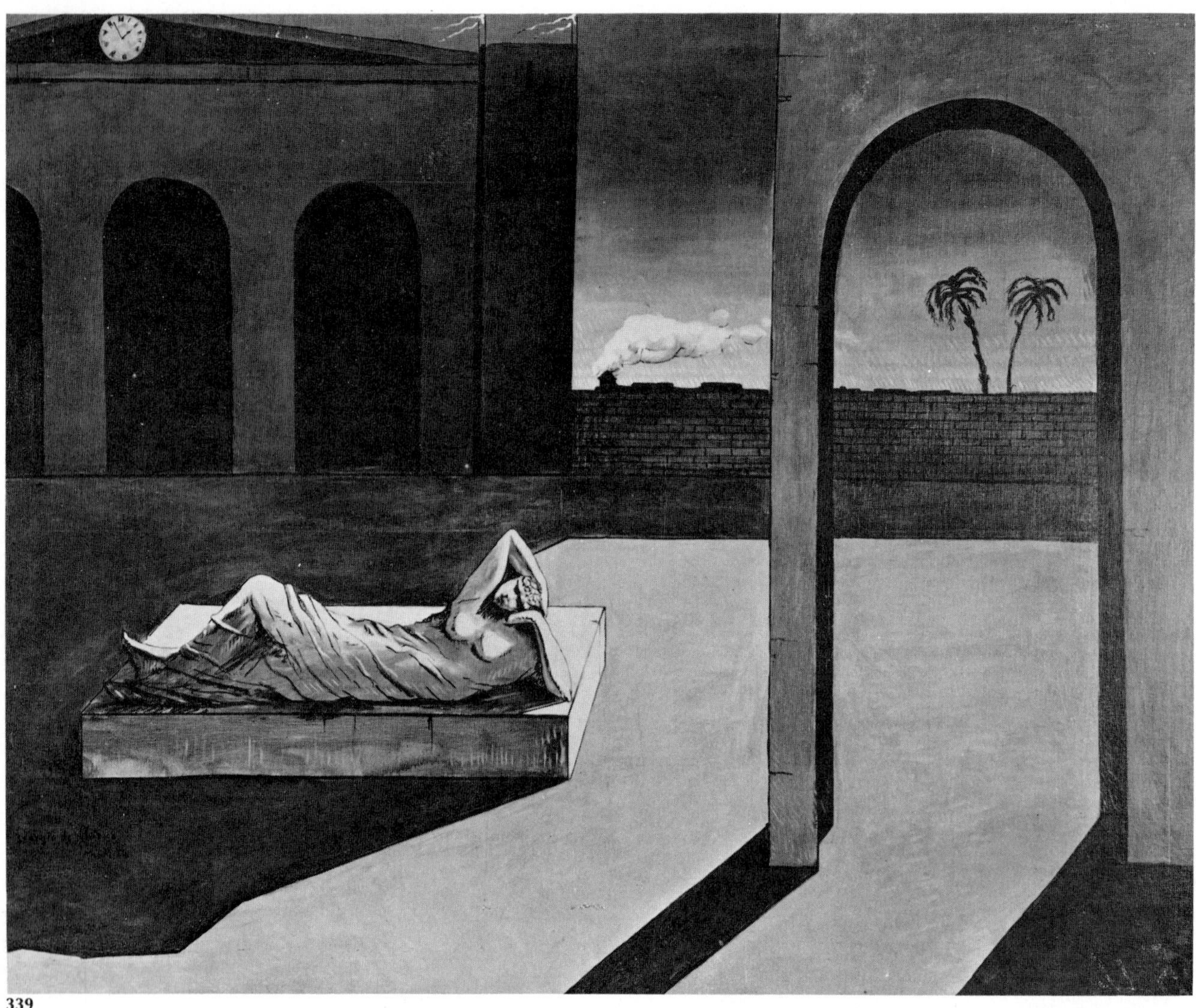
339

subject reappeared as a dominant element in painting. Symbolism also emerged as a major consideration, and the term *Surrealism* was coined to identify a nonrational intuitive manner of working, recreating chance relationships and strange combinations of symbols that often occur in dreams. Two main styles developed. The first was based on earlier developments in the work of the Italian Giorgio de Chirico, in which objects were executed in a pristine manner, with unexpected settings and relationships. De Chirico created strange classical landscapes that seem familiar yet abandoned of all life, their fragments of architecture and sculpture surrounded by a vacuum (Fig. 339). Such works, beautifully composed and meticulously painted, relied heavily on balance and contrasts in value, with little texture and no obvious rhythm in the sense of flow or movement. The static quality was an essential element in the content. The second style, sometimes called "organic surrealism," moves close to Abstraction in its pursuit of forms not dictated by the conscious mind. The personal symbolism of the Spaniard Joan Miró with shapes floating in space is not unlike the later work of Kandinsky (Fig. 340). (See also Figs. 15 and 85, pp. 12

339
Giorgio de Chirico. *The Soothsayer's Recompense.* 1913. Oil on canvas, 4′5⅜″ × 5′11″ (1.36 × 1.8 m). Philadelphia Museum of Art (Louise and Walter Arensberg Collection).

340
Joan Miró. *Carnival of Harlequin.* 1924–1925. Oil on canvas, 26 × 36⅝″ (66.04 × 92.96 cm). Albright-Knox Art Gallery, Buffalo, NY (Room of Contemporary Art Fund, 1940).

and 58.) Here the predominant design qualities are rhythmic movement and a strong linear quality along with variety of shapes and an overall texture.

The trend begun by Kandinsky reached full fruition in the nonobjectivity of the *Abstract Expressionists,* whom we have already described in connection with Jackson Pollock (Fig. 335). While *Abstraction* concerns the essence of a recognizable object, sometimes discarding all reference to the object itself, *nonobjective* painting disregards any reference to an object at all, beginning with forms, lines, and rhythms whose reference to recognizable forms is purely coincidental. (See the discussion of nonobjective shapes in Chapter 4, p. 57.) As a movement, Abstract Expressionism arose in New York in the aftermath of World War II. Its predominant design characteristics are dynamic rhythms and jabbing colors and shapes. The term *action painting* characterizes its radical departure from previous modes, and its enormous canvases and vitality made it one of the first American developments to attract worldwide attention.

We have noted the influence of *Op Art* in the work of such painters as Vasarely (Fig. 125 and Pl. 7, pp. 83 and 105) and Bridget Riley (Fig. 67, p. 45). Primarily concerned with the science of optics, these works are of interest to us for their experiments with color, shape, and line, and the resultant sense of movement and rhythmic quality. There is no subject, but there is strong form and a content involved with the exploratory nature of the concept of form. Often there is predominant visual texture as well. It is this group of works that comes closest to the critical evaluation of being "pure design," though the assessment is obviously unfair since there was a great deal more involved in the artists' purpose.

340

341

Op art moves into *Minimal Art* by logical progression. Once subject had disappeared, it was logical to experiment in another way, by arriving at a work of art by the least possible means. This meant resorting to color and shape, no more. Sometimes even shape was not evident, as in the Color Field Painting that developed from this general trend (Pl. 19, p. 112). Balance, emphasis, and unity are obvious, and sometimes a linear element is invoked (Fig. 341). On the whole, however, Minimal painting reduces painting to the simplest terms, again coming close to pure design. Still, once again, it is dangerous to make statements about the artist's intent. In Figure 341, Frank Stella has titled three starkly geometric forms after Colorado mining towns, perhaps telling us that even in Minimal painting, the work may not be as nonobjective as it seems.

As we stated at the beginning, this is not meant to be a survey of contemporary painting. If it were, we would have to include many more movements and trends. It is instead a tracing of design qualities through the works of the early twentieth-century artists, with the intent of following the thread of design into the work that is being done today.

Recent Trends in Painting

If there is one trait that unites the paintings of the last half of the twentieth century, it is a swing away from abstraction to a more obviously human orientation—figuratively, emotionally, and historically.

The most startling leap was from nonobjective painting to *photorealism* in the 1960s. The invention of the camera had exerted considerable influence on earlier painters, making it seem both unnecessary and useless to attempt in paint what the camera could accomplish in a fiftieth of a second. Now, after several decades, painters began to use the camera as an ally. The reasoning is that photographic images, movies, television, and magazines are as important a part of our reality as actual phenomena; therefore the artist paints as the camera views the world. Chuck Close tries to make it clear that he is making paintings from photographs and that his results are not the way the human eye sees them. His portraits show every hair and wrinkle (Fig. 342). Neil Welliver, in painting landscapes, seems to be working in a traditional representational way, but he emphasizes the flatness of the picture plane and the fluidity of paint, at the same time composing his subject into beautifully balanced compositions (Fig. 343).

341
Frank Stella. Left to right: *Lake City, Ophir,* and *Telluride.* 1960–61.
Metallic copper paint on canvas.
Courtesy Leo Castelli Gallery, New York.

342
Chuck Close. *Linda.* 1975–76.
Acrylic on canvas, 9 × 7′ (2.74 × 2.13 m).
Courtesy the artist.

343
Neil Welliver. *Cedar Breaks.* 1976.
Oil on canvas, 8 × 8′ (2.44 × 2.44 m).
Pennsylvania Academy of Fine Arts, Philadelphia.

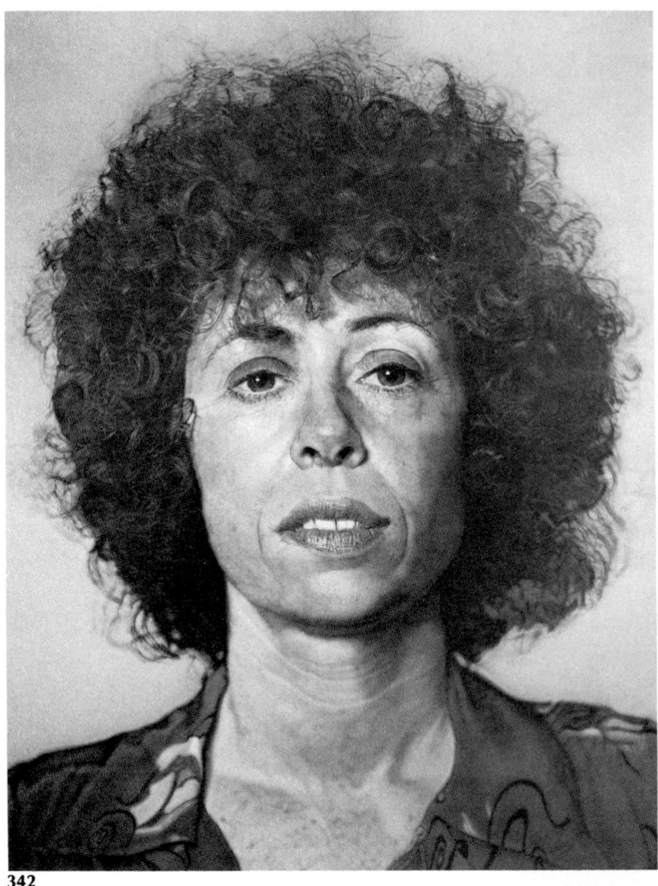
342

343

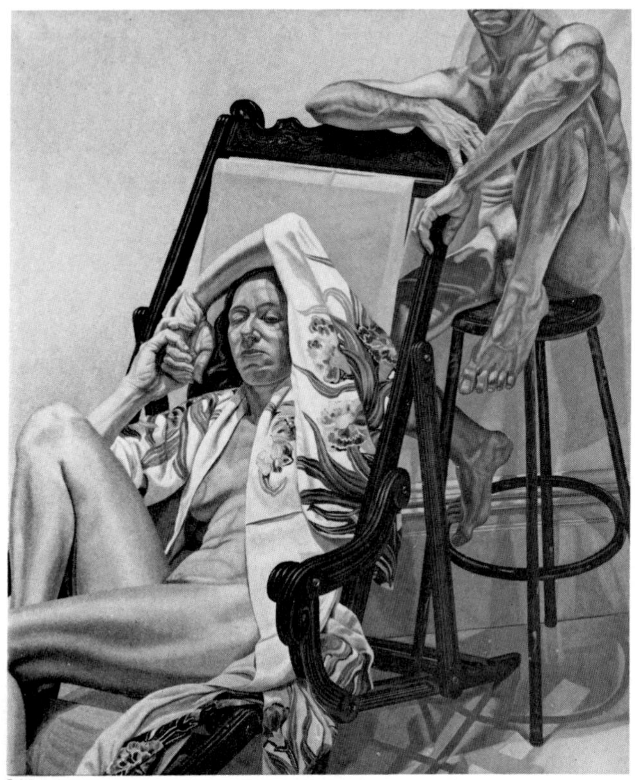

344

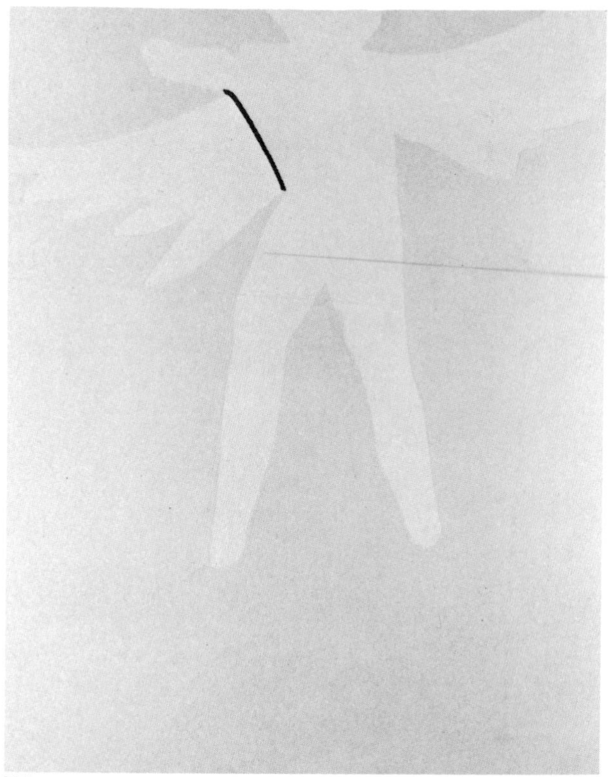

345

Philip Pearlstein is of particular interest because he combines the superficial aspects of photorealism with a personal philosophy quite in opposition to that of Close. "I'm interested in abstraction," Pearlstein tells us. "Subject matter never interests me."[4] As the motif for his abstractions, he has chosen the nude and he paints it from what he calls "a cool and detached point of view devoid of sentimentality." He counteracts the "nude's natural eroticism" with a cold, objective, almost clinical attitude, and the results are beautifully modeled forms arranged in intricate compositions of photographic clarity. In Figure 344 the composition is strongly diagonal, with the implied space characteristic of Pearlstein's work. We see not people but forms—the smoothly flowing muscles of a thigh and the intricate veining of a foot. The carving on the chair and the floral design of the wrap are all there but with a strong design quality that transcends their realism. The balance of dark and light, the diagonals of stool legs and the chair brace that counteract the dominant diagonals of the figures, the visual textures of light on skin—all of these show Pearlstein as a master of design as well as of technique.

Some of the most articulate of recent trends are grouped under the term *Post-Modernism.* Moving away from the depiction of the human face and figure, they express a revived interest in human *values.* One category taking the name of New Image Art tends toward personal mythology translated into semiabstract forms. Often the subject matter seems to have emotional overtones that dissolve into animals with symbolic appendages and subjective imagery. Lois Lane's work, for instance, contains delicate

344
Philip Pearlstein. *Female Model on Deck Chair, Male Model on Stool.* 1981.
Oil on canvas, 6 × 5′ (1.83 × 1.52 m).
Collection Reynolda House, Winston-Salem, N.C.

345
Lois Lane. *Untitled.* 1980. Oil on canvas, 6′3″ × 5′ (1.91 × 1.52 m).
Private collection.

346
Harry Koursaros. *Pythian Maidens.* 1981.
Oil and acrylic on canvas, 4′6″ × 4′6″ (1.37 × 1.37 m). Private collection.

[4] Paul Smith, "Philip Pearlstein's New Paintings," Arts Magazine, April 1982, p. 81.

shapes and forms that seem charged with private experience and hazy mythological associations (Fig. 345).

Another group works under the designation of *Pattern and Decoration.* These painters declare in favor of design and sensuous ornamentation, and their works are vividly, even garishly, colored, borrowing images from Oriental rugs, Chinese porcelains, and Islamic decor. Design quality is of primary concern here; Harry Koursaros paints meticulous allover patterns with strong mythological implications but our first impression is one of flowing rhythms, beautiful balance, and an overriding sense of design (Fig. 346).

Our purpose has been to trace the importance of design in painting. We have, of course, only touched on the wealth of material available. The important point is that painting, although one of the most eminent of the fine arts, is grounded firmly in design, and the painter's knowledge of design and personal use of the elements and principles has a great deal to do with the validity of any individual work of art.

346

17 Sculpture

In the consideration of sculpture, we move into the three-dimensional application of the elements and principles of design. Sculptures exist in real, not illusionary, space. We perceive them in the same manner in which we perceive objects in the natural world, and we frequently relate to them in space in the same way that we relate to objects in our physical environment. We approach, we draw away, we move around them, and sometimes move over or through them (Fig. 347).

Categories of Sculpture

Sculpture may be created by many methods, from riveting to modeling in clay. The tools of the sculptor frequently include implements for working metal, glass, and plastic, as well as the traditional range of mallets, chisels, and gouges for shaping wood and stone (Fig. 348). Although many contemporary sculptures defy formal classification, tradition divides sculpture into two categories: *freestanding* and *relief.*

Freestanding sculpture, or sculpture in the round, is free of attachment to any background. Sometimes freestanding works are mounted permanently in niches or other settings, but more often they are situated so the viewer can move around them. George Sugarman's *Kite Castle* (Pl. 28, p. 263) rests in New York's Hammarskjöld Plaza, where it creates a lively relationship with the cityscape. Its forms and spaces interact with the buildings that surround it, the space of the plaza, the pedestrians who move around and through it, even the backdrop of passing vehicles. The viewer can observe it from an infinite number of angles, both on the ground and through the windows of adjacent buildings—and over periods of extended time. Each different viewpoint changes the configuration of solids and spaces.

Relief sculptures are usually attached to a background or are carved from it. The carving may vary in depth, the two traditional divisions being *bas-relief* (low relief) and *haut-relief* (high relief). In the doors for the Baptistry of the Cathedral of Florence, Lorenzo Ghiberti used both for intricate

347

348

347
Raffael Benazzi. *Work No. N.Y. 44.* 1979. Black walnut, 34¼ × 26 × 14" (87 × 66.04 × 35.56 cm). Private collection.

348
Assortment of mallets, chisels, and gouges used in carving and sculpture.

349
Lorenzo Ghiberti. *Gates of Paradise.* East doors of the Baptistry, Florence. 1425–1452. Gilt bronze, height 18'6" (5.64 m).

349

purposes of design (Fig. 349). One of the great masterpieces of bronze relief sculpture, these doors were created during the early Renaissance, in the late medieval style of representing Old Testament subjects, including more than one incident in some of the panels. Separating the episodes within a panel required consummate skill, and Ghiberti accomplished the feat by using various levels of relief to imply both action and distance, at the same time achieving a rich textural surface. Figures in the foreground are in haut-relief verging on roundness, whereas the background slopes gently to relief so low that it gives the effect of aerial perspective, often articulating a second episode on a different plane. In this treatment, Ghiberti employed Renaissance discoveries for depicting depth, making his work a technical milestone as well as an artistic one. Though only $31\frac{1}{4}$ inches (79 centimeters) square, many of the panels contain more than a hundred figures, as well as ships, architecture, and details of landscape. Viewing the two doors as a total design, we are impressed by the overall balance—of arched architectural details, grouped figures, vertical lines, and deep shadows. The total composition is bordered by a band of human figures interspersed with plant and animal forms in pulsating rhythm, and separated from the highly textural panels by bands of smooth gilt bronze. The effect is one of opulence tempered by dignity.

Ghiberti's doors were cast after being modeled in wax, a medium that made possible the wealth of intricate detail. As we mentioned in Chapter 11, various materials can be cast; however, the creation of a work of sculpture involves specific considerations. The mold for casting can be a simple depression into which liquid material is poured, resulting in a solid mass when hardened. For works of metal and clay, however, a hollow cast is preferred, since this will result in a thin layer of material, minimizing the danger of cracking and resulting in a work of considerably less weight. Hollow casting necessitates a mold composed of at least two sections—one for the outer surface and one for the inside. The classic method for hollow casting metal, especially bronze, is the *cire-perdue,* or lost wax technique.

In cire-perdue casting, the sculptor builds a model of wax around a core of some nonmelting material, such as clay. Next, an outer mold, usually of clay, is applied to the wax model, conforming to it in every detail. To make the cast, the wax is melted out and replaced with molten metal. Several identical sculptures can be produced from the same mold. Furthermore, the sculptor is not confined to the compact form required for materials that could break easily, but is free to make extensions into space as the design requires. Most of the monumental bronze sculptures in parks and plazas were made by the cire-perdue method (Fig. 219).

Another popular casting method depends on molds made of damp sand, which is solid enough to hold a shape but will release the cast material after it has hardened. Bronze, plaster, plastics, and concrete are the materials often cast by this technique, and the surface texture resulting from adhering sand particles can be left or smoothed. Panels for exterior walls of buildings can be relief cast by pouring wet concrete onto flat sand molds modeled in reverse. This is the method that was used for the relief panel on the building in Figure 151, p. 99.

With the advent of plastics and the sculptor's use of the welding torch, sculpture has burst beyond the limits of traditional categories. Some sculptors comb junkyards and dumps for interesting castoffs and use them as ingredients for new forms without reference to their original purpose.

Attributes of Sculpture

As with painting, three attributes generally are applied to sculpture: subject, form, and content. It is difficult to separate the three in painting; it is almost impossible in sculpture. For one thing, in a three-dimensional work, the form *becomes* the work. In analyzing how attributes operate in a piece of sculpture, the overall significance of form must be kept in mind.

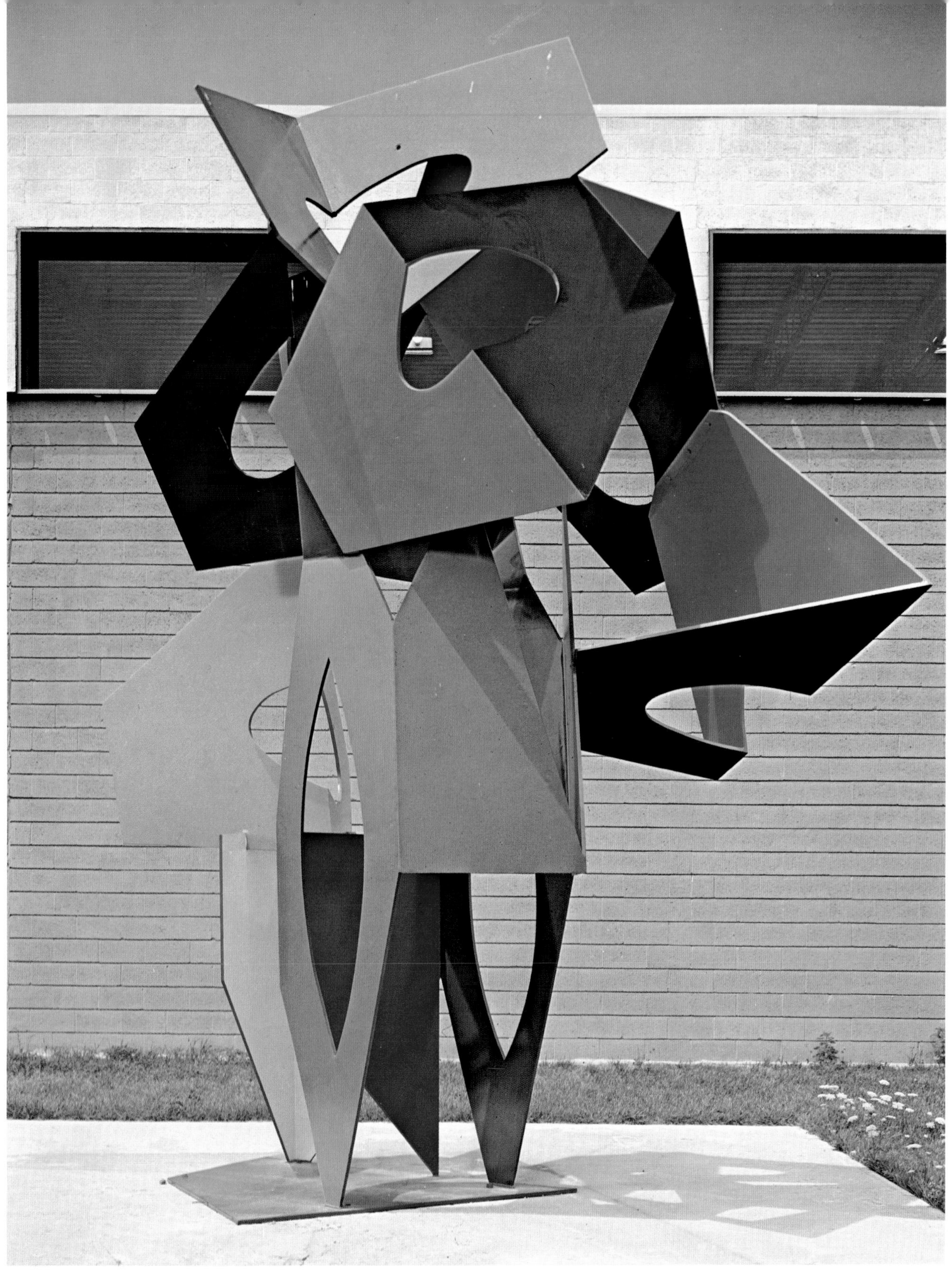

Plate 28
George Sugarman. *Kite Castle.* 1973–74. Painted steel; height 18′ (5.49 m). Hammarskjöld Plaza, New York.
Courtesy Robert Miller Gallery, New York.

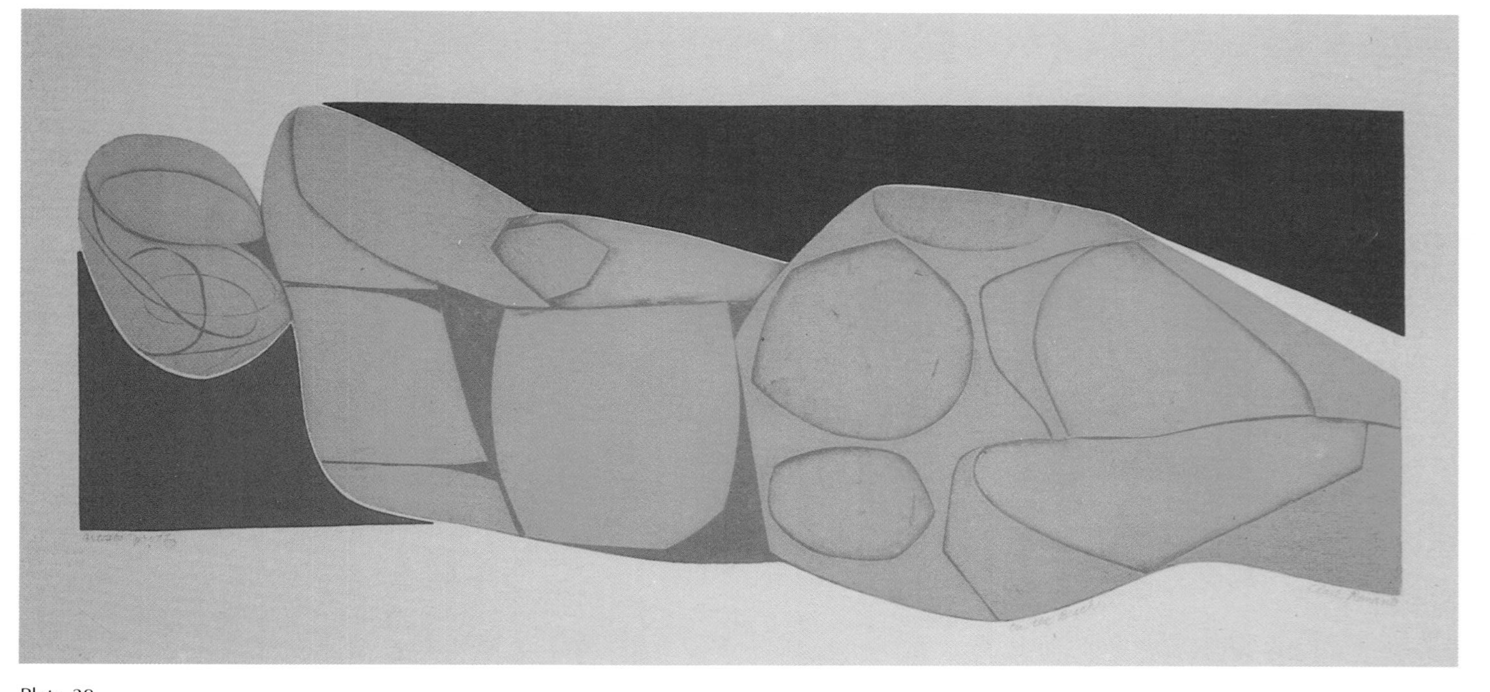

Plate 29
Clare Romano. *On the Beach II.* 1969. Color collagraph of cardboard, papers, and sand; $11\frac{5}{8} \times 29''$ (29.53×73.66 cm). Associated American Artists, New York.

350

For 25 centuries sculpture has been involved with *subject,* usually freestanding human or animal forms and the qualities emanating from them, often religious or superstitious. One of the oldest and most famous of the human subjects is a stone figure less than five inches high that was unearthed in central Europe (Fig. 350). Subject is inseparable from *content* here, for the tiny but ponderous Venus was almost certainly a fertility figure. Similarly interrelated are the subject and content of the great body of mythological figures depicted in sculptures all over the world. In Figure 351, for instance, we see a depiction of the Hindu god Shiva. To his followers, Shiva is the center of the universe, its root and support. He is both the creative and destructive flow of life rushing through it; he is motion and calm, light and dark, male and female, ascetic and lover. As might be expected, interpretations of Shiva in East Indian art take widely varying forms. The Eastern artist is not concerned with how a figure looks so much as with the realization of the inner god and spirit. Divinity is always shown with chest expanded, the body filled with the breath of life. Shiva is variously represented as a dancer with many arms, a many-faced pillar, an erect phallus bearing a single face, and a bull which, with its intimations of sexual potency, is at once the god's favorite vehicle, his mount, and his most devoted subject. The depiction in Figure 351 imbues the subject with its ultimate *content* by showing the god as half-woman, with the sacred bull alongside.

The sculpture of ancient Greece represents the ideal from which many subsequent sculptors derived inspiration. Here the subject matter was primarily of the gods or of athletes, human forms of exceptional beauty (Fig. 352). The discus thrower in Figure 352 is the embodiment of imminent action, from the tautness of the leg muscles to the tension in the arms and chest. The work has come down through the centuries as the essence of the

351

352

350
Venus of Willendorf. c. 30,000–25,000 B.C. Stone, height 4⅜″ (11.18 cm). Museum of Natural History, Vienna.

351
Cholan, Tanjore District. *Ardhanarisvara,* Indian. 850–1100 A.D. Black granite, height 44$^{5}/_{16}$″ (112.5 cm). St. Louis Art Museum.

352
Myron. *Discobolus* (Discus Thrower). Roman copy after bronze original of c. 460 B.C. Marble, lifesize. National Museum, Rome.

353

354

353
Seymour Lipton. *Sanctuary.*
Nickel silver over steel,
height 29¼" (74.3 cm).
Museum of Modern Art, New York
(Blanchette Rockefeller Fund).

354
Dance mask from West Bamileke,
Banga-Djang region, Africa.
Late 19th-early 20th century. Wood,
height 26½" (66 cm).
Rietberg Museum, Zurich
(Von der Heydt Collection).

355
Gian Lorenzo Bernini. *David.* 1623.
Marble. Galleria Borghese, Rome.

ideal athlete, yet athletes today tell us that taking this pose could very well upset the balance of a person about to throw a discus. In spite of this fact, the essence remains. Subject, form, and content have combined to produce a great sculpture, and practical considerations do not seem of particular importance.

What we feel in the discus thrower is a *kinesthetic,* or *kinetic,* sense. This is a reaction to motion, in which we feel within our own bodies the action that we see in someone else. The kinetic sense is familiar to anyone who enjoys dancing or athletics, even as a spectator, and it was a major element in the content of Greek sculpture. When we realize that these works depict the people who originated the Olympics, who felt that the body should be a fitting vehicle for the spirit and the mind, we understand why their human figures are muscular and active and why even the horses that pranced around the frieze of the Parthenon were spirited creatures of strength and beauty. This tremendous force was the content as well as the form.

The active figures of Greek sculpture necessarily have an *open form,* one in which space flows in and around the positive masses. The work in Figure 353 has a *closed form,* coiling in upon itself in a modified spiral. The title, *Sanctuary,* makes clear that the form and content are inseparable. The spiral, of course, provides radial balance. The texture of the surface also plays an important role, providing the viewer with a tactile experience. There is an interplay of negative and positive space, but it, too, contributes to the flowing inward, the convergence of all elements toward the center of emphasis.

Entirely different in purpose is the closed form of the Bamileke mask in Figure 354. In this case the form is distinguished by perfect bilateral symmetry. Design elements of immense importance are the linear treatment balanced between top and bottom, the stippling distributed throughout, and the deep carving, which provides strong light and shadow. Here again, we have an active tactile experience.

One of the most illuminating ways to understand content is to compare the works of two different artists on the same subject. Unlike our comparison of Cézanne's different approaches to Mont Sainte-Victoire, which charted his personal reactions and development, this sort of comparison demonstrates how the creative intellect is expressed through two entirely different channels. In Michelangelo's *David* in Figure 13 we see a youth of dignity and composure, standing confidently as he awaits the confrontation with Goliath. The form is closed, and the style reminiscent of the Greeks, by whom Michelangelo was strongly influenced. A hundred years later, Bernini did a sculpture of David that has become equally famous. Bernini was greatly influenced by Michelangelo, but he developed his own unique style early and became an impressive figure in the use of the opulent swirling forms of the Baroque (see Fig. 292, p. 216). It was said that he used space as if it were a plastic material to be molded, his figures surrounded by its fluid forms, which circled and enveloped them in a theatrical interplay of stone and light. His *David* does not stand calmly (Fig. 355). He swings his muscular arms at the moment of releasing the stone from the sling, his brows drawn together, lips compressed, every fiber of his body totally involved. The form is open and dynamic.

355

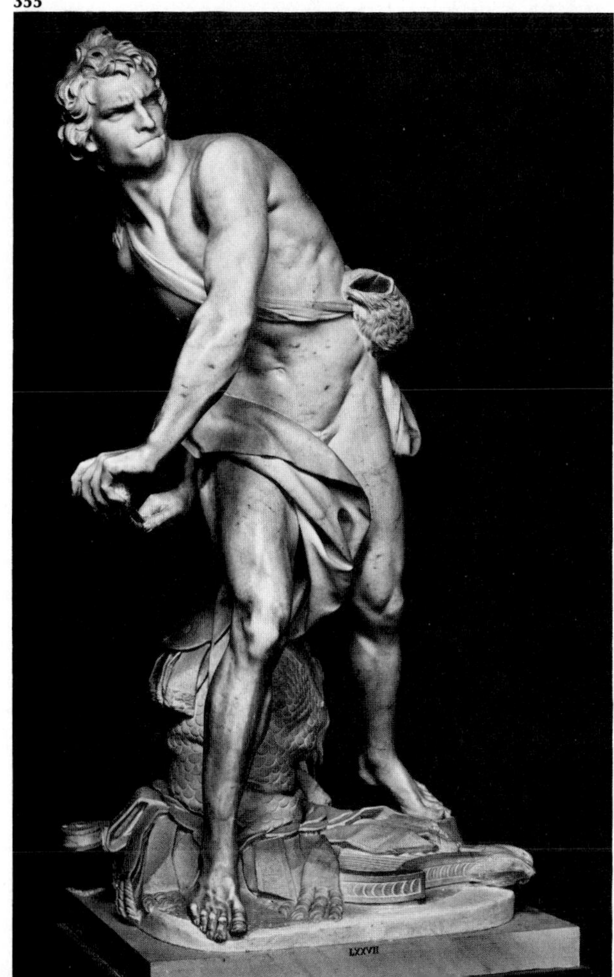

356

357

356
Donatello. *Madonna and Child.* 1448.
Bronze, height 5′3″ (1.60 m).
Il Santo (Church of St. Anthony of Padua).

357
Simon Qissualu Aliqu. *Femme et bébé* (Woman and Baby). c. 1965.
Povungnituk, Quebec. Soapstone.
Courtesy Canadian Minister of Indian Affairs and Northern Development.

358
Gargoyles on the face of Washington Cathedral, Mount St. Alban.
Washington, D.C.

Such biblical subjects provided material for sculptors for centuries, and none was more loved and more variously depicted than the subject of the Madonna and Child. We have buxom blond madonnas from the northern artists, and slim olive-skinned madonnas from Italy and Spain, for this is a subject touching the heart of humanity and adapting readily to personal interpretation. In Figure 356 we see the Madonna cast in bronze by one of the great sculptors of the Renaissance, Donatello. The Madonna is a queen, clothed in the opulent robes of the Italian Renaissance, presented to us frontally in full majesty, her lap forming a throne upon which she brings forth her son. This universally appealing subject has entirely different *form* and *content* in a representation by Eskimo artist Simon. In his soapstone carving (Fig. 357), the mother is protective, sheltering the child from the elements of a harsh northern country. The work, however, is not harsh or crude, but filled with curvilinear rhythms; the very mass and simplicity of its form evoke its elemental setting. Form and content, thus, are not only attributes of an individual work but can be expressions of the time and place in which it is created.

Light and Sculpture

In drawing or painting, shape is translated into mass by means of shading or tonality (see Figs. 99 and 100, p. 67). In sculpture, this transformation takes place as a result of light.

The placement of sculpture is therefore crucial. Outdoor sculpture is positioned in open courts and plazas, where the full light of day will strike it, changing its contours as the sun moves throughout the sky. The ancient Greeks made a fine art of moldings—simple chiseled borders that adorn their buildings—because they could depend upon the bright Greek sun to carve them into sparkling accents of light and shadow. Look again at the Parthenon in Figure 194 (p. 149) and try to imagine it without the impact of light. The triglyphs (short vertical grooves in groups of three around the frieze at the top) would disappear without the shadows in the grooves, and the supporting columns would appear smooth. The grooving of the columns was an overture to the sun, for it is only light that gives the grooves visual substance. The play of light dramatically articulates the forms on the Washington Cathedral in Figure 358. Not only the moldings and arches but the gargoyles are dependent upon light for their form. Observe the differ ence in the two gargoyles: one, drenched in light, is *outlined* by shadow; the other one, placed so shadow engulfs its underside, is outlined in light.

358

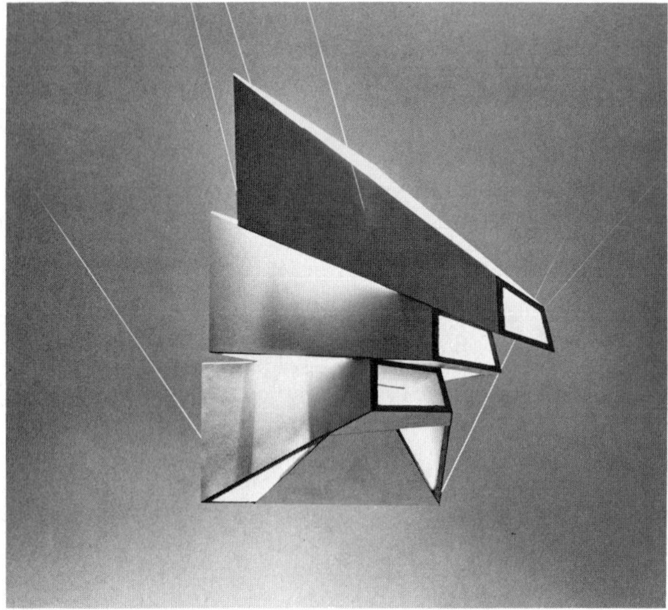

359

360

359
Steve Keister. *U.S.O. #66.* 1980. Formica and acrylic on plywood, 30 × 13 × 30″ (76.2 × 33.02 × 76.2 cm). Blum Helman Gallery.

360
Umberto Boccioni. *Unique Forms of Continuity in Space.* 1913. Bronze (cast 1931); 43⅞ × 34⅞ × 15¾″ (111.3 × 88.4 × 39.9 cm). Museum of Modern Art, New York. (Lillie P. Bliss Bequest).

361
Naum Gabo. *Construction in Space with Balance on Two Points.* 1925. Plastic, glass, metal and wood; 26½ × 40″ (67.3 × 101.6 cm). Base 19¹¹⁄₁₆ × 10⅝″ (50.0 × 27.2 cm). Yale University Art Gallery, New Haven (gift of H. Wade White).

362
Constantin Brancusi. *Bird in Space.* (1928?) Bronze (unique cast); height 4′6″ (1.37 m). Museum of Modern Art, New York. (anonymous gift).

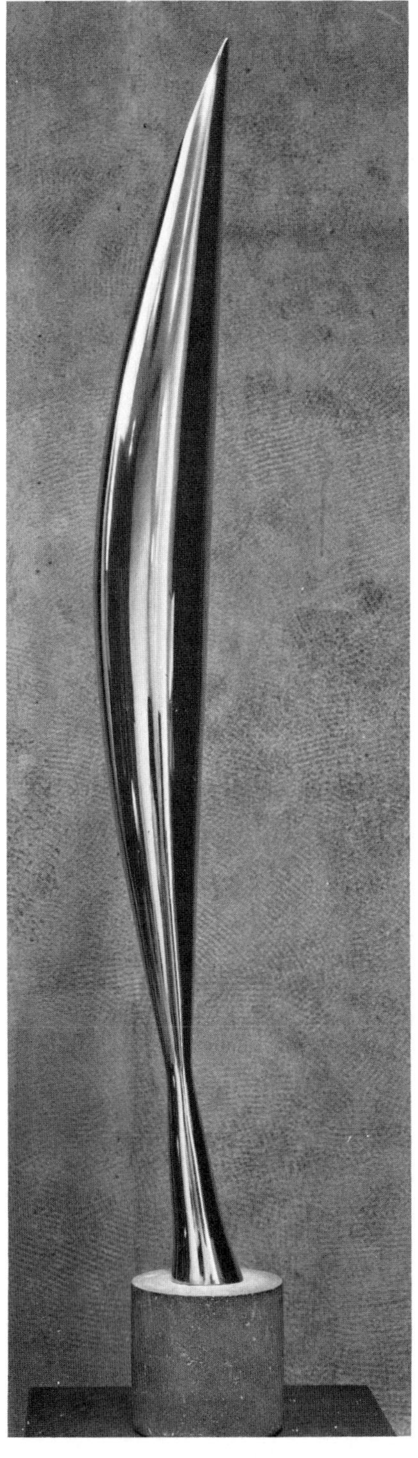

361

When sculpture is installed indoors, the source of light is more static and therefore must assure maximum effect. Some contemporary artists install moving lights as part of their work, providing the kind of dynamics that comes from changing sunlight. Others, like Steve Keister, engage light as the major element of the work itself (Fig. 359).

Directions in Contemporary Sculpture

Twentieth-century sculptors have experienced the same release from traditional forms as painters have, and some of the movements that we discussed in painting have counterparts in sculpture. Cubist sculptures, as we see in Boccioni's work in Figure 360, bear a definite kinship to Duchamp's *Nude Descending a Staircase* (Fig. 336, p. 251). There were also movements indigenous to sculpture, such as *Constructivism,* which emerged after World War I and which was described as an attempt to release earthbound masses from the pull of gravity (Fig. 361). As with painting, there were numerous *-isms,* most of them of interest today more for their experimental nature than for their aesthetic importance. *Abstraction* was as strong and as revolutionary a force in sculpture as in painting. Brancusi's *Bird in Space* (Fig. 362) created a sensation when it appeared in 1919.

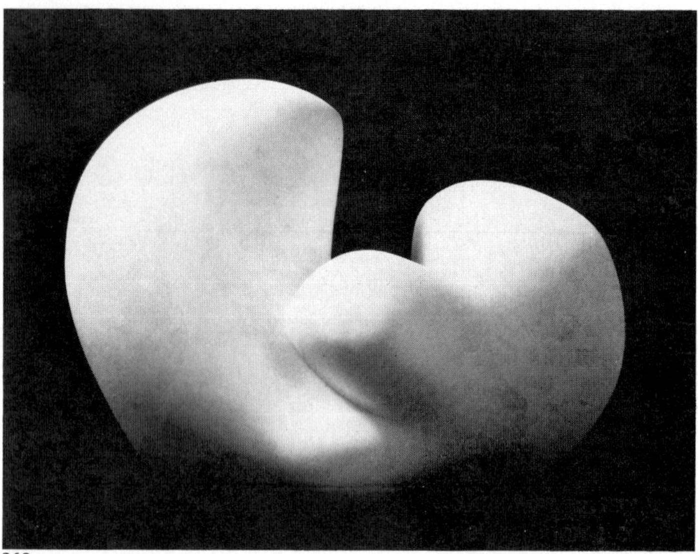

363

Like Kandinsky, Brancusi had a deeply rooted personal philosophy, to which he gave direct expression in his work. Brancusi gave special significance to the base of his pieces. For example, he felt that in a sculpture of high finish such as *Bird in Space* there should be a base of natural rough-hewn character, not only for textural contrast, but also to provide a spectrum of surfaces to suggest symbolic emergence—the plant from the soil, the child from the seed within the mother, fruition from chaos. Another influential figure, Jean Arp, used abstraction with a similar connotation of growth. *Human Concretion* (Fig. 363) does not rise from a base but emerges in the manner of a fetus, organically, its fluid forms and smooth surface suggesting cell division. Though stylistically very different, the works of Brancusi and Jean Arp show a strong sense of rhythm and balance, a particular interest in proportion, and a fundamental involvement with the expressive quality of texture.

Abstract Expressionism finds its sculptural counterpart in the work of contemporary sculptor Judy Pfaff (Fig. 364). She wraps materials like plastic, contact paper, and Mylar with wire, tree branches, and reeds, arriving at the same kind of weaving in and out of lines and forms that we saw in the work of Jackson Pollock (Fig. 335, p. 250). Employing brilliant, sometimes luminous colors, Pfaff creates an all-enveloping abstraction that occupies and encloses space at the same time that it transmits an emotional experience of the artist.

363
Jean Arp. *Human Concretion.* 1935.
Original plaster, 19½ × 18¾″
(24.1 × 47.5 cm). Museum of Modern Art, New York (gift of the Advisory Committee).

364
Judy Pfaff. *Dragon.* February 4–April 5, 1981.
Mixed-media installation at Whitney Biennial, the Whitney Museum of American Art, New York. Courtesy Holly Solomon Gallery for Photos, New York.

365
Bryan Hunt. *Caryatid.* 1980–1981.
Cast bronze on limestone base,
52 × 33 × 29½″ (1.32 × .84 × .75 m).
Courtesy Blum Helman Gallery, New York.

Contemporary Trends

Many contemporary artists work in both painting and sculpture; others, like Judy Pfaff, combine the two in an entity known as an "environment." Whether individual works of sculpture or comprehensive environmental constructions, they exhibit many of the same characteristics as Post-Modern painting—new images, an emotional quality, and a highly mythological and symbolic ambience. There is emphasis on motion and light, with lively subjects transmitted in rigid materials, as in Bryan Hunt's series of cast bronzes inspired by waterfalls (Fig. 365). When the human figure is

364

365

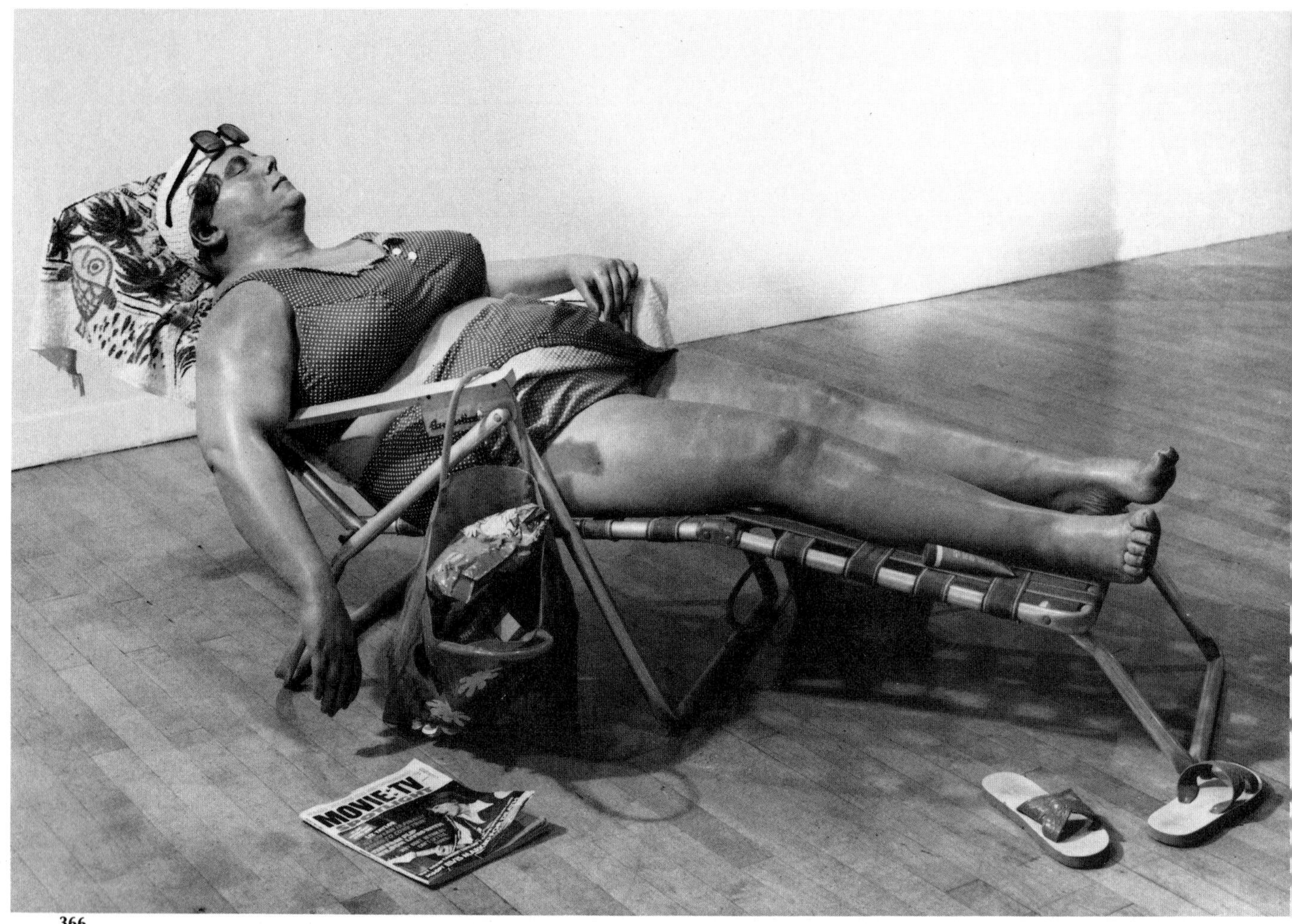

366

366
Duane Hanson. *Woman at Beach on Lounge Chair,* or *Sunbather.* 1971.
Polyester and fiberglass, polychromed; lifesize. Private collection.

367
Alice Aycock. *The Machine that Makes the World.* 1979. Mixed media, 38 × 21 × 8′ (11.58 × 6.39 × 2.44 m)
Collection of the artist.

368
Yaacov Agam. *Space Divider.* 1980. Gold plated brass; 8¾ × 8¾″ (22.1 × 22.1 cm).
Published in a limited edition by Diverse Dimensions Art, New Rochelle.

depicted it has none of the idealism of past eras but is shown with merciless fidelity in all its unsightly mediocrity, a commentary on the cruder aspects of contemporary society (Fig. 366).

Alice Aycock calls her constructions "pseudo-architecture," stating their object to be the restoration of that sense of compulsion that sweeps us away from ourselves to a wish to be ourselves more completely and deeply. In Figure 367 she has employed several architectural motifs, including a nearly impenetrable labyrinth, to express the power of bureaucracy and other social institutions to constrict human freedom.

Yaacov Agam is well known as an Op painter, yet he, too, now moves toward an interpretation in three dimensions of the light and movement that permeate his canvases. His *Space Divider* (Fig. 368) has a definite affinity to Op paintings (see Pl. 7, p. 105), but swinging on a single axis, it captures the perpetual state of flux and motion implicit in the creation of the universe.

367

368

369

Finally, light becomes the medium of Larry Bell's installation in Figure 369. Here, 56 plates of glass challenge the senses with ever-changing movement and light that seem to dematerialize the surrounding world. Whether this can be called sculpture in the strictest sense is debatable, and this, in itself, is characteristic of contemporary art. Dividing lines dissolve—between art and technology and between the categories of art—as artists reach out and down, probing the depths of human thought and emotion, expressing human experiences in highly subjective terms. The emphasis is on the totality of human life as it grows from within and is nurtured by experience. This is the basis from which sculpture emerges, and its materials are mass, light, rhythm, space, texture, emphasis, and scale—the ingredients that establish it irrevocably as both art and design.

369
Larry Bell. *The Iceberg and its Shadow.* 1975. Glass, variable measurements, 60 × 3⁄8″ (1.52 × .95 cm).
MIT Permanent Collection (gift of the Albert and Vera List Family Collection).

18 Printmaking

The field of printmaking is a transitional area between art and design. We have noted that allover fabric design is applied by printing processes, and we will find that printmaking is the medium for much of graphic design—posters, book illustration, and magazine advertising. Defined as the production of original prints, printmaking is classified as a fine art.

A print is a work of art created by an indirect transfer method. Rather than making an image directly on a ground, the artist works on a "master" surface with the image usually in reverse. From this master, many impressions can be made on paper (Fig. 370). The principle involved is identical with that of the common rubber stamp.

Because it is general practice to strike a number of impressions from a single master, prints often are referred to as *multiples.* The artist creates an image on a plate, stone, screen, or other surface, then supervises the printing or undertakes it personally. The number of impressions, known as the *edition,* possible from a single original will vary with the material. A linoleum cut yields relatively few prints before the soft material begins to wear and the quality of the impressions diminishes. A steel-faced metal plate, on the other hand, is capable of striking many thousands of fine-quality prints. As a rule, prints are numbered as they come from the press, with the earlier impressions being the finest and therefore the most desirable. The artist will hand sign each print that meets with his or her approval.

370

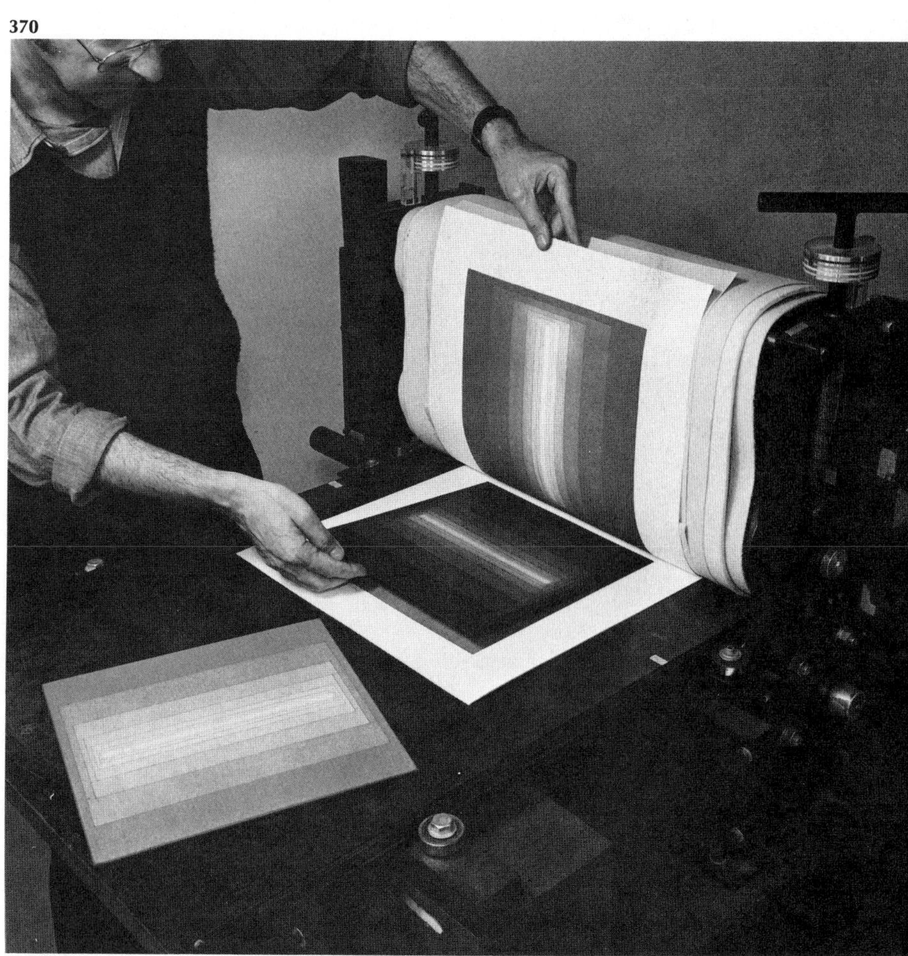

370
Photograph of print being pulled.

Prints begin with a drawing and incorporate the same compositional principles as paintings. Line, shape, texture, or value may be the predominant element according to the printing technique used. Some have obvious decorative qualities (Fig. 371), while others are graphic or filled with emotional impact (Fig. 372).

Prints as works of art should not be confused with reproductions. A *reproduction* is a copy of a work done in some other medium, usually painting. While good-quality reproductions may be suitable for educational purposes, they can in no sense be considered works of art, since the artist had nothing to do with them. A print, on the other hand, is an original that may exist in several versions. It resembles, in this sense, a bronze sculpture for which there may be a number of castings from the mold. Sometimes the printmaker varies the image between impressions, so each print is a bit different from the others.

Attributes of Prints

Like painting and sculpture, prints have *subject, form,* and *content;* however, the techniques of printmaking are so varied and specialized that they dominate these attributes. One might say that the technique *is* the content in many cases.

Historically, *subject* matter has been of major importance to prints since the earliest wood-block prints illustrating books, playing cards, or religious images (Fig. 373). In all three prints shown thus far in this chapter, subject plays a predominant role. The print by Mungituk, an Eskimo working in northern Canada, predates the American moon walk by several years (Fig. 371). The flight of wild geese over the Arctic is an event of wild rejoicing for Eskimos, as geese are highly prized as a source of food. In this whimsical print, the man is being transported bodily by geese amid much honking and flapping of wings. The subject was carved into a slab of soapstone as bas-relief, then inked and printed on paper. The texture of stone and act of carving it give the work its *form,* a simple decorative composition.

371

371
Mungituk. *Man Carried to the Moon.* 1959. Stone relief print, 19⅛ × 15" (48.58 × 38.1 cm). Brooklyn Museum, New York (Dick S. Ramsay Fund).

372
Käthe Kollwitz. *The Prisoners.* 1908. Plate 7 of *Peasant War* (Die Gefangenen). Etching and soft ground, 12⅞ × 16⅝" (32.7 × 42.2 cm). Print collection, The New York Public Library (Astor, Lenox & Tilden Foundations).

373
Illustration from *The History of Sir Richard Whittington Thrice Lord Mayor of London.* 18th century. Woodcut. British Library, London.

372

373

Although German artist Käthe Kollwitz was both a painter and sculptor, it was her powerful work in printmaking that established her unique place in the field of art. Married to a doctor who served the poorer classes of World War II Berlin, she not only became his helper and confidante but also dedicated her artistic talents to chronicling the anguish of all who suffered. Anguish permeated her own life. As a Jew, she was in constant danger of being sent to a Nazi concentration camp, and she lost her husband in the bombing of Berlin. The dramatic contrasts and forceful drawing displayed in her prints express the *content* by which the subject matter of her work is overwhelmed, a content evolving from an immense experience of compassion and sorrow. Her etching shown in Figure 372 is one of a cycle set in an earlier period, during the Peasant War of 1525 in which the peasants of southern Germany, after years of inhuman slavery, revolted against the nobility and the Church. The strong contrast in tone and texture accentuates the sense of dejection and confusion in the expressive drawing from which the print was made.

The woodcut in Figure 373 is totally involved with subject since it is an illustration for a book. The book tells the story of a boy who went to London to find his fortune and gave his cat to an outgoing vessel. After a wretched life as a kitchen slave, he was leaving the city when he heard the bells ringing, warning him to go back. He thereupon discovered that his cat had been sold for a high price in Barbary; he was given the money, and ended up as Lord Mayor of London. Richard Whittington did, in fact, exist. He was Lord Mayor three times in the early fifteenth century, became a confidant of the king, and left all his money to charity. The woodcut technique conveys a solid simplicity particularly suited to the depiction of a story over five centuries old.

Printmaking Processes

Most printmaking processes can be placed in one of four basic categories: *relief, intaglio, lithography,* and *serigraphy.* However, today there are many variations, with considerable overlapping.

Relief

Relief describes any process in which the image to be printed is *raised* from the background on the printing surface and takes the ink directly (Fig. 374). The inked image is then transferred to the paper by pressure. The oldest printmaking processes are the relief methods. In their most typical form relief prints preserve the qualities of the material from which they are made, translating these qualities into an artistic expression. The most common methods are *woodcut, linocut,* and *engraving* on wood or plastic.

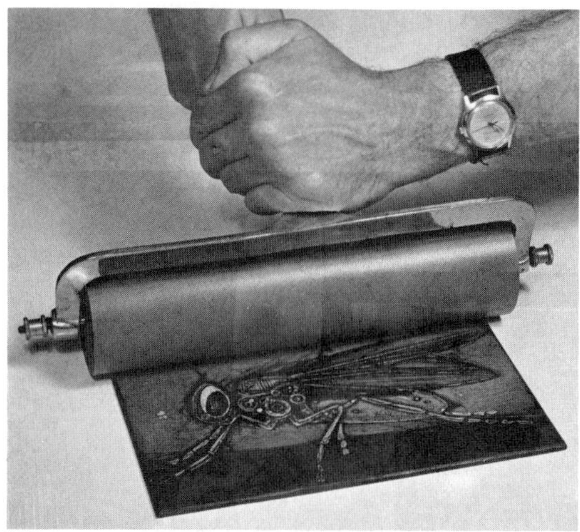

374

375

374
Inking a collagraph.

375
Basic tools used in making a woodcut.

376
Ernst Ludwig Kirchner. *Head of Ludwig Schames.* 1917. Woodcut. Printed on black sheet; $23\frac{7}{8} \times 16\frac{1}{8}$" (58.0 × 41.1 cm). Composition, $22\frac{15}{16} \times 10\frac{3}{16}$" (58.2 × 26.0 cm). Museum of Modern Art, New York (gift of Curt Valentin).

377
Henri Matisse. *Seated Nude.* 1906. Linoleum cut, printed in black; $18\frac{3}{4} \times 15$" (47.63 × 38.1 cm). Museum of Modern Art, New York (gift of Mr. and Mrs. R. Kirk Askew, Jr.).

Woodcuts have a forthright charm that has never been surpassed. The basic technique is simple. The image to be printed is projected or sketched on the side of a block of even-grained wood, then the areas that are *not* to be printed are cut away with knives or gouges (Fig. 375). The block is inked and the image transferred to paper by pressing or rubbing. Because they are cut primarily *with* the grain, woodcuts have a hand-hewn look that emphasizes the feeling of the wood itself (Fig. 376). Sometimes knots are left in the wood to become a part of the design. In any case, a woodcut possesses characteristics that cannot be imitated in any other medium.

Linocuts are made from heavy linoleum blocks, generally made by gluing thick linoleum to plywood (Fig. 377). The technique is the same as for a woodcut, but the actual cutting may be easier, because the smooth linoleum has no resistant grain. The resulting print may have fine smooth lines or may be rough to approximate the effect of wood. Color prints involve several blocks, each planned for a single hue. In printing, the various blocks are *registered* or lined up, so that they print in exactly the right image area. This technique is also possible with a woodcut.

376

377

The Eskimo printmakers of Cape Dorset, on west Baffin Island in Hudson Bay near the Arctic Ocean, have perfected a number of unique processes, including the type of print from stone reliefs exemplified by Mungituk's work (Fig. 371). For their *stone cuts,* these artists polish a large stone, trace an image upon it, then carve away the background areas from the stone. After the raised portion of the stone has been inked, they lay a sheet of paper on it and rub with the fingers on a sealskin pad, thus transferring the image. Contemporary Eskimo artists are receiving increasing recognition for their bold, stylized, and charming prints.

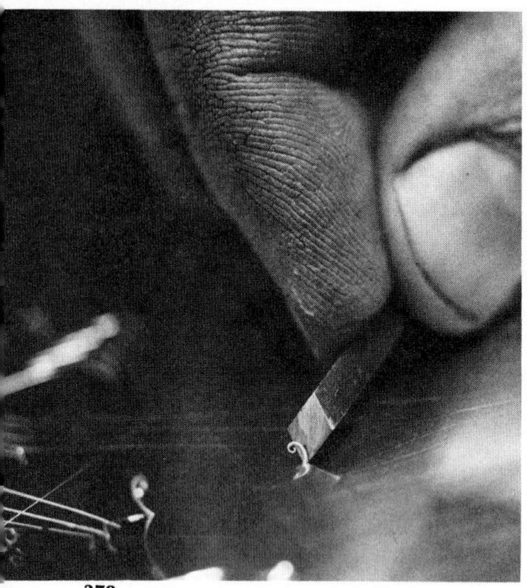

378

379

380

378
Burin in use, showing the curl of metal that is sometimes left on the plate, softening the effect of the finished print.

379
Thomas Bewick. *Bison.* Engraved wood-block. Los Angeles County Museum of Art (anonymous donor).

380
Thomas Bewick. *Bison.* 1800–1814. Wood engraving, 2 × 2¾" (5.08 × 6.99 cm). Los Angeles County Museum of Art (anonymous donor).

381
Sir Reginald Malyns and Wives. c. 1385. Rubbing of sepulchral brass at Chinnor, Oxon, England. British Museum, London.

Wood engravings differ from woodcuts in that they are cut from the *end grain* of the wood. A fine steel tool called a *burin* (Fig. 378) allows for finer lines and greater detail than is usual in woodcuts. The process is still relief, because the fine lines show white against the dark background that is inked and printed (Figs. 379 and 380). Lucite sometimes replaces wood, again making for smoother cutting.

Strictly speaking, *rubbings* are not art prints, since the "printmaker" is not involved in creating the master image. Rubbings are impressions taken from preexisting relief surfaces. Popular subjects have included gravestones, manhole covers, metal doors, and similar reliefs (Fig. 381). In making a rubbing, one fixes a piece of paper over the relief surface and rubs across it with charcoal or some other soft drawing material. Only the raised surfaces take an impression from the charcoal, with the depressed areas remaining white. Rubbings have great value in providing a reproduceable record of works that may be difficult to photograph or that will wear with time. Quite apart from this, they offer a splendid introduction to the potentialities of the relief process. It could even be argued that rubbings *are* original works of art, since they imply a creative act that was not envisioned by the artist who made the relief. The overall effect of the rubbing is quite different from that of the stone or metal original.

381

382

383

382
Martin Schongauer. *St. Michael.* c. 1480–1491. Engraving, 6⅜ × 4½″ (16.19 × 11.43 cm). British Museum, London.

383
Egon Schiele. *Portrait of Franz Hauer.* 1914. Drypoint, 5⅛ × 4¼″ (13.02 × 10.8 cm). Courtesy Fischer Fine Art Ltd., London.

384
Jim Dine. *Five Paintbrushes State 1.* 1972. Etching, 30 × 40″ (.76 × 1.02 m). Courtesy Petersburg Press, London. © Jim Dine 1972.

Intaglio

The term *intaglio* comes from the Italian word *intagliare,* meaning "to incise." It describes a printing process that is, in essence, just the reverse of relief, in that the parts to be printed are etched *into* the plate and are lower than the surface. Ink is retained in the incised areas rather than on a raised surface. Intaglio hand processes include metal engraving, drypoint, etching, aquatint, and mezzotint.

Like woodcuts, *metal engraving* has historic precedents, having descended from the medieval practice of decorating metal, such as armor, with incised designs. Metal engravings are executed with sharp tools (burins or gravers) on sheets of copper, zinc, or steel. Whereas the wood engraving prints an inked background from which white lines have been cut, the metal engraving is basically a composition of dark lines that have been incised and then inked, with the plate surface wiped clean to provide a white background. Metal engravings thus have a quality not unlike ink drawings (Fig. 382).

In making an engraving, the V-shaped burin is pushed into the surface of the metal plate to gouge out the lines of the design, after which ink is rubbed into these grooves. The artist then wipes the surface clean, places it face up on the bed of a press, lays dampened paper on the inked plate, covers the paper with a felt blanket, and applies pressure with a heavy roller. The roller forces the paper into the grooves, and the ink is transferred to the paper.

Before the invention of the camera, engravings were widely used to reproduce paintings and print book illustrations. Copper engraving is still employed for seals on official documents, postage stamps, paper money, and fine stationery.

The process for *drypoint* is much the same as that for engraving except in the preparation of the plate. Drypoints generally are executed on copper plates with needlelike instruments that have steel or diamond points. The resulting lines differ in effect from those made by the burin (Fig. 383). Instead of being pushed into the surface, the tool is drawn across the plate to raise a *burr* or tiny curl of metal along the edges of the lines. When the plate is inked, this burr retains the ink, so that the printed image has a velvety appearance recalling the darker accents in a fine pencil drawing.

The term *etching* derives from the German word *essen,* meaning "to eat." In this process the lines of the image are eaten into the metal plate with acid, instead of being gouged out with tools.

To produce an etching the artist coats a polished metal plate with a protective film of waxlike substance to produce the *ground.* The lines of the drawing are then scratched into the ground with a blunt needle, exposing the metal in the areas that are meant to print. The plate is immersed in an acid bath, and the acid eats into the exposed lines, etching them permanently. Finally, the plate is inked and printed in the same manner as an engraved plate. Used originally for decorating metal, such as armor, the etching technique came into use as a method of illustrating books in the sixteenth century. Etchings generally are characterized by a somewhat softer line than engravings (Fig. 384). It is said that in place of a sketchbook, Rembrandt carried a metal plate with him, making his sketches with an etching needle and then inking and printing the plates when he returned to his studio.

384

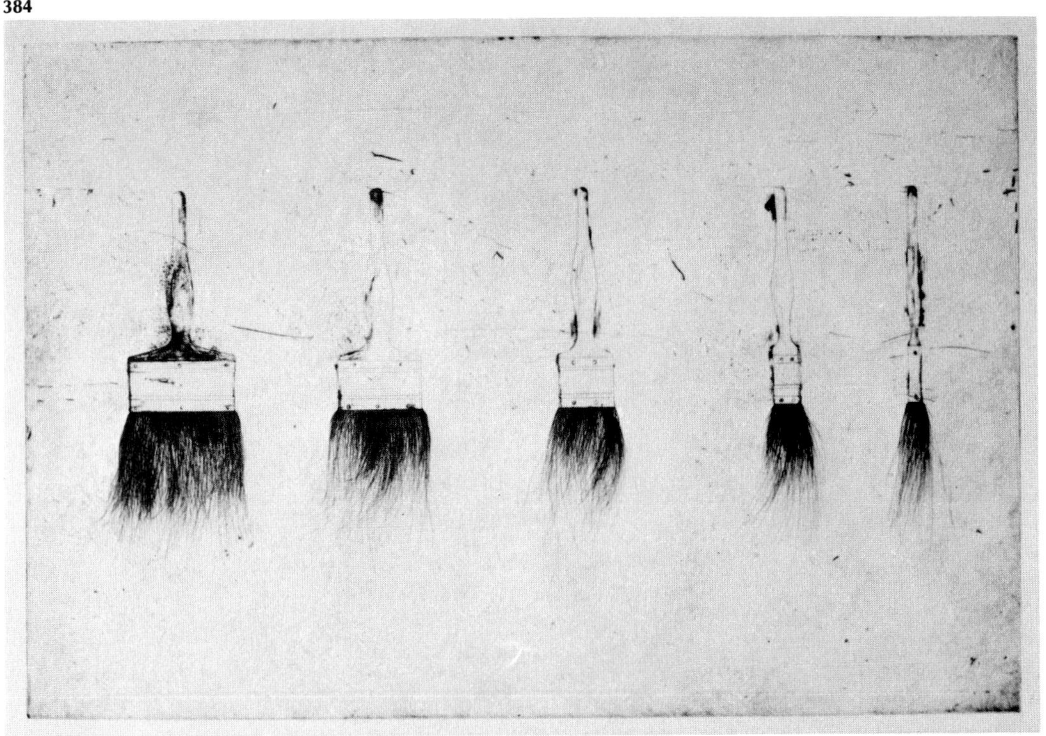

Aquatint is a process by which subtle tones are created on an intaglio plate. All linear elements of the composition are first etched on a metal plate, after which the plate is covered with a powdered resinous substance by one of several methods. After the particles have covered the plate evenly, the plate is heated so the resin will melt and adhere to the metal surface. The next step is to submerge the plate in acid, which will bite the particles of metal not covered by the resin, resulting in a fine textured tone. When the plate is removed, the lightest toned areas will have been established. For darker areas, the plate is submerged at intervals, the light areas then being stopped out with acid-resistant varnish, until the full succession of tonal values is achieved. The resulting print will have a soft quality unlike that of any other printmaking process (Fig. 385).

A velvety tone characterizes *mezzotint,* another variation on the etching technique. Here the artist first works over the entire plate with a *rocker,* a tool with many sharp cutting teeth, to dig up the surface and produce an allover covering of burrs. If the plate were printed at this stage, the burrs would create a uniform black tone. To build intermediate tones the artist partially removes the burrs with a *scraper;* highlights result from smoothing away the burrs completely. Mezzotint prints usually have a dark, rich, brooding quality (Fig. 386).

Lithography

Lithography is known as a *planographic* process because it employs a flat surface with neither raised areas nor depressions. The main printing medium of this process is the basic *lithograph,* but *monoprints* are also considered planographic. The invention of lithography is credited to the German Alois Senefelder, who used a special limestone in his native Bavaria for drawing images, thus introducing a new printing process based on chemical rather than physical properties (Fig. 387).

385

385
Mary Cassatt. *In the Omnibus.* 1891. Color aquatint with drypoint and soft ground, 14⁵⁄₁₆ × 10½″ (36.35 × 26.67 cm). Cleveland Museum of Art (bequest of Charles T. Brooks).

386
Chuck Close. *Keith.* 1972. Mezzotint, 4′4″ × 3′6″ (1.32 × 1.07 m). Courtesy Parasol Press, New York.

387
Pierre Auguste Renoir. *Portrait of Louis Valtat.* c. 1904. Original lithograph, 9′10″ × 7′10″ (2.98 m × 2.38 m). Collection Jack Rutberg Fine Arts, Los Angeles.

The lithographic process depends on the mutual antipathy of grease and water. The artist draws on a stone with a grease pencil or with a brush dipped in a greasy paintlike substance. Next, the stone is treated with a solution of gum arabic to which a small amount of nitric acid has been added. Finally, after excess drawing substance has been removed, the stone is moistened with water, then inked with a roller. The areas treated with gum arabic accept the water; the greasy image areas accept the greasy ink. Thus, when ink is rolled onto the surface of the stone, it is retained by the drawn areas but does not adhere to the wet surfaces. The artist places damp paper onto the stone and applies pressure, thereby transferring the image to paper. Bavarian limestone remains the classic ground for lithographs. In recent years, however, many lithographers have used zinc plates to make their prints, resulting in unique textural characteristics.

Each of the printmaking techniques described has its counterpart in commercial photomechanical reproduction—the means of printing books, magazines, newspapers, posters, and so forth. The corresponding

386

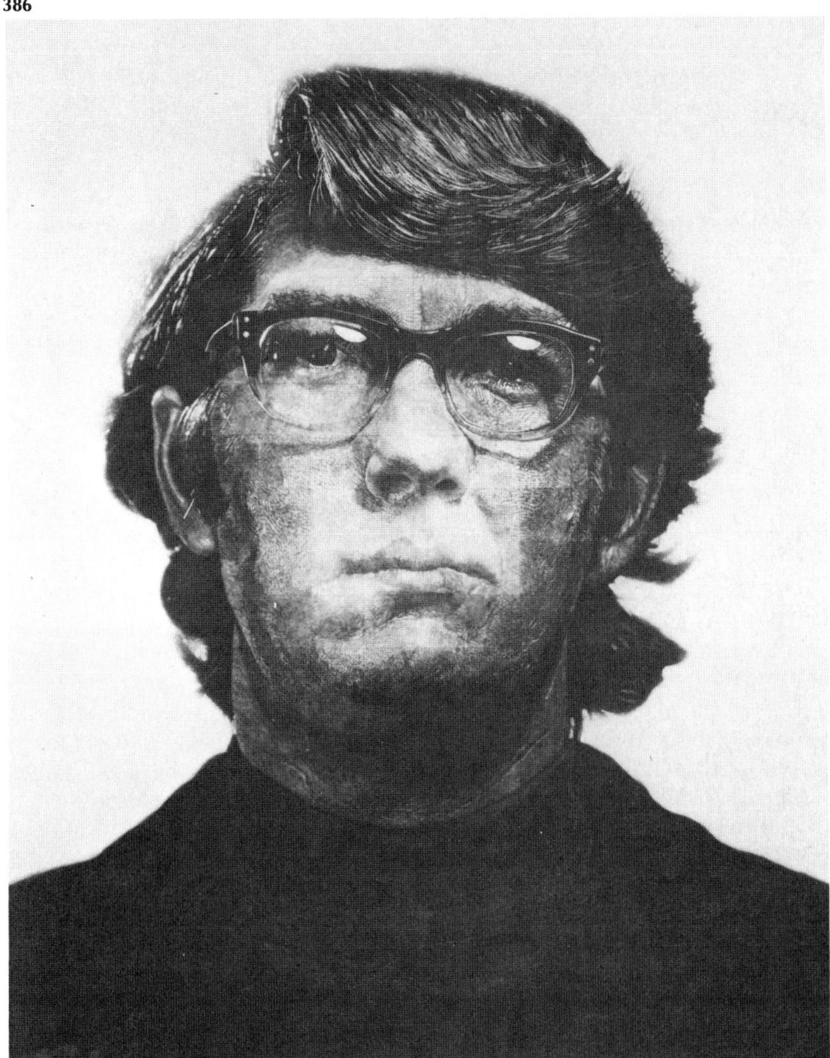

387

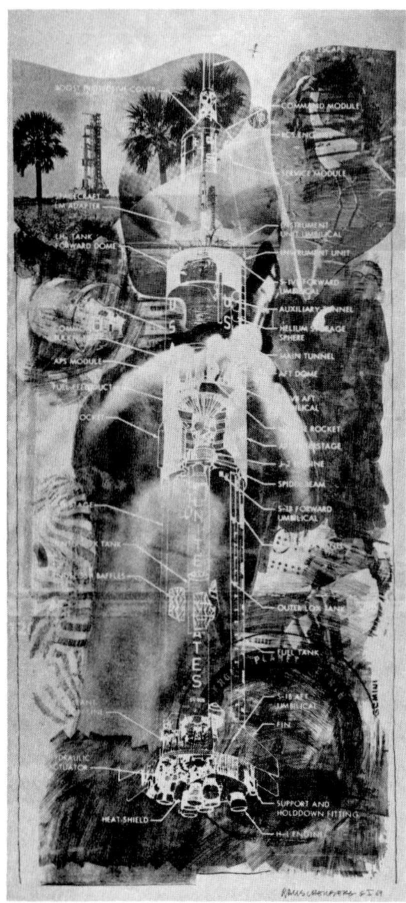

388

389

388
Robert Rauschenberg. *Sky Garden.* 1969.
Six–color lithograph-silkscreen,
7′5″ × 3′6″ (22.6 × 10.7 cm).
Edition of 35. © Gemini G.E.L., 1969.

389
Edgar Degas. *Le Bain* (The Bath). c. 1880.
Monotype, 8⅜ × 6 7/16″ (21.27 × 16.35 cm).
Den Kongelige Kobberstiksamling, Statens
Museum for Kunst, Copenhagen.

390
Andy Warhol. *Hand Colored Flowers,*
One from a portfolio of ten. 1974.
Silkscreen and watercolor,
41 × 21″ (1.04 × .53 m).
Published by Castelli Graphics
and Multiples, Inc., New York.

391
James Rosenquist. *Whipped Butter for Eugen Ruchin.* 1965. Silkscreen,
24 × 19⅞″ (61.0 × 50.3 cm).
Collection of Rosa Eman.

planographic process in printmaking is *offset lithography,* or simply *offset.* The text and illustrations for this book were offset printed.

Photolithography is a commercial technique used by many artists because of its extensive possibilities for experimentation. Briefly, it is the process of creating an ink-receptive image on a surface by means of photographic processes. Stone, zinc, or aluminum is given a light-sensitive coating, then an image is created on film or acetate and projected onto the plate, after which it is exposed to light. The coating in the light-exposed areas hardens and accepts ink, while the coating in the unexposed areas washes away. The surface is desensitized in these areas with a special preparation, then the plate is inked and printed like any other lithograph. The detail possible through the use of photographic images extends the range of subject and composition considerably (Fig. 388).

A *monoprint* or *monotype* is made by painting on a flat surface of metal or glass with either paint or ink. The printing paper is pressed onto the colored surface and then peeled off, resulting in a slightly different effect than could have been achieved by painting directly on the paper (Fig. 389). While it is theoretically possible to take more than one impression, the monoprint, as the name implies, is usually a single work.

Serigraphy

390

Serigraphy, or *screen printing,* is a stencil technique, which means that an image is transferred to a ground by applying color or tone around or inside a pattern. Except for its application to paper rather than to cloth, the technique of serigraphy for art prints does not differ at all from the fabric screen printing described in Chapter 14.

The term *serigraphy* means literally "writing on silk," and silk is the traditional material for this process, although others, such as nylon, have come into use. Because color printing is relatively easy, screen prints usually are characterized by bright, multiple colors.

To make a print, the artist first stops out on the screen mesh all the areas that are not to print in a particular color. Next, ink or dye in that color is forced, with a squeegee or roller, through the open areas of the screen onto the paper. Each color requires a separate screen and individual inking action. There is no limit to the number of colors that can be printed on a single sheet, provided the different screens are registered properly. Many artists have discovered that screen printing offers a fertile area for exploration. The basic process easily combines with oil painting, watercolor, drawing, and other techniques (Fig. 390).

Photoserigraphy is responsible for an entirely new type of lithographic print. The screen is coated with an emulsion by drawing the squeegee over it, then a film positive is secured to the glass on a light table and the screen placed over it. After a two- to five-minute exposure to light, the screen shows a pale latent image. The screen is now washed down with water, washing out the unexposed parts of the image and leaving the other areas hardened as a resist coating. The screen is then printed in the usual fashion. As in photolithography, the detail possible is practically unlimited (Fig. 391).

391

392

Contemporary Trends in Printmaking

Collagraphy derives its name from collage and it can incorporate both relief and intaglio methods. While most printmaking processes are subtractive, involving the cutting away of lines or areas, collagraphy is *additive,* resulting from the building up of a surface from nearly any material the artist finds interesting, including "found" objects such as coins, keys, and bits of machinery. Certain advantages make collagraphy a natural process for contemporary artists. The plate may be easily altered, affording freedom to invent and develop ideas. The possibilities for texture are limitless, and there is a sense of building that appeals to the creative mind. Collagraphy is often brilliant in color as well (Pl. 29, p. 264).

Much of contemporary experimentation is concerned with *combining traditional techniques.* Etching, in particular, lends itself to combination with other processes involved in printing from plates. Aluminum plates, lithographic stones, and several silk screens have all been combined in one production (Fig. 392).

Printmaking and Design

392
John Baeder with Madeleine-Claude Jobrack, platemaker and printer. *Empire Diner.* 1976. Photoetching, 8⅝ × 13⅝" (21.91 × 34.61 cm). Courtesy the artist.

Any discussion of printmaking focuses naturally on techniques and processes, seeming to relegate the elements and principles of design to a place of lesser importance. This is not the case, however, for the technique *is* essentially the design quality of any print and the artist absorbs the elements and principles of design into the basic process. As we mentioned early in the chapter, the character of a woodcut, a lithograph, or an etching is totally bound up with form and content, and it is also inextricably a part of design. The design qualities of each type of print are dictated by its distinctive texture and by the technique with which it was made. The elements of shape and color are important in many cases, and in etching and engraving, line is the primary means of expression. Proportion and scale are determined by the size of the print, which in turn is dependent upon the intentions of the artist and upon the equipment at hand. The prints illustrating this chapter display rhythm, emphasis, balance, and variety, and the requirements of each specific technique or medium make for unity of design. Printmaking is highly technical and often commercial; in many cases it involves pure design, but it can also be an art form meeting the highest aesthetic standards.

Graphic Design

The word *graphic,* in its broadest sense, refers to anything written, drawn, or engraved. Under this definition the term *graphic design* could apply to any of the visual arts, especially those that involve a two-dimensional surface. Drawing and printmaking, in particular, often are described as graphic arts. However, the goals of a painter or draftsman and those of an advertising designer are quite different, as are the problems encountered. Therefore, a more specific and generally accepted categorization limits the term graphic design to work intended for commercial reproduction.

For our purposes, graphic design will be defined as the selection and arrangement of elements for a printed format. The elements are words and images, which in design terms are called *type* (letters and words), *halftones* (photographs), and *line art* (drawings). Usually graphic design has some definite purpose, for instance, to sell a product or an idea, to make a book readable and attractive, or to call attention to something. Printed advertising, package design, and the design of such things as television commercials, books, magazines, and record jackets all are examples of today's graphic design.

A significant difference between graphic design and most other forms of design is the audience to which it is directed. The painter, the sculptor, the photographer, and the craftsman can aim their designs at a limited and usually sophisticated market. However, the graphic designer must be concerned with reaching out and influencing great numbers of people. Except for the limited-edition collector's book, every other design medium discussed in this chapter will be expected to have a mass audience. Every creation of the graphic designer is meant to sell something—either itself or another product. Thus, the graphic designer must be very much aware of how people react to shapes, sizes, lines, textures, colors—and ideas.

As suggested above, graphic design is essentially a two-dimensional medium. Even when the actual product takes on a third dimension, as in packaging or books, the design will be conceived in planar terms. This is because every design must be *printed* by commercial methods and thus must run through a press. Regardless of how the final product may be assembled, the basic design unit is flat.

Many designers work interchangeably in various fields, moving freely back and forth from one to another. While the basic character of each may be different, the manner of applying the elements and principles of design is quite similar.

Books

A fine book holds a unique place among the world's treasures. Not only can it provide a record of great ideas and literary composition, but it may also be a work of art in itself. A combination of beautiful papers, ink, type, illustrations, binding, and cover can produce an aesthetic expression worthy of the most noble content.

Books have a history almost as old as civilization. The ancient Egyptians threaded their hieroglyphs through their paintings as a running commentary, using the thick stem fibers of the papyrus plant to make scrolls. After the beginning of the Christian era, the practice of creasing parchment scrolls into flat sheets led to the development of the *codex,* the predecessor of the bound book. During the Middle Ages devoted monks kept Western culture alive by painstakingly copying and recopying the texts of Christian-

393
Nine Pairs of Divinities. Codex from the Mixtec culture, Mexico. 14th–16th century. Vatican Library, Rome.

394
Magazine page layout design for *Redbook Magazine.* 1981. Designer: Paula Laniado. Artist: Braldt Bralds.

ity, as well as those of ancient Greece and Rome. These manuscripts often were *illuminated,* or hand-painted, with intricate pictures and designs. The custom of illuminating manuscripts was also practiced in the Far East.

In the New World elaborate and colorful codices were made by the Mixtec and Aztec cultures in Mexico (Fig. 393). Only eight codices survive from the pre-Columbian era because the conquering Spaniards, considering the writings to be "heathen," destroyed the remainder.

The modern book evolved largely because of the development of printing technology and photography. Ideally, a book should be an entity in which format, text, and illustrations—in other words, form and content—are sensitively coordinated to achieve a unified whole. Generally, the graphic designer has little control over the text, and often he or she has no choice in the selection of illustrations. Both may be presented as the "given" around which the designer must create. The task, then, becomes one of interpreting the written material and finding the most effective physical means of presenting the book's contents. To do this, the designer manipulates text design, layout, paper, and cover (Fig. 394).

393

394

TOMATO *fandango*

A SHORT STORY
BY SARA CLAYTON

With no father in our families, my friend Pan and I knew few men, but we thought there must be some who were capable of experiencing the spirit of the fandango—whatever that was

The summer Pan and I were twelve, I decided that when I grew up I wanted to have a laugh and a smile like her mother's. My own laugh was a delirious trumpeting that contorted my face into a wizened, pre-sneeze squint. Claire McKee's raspberry mouth would smile and nudge both cheeks up into rosy crescents; her laugh was a vigorous, musical noise that sounded like "hallelujah-hurrah." It seemed to orbit Pan's and my heads and affect us like the full moon.

Laughing or talking, Mrs. McKee gestured with her hands, fanning her fingers and scooping the air gracefully. Her style, like her laugh, was sensational: She wore skirts and blouses the way other mothers did, but she'd wrap a scarf around her waist or knot a silky cord loosely at her throat, or maybe twist a length of fabric around her head like a flashy halo and force her chestnut curls to spiral out like corkscrews. She wore jewelry too. A magazine ad I saw once pictured a cluster of elegant men and women embracing in tropical surroundings, and printed below were the words: "Experience the Spirit of the Fandango." I remember thinking that Mrs. McKee would probably be able to do that, although I wasn't exactly sure what it meant.

Claire McKee taught high-school chemistry and (*Continued on page 156*)

Design
Through
Discovery

Design
Through
Discovery

Design
Through
Discovery

DESIGN
THROUGH
DISCOVERY

Design
Through
Discovery

Design
Through
Discovery

395

395
There are thousands of different type faces available today. Illustrated here are: Baskerville, Prisma capitals, Swinger Shadow, Andrich Minerva italic, LSC Manhattan, and Helvetica.

396
Book jacket design for *The Buried Life: A Nun's Journey* by Midge Turk. World Publishing Co. Designer: Alan Peckolick.

397
Gyo Fujikawa. *We love to have a heart-to-heart talk!* 1978. Watercolor, 7½ × 8″ (19.05 × 20.32 cm). Collection Gyo Fujikawa Square Board Book Line.

Text design can be quite complicated. The designer must choose a *typeface* and its size, a *display typeface* for such things as chapter titles and headings, perhaps a decorative numeral or initial letter. The size and shape of the page, the margins, and the space between various elements must be determined. If the book has illustrations, either line drawings or halftones, these and their captions must be integrated into the total design. All these elements work together to create unity.

Typefaces have developed considerably since Gutenberg invented movable type in the fifteenth century, and today the range of possible faces is extraordinary (Fig. 395). Standard book design makes use of only a dozen or so, with somewhat more flexibility in the display faces. This text is printed in a typeface called "Optima," with some of the principal headings in "Broadway."

Type design must be consistent with the overall design of the book and appropriate to its content. Closely related to the choice of a typeface is the question of *layout*. Design of the title page is crucial, for it usually provides the reader's first impression of the interior of the book. The layout of every page is likewise important. The arrangement of text and illustrations, titles and subtitles, and the spacing of lines within the text all play a part in the book's visual attractiveness.

The first thing one notices about a book is its "package"—the dust jacket or paper cover that encloses the book. The main purpose of exterior design is to attract the attention of the potential buyer and to make the book's contents seem interesting. In the highly competitive field of book merchandising, covers and jackets are planned to be as conspicuous as possible on the crowded shelves and display racks of bookstores.

The cover designer's primary task is to interpret the book's content in an effective manner. There are several possibilities. The designer may choose to use a literal or symbolic representation of the contents (Fig. 396), an abstract design that alludes to the contents, or a striking combination of type alone, with no imagery. Cover design is vital to a book's success, for if one is never stimulated to pick up the book, one may never discover the treasures it contains.

A special category of books are those designed for children, which usu-

396

397

ally feature colorful and fanciful illustrations (Fig. 397). The typical book for young children has a limited text and stresses the pictures as much as or more than the words. Since the book will be aimed at novice readers or those who do not read at all, the designer must strive for immediate visual impact to engage the young audience. All design considerations are planned around the illustrations, although the various elements—type, page size, margins, and so forth—must be joined in a unified whole.

Magazines and Periodicals

The magazine designer works with the same elements as does the book designer; these include type, illustrations, shapes, and spaces. There are, however, certain differences between the two media. For one thing, the magazine designer usually has much more control over the choice of illustrations and may be able to commission a photographer or illustrator for a particular article. Another difference between magazines and books is one of "tone." Magazine design tends to be more casual, more flamboyant, more colorful. The designer can follow styles and fashions closely without

398

399

Why McDonnell Douglas Is Going Dutch
The Instant Millionaires of Tyler, Texas
Sea-Land's Punishing Victory at Sea
$2.50
June 1, 1981
FORTUNE
COKE
STRIKES
BACK

398
Magazine illustration for *Body Language,* by Marilyn Mercer. *McCall's Magazine.* Designer: Carveth Kramer.

399
Cover for *Fortune Magazine.* 1981. Designer: Ronald N. Campbell. Publisher: Fortune Magazine.

400
"Peanuts" by Charles M. Schulz. © 1968 by United Feature Syndicate, Inc.

fear of obsolescence, because the magazine, unlike the book, will probably be thrown away in a few weeks.

A magazine by its very nature is meant to be read in odd moments and in spurts—in the dentist's office, under the hair dryer, or while dinner cooks. Thus, the layout will be designed in such a way that one's eye is caught and then moved along from place to place. Except for scholarly magazines and the like, the visual design should be striking enough to exist alone, so that one can scan the illustrations and ignore the text (Fig. 398).

The cover of a magazine must be even more attention-getting than that of a book (Fig. 399). As a rule, people decide quickly about which magazine they will buy—while rushing to catch a train or checking out at the supermarket, for example. The vast display of publications vying for attention makes the choice extremely difficult, so the designer must capture attention immediately with a striking cover.

Magazines rely heavily on illustrations as a design element. There is one realm of illustration, however, associated with magazines and newspapers, that exists in a class all by itself. That is the *cartoon,* a category encompassing the political satire cartoon, the humorous cartoon, and the comic strip. Many different styles of cartoon illustration exist, and there have been changing fashions over the years. Recently, one of the most popular styles has been the simple outline drawing, in which characterizations are created by the most basic means. The classic example of this type is "Peanuts" (Fig. 400).

400

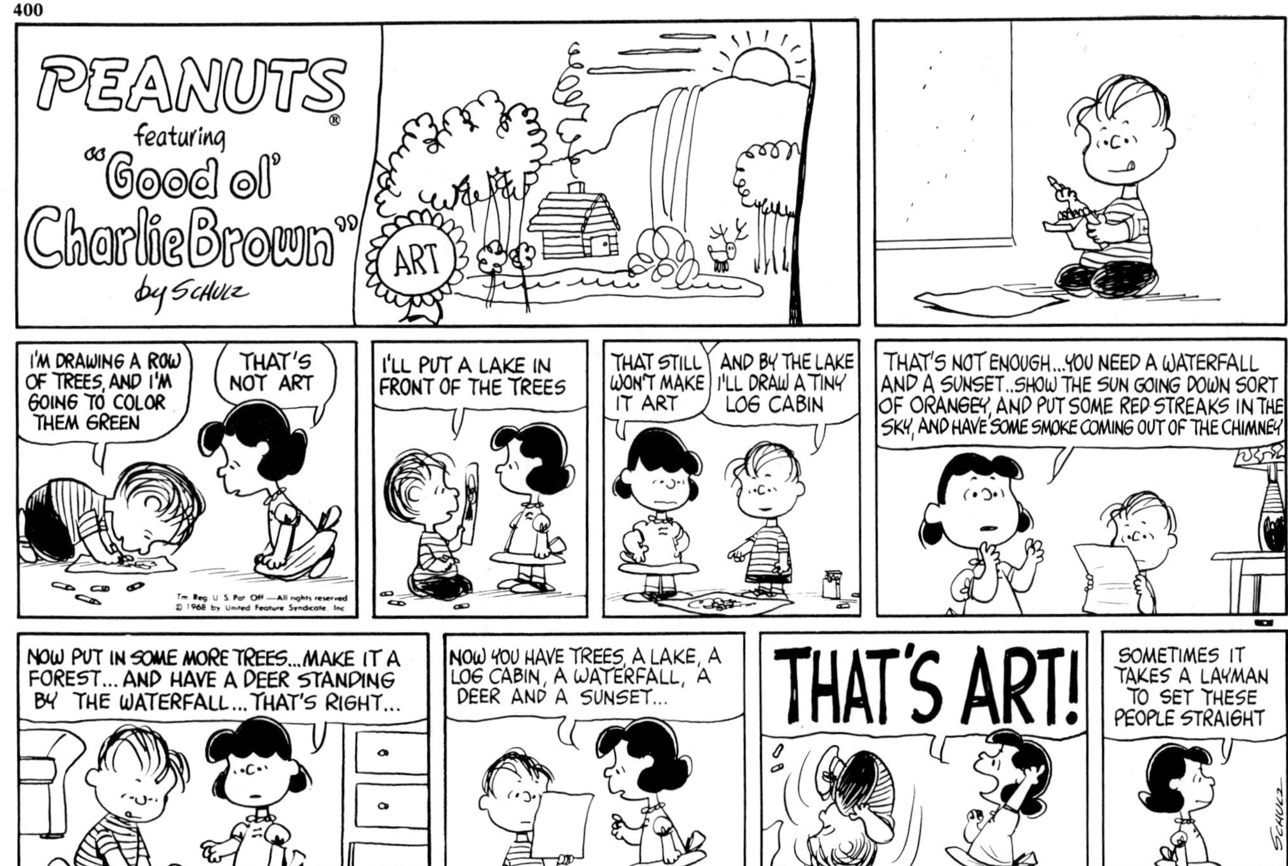

401

Record Jackets

The covers for record albums also attract the consumer's attention. Buying recorded music is usually a pleasure, and this enjoyment can be heightened by looking through a file of attractive albums. If a person does not have a specific selection or a certain artist in mind, the design of the jacket can influence the purchase. Although photography plays an important part in album design, it is interpretive photography, and many albums show stunning use of the photographic medium (Fig. 401). Others feature bold and colorful illustration. Often the album cover is a visual interpretation of the music involved and thus becomes a high form of evocative graphic design (Fig. 402).

Advertising

Advertising art has existed since about 3000 B.C., when the Sumerians employed pictures to advertise their wares. The elaborate wrought-iron signs still hanging over shops along many medieval streets in Europe were essentially an advertisement of the goods or services to be found within.

Advertising is related to production, for only when goods are plentiful is it necessary to seek buyers for them. The advertising industry, then, is a natural outgrowth of the Industrial Revolution with its mass production of all kinds of objects. The earliest known advertising agency opened its doors in England in 1812, and within a century and a half the advertising industry has grown into a giant multimillion-dollar business.

Until well into the twentieth century, foodstuffs and other goods were marketed in barrels, tubs, or sacks with no indication of the source of

401
Front and back album cover for recording of "Chicago." Designer: John Berg.

402
Record jacket for *Broadway Magic* for CBS Records. 1981. Photographer: Joseph Abeles Collection. Art Director: Karen Katz.

403
Logo for the Bell System, as it has appeared successively since 1889.

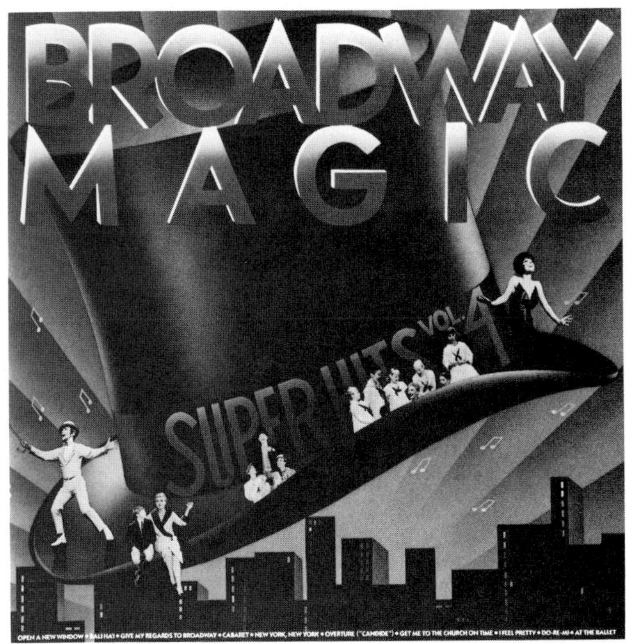

402

supply as far as the consumer was concerned. The trademark was developed as a kind of reward for products of excellent quality and a means by which the buyer could be assured of purchasing goods of similar quality in the future. Actually, the trademark became a stepping-stone for manufacturers developing their own businesses, for it quickly established their identities and provided them with an opportunity to extend their reputations. The logo (Figs. 322 and 323, p. 238) is a natural outgrowth of the trademark. Styles in trademarks change through the years, yet the identity remains constant (Fig. 403).

403

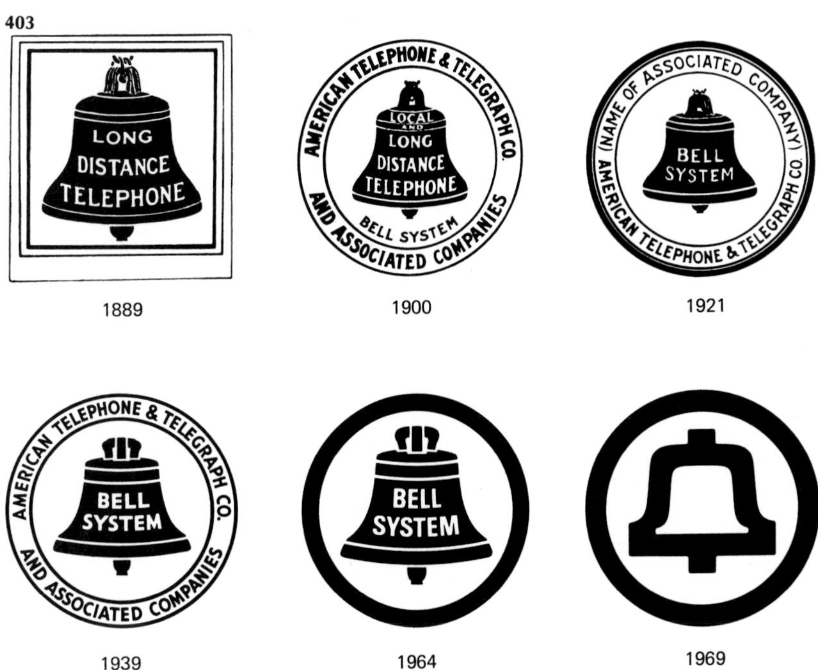

Most advertisements consist of two elements: the words or *copy* and the illustration. The role of the graphic designer is to arouse curiosity or interest to the point that a reader will stop to examine the copy. It is vital that the ad be addressed to specific people, to fill specific needs or interests, or to help achieve specific goals. The ad in Figure 404, telling of a series of educational programs on television, is directed to parents. The most compelling reason for spending money is the conviction that the object or service to be purchased is more necessary than the money itself. Even with money spent for the necessities of everyday living, the actual selection of varieties and brands provides wide scope for advertising.

Consumers engage in two kinds of spending: spending for *basic* necessities and *discretionary* spending, which concerns the purchase of items that make life more comfortable, satisfying, or attractive. To design an ad that will touch the vulnerable spot closest to the consumer's dreams requires an exploration of the motives to which those dreams are geared. There are many kinds of motives: the desire to create or build, to protect or conserve, to acquire property, to achieve power, to move up the social scale, or simply to be comfortable (Fig. 405).

The public is exposed daily to at least two *kinds of advertising:* direct and indirect. *Direct* advertising is used when the seller expects immediate returns. Department stores, supermarkets, and other retail outlets take this approach, especially when they have special sales. *Indirect* advertising, on the other hand, is effective for building a reputation and establishing the desirability of a product or service, with an emphasis on future as well as immediate results. A subcategory of indirect advertising is the *institutional ad,* which has as its aim the creation of goodwill for a particular firm or organization. A subtle form of institutional advertising is the sponsorship of some artistic endeavor—drama, art, or music, for example—along with a quiet mention of the company's participation (Fig. 406).

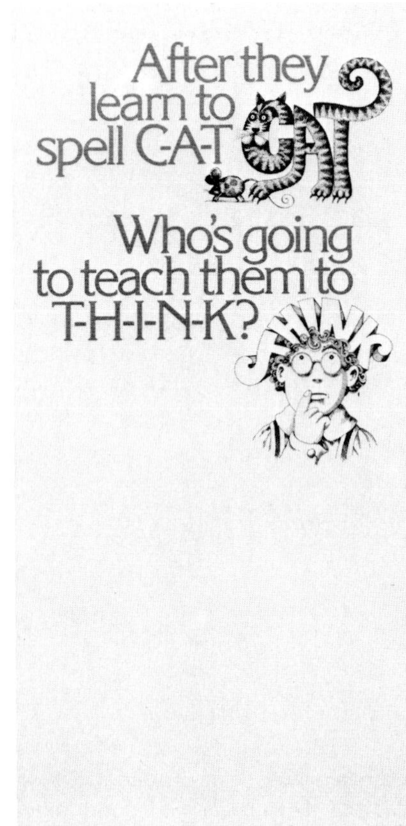

404

405

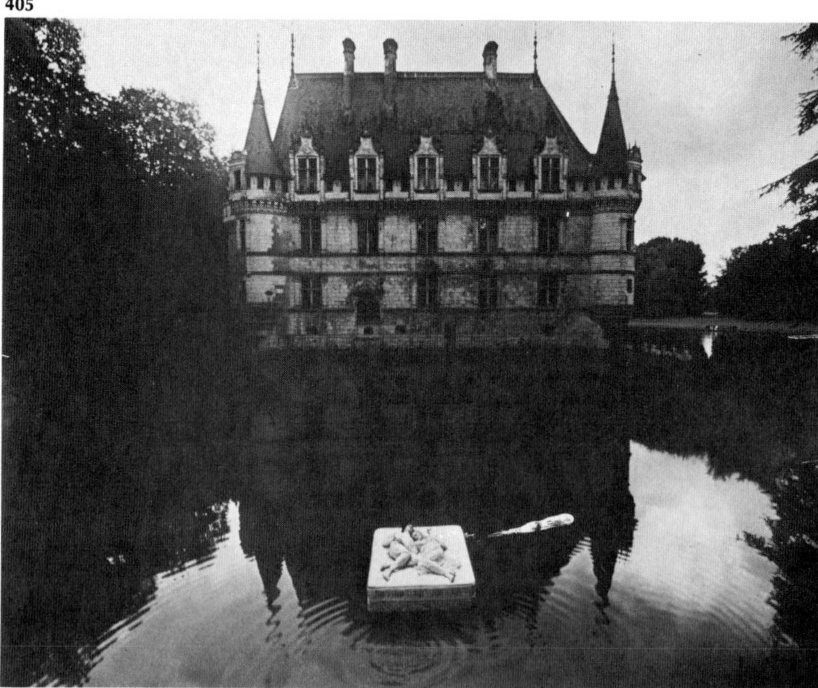

404
Brochure cover design for Gene London's Children's Broadcasts on CBS.
Designers: Lou Dorfsman and Ira Teichberg. Artist: John Alcorn. For CBS Television Stations Division.

405
Ad for Beautyrest mattress. Designers: Matt Basile and Jerry Sandler.

406
Ivan Chermayeff (Chermayeff & Geismar Associates). *Crime and Punishment,* poster for *Masterpiece Theatre.* 1981. Ink and chalk on paper, 22 × 36" (55.8 × 91.4 cm). Mobil Oil Corporation Collection.

When the designer is presented with a product or service to be advertised, the process of decision making begins. With the type of consumer in mind, one must first of all determine the kind of approach most likely to be effective. In general, there are two broad categories of approach: factual and imaginative.

The *factual* approach usually proves best in reaching the no-nonsense individual or in promoting a product with a serious mission. Visual design focuses on a realistic representation of the product, and this can be done in many ways. For example, a product can be depicted alone, in a decorative setting, in actual use, or in combination with the results it is supposed to yield.

The *imaginative* approach may feature something totally unrelated to the product, with the ad serving mainly as an attention-getting device to introduce the product's name. It can also rely on imagination to convey that the purchase of a certain product will bring rich rewards in social satisfaction and prestige.

406

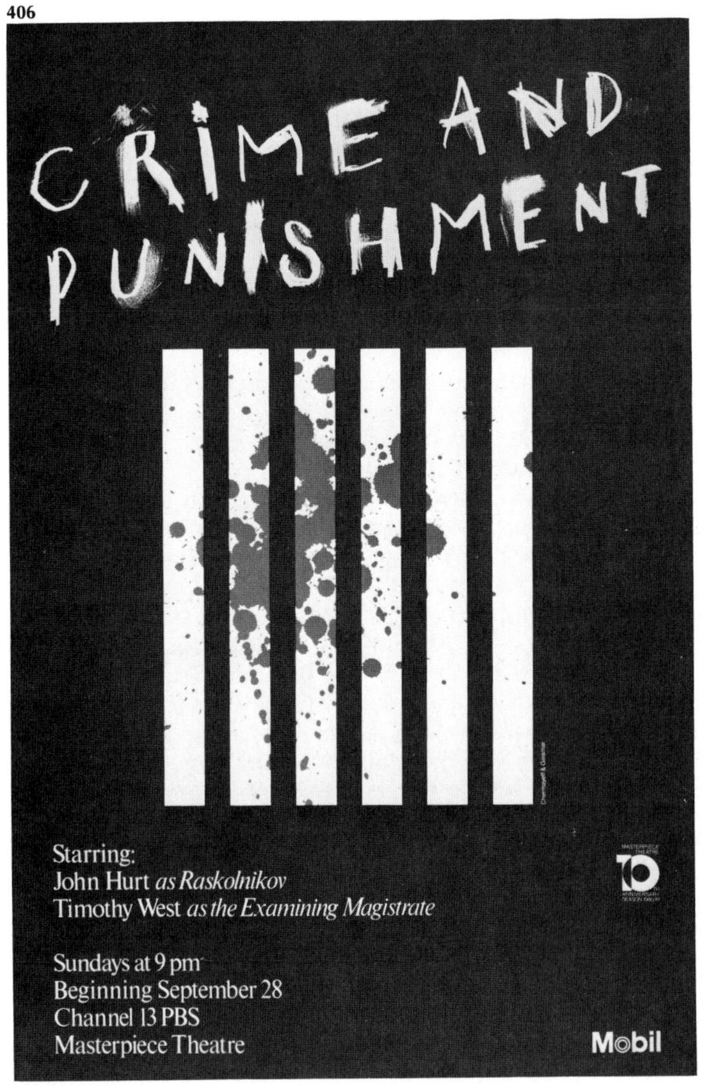

In either instance, the advertisement begins with a layout, which means the total design of the ad, including illustrations, blocks of type, display type, white areas, the entire composition—in other words, texture, shape, value, space, and balance. Many ads depend on a provocative headline in large, bold type to capture attention. Color may be important to the success of an ad, although its use is not always possible because of the limitations of advertising budgets.

The principles of design apply to every aspect of design graphics. Type and illustrations must be in proportion to one another, and colors and shapes should be arranged for a sense of total balance. Variety in type size and style as well as in visual textures adds to the overall effect. Unity is, of course, of the utmost importance in focusing the viewer's attention on the primary object, the product advertised.

Newpapers and magazines, along with television, carry the greatest burden in presenting advertised products to the consumer, but sometimes other outlets may be more suitable for a particular situation. Outdoor advertising is a challenge to the designer, for the viewer is on the move and frequently in a hurry, so the idea must be concise and presented clearly to achieve an impact.

Buses, trains, and terminals sell advertising space for the placement of posters. The poster requires a design that will attract immediate attention, with clear lettering and usually with bright colors or some appealing image (Fig. 407). Unlike most other types of advertisements, posters may be collected by individuals to decorate their homes.

The television commercial has the potential of reaching eleven million homes in the United States during the average minute of evening programming. Since television is most effective in *showing* what is to be sold, the designer bears most of the responsibility for the advertising. All the advantages of association and symbolism used in magazine advertising are adapted even more readily to television, with the bonuses of dramatization, action, music, and characterization. Besides being familiar with the principles of graphic design, the television designer must have some knowledge of film techniques. A well-conceived commercial may be more entertaining than the programs it supports.

Designing an effective advertisement is a matter of ideas, and finding an effective idea in a highly competitive market can be a rigorous matter. Frequently, in the effort to attract attention, an advertiser makes claims beyond the capabilities of the product. Sometimes a claim is deliberately so extravagant that most people do not take it seriously, yet with the millions of different personalities to whom it will be exposed, this approach can be risky. Humor is an asset in advertising, but ridiculous claims invite misinterpretation by those who cannot see the humor. In designing advertising, the artist must be guided by the primary responsibility of integrity. Only by honest representation of the product can the designer protect the prospective consumer and sustain the reputation of the product.

407
Poster for New York's Metropolitan Transportation Authority. New York Metropolitan Transportation Authority; Howard York & Associates; and Michael Bosniak, MTA.

408
Package design for Neo-Art, Inc. 1981. Designer: Zengo Yoshida. Artist: Sen Maruyama. Zenn Graphic Design, San Francisco.

Packaging

The widespread practice of self-service shopping makes package design as important as advertising. A customer faced with a shelf of similar products tends to select the one whose package seems most attractive. The design of a package performs several functions. First, it helps to sell the merchandise by identifying it and distinguishing it from competing articles. It also facilitates a better display, making it easier for the merchant to put the article before the public. Packaging may also improve the appearance of the merchandise and help to keep it clean.

The packaging designer must keep several factors in mind in creating a new design. A successful package must above all serve the needs of the product, protecting the contents while at the same time being easy to handle. A group of packages should stack easily with no loss of space, so that a merchant will be predisposed to give them visible display.

From an advertising point of view, the package must immediately attract the customer's attention. The best way to start a new design is to gather together all the competing products and analyze their packaging. This will make clear the similarities, the weaknesses, and the good qualities to be surpassed. A color not previously used may attract attention; a totally new concept can make a product stand out.

Emphasis is vital to package design. The name of the product must be clear, preferably in print that contrasts with its background. Shapes and illustrations on the package should relate to the contents in some way (Fig. 408). For example, in the packaging of household products, the stress is usually on health and cleanliness, whereas containers for foodstuffs may emphasize the "natural" origins of the food.

A practical consideration in package design is ease of opening. Too many designers invent fancy openings that turn out to be more trouble than the conventional ones.

407

408

One of the most fascinating and challenging assignments for the graphic designer is the task of designing a "corporate image" (Fig. 409). This involves creating a visual impression that carries through every aspect of a company's business, with integrated designs for packaging, shipping materials, advertising, labels, stationery, brochures, warranties, and even the decor of the corporate headquarters. The designer who takes such an assignment knows that the entire consumer market—perhaps millions of people—will learn to associate the company with that particular design. Such a responsibility can be a designer's dream come true, for in a single design lies total control of the visual aspects of a company's operation.

We have seen how the elements and principles of design operate in every aspect of graphic design, with particular stress on their use to attract attention through variety and emphasis. Perhaps the most pertinent point to be made here is the fact that the same elements and principles that the master artists have used through the centuries to create works for us to enjoy quietly at our leisure become dynamic forces in the highly competitive world of twentieth-century commerce.

409

409
Corporate identity and packaging program designed for Tom's Natural Soap by A. R. Williams & Associates, South Lynnfield, MA. The total design concept includes shipping cartons and letterhead (designer: Rod Williams); a poster (designer: Rod Williams, Frederick Pickel, and John Evans); and packaging (designers: Rod Williams, Fred Ribeck, Fred Pickel, and John Evans).

20 Photography

As design, photography is unique in requiring little manual dexterity. Until well into the twentieth century, it was considered simply a means of recording events, but in recent decades it has become a technique used in painting, printmaking, and sculpture. More important, it has taken its place as a powerful yet sensitive medium of expression.

More than any other art form, photography is allied to science and technology, a relationship that makes it a particularly appropriate medium for the twentieth century. The *art* of photography is a collaboration between the artist and some highly sensitive mechanical equipment, the most important of which is the camera.

The Camera

In simplest form, the camera is a light-tight box with an opening at one end to admit light and a receptive ground at the other to take the image. The diagram in Figure 410 shows the essential features of all cameras. Light enters the camera through the *aperture*. The amount of light entering can be controlled by the *diaphragm,* which regulates the size of the aperture, and by the *shutter,* which determines the amount of time during which light may enter. A *lens* gathers and refracts the light, throwing it onto the light-sensitive field at the back of the camera, the film.

Differences in cameras result mainly from the quality of their lenses and from the distance between the lens and the film (the *focal length*). The most sophisticated equipment is that which allows the photographer maximum control in distance, shutter speed, and diaphragm openings. Special lenses permit photographs of very broad vistas (*wide-angle* lenses), of subjects that are very far away (*telephoto* lenses) or very close to the camera.

After a photograph has been exposed, the film is removed from the camera, developed, and, except for transparencies, printed on special paper. It is in these steps that recent developments have given the photographer unprecedented latitude for creation.

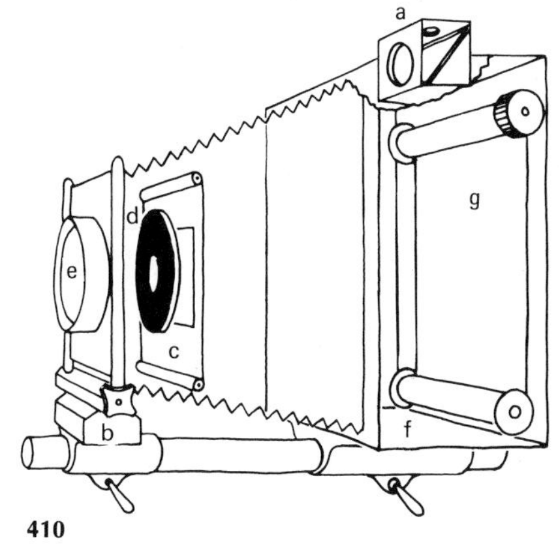

410

Attributes of a Photograph

Like paintings and prints, photographs have the attributes of *subject, form,* and *content*. Historically, subject was the photograph's reason for being, since it was presumed to capture things, places, and people with more accuracy than any painting or drawing. We know now that this is not necessarily true. Variations in setting and use of different lenses can cause distortion, and a photograph quickly snapped can catch a person in an uncharacteristic gesture or expression. As an art form, photography is more concerned with capturing essence or mood, in other words, *content*.

Contemporary photographers also find challenge in new *forms* made possible by manipulation of light and angle. A photograph can become a total abstraction, dissolving into interesting design (Fig. 411). It can be-

410
Diagram of the essential parts of a camera: *a* viewfinder; *b* focusing system; *c* shutter; *d* aperture with diaphragm; *e* lens; *f* light-tight box; *g* film.

411
Enrico Ferorelli. *The Alps.*

411

412

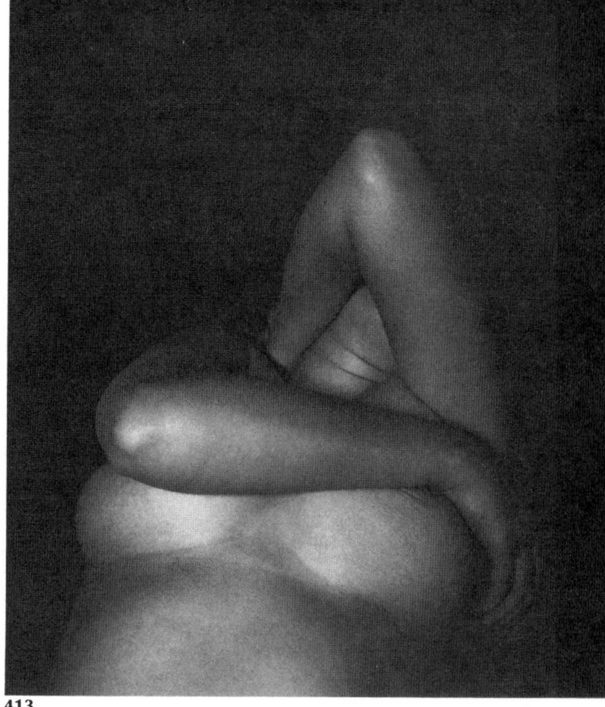

413

412
Art Kane. *Greeting*. For Eastern Airlines.

413
Harry M. Callahan. *Eleanor*. 1948. Photograph. Courtesy the artist.

414
John L. Huszar. *Double Portrait, Georgia O'Keeffe and Ansel Adams*. 1980. Taken during the filming of a documentary on Adams.

415
Roman Vishniac. The hormone thyrotrophin (thyrotrophic hormone TTH) from the thyroid. Magnification 18000 ×.

come an abstraction in another way, by making a general statement of content far beyond the contours of a specific model. A photograph of a child, for instance, may be a portrait of a particular child, but it may also be a symbol of childhood, a commentary on impishness or innocence, a contrast in light and shadow, a study of form, or possibly all of these at once. By making the subject slightly out of focus, Bert Stern has translated, through the depiction of a specific mother and her baby, the mystical essence of motherhood (Pl. 30, p. 313).

The entire field of news photography whirls around *people* and what happens to them, and volumes have been filled with the results, some of them historic documents, some masterpieces of character study, some epics of dramatic action. For the designer with camera in hand, the human form and face offer every possible combination of elements and principles. The beauty of human relationships can be captured in a photograph more poignantly than in the most eloquent words (Fig. 412).

Harry Callahan is one of several photographers who have seen in their wives the continual unfolding of the mysteries of woman, and have documented them in hundreds of studies. For Callahan, his wife Eleanor becomes the symbol of womanhood, of the essential life force, of fertility and richness. She is the center of his life, and he makes her the center of the world, the standard against which all other things are measured and all

414

415

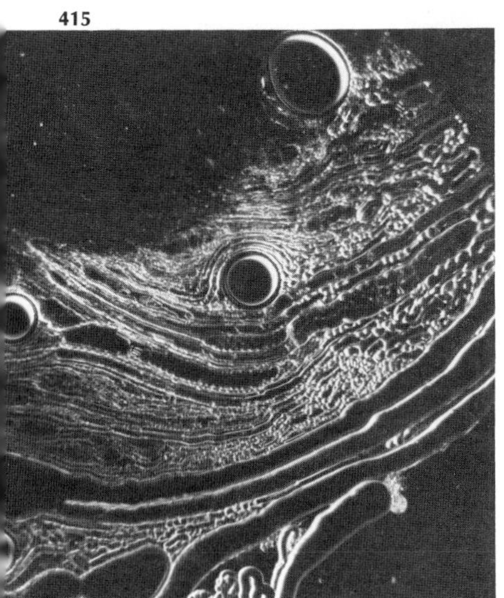

forces react. In Figure 413 he has composed her into a traditional triangular design with angles and curves in opposition, and a lively play of highlights against a dark background.

The human body lends itself to tremendously diverse designs, yet the ultimate expression of human life remains the character study of an individual. In Figure 414 we see two people who have had long creative careers: Ansel Adams, an eminent photographer of nature and landscape, and painter Georgia O'Keeffe (see Pl. 1, p. 21), whose husband, photographer Alfred Stieglitz, is credited with making photography into an artistic medium. No photographic study could be more eloquent than this portrait of two friends, each with a lifetime of artistic experience depicted in a face. Even with such content, however, the photographer took care to compose an excellent design. O'Keeffe's dark coat is repeated in Adams' glasses and the shadows in his shirt, while his own light clothing is balanced by her hair and hands. A background whose middle value plays through the shadows in the faces gives unity to the extremes of light and dark.

Photographing *nature* can mean capturing the Grand Canyon at sunrise or exploring the wonders beneath the sea. It can also mean investigating what goes on under a microscope. In Figure 415 the photographer has found tremendous variety in shape and texture in the thyrotrophic hormone TTH. Intense magnification opens up an entire world of beautiful designs, as David Cavagnaro and his wife Maggie discovered during three years of studying the miracles of the California grasslands, watching the journeys of insects through the changing seasons, and observing the effects of weather on seeds and grasses (Fig. 416). They saw in this small world the biological and philosophical secrets of the universe.

Many artists find remarkable design in the most commonplace natural subjects, using them to evoke worlds of dream and memory (Fig. 417). The changing lights as well as the marvelous textures, lines, and rhythms of the natural world present the perceptive photographer with a limitless supply of subject matter for personal interpretation.

Painters often choose *still life* subjects as a means of showing skill at rendering textures and lighting effects. Philip Molten found such a photographic opportunity in a piece of abandoned machinery, with its interplay of curves and straight lines. The particular moment presented him with a vibrant interaction of light and shadow, not only in the subject itself, but also in the strong verticals of the tree trunks in the background (Fig. 418).

416

416
David Cavagnaro. 1970. Photograph. Dew-Covered Dry Grasses.

417
Alen MacWeeney. *Wicklow Trees.* Ireland, 1965–1966.

418
Philip L. Molten. *Cast-Off Machinery,* Wawona, CA. 1971.

417

418

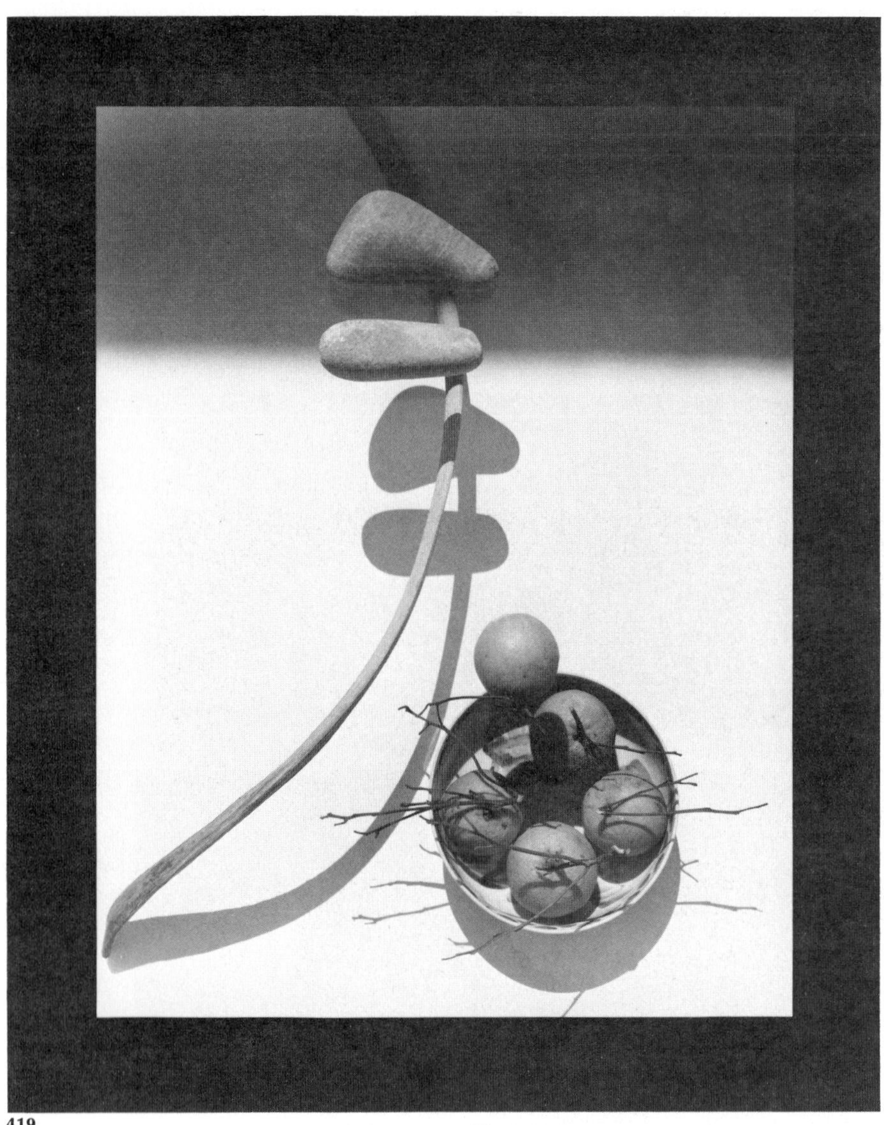
419

419
Laurence Bach. *Still Life #1.* 1980. Private collection and the Philadelphia Museum of Art.
420
Ron Tarver. *The Fireman.* 1981.
421
Yale Joel. *Illusion of Speed.* 1965. Photograph taken with panning camera.

The French expression for still life is *nature morte,* literally "dead nature." This sums up the greatest challenge to the still-life photographer, the need to imbue inert objects with an energy that gives them interest. Some photographers do this with lighting, giving uncharacteristic weight or gentleness to familiar articles. Laurence Bach arranges objects on a sheet of glass or suspends them in midair, to achieve shadows, reflections, and the illusion of floating in space. Many of his objects are rocks, pottery shards, or debris picked up on the Greek island where he spends his summers. During gray city winters he uses studio lights to recapture the sunstruck reality of his summer dreams (Fig. 419).

Much news photography inevitably conveys *motion,* since it is taken in the thick of action (Fig. 420). In other cases, the feeling of action is contrived. In Figure 421 the model was motionless, but the camera was rotated on a tripod during the exposure. Once again the old adage that the camera never lies has moved into the realm of legend.

420

421

422

Even more dramatic proof can be seen in the photograph of New York in Figure 422. This image was recorded by a Zoomar camera, which registers a complete 360-degree view in one exposure. The approaches to the Brooklyn Bridge in this image swoop and bend like dancers moving to an unheard tune. The unique combination of size, shape, and image that characterizes the *form* of the work also provides the fantasy of its *content.*

The difference between a photographic record and a photographic work of art lies in the affinity that grows between the photographer and the subject, be the subject a person or a place. Sometimes a photographer produces a body of exceptional work about one special place in the world simply because there is a *resonance* there, a vital force that awakens memories, dreams, associations, and the full force of artistic creativity. In such cases, the resonance becomes the content of the work. This quality also stimulates the photographer to see the textures, rhythms, emphasis, shapes, and balance that he combines in his compositions.

Eugène Atget was a commercial photographer, who dedicated himself to creating a body of photographs that would describe the authentic character of French culture in all its aspects. Into the nearly ten thousand photographs in his collection, he poured his love and appreciation, allowing his perceptions to change and grow throughout a lifetime. Typically expressive is the photograph of a chapel shown in Figure 423. The chapel could have been photographed from any angle, the most obvious of which would have been one showing the front door. Instead, Atget saw in the gnarled tree at the rear a dramatic force whose writhing forms against the sky are reminiscent of a crucifix. By positioning his camera for ultimate impact, the photographer infused his work with texture, variety, and mass, and with content far beyond the forms of the image.

423

422
The Brooklyn Bridge. Photograph taken with the Zoomar 360 Panoramic camera.

423
Eugène Atget. *Route Amiens.*

Plate 30
Bert Stern.
Allegra Kent with Daughter Trista.
1961. Photograph.
Collection of the artist.

Plate 31
Scene from the Broadway musical *Dream Girls.*
1981. Lighting designer: Tharon Musser.

Plate 32
Yves St. Laurent costume mixes geranium red pants with fuschia tunic, raspberry hat, lime green and grape touches at the neckline and a coat of midnight blue.

Plate 33
Living room of guest house of Pat Montandon.
Michael Taylor, designer. Photograph by Russell McMasters.

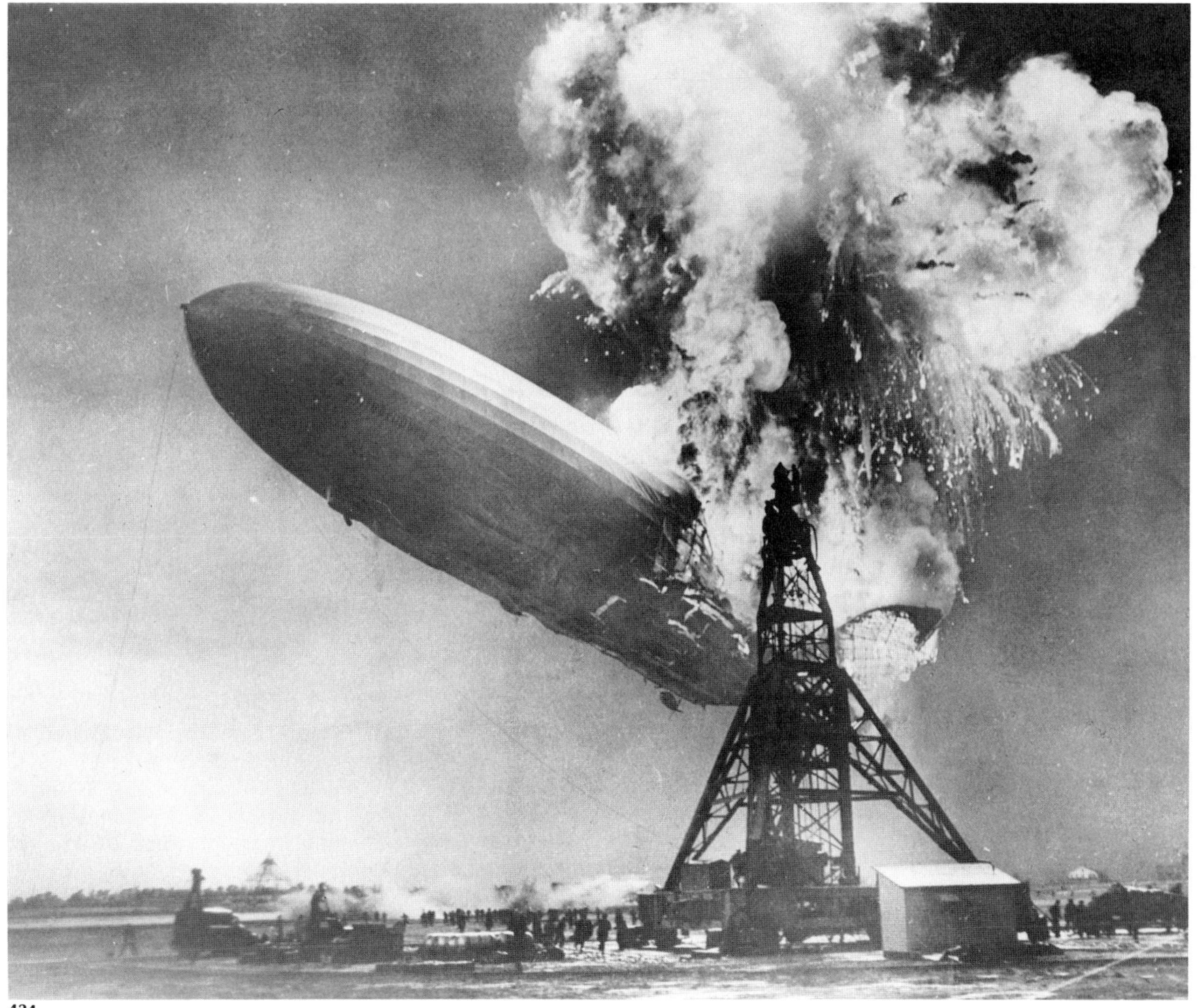

424

Purposes of Photography

Every scientific or adventurous expedition is *recorded* by its own photographer. It is because of the photographer that the world sees the mountaineer erecting a flag on top of Mount Everest, or shares in the wonder of wild animals in Africa. History books and museums are enriched by photographs of historic personages, and every American president has a personal photographer on his staff. We know of earthshaking events through the work of the news photographer. In recording such sights as the one in Figure 424, the photographer takes a place as a chronicler of history, a producer of documentary evidence.

As we saw in Chapter 19, the role of photography in advertising is to *stimulate* interest. Proceeding on the theory that to see a thing is to want it, advertisers use photographs lavishly in magazines, newspapers, and mail-

424
Sam Shere. *Explosion of the Hindenberg,* Lakehurst, NJ. 1937.

425

426

order catalogs, as well as on posters and billboards. The issue becomes one of who can produce the most effective photograph of the product, whether it is a jar of peanut butter or a mink coat. An ingenious presentation, a unique setting, effective lighting, a humorous twist—any of these could be the critical element that would influence people to buy. Certainly photography is the single most important factor in the advertising of the travel and airlines industries (Fig. 425).

Photographs are the most obvious visual aid in *clarifying* material presented in articles and books. For generations, textbooks were dull affairs consisting of printed words and diagrams. Then someone conceived the idea of making the text come to life with photographs. History books printed color photographs of monuments and sites of battles, even including reproductions of works of art representative of a given period. In this way, the student became aware that history was more than an assortment of dates and battles, that it included people and their creative efforts as well. In books on science, theories and experiments are now punctuated with attractive pertinent photographs, and books on math and languages find visual ways of expanding a field and its appeal. Needless to say, a book on visual arts would be ineffectual without illustrations. We offer this book as an example of the importance of photographic accompaniment.

Photographs can *evoke* moods, memories, and humor. They can also evoke a sense of glamor, an elusive quality that perhaps cannot be captured in any other way. The photographer of royalty must present to the public characters that will command respect, as well as the image of a world fantasized by the average person. Such a world was the Hollywood of the thirties, wherein stars were made into gods and goddesses and people flocked to the theater to be lifted from the drabness of a post-Depression world. George Hurrell was the master of this magic, taking hundreds

425
Bert Glynn. *New Zealand.* For Pan American Airways. 1971. Poster design: Ivan Chermayeff and William Sontag.

426
George Hurrell. *Rita Hayworth.* c. 1940.

427
Heribert Brehm. *Sewing Machine* (*Half series*). 1980.

427

of photographs at a single setting, employing dramatic lighting and skillful retouching with dazzling results (Fig. 426).

We have seen how photographs *express* the photographer's feelings about a place or person, but they can also be used to express ingenuity. Through photography West Germany's Heribert Brehm has found a unique way of expressing his views on women. He states: "In them I seek the obscure, the strange, the bewitched. In my photographs nothing is real and all is fantasy. I am a fantastic photographer"[1] (Fig. 427).

Light as the Designer

Just as there is no color without light, so there can be no photograph without it. The effects of light go far beyond the exposure of the film, however, and every photographer with a consciousness of design finds light a valuable ally. Light delineates tactile texture and produces visual texture, accenting, highlighting, and silhouetting as the artist desires. It is lighting that creates shape and value, as in the Atget chapel in Figure 423, in which the tiny stone cross is bathed in light in contrast to the monumental forms of the ancient tree. It is light again that makes possible the shadow shapes so important to the Bach still life in Figure 419.

[1] David Markus, "Flash! Brehm's Better Halves," *American Photographer,* September 1981, p. 54.

428

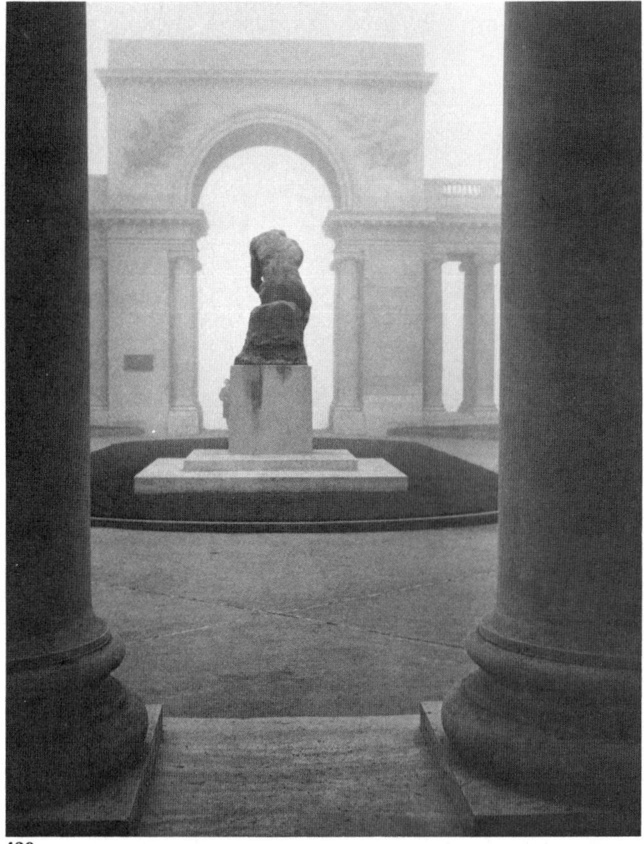

429

428
Paul Caponigro. *Canyon de Chelly, Arizona.* 1970.

429
Philip L. Molten. *California Palace of the Legion of Honor,* San Francisco. 1960.

430
J. Seeley. *Skytrip #3.* 1979. Photoscreen print, 22½ × 30" (57.2 × 76.2 cm). Courtesy Diane Barton Collection.

Light was an influential partner in the creation of the photograph in Figure 428, of a subject that has been photographed thousands of times. It required the eye of a designer to see the possibilities of dark shadow over brilliant stone, of clumps of dark pinon against horizontally striated cliffs. The focus is on the manmade buildings, but the eye is led dramatically to them by the ascending and descending dark shapes. Nature is monumental and enduring, and man's works are small and transitory: this is the content of the work, eloquently expressed by the eye and hand of an artist who knew the power of designing with light.

Special Effects

The photographer sometimes uses special effects in order to create a mood, an abstraction, or a distortion. Such effects can be given by special filters, an unusual angle, contrived lighting, or simply the grasping of a moment when unusual natural conditions prevail. The photograph in Figure 429 falls in the last category. Here a portion of the California Palace of the Legion of Honor is bathed in fog. A bronze cast of Rodin's statue *The Thinker* sits brooding as though on the brink of the world, an arch leading into nothingness just beyond him. We view him between two giant columns with the uneasy feeling that if we step through into the court, we, too, may be led to the brink. The view of the Brooklyn Bridge in Figure 422 presents another example of a special effect, this time maneuvered by the use of special equipment. As technical knowledge has expanded, the scope of the camera—and the photographer—has reached new horizons.

Special Techniques

As opposed to effects made possible by the use of regular photographic equipment, special techniques are ways in which contemporary artists combine photographic processes with other forms of art. We noted in Chapter 18 the combination of photographic images and printmaking techniques. Many artists combine such images with paintings in a kind of collage; others use them on Styrofoam figures to take photography into the realm of three dimensions. One of the most individual styles is the one in which J. Seeley combines photography with the materials of graphic design (Fig. 430). All of Seeley's images begin as photographs made with conventional camera and film. They are then transferred to continuous tone film, where everything is black and white, and the total result is built up gradually, by tearing up parts of images, discarding others, substituting, and finally rephotographing with screens, patterns, and masks. The results are eerie images, the product of an artist's intuition, brought to life by experimentation.

430

Film and Video

Any consideration of photography as a design medium must take into account the vast potential of motion picture film and video.

The motion picture began as a substitute for theater, bringing dramatic productions to thousands of people who would never see the professional stage. It soon became obvious, however, that film had certain distinct advantages over live theater, at least from the standpoint of production. Film could be shot anywhere in the world with evocative views to set the mood and a sound track to provide appropriate musical background. The rapport between actors and audience was lost, of course, and the final result, which blended months of work and diverse shots into a unified whole that was shown smoothly and without interruption, was in actuality more closely related to the novel than to the stage drama. In the end, the film became an entity in itself, in which every element and principle of design could contribute, from texture to emphasis, not only in the settings and the photography but in the direction of the action. Film festivals set high standards, so that the performance of the actors became only one aspect in a many-faceted effort.

With television, film could be viewed in the comfort of one's home, allowing free movement and activity among the audience, and a totally informal approach. Since the invention of video, laser beams or electronic devices transmit images from the television set to tapes or discs that can be seen at the viewer's convenience, in full color on the television screen. A video recorder can even capture material from one television channel while the viewer watches a different one.

Both film and video have long moved beyond the area of dramatic production. The educational potential was recognized early and has been developed, particularly by public television stations, which present a wide range of documentary films in all fields of knowledge. News broadcasts are taken for granted as viewers cease to marvel at the miracle that unites people all over the world in shock, anguish, or rejoicing as they witness events taking place thousands of miles away.

Probably the highest artistry is achieved in cultural productions, works of art in themselves, transmitted to the home screen through the skill of the photographer. The bonus of intermission interviews with performing artists, with casual background shots and telling closeups, brings the world of concert and theater into a personal relationship with the viewer. Analyzing the broadcast of a symphony concert could become a dissertation on design. The closeups of hands performing on various instruments, the character studies of individual players, the textural shots of the total orchestra superimposed over the dramatic focal point of the performing conductor—all of these provide a montage of the elements and principles of design. Complementing the artistic qualities of the music are the visual rhythms of violin bows moving in unison; the balance and proportion of long-range shots and closeups of individual performers; character shots of the conductor's face, expressing absorption in the composition; the contrasting values of light faces and metal instruments against dark clothing; the shapes of instruments; and the space swirling around the performers in the immense hall. Here is artistry at its finest, displayed in consummate musical skill and, less obvious but equally important to a viewing audience, in the sensitivity of a staff of skilled photographers and designers.

21 The Performing Arts

The performing arts are the arts associated with acting and music: theater, film, television, dance, opera, and all types of musical expression. The people most prominent in such productions—those who speak the words and interpret the movements or the music—often are referred to as artists. The *visual* artists involved may never appear before an audience, yet, as we indicated in the previous chapter, their roles are crucial to any production. It is their function to provide the setting, the costumes, the lighting, and the photographic interpretations that make the performance a successful artistic as well as dramatic presentation.

Set Design

Some types of performance require no setting. The melodic lines of a string quartet could be appreciated just as well on a bare stage, in an empty loft, or in a meadow (Fig. 431). The art of mime traditionally is practiced on an empty stage with no props, with the performer made up in whiteface (Fig. 432). Since the effect of mime depends largely upon the viewer's imagination and since meaning derives solely from the mime's postures and facial expressions, visual clues could be distracting.

431

432

431
A string quartet practicing in a meadow.

432
The mime Marcel Marceau in "Bip as a Street Musician."

433

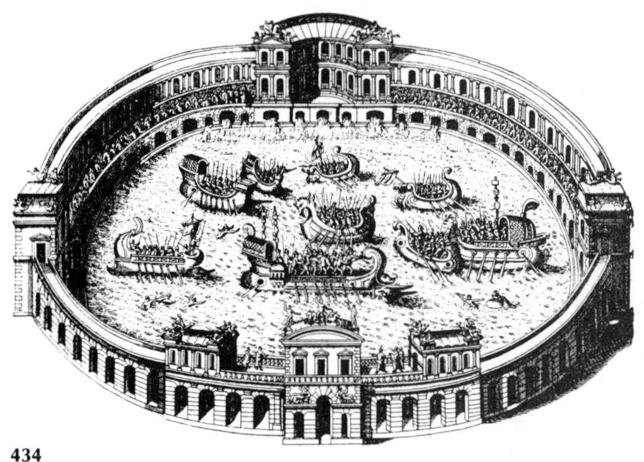
434

433
The theater at Epidaurus staging its festival of classical Greek drama.

434
A whimsical 19th-century reconstruction of a staged sea battle in the Roman Colosseum. Courtesy The New York Public Library, Astor, Lenox, and Tilden Foundations.

435
Sleigh scene from "The Nutcracker" as staged at Lincoln Center, NY. © 1982 by Jill Krementz.

436
Diagram of a stage set on a parallel axis.

437
Diagram of a raked stage set.

In Shakespeare's time sets were simple, even for his productions. Two doors at the rear of the stage allowed for exits and entrances, and there was a screened area, called the "discovery area," in which people could be discovered or revealed for dramatic effect. A trapdoor in the stage allowed for the appearance of ghosts and similar phenomena. Costumes were elaborate versions of contemporary dress, not adaptations from the period in which the play was set. Furthermore, young boys played all the female roles since it was unseemly for women to appear on stage.

All modern theater derives from the classic Greek theater, yet it, too, was simple in production. Plays were performed outdoors in an open amphitheater, with no real sets (Fig. 433). The Romans, on the other hand, produced theatrical spectacles, flooding the Colosseum to stage realistic sea battles (Fig. 434).

Twentieth-century theater embraces both extremes with many variations in between. There are two requirements for an effective set. First, it must be expressive of the production—its spirit, mood, historical period, locale, social stratum, and season. Second, it must be practical and meet

435

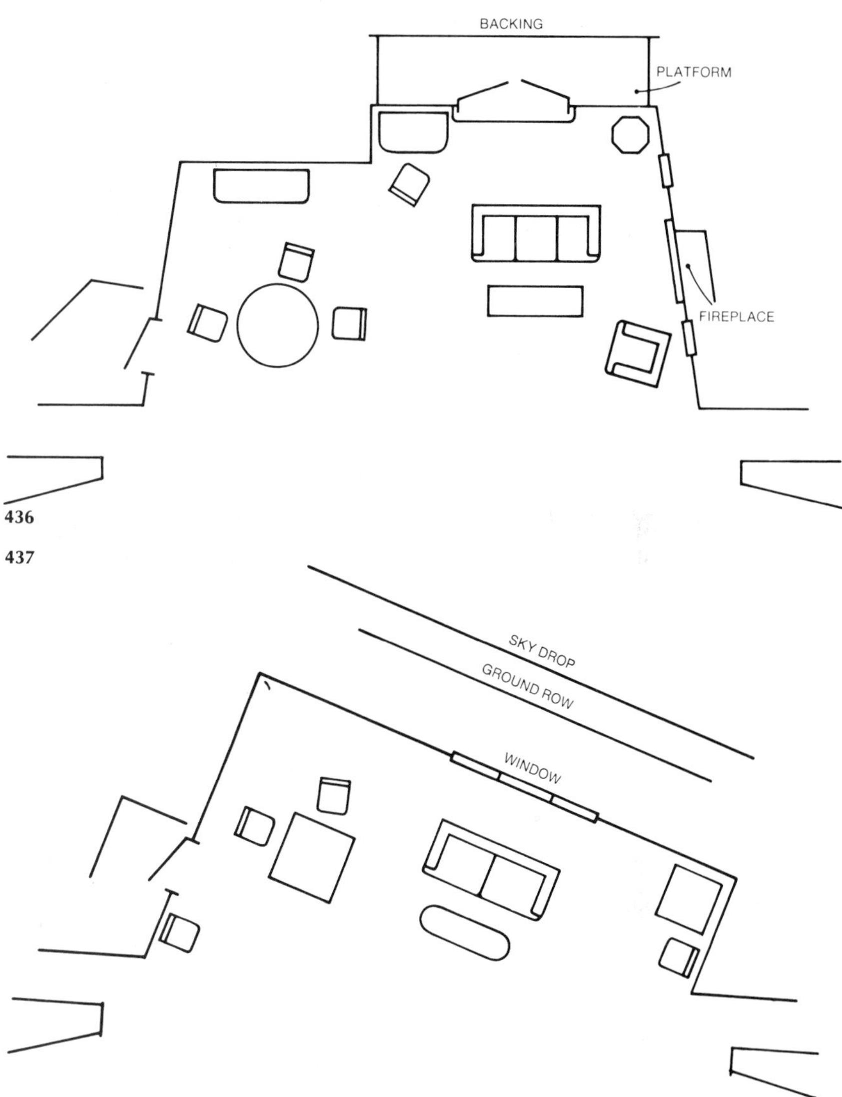

436

437

the needs of the action. Doors must be wide enough to permit the passage of players in costume, banisters must be strong enough to be leapt over or slid down, balconies must support whatever action takes place upon them. Special effects may have to include making a personage fly through the air as in *Peter Pan,* a swan glide across the stage as in *Lohengrin,* or a sleigh soar upward as in *The Nutcracker* (Fig. 435). All of these considerations must be met in addition to producing a set that will lend itself to rapid construction, be easy to shift and store, and stand up under continued use.

The elements and principles of design come into play with the first decisions of the director and the designer. If the play is formal, the set will be *conventional,* that is, on an axis parallel to the footlights (Fig. 436). Such a layout would be most appropriate to classical Greek drama, Shaw, Ibsen, and O'Neill, for example. A *raked* set offers the informality suitable to modern comedy, fantasy, and domestic drama; it also limits the space for action (Fig. 437).

438

438
Macbeth by William Shakespeare. Produced by Yellow Springs Area Theatre, Ohio, directed by Paul Treichler.

439
The Importance of Being Earnest by Oscar Wilde. Produced by Yale University Theatre, directed by Frank McMullan, sets by John Ezell, costumes by Barbara Douglas. Yale School of Drama, New Haven, CT.

440
Waiting for Godot by Samuel Beckett. Produced by Virginia Museum Theatre, Richmond, directed by Robert S. Telford, sets by William J. Ryan, costumes by Anthony Eikenbary.

Once *orientation* is established, the *architecture* must be designed. Plays may take place in one room, in which case the number and position of doors are crucial to the smooth flow of action. Opera sets, on the other hand, may have sweeping staircases, elaborate exterior architecture with balconies and towers, or mountains on which raging storms take place. Shakespearean productions have been presented in every conceivable architectural setting, ranging from medieval castles to outdoor amphitheaters in which scenes are changed by switching lighting from one level of lawn to another. One of the most effective sets for *Macbeth* is the one shown in Figure 438, in which all the brooding masses and mysterious recesses of a medieval castle are implied with one simple pointed arch.

The *symbolism* of the pointed arch exemplifies the artistry of set design. Every setting must be conveyed with minimum means because it is background and must never overwhelm the action. Suggestion of time, place, climate, and mood must be accomplished with symbols or details. Associations with objects in a room tell us much about the characters in a play. Sports equipment, a desk and file, an easel or piano, a small table lit by candlelight—each of these informs us concerning the world we are about to enter. In the set in Figure 439 we are told, by the use of a few dominant symbols, that we are going to be transported into Victorian England. Strong *textures* are used for the window, which provides visual *emphasis* by accenting the center of the stage and by providing contrast between light and dark *value*. Textural interest is repeated over the window and in the lighting fixtures as well as in the columns at each side of the stage. The furniture, while consistent in period, is relatively simple. There is no patterning on walls, floor, or furniture; they are simply a background for the period costumes and the action. At the particular point shown, the action is staged with ultimate effect, the central figure with the dark costume being outlined against the light window and the other actors being balanced in *mass* and *space* at either side.

In addition to imparting information, symbolism is employed to establish *mood*. In Figure 440 the set is for a modern play of psychological tension, and the jagged opening that frames the action gives us an immediate clue to the fact. The dejected tree is the point of emphasis, warning us that this is not to be a lighthearted trifle but a work of serious concerns.

The means of creating mood are directly involved with the elements and principles of design. We do not look for visual *line* in a play production, yet it is always there, in the figure who is commanding our attention at any given moment; in the line that relates the tops of the heads within a group; in doorways, arches, pillars, and furniture. Horizontal lines are stressed in a set implying rest or repose, vertical lines convey a sense of vigor and aspiration. As in Figure 440, jagged lines imply tension.

439

440

441

The elements of design concern action on stage in addition to setting, and the most effective dramatic expression involves both. *Mass,* for instance, can accentuate the importance of an actor: he or she can be dressed in a voluminous costume or placed beside a big piece of furniture. Groups of people provide mass according to their placement—a group upstage will be a smaller mass than the same group in a downstage area. Regular or symmetrical masses, with people balanced against one another within the "frame" of the stage, give a feeling of formality and dignity, whereas a diffused mass, with people scattered about the stage, connotes confusion. Mass and line alone can create an effective set (Fig. 441).

Color is a shared tool of set designer, costume designer, and lighting designer. It is, of course, the most obvious means of giving attention to a single actor. A costume in bright colors or a light or dark color in *contrast* to the rest of the cast will ensure that an actor is the center of interest. The stage is also a primary example of using the *emotional impact* of color. Bright warm colors immediately give the impression of warmth and gaiety, whereas dark colors convey a sense of foreboding. These are not rules, of course. It is the contrast and emphasis that give a color character on stage.

The theater embodies the art of entertainment, and variety is its essence. Different levels of action, the distribution of actors about the stage, imaginative devices for moving the action about: all contribute to the overall composition of the production. In addition, of course, there must be variety in the set without its becoming distracting.

The stage is essentially a visual phenomenon. It is at the same time

441
The Shoemaker's Prodigious Wife by Federico García Lorca. Produced by Virginia Museum Theatre, Richmond, directed by Robert S. Telford, setting by Ariel Ballif.

442
Charles Ryder (Jeremy Irons) visits the Lido with Cara (Stephane Audran) in Granada Television of England's dramatization of Evelyn Waugh's novel *Brideshead Revisited.*

443
A scene from Federico Fellini's 1965 film, *Juliet of the Spirits.*

442

443

pictorial and three-dimensional. The interaction of these two factors provides a challenge that can be one of the most stimulating areas of design.

Lighting Design

Even the most skillful of set designs would be rendered ineffectual without the reinforcement of lighting. A play that has no set at all can be made visually dramatic through the striking use of light.

There are two overall kinds of lighting on a set: *general illumination,* which makes it possible for the audience to see the action, and *specific illumination,* which molds and models to control audience reaction. Lighting can serve a variety of purposes.

Although it is important that the audience see the performance comfortably, it need not always see everything equally well. The action must be visible and, when the stage is empty, that segment of the set that is significant at the moment must be visible. Sometimes a set will have several rooms or areas, with the action taking place in different spots. Selective lighting could then be used to build a sequence of events.

Seasons, weather, and localities all require individual lighting effects. Compare, for example, the harsh light of the tropics to the hazy light of London in the fog. Late afternoon and moonlight could be suggested by shadows, the hot light of noon by a light coming from directly overhead. With no verbal clues at all, lighting can create an atmosphere that sets us in a particular time, place, and climate.

The true artistry of the designer is realized in the use of light to create a living composition that changes with every movement of the performers. Light in this sense is the means of breathing life into a set, of giving form to the work and bestowing unity upon the whole.

As with music, light can manipulate an audience without the viewers being consciously aware of it. A flood of warm, rosy light raises the spirits and implies gaiety, whereas a dimly lit setting may suggest the sinister or the supernatural. A sudden flooding of light predicts a moment of triumph. Shadows set the mood for violence. Designers today have the capability for many special lighting effects (Pl. 31, p. 313).

Costume Design

The costume designer is immensely influential in establishing the visual and emotional qualities of a work. Before the first word is spoken, the audience gains an impression from the actors' clothing.

Sometimes the goal of the costume designer is meticulous historical accuracy, as for a classical play set in sixteenth-century France or a television drama recreating World War I England (Fig. 442). At the other extreme, costumes sometimes are meant to have a jarring, unsettling effect. In large part the surreal quality of a scene from Fellini's *Juliet of the Spirits* (Fig. 443) derives from the visual shock of seeing a young woman dressed half like a bride and half like a chorus girl dancing with an old man in a black cape. In the first case, the audience "believes" the play because the costumes seem *right*; in the Fellini scene, the audience reacts because the costumes seem *wrong*.

444

Costume may in some circumstances transcend its usual role to become something else entirely. In the "Small House of Uncle Thomas" sequence from *The King and I* (Fig. 444) the long flowing scarves held by the performers serve as a kind of set for the playlet.

Finally, a coordinated ensemble of costumes can function as a dramatic visual composition, almost like a painting within a play. This was true of the costumes Cecil Beaton designed for the famous Ascot Gavotte number from *My Fair Lady* (Fig. 445). All the performers were dressed in combinations of black and white as a witty commentary upon the sameness and boredom of upper-class amusements during the period in which the play was set. The starkness of the costumes and the stilted movements of the actors created a stunning tableau.

444
The "Small House of Uncle Thomas" sequence from the Twentieth Century-Fox film production of *The King and I*. © 1956 Twentieth Century-Fox Film Corporation. All Rights Reserved. Courtesy Twentieth Century-Fox.

445
The "Ascot Gavotte" number from the Broadway production of *My Fair Lady*.

446
The Nikolais Dance Theatre production of *Grotto*, premiered in February 1973 at the Brooklyn Academy of Music. Choreography, costumes, and lighting by Alwin Nikolais.

The Overall Production

Visual design in the performing arts reaches a peak when the entire production is controlled in such a way as to achieve a sense of perfect unity. Good examples of this are the offerings of the Alwin Nikolais Dance Theatre (Fig. 446). For these presentations, every aspect, visual and musical, is coordinated. The costumes blend with the sets, which are often masses of stretchy fabric. The movements of the dancers are choreographed so as to exploit the visual qualities of the costumes. Such a performance springs from a concept of the performing arts as a totality.

445
446

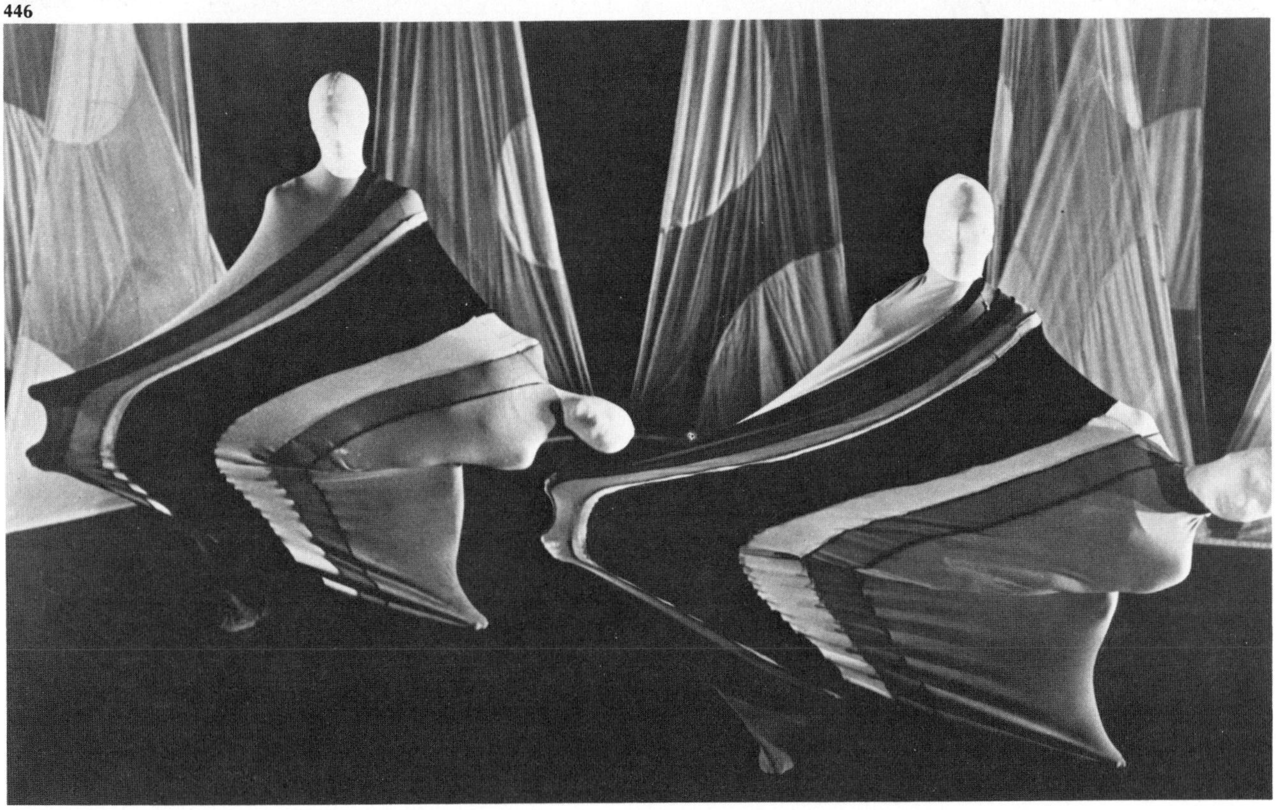

447

Total design is no more evident than in a production by Maurice Béjart's Ballet of the Twentieth Century set to the music of Beethoven's Ninth Symphony (Fig. 447). Even without the dancers, Beethoven's composition allows for a massive production involving orchestra, chorus, and soloists. The choreography introduces such elements as movement, visual rhythms, setting, costumes, and relationships among the groups of performers.

Design for the performing arts is one of the most exciting and glamorous of the many realms of design. Applying the same principles that govern other fields, the designer here gains the exhilarating experience of delving into make-believe, as well as the heady reward of applause.

447
Maurice Béjart's Ballet of the 20th Century in a production of Beethoven's Ninth Symphony.

Part Four

Design for Environment

22 Apparel

Environment is the sum of all the circumstances and conditions that influence our life and development. It is our personal domain, the vantage point from which we interpret ourselves, and from which we gather strength to make our contribution to society and to the world. In relation to our environment we are all designers as we exercise the choices that make us and our society what we are.

In considering design for environment, we will begin at the center and work outward. In this centric interpretation, the center is ourselves, the personality we present to the world. Since our concern is primarily *visual,* our interest will be focused on how we look and thus, to a large degree, on what we wear.

A multimillion-dollar industry has grown up around the design of clothing. Although it seems fairly certain that human beings have worn clothing in some form for at least seven thousand years, it has been only in the past two centuries that people have been able to buy ready-made clothing. Before that time clothing either had to be made in the home or ordered specially from a tailor or dressmaker.

Most apparel designers are motivated by a keen interest in the human body as a medium. They are fascinated by the interaction between fabric and movement, and the coordination of lines of garments with the lines of the human form. The clothing designer uses the body as a painter uses canvas, arranging lines, shapes, spaces, colors, textures, and patterns to achieve a satisfying design.

Purposes of Clothing

The Book of Genesis teaches that clothing was invented when Adam and Eve, having eaten of the Tree of Knowledge, saw that they were naked and felt shame. Some archaeologists believe that the first stimulus for wearing clothing was the desire for *power* against one's enemies or one's prey. Probably the earliest manifestation of this was body painting and tattooing (Fig. 448). Today uniforms such as those worn by the police and the military denote power. Another example of modern attire that designates power or authority is the miter, the tall headdress worn by the Pope and other high church officials.

448

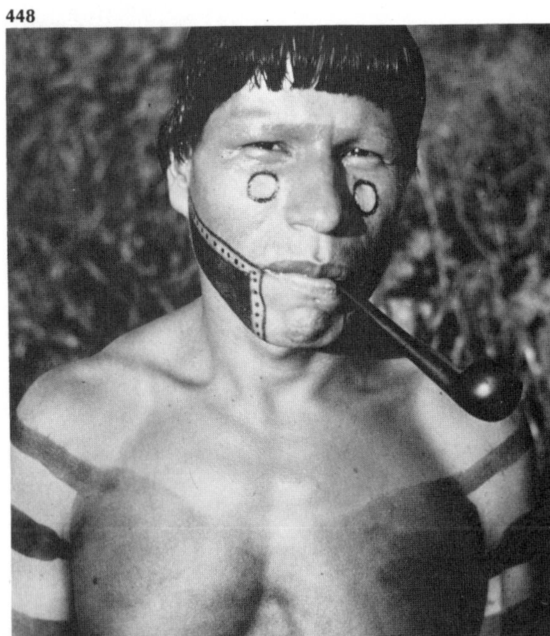

448
Karaja Indian of the Amazon River area, Brazil, with tattooed face and body painting.

Status may imply political power, as would that of a tribal chieftain or a reigning head of state, but in many cases status means rank alone. A religious habit, for instance, marks the wearer as having a certain social status, as do a judge's robes or academic attire.

For years, social status symbols have been, for men, the Brooks Brothers suit or custom-tailored English tweeds (Fig. 449); for women, the Chanel suit or, more recently, the Halston dress (Fig. 450). Since material wealth and knowledge of prevailing fashion are among the major indicators of status in our culture, fashionable and expensive clothing are often used to convey status.

Although nearly all members of the animal kingdom are admirably equipped by nature for protection from the elements, human beings must adapt their *clothing* to the changing needs of climate. Extreme atmospheric conditions may demand special protection for the body. An entirely new field of apparel design opened up with the era of space exploration (Fig. 451). Here designers had to take into consideration protection against very severe heat, cold, and pressure; to provide for self-contained breathing, communications, and eliminatory apparatus; and to allow at the same time for maneuverability. The designer of clothing for space travel or other specialized purposes must put function above all other concerns, with little or no consideration of style, fashion, and visual appeal.

449

450

449
Amateur Point-to-Point race spectator. Suffolk, England.

450
A dress by Halston is a status symbol for the contemporary woman. 1981.

451
Astronaut Walter Cunningham, wearing a space pressure suit, 1964. Courtesy NASA.

452
George Stavrinos. Illustration for Bergdorf Goodman ad. 1979. Courtesy of the artist.

451

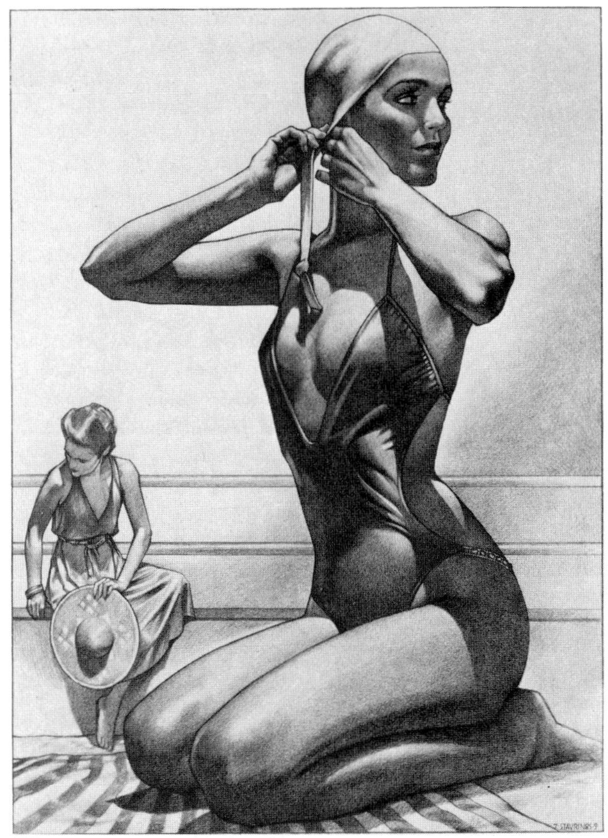
452

Standards of *modesty* have varied from time to time and from place to place ever since Adam and Eve, according to tradition, donned fig leaves. In many tropical cultures clothing has been deemed adequate if it covers the genitals, and no thought is given to concealing a woman's breasts. The early missionaries in Hawaii and the South Sea Islands caused a major upheaval among the native people in urging the women to wear "muumuus" in place of the standard half-sarong.

Possibly the most rigid standards of modesty ever known prevailed in England and the United States during the middle and late nineteenth century—the Victorian era. For a period of several decades it was unthinkable for a woman to show an ankle, much less a leg, or even to mention these words in public. Gowns were designed on a hoop or bustle superstructure that completely denied the form underneath, so that a woman's torso appeared to be floating along on a wheeled cart. Today our standards of decency are a great deal more relaxed. To be sure, in some Moslem countries the women still wear veils covering their bodies and faces, but this is changing rapidly.

The criteria for modesty can vary even in the same place at the same time. A woman in a bikini or a man who is shirtless would seem out of place and "immodest" on a city street, whereas they would pass unnoticed on the beach. With nude bathing acceptable on many of the beaches of the world, the design of beachwear is not concerned with modesty. Swimsuits are intended to enhance the human body at its ultimate exposure and attract attention to its contours (Fig. 452).

453

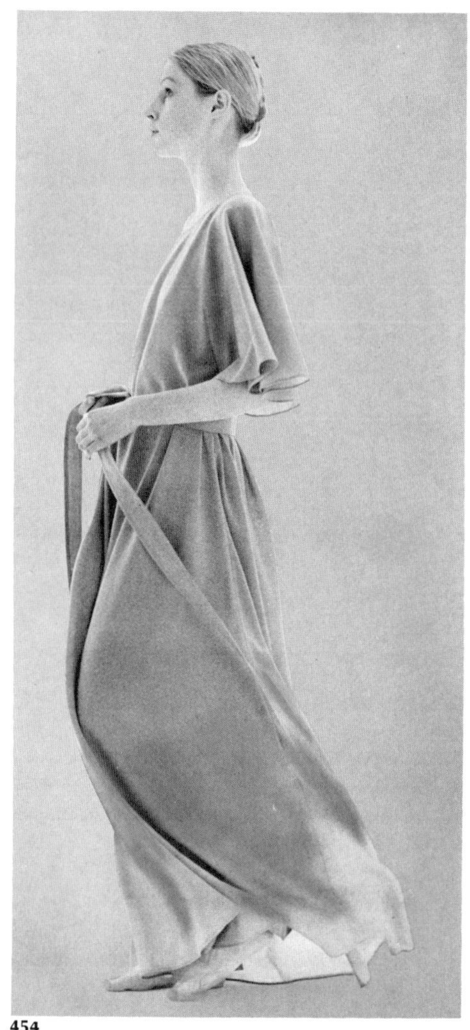

454

453
Hyacinthe Rigaud. *Louis XIV.* 1701. Oil on canvas, 9′½″ × 6′5⁄8″ (2.75 × 1.84 m). Louvre, Paris.

454
"Perhonen" dress. 1971. Designed by Vuokko Eskolin-Nurmesniemi for Vuokko Oy, Helsinki.

455
"The Great Sweater Dress," designed by Kimberly Knits.

456
Crossover swimsuit in textured rib with "Lycra" spandex. Designed by De Weese for Dupont.

457
Bill Blass. Evening gown of velvet, partially threaded with clear cellophane. 1982.

For the last 150 years or so, the fashion industry has catered primarily to women. Nature, however, has always been more lavish in the *adornment* of the male; generally, it is the male who seeks by his appearance and behavior to attract the attention of the opposite sex. This is apparent in the plumage of birds. The gay feathers of the male are fundamental to the ritual of mating, while the female's neutral coloration aids in the protective function she performs for her brood. Until the nineteenth century the human male took his cue from nature. The Georgian man spent at least five times more on clothing than his wife did. Fine laces, furs, brocades, satins, velvets, and ribbons were all part of masculine apparel from the time of the sixteenth century. This elaborate style reached the pinnacle of elegance during the reign of Louis XIV in France (Fig. 453).

During the nineteenth and early twentieth centuries, men in Western societies, whose clothing had become conservative in color, cut, and fabric, were overshadowed by the more decorative women. The classic example of this was the formal party or ball, where the men would be dressed identically in black dinner clothes, while the women sought to outdo one another in lavish gowns, opulent fabrics, precious gems, and bright colors.

Elements and Principles in Apparel Design

All of the elements and principles of design apply to apparel. Some—line and rhythm, for example—must be considered in relation to the line of the body that will be under the garment. In the field of apparel, line has two meanings: the overall line of the garment and the internal lines that may be part of its design. A garment with vertical lines tends to make the body seem taller and slimmer (Fig. 454), whereas one having predominantly horizontal lines will create a shorter, broader impression. Designers often use horizontal lines to shorten a long waist, give fullness to a thin neck, or widen too-narrow shoulders (Fig. 455). The impression of virility in a male figure may be enhanced by broadening the shoulders and slimming the hips. Diagonal lines may heighten the effect of a body's rhythmic movements (Fig. 456).

Shape can be surprisingly varied in apparel design. A garment may hug the body, fall from the shoulder, or billow out in a form all its own (Fig. 457). Although today's designs have their full share of variety in size and shape, they are characterized by a simplicity and comfort not always experienced in the past. Overemphasis on tiny waists and feet has given way to a sense of practicality that, on the whole, allows the human form a natural appearance and freedom of movement.

455
456

457

Texture and *pattern* in clothing design relate primarily to fabric and its construction. Tactile textures can range from the sleekness of a nylon swimsuit to the deep pile of a shaggy fur coat. With increased interest in hand weaving, texture often becomes one of the most stunning aspects of a garment. Visual textures emerge from varied fibers, the myriad textile patterns available, and the ways in which they are combined. Both tactile and visual textures result from trim, such as braid, lace, ruffling, sequins, and beading.

Unity and *variety* are, as in other fields, the overriding principles of apparel design. A costume is composed of many pieces and accessories, and some unifying element is needed if they are going to result in a harmonious effect. The unity may be in color, fabric, pattern, style, or a number of other things. The Yves Saint Laurent costume in Figure 458 assembles many diverse elements—colors, fabrics, shapes, and patterns. All of these elements blend because of the underlying theme of ornate peasantry, a kind of ethnic opulence.

Balance is basic in apparel design since the designer is working with a "support" that is symmetrical. Most Western clothing reflects this symmetry by a formal balance, but many other cultures use asymmetrical balance

458

458
Jacket, tartan dress, and wool shawl designed by Yves St. Laurent for his 1976–1977 winter collection.

459
One-shoulder evening robe by Mary McFadden features "marii" pleating with dropped waist picot detail and diagonally worn strand of simulated pearls. 1982.

460
Large scale designs provide drama in a costume by Oscar de la Renta for Martha. 1981.

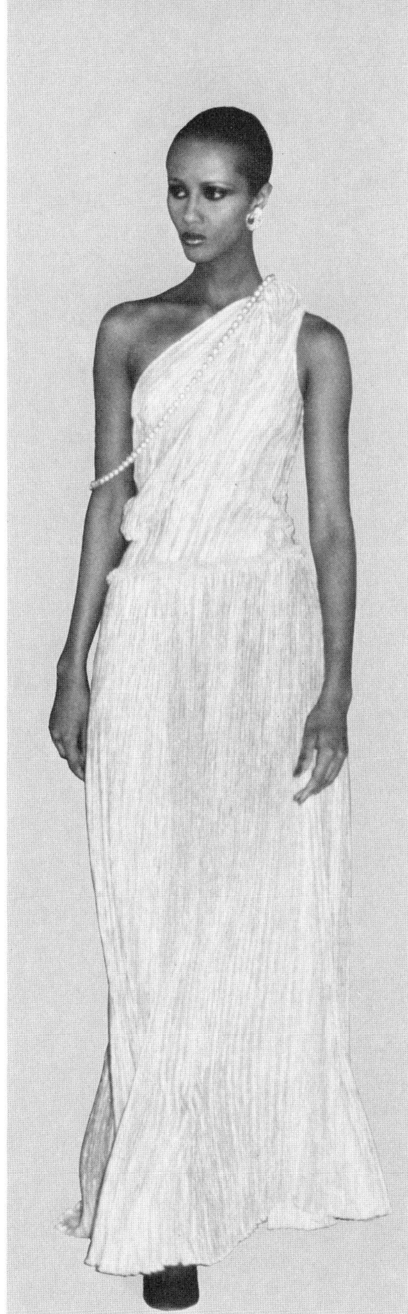

459

as a basic style, notably in the East Indian sari and the tropical sarong. When a Western designer uses asymmetrical balance, the results can be striking (Fig. 459).

Proportion comes into play in designing clothing because apparel is automatically in *scale* with the body. Generally speaking, tall people can better carry oversize garments or large-scale designs (Fig. 460) than can small people, who would be overwhelmed by them. Conversely, a large person might seem ridiculous wearing a dainty, ruffled dress.

Color has always been an intrinsic part of apparel design, and this was never more true than today. As recently as two decades ago, certain color combinations—such as blue with green or red with pink—were considered unthinkable. Now rules no longer exist. To some extent colors vary with styles and with seasons, but clothes in a spectrum of hues are always available (Pl. 32, p. 314).

460

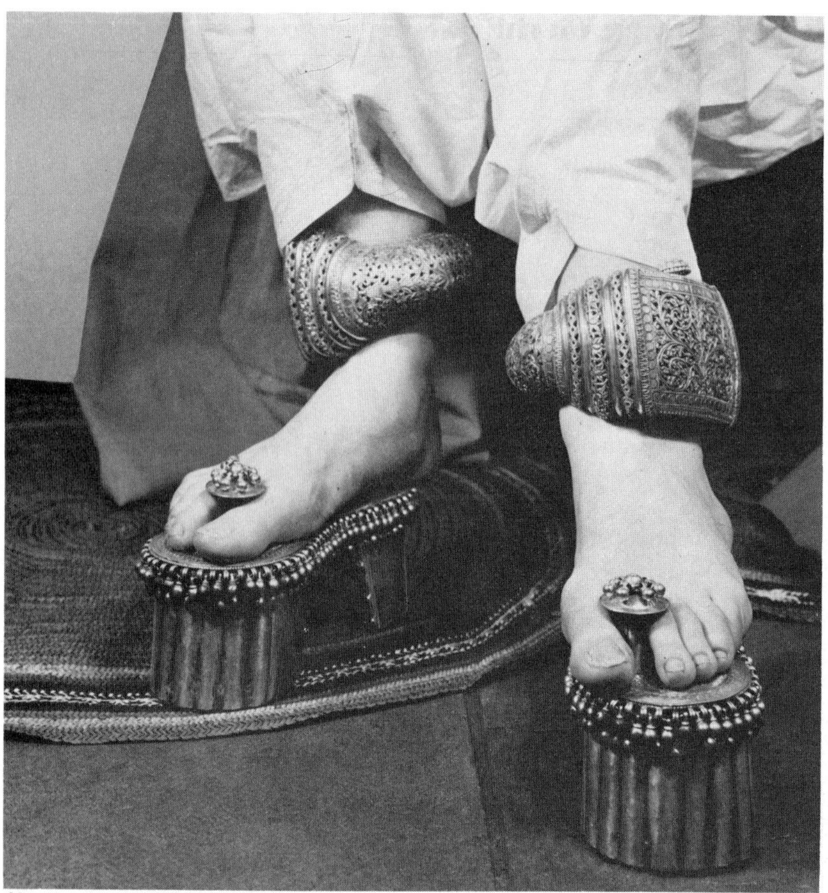

461

462

Apparel and Life Style

461
Silver anklets and chopins, part of the traditional adornment for women in North Africa. Collection Traphagen School of Fashion, NY.

462
Denim overalls by Town Set, Division of Country Set, fabric by E. I. DuPont de Nemours & Company.

463
"Pujahdus" ensemble designed by Vuokko Eskolin-Nurmesniemi, 1975.

464
High-waisted daytime costume by Pierre Cardin.

In the not-too-distant past, North African and Oriental women of high standing wore *chopins* or platform shoes like those shown in Figure 461, which made it difficult for them to walk, much less run. This type of accessory helped to emphasize a woman's station in life. She could be waited on and need do nothing for herself; therefore, her costume flaunted this helplessness.

Western women today lead busy, energetic lives that necessitate easy-to-wear, comfortable clothing. We have only to imagine a hoop-skirted Southern belle attempting to board a commercial jetliner to understand how drastically our mode of living influences apparel.

Today both women and men can adopt the occupation and life style that suits them best, and there will be appropriate clothing available for them. Some women prefer the hardworking, no-nonsense approach of blue jeans and overalls (Fig. 462), others the comfort of free-and-easy non-clinging apparel (Fig. 463).

Although the business suit for both men and women still prevails in city offices, new materials have made it more comfortable, and, for men, the turtleneck top frequently replaces a formal shirt and tie. Outside the office, male apparel ranges widely in color and style.

Influences on Clothing Design

Like designers in other fields, the couturier seeks the world over for sources on which to draw. A thorough knowledge of the history of costume is essential in clothing design. For instance, the ancient Greek chiton was revived in Napoleon's day (Fig. 158, p. 114), later becoming the basis for the Empire waistline that reappeared in evening wear and lingerie. Even today, when clothing tends toward the relaxed, natural lines of the body, the high waistline of ancient Greece is sometimes used with striking effect (Fig. 464). The full skirt of European courts was translated into the hoop skirt of the antebellum South, and variations can still be seen in bridal gowns and ball dresses. Styles derived from a South Sea island or the Italian countryside turn up on patios in suburbs across the United States. Oriental influence can be found in slit skirts, frogged openings, and mandarin collars. Fabric design has been affected by East Indian and Persian colors and designs.

463

464

465

In introducing one of his fall collections, designer Yves Saint Laurent said the clothing "incorporated all my dreams—all my heroines in the novels, the operas, the paintings." In that particular collection there were influences derived from Morocco, Austria, Czechoslovakia, and Russia, all combined in a style characteristic of the designer.

Film and television have had a vital impact on apparel design. After *Dr. Zhivago* there was a great influx of boots, fur hats, and fitted coats in the Russian style. Later, when *The Great Gatsby* premiered, designers rushed to their drawing boards to create a line of F. Scott Fitzgerald fashions in soft pastel colors (Fig. 465). The film received mixed notices, but the fashions were a tremendous success.

Contemporary Trends in Apparel Design

Twenty years ago women anxiously awaited each new season to find out what length the skirt would be, as hems seesawed from mini-skirts halfway up the thigh to maxis reaching toward the ankle. Twenty years before that, a woman needed a hat to wear with every costume, along with matching purse, gloves, and high-heeled shoes.

During the past twenty years, women have freed themselves of the bond of fashion dictates, finding the skirt length that suits them best and wearing pants on most occasions, discarding gloves and hats for dress almost entirely. Today, after a period of extreme casualness and a studied disregard for traditional dress, the trend is toward a kind of nostalgic romanticism. The same impulse that has brought New Images to painting and sculpture, with emphasis on symbols, color, imagery, and emotion, is finding its way into fashion design, with a distinct trend toward symbols and images of the past. Blue jeans are still worn for the active life, but the art of dressing up has returned as an important part of social life. Men wear bright colors, blousy pants, and ruffled shirt fronts, and women don costumes that make them look—and feel—exotic or romantic (Fig. 466). Most important, the dictates of fashion no longer exist. Designers are saying "Let people go their own way" and are supplying the designs so they can do just that.

465
Mia Farrow and Robert Redford in a scene from *The Great Gatsby.* Copyright © 1974 by Newdon Company. All rights reserved. Courtesy Paramount Pictures Corporation.

466
Lanvin design in the romantic mood for the salon of Elizabeth Arden. 1981.

A designer of clothing can build a career creating clothes for a specific purpose, as in the design of sportswear, or of boots and shoes. Or a designer's work may be motivated by a fascination for adapting motifs from faraway places to fashion designs for twentieth-century urban life. Whatever the motivation of the designer, one overriding consideration must govern anyone designing apparel: the garment should make the wearer feel good. In our choice of clothing we create an intimate portable environment that can determine as well as reflect our state of mind.

466

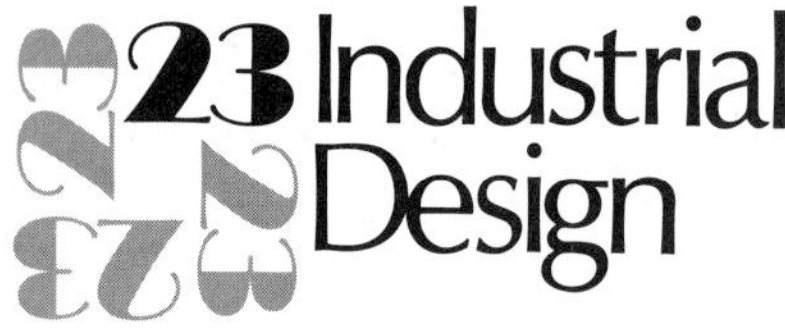

23 Industrial Design

Industrial design is the field in which products are created for mass manufacture, products that become basic components of the environment. In this area of design, the emphasis changes, for, although the visual aspects are still important, the primary consideration must be how well the object serves its purpose. Whether that purpose is to mix a cake, plow a field, dispose of garbage, or drill a tooth, the person who uses the object will expect it to operate efficiently; consequently, the industrial designer must have a background in technology as well as in design.

Although goods were produced for mass consumption by European guilds as early as the twelfth century, the term *industrial design* was not used until machines turned out objects in vast quantity. The Industrial Revolution of the late eighteenth century marked, in fact, the turning point: instead of being meticulously handcrafted, objects were now reproduced in infinite quantity. Perhaps the most negative effect of such technical development was the fact that for years the design of any given object was the work of the person who ran a machine rather than of anyone with aesthetic training. Consequently, items for all kinds of uses were elaborately, but distastefully, ornamented in demonstration of the virtuosity of the machine.

467

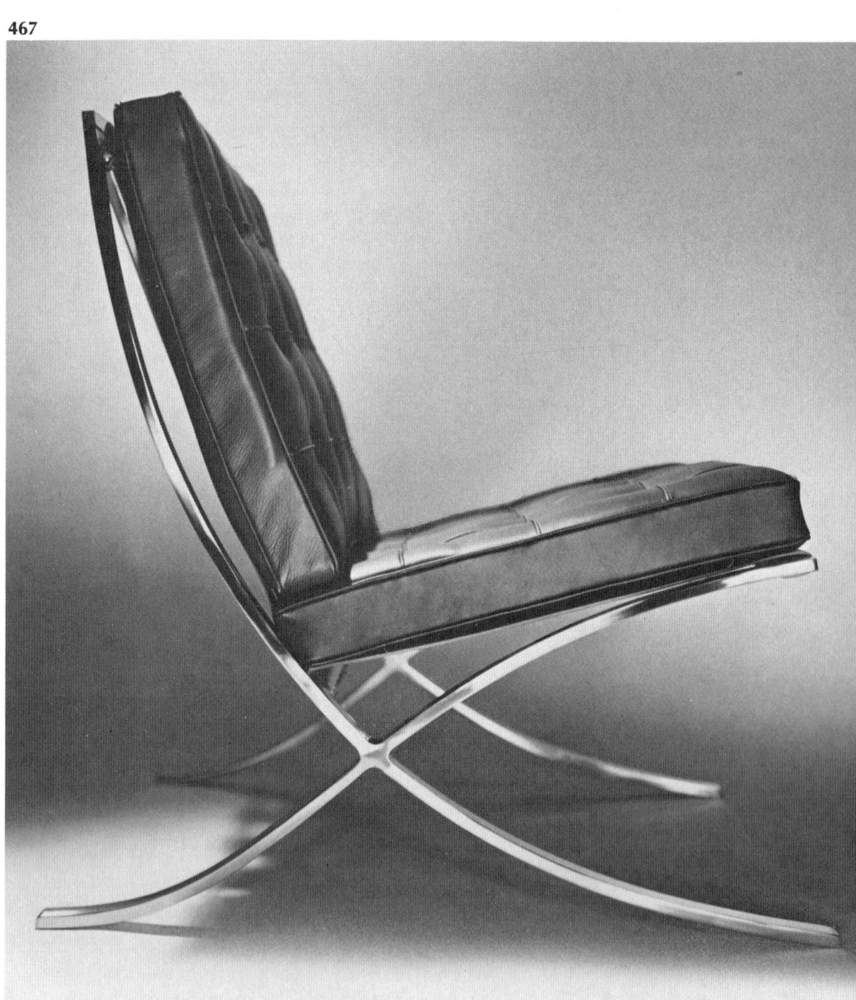

467
Ludwig Miës van der Rohe. "Barcelona" chair. 1929. Steel and leather.

468
Raymond Loewy. Coca-Cola bottle.

The first voice to speak out seriously against this situation was that of the Englishman William Morris, who was associated with the Arts and Crafts movement in England and the United States during the late nineteenth century. Through his firm, Morris and Co., he produced textiles, wallpaper, and household furnishings that embodied his high standards of design. The *Deutscher Werkbund,* founded in Munich in 1906, and the Design and Industries Association, which emerged in London in 1915, represented private industries that tried to infuse technology with aesthetics and thus establish new design standards. A few years later the Bauhaus continued the effort with the collaboration of trained designers and skilled engineers (Fig. 467). It was not until Raymond Loewy founded his design studio in 1927 that America was involved in any kind of design aesthetics. Loewy, born in France and originally an illustrator, transformed the face of America with such designs as the Frigidaire, a streamlined engine for the Pennsylvania Railroad, the Farmall Tractor for International Harvester, Studebaker cars, and, perhaps most far-reaching of all, the Coca-Cola bottle (Fig. 468).

468

The idea of corporate design, as opposed to designs by individual designers, came from Europe in the 1950s. Braun, the German maker of electrical goods and home appliances, and Olivetti, the Italian manufacturer of typewriters and communications systems, were so dedicated to a policy of good design that for many years everything good in industrial design seemed to originate with one or the other. The Olivetti showroom in New York exemplified the credo of its founder, that a typewriter or any other object of industrial design should be practical and elegant at the same time. Gradually large American corporations followed suit.

Today there is increasing interest in the "small designer" working closely with museums and artists. J. Stewart Johnson, curator of design at the Museum of Modern Art, has been quoted as saying that design has the same validity as the pure arts, a term frequently applied to such arts as painting and sculpture. In any case, consumers have become increasingly discriminating, and the demand for attractive appearance as well as efficient function has changed the face of the design industry.

Characteristics of Industrial Design

Industrial design differs from other fields of design in several ways. In corporate industrial design, the designer works as a member of a team, and major decisions concerning economics and marketing will have been made before a project ever reaches the designer. An individual rarely receives recognition for a design in such a situation. In addition, the industrial designer is restricted by the machinery available. To be economically feasible a product must be designed with existing equipment or require retooling only within practical economic limits. A third difference is in the gap between the designer and those who buy the finished product. A profile of consumer needs may be projected, but the designer must learn whether the design was satisfactory by indirect means—by looking at sales charts, for example, or by seeing the product used by customers. Furthermore, the general public is far more critical of industrial design than of works of art. The same person who will stand before a painting apologizing for a lack of background to appreciate it will speak out emphatically about the faults of a power saw or an electric razor.

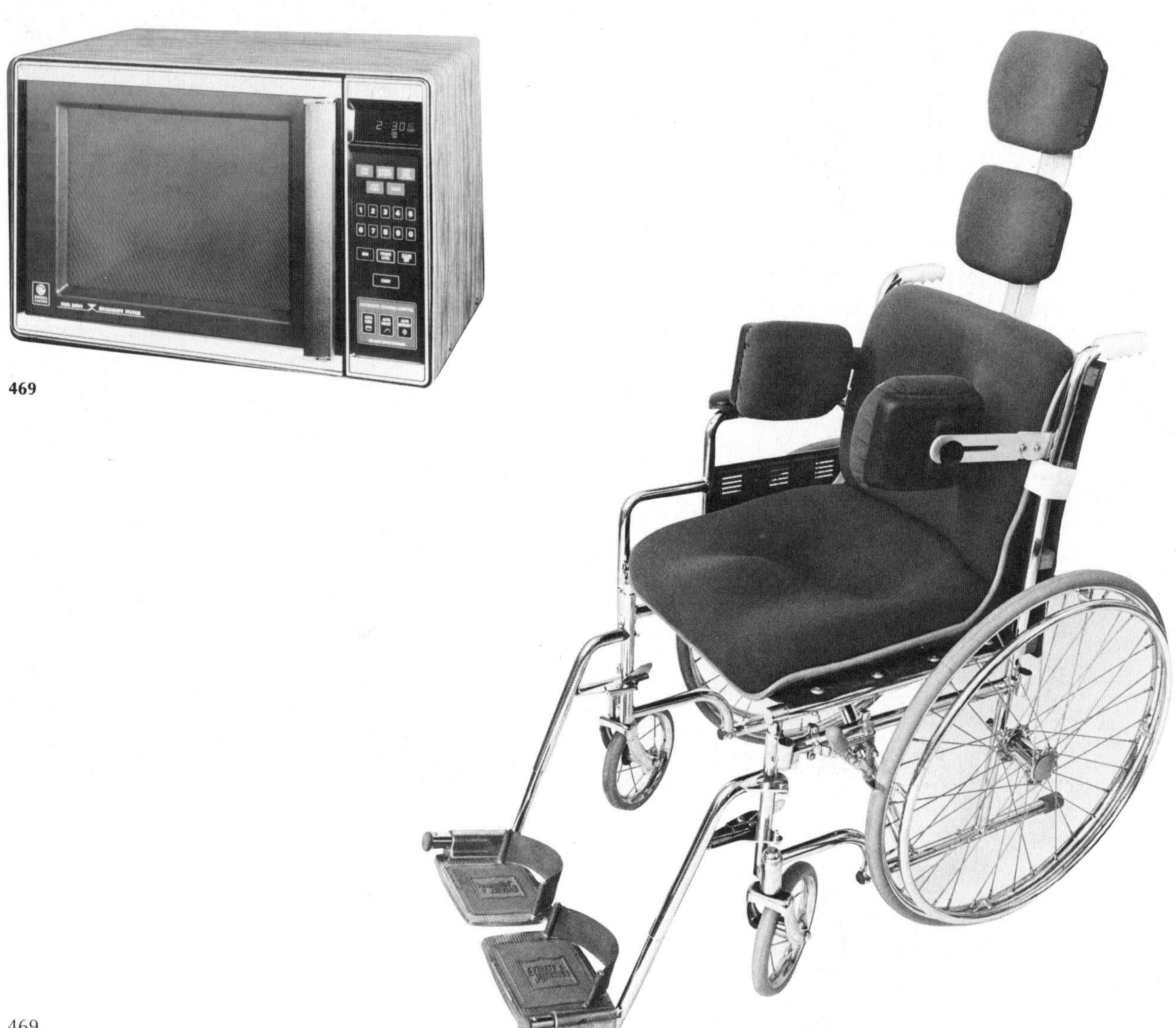

469

470

469
General Electric Dual-Wave Countertop Microwave Oven. 1982.

470
Frank Low and Robert Burridge, for Contourpedic. Custom wheelchair. 1975. Chair was designed with plastic bags filled with foam beads to conform to the contours of the body.

471
David Gammon. *Turntable.* 1964. Aluminum and acrylic, height 6¾″ (17.15 cm). Manufactured by Transcriptors. Museum of Modern Art, NY (gift of the manufacturer).

472
Super Swallowtail (SST). Designed by Chris Price, Chris Wills, and Bob Wills for Wills Wing, Inc.

With increasing technology and high competition among manufacturers, the field of industrial design has assumed a new role: the generation of need. Before industrialization, consumers knew what their basic needs were. Now, with increased affluence, the public is able to buy luxury items and is seduced into doing so by the sales campaigns of manufacturers, which claim that such novelties as a microwave oven, a Polaroid camera, and a Citizen's Band radio count among life's basic necessities (Fig. 469).

The manufacturer, through the designer, continually molds our choices and our taste and thereby our motivations for buying certain things. Shapes, colors, and textures can make a product look more contemporary than its rivals, more elegant, more comfortable, or more sporty. Whatever our preferences, they inevitably conform to what is available, and what is available becomes the decision of the designer and the manufacturer who sponsors the design.

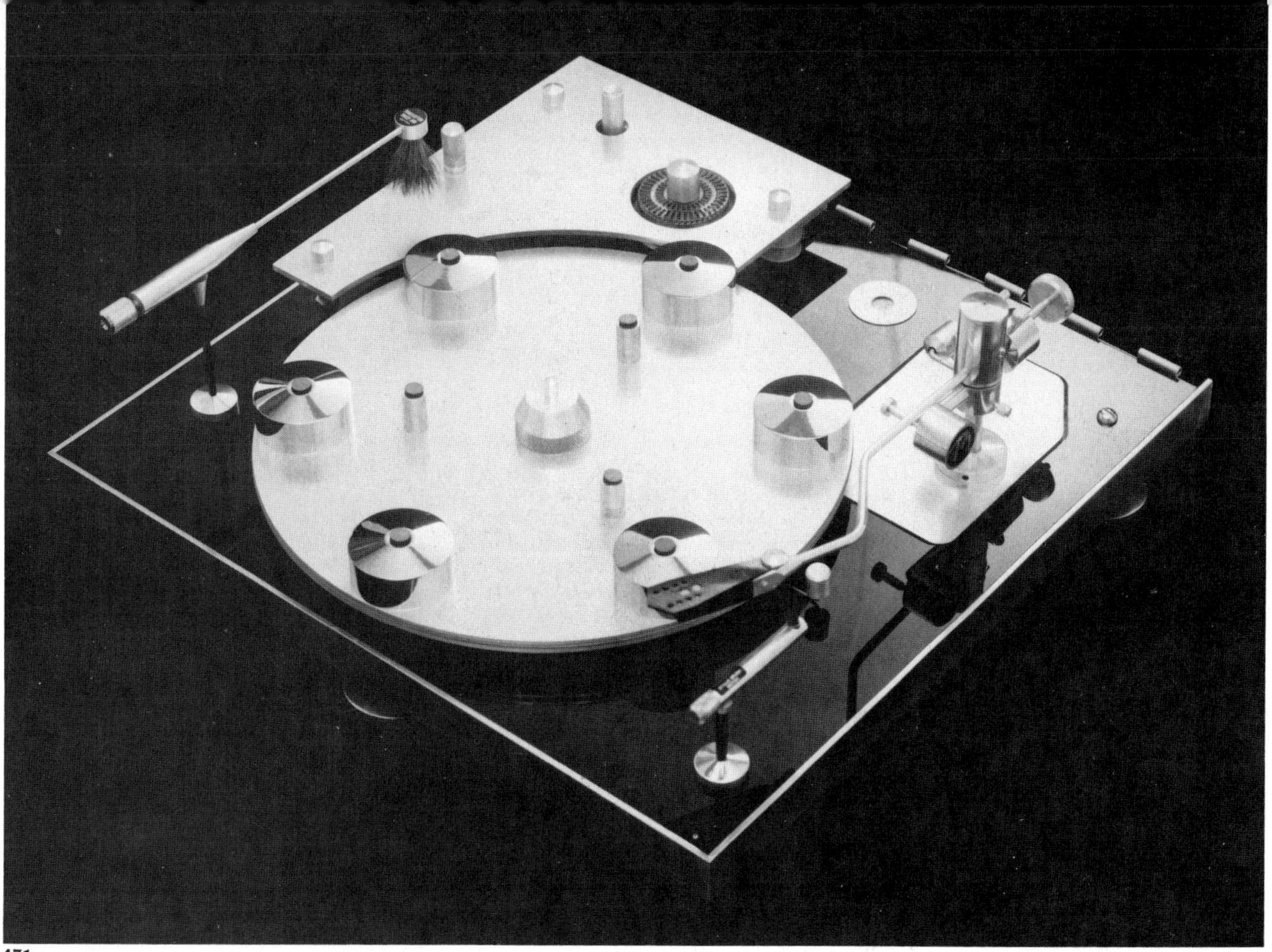

471

472

At its best, industrial design can answer genuine needs. In the United States alone, hundreds of thousands of people are chronically confined to wheelchairs. Until now, the two major problems have been balance (especially when the lower anatomy is paralyzed) and pressures on limbs forced to stay in the same position. Painful skin ulcers were the least of the difficulties that might arise with improperly fitted equipment. At worst, the pressures could result in amputation or even death. A team of designers researched the problem and came up with the chair in Figure 470, the contours of which can be custom-adapted to each patient. Although function was the primary concern in its design, the wheelchair is also more attractive than previous models.

Categories of Industrial Design

Products designed for mass production could easily number in the millions. All, however, fall into one of four broad categories.

Consumer products are the objects that people use in their homes and their recreational activities. They include electrical and other appliances, plumbing fixtures, lighting equipment, garden implements, radios and television sets, stereo components (Fig. 471), luggage, furniture, sports gear (Fig. 472), toys, and children's vehicles.

473

Commercial and service equipment encompasses the fixtures for stores and offices, gas stations, restaurants, barber and beauty shops, and similar enterprises. The items range from desks to scales and typewriters, data processing equipment, and computers (Fig. 473).

Durable goods are such things as heavy equipment and machine tools, agricultural machinery and equipment, industrial furnaces, and power generators.

Transportation design embraces all modes of transportation, from airliners to sailboats and yachts. Included in this category is automotive design (Fig. 474).

The Industrial Designer

473
The Apple II Plus personal computer system equipped with a monitor and a Disk II floppy disk drive.

474
Renault *Elf.* 1982 RE 30B.

475
Total design concept for CBS Television Network. 1981. Designer: Marie-Christine Lawrence. Artists: John LeProvost and Jim Dessing.

Industrial designers have a certain advantage over designers in other fields. While painters, sculptors, potters, and weavers might hope that a few hundred people will be touched by their creations, industrial designers face the dizzying prospect that *millions* may use and enjoy one of their designs. For example, the designer of a telephone could within reason expect that virtually every person in the United States will at some point pick up that telephone and talk into it, perhaps several times a day. Our very concept of what a telephone is could be shaped by the output of one person's creativeness. The person who designs a bicycle or a toothbrush might see that design exported around the world to serve literally billions of people.

Industrial design is, above all, a balanced combination of creative and practical concerns. To original ideas must be joined the technological knowledge to translate those ideas into large-scale production. A designer should be familiar with all the standard processes of manufacture and be able to see ways of improving a product within the framework of the present machinery and practices of the manufacturer.

Designers can belong to a manufacturer's staff, or they can work independently, taking commissions from firms needing their services. An independent designer can build up a reputation for a certain type of product through a series of successes, or establish a reputation for widely varied designs or for total design concepts (Fig. 475).

474

475

476

The Design Process

Although the design of an industrial product follows much the same creative process as design in other fields, there are many special considerations. Usually the first step is an extensive research program to determine whether a given product would be successful. Mass production requires such an enormous outlay in tools, machinery, labor, materials, and marketing that the manufacturer cannot afford mistakes. An independent craftsman who has a design failure can simply discard the product and start again. The mass producer who markets a product people will not buy may face bankruptcy. For this reason, extensive research will attempt to answer many questions before any money is committed to design: Who will buy the product? Why do they want it? What features will be most popular? How much will the consumer pay? Can the product be made commercially successful at that cost? What features does the competitor's product have, and can one improve upon them?

Even the best research will not be infallible. In 1958 the Ford Motor Company unveiled the culmination of a gigantic research effort that had sought to discover precisely what the American driver wanted in an automobile—the best engineering features, the most comfortable interior, the most attractive exterior design. The result was a classic failure of industrial design: the Edsel (Fig. 476).

After research, the next step is analysis of the problem. This phase includes all aspects of materials, color, structure, production, cost, and marketing. The merchandising requirements of a particular product often have a significant effect on its design. Perhaps it will be decided that a certain product will appeal only to affluent people and should therefore be advertised in expensive magazines. This may change the pricing of the product as well as its materials and design.

Once the general characteristics of a product have been established, the more concrete design process can begin. The designer will usually start with sketches, proceed through several stages of models in clay or some working material, and finally develop a *prototype* of the finished product. This is the stage at which the elements and principles of design are applied. The prototype is a trial run for both the product and the process of manufacture. It may be made of cheaper materials than the final piece, but it will be exactly the same in all other details. Flaws of shape, structure, engineering, and manufacturing can be eliminated at this stage.

Materials and Techniques

All the materials discussed in Part II of this book appear in some phase of industrial design. In the twentieth century, however, metal and plastics have assumed a dominant role because they lend themselves so easily to machine shaping.

The techniques used in industrial production are so sophisticated and so varied that it is almost impossible to generalize about them. They do, however, fall into several broad categories. *Casting* in molds is one of the most common techniques used. *Extrusion* calls for a molten material to be forced through shaped openings, after which it hardens upon cooling. *Stamping* is a fully automatic process in which material, usually metal, is

476
Ford Edsel, 1958.

477
A century of telephone design. Liquid Telephone, 1876; The Butterstamp, 1877; The Blake Transmitter, 1880; Common Battery, 1900; Desk Set, 1910; Desk Set, 1928; "500" Type Desk Set, 1949; Trimline, 1976; Design Line—Sculptura, 1977.

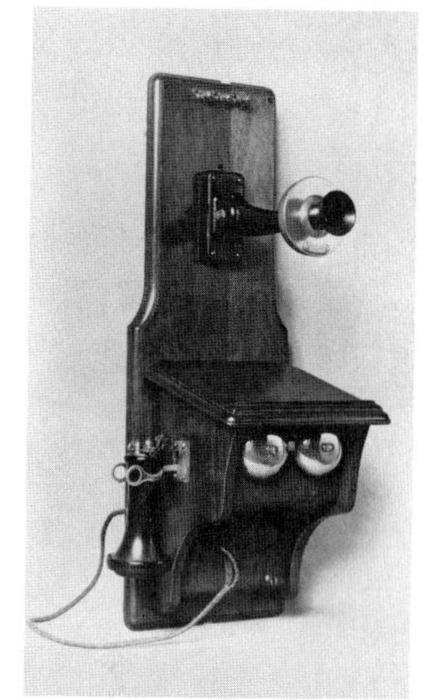

477

cut, shaped, and combined into the desired form. *Lamination* and *fabrication* in industrial terms resemble the processes as they apply to plastics (see Chapter 12). The industrial designer cannot hope to make intelligent decisions without becoming totally familiar with the range of manufacturing processes possible for the object to be designed.

Contemporary Trends in Industrial Design

Products available today are so diverse in appearance and function that we cannot isolate a particular "style," yet there are certain trends visible in many areas of industrial design. A general tendency toward streamlining and *simplification* has been obvious for some time. In Figure 477 we see this trend embodied in the metamorphosis of the telephone over a century. Not shown are the cordless model that makes it possible to roam about the house while talking, and the newest model that can be worn on the wrist, much like a watch.

Compactness has become important as our world grows increasingly crowded. Forms are smoother and more geometric, often fitting together as

478

479

478
Nick Roericht. *Stacking Tableware.* 1963. Porcelain. Manufactured by Rosenthal China Corporation, Thomas Division, Germany. Museum of Modern Art, NY (gift of the manufacturer).

479
Coffee grinder. 1965. Plastic and metal housing, height 7½″ (19.05 cm). Manufactured by Braun A. G., Germany. Museum of Modern Art, NY (gift of the manufacturer).

480
Marco Zanuso and Richard Sapper. *Doney 14.* 1962. ABS with transparent casing. Museum of Modern Art, NY (gift of the manufacturer).

square or circular units. Tools and appliances that perform several different functions on the same motor save both space and money.

Another trend is toward *modular* design, composed of repetitive units that can be interchanged. This type of design can apply to buildings, furniture, and many other aspects of the environment. Cups and dishes that fit together into a neat stack not only save space but are also less likely to break (Fig. 478).

Until recently it was considered desirable for all working parts in machinery or appliances to be concealed. Today there is a tendency toward greater *visibility* of merchandise and its component parts. The coffee grinder in Figure 479 has transparent compartments so one can see the coffee granules. Consumers are also choosing appliances of more straightforward design, without panels of wood-grained plastic and pseudo–period cabinets, for example. An expression of both of these trends is the transparent television set in Figure 480.

480

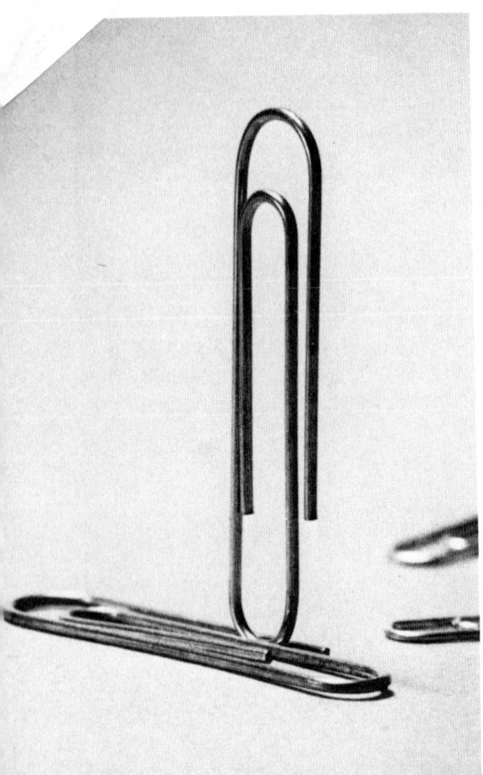

481

Industrial Design and Environment

Recently a group of prominent industrial designers were asked to select examples of objects they felt were well designed. The examples ranged from a convertible Karmann-Ghia to a coat hanger that screws to a wall, but most of the items considered most praiseworthy were simple things that we use every day. One designer cited them for their "dailiness," meaning that we would miss them if they weren't there, without quite knowing why. In this group was the paper clip, a simple bent piece of wire that has become a necessity for home, schoolroom, and office (Fig. 481). Other designs worthy of note are the safety pin, the clothespin, and the thumbtack. The thermos, the parachute, blue jeans, the lead pencil, and the red-clay flower pot were also allotted a share of the praise (Fig. 482). Some designers cited the designs they felt were bad—childproof bottle caps that are impossible to open except by a contortionist, blenders with too many buttons, statuettes that can be fastened to dashboards with suction cups.

The important point is the fact that the products that are well designed not only last but become so indispensable that we scarcely think of them as having been designed. They are necessities whose form and function are inextricably linked. The electric light bulb could be placed in this category, although it represents the work of a genius. Genius certainly has its place in industrial design, but the ability simply to see a need can be the key to a design of lasting importance.

Industrial design has a special relationship to the environment by virtue of mass production. Most things outlive their usefulness by wearing out mechanically or by becoming outdated. At a time when we are deeply concerned about the quality of environment, it becomes necessary to plan ahead for the disposal of a product even while it is being designed. Each year the United States manufactures 60 tons of products that cannot

482

481
Paper clips.

482
Montage of jeans, lead pencils, thermos, and red clay flower pot.

be recycled. Such colossal output results in 3.5 billion tons of waste annually that must somehow be absorbed into the landscape. The first disposable drinking cup was marketed in 1910, but it was only in the 1950s that the term *disposable* came into general use. It did not take long for us to discover that the term is inaccurate. "Disposable" objects rarely disappear; they simply convert into the clutter along streets and roadsides. Someone has suggested that later civilizations will identify as the one characteristic artifact of our culture the metal pull-top from a soft-drink can.

Thus to standards of function and attractiveness we would add one other criterion of successful industrial design: disposability. The disposal of material objects must be seen as an imperative consideration in modern design, especially in light of the overwhelming presence of mass-produced items in contemporary culture and their impact on the environment.

24 Interiors

The interior designer is concerned with creating spaces for human activity. Encompassing *interior decoration,* the arrangement of furnishings to satisfy specific tastes, *interior design* involves not only furnishings but also the articulation of interior space, the structure molding it, and the experiences, character, and personality of the people who move within it. Whether planning enormous areas for sports events, conventions, or cultural affairs, or an intimate apartment, the interior designer composes environment.

The Home

Our home is the most intimate of the spaces in which we spend our lives. The character of a home develops through a series of choices regarding color, line, texture, shape, and size, which reflect the attitudes and personalities of its occupants and modulate with the changing quality of those occupants' lives. This capacity to express the life within a space is the basic precept of interior design. A weaver's home may have a loom in the living room (Fig. 483), a musician's, a grand piano. A painter or potter may make the studio the center of the home. A person active in the theater may have a wall filled with signed photographs. Treasured heirlooms may determine the character of an entire house. We can tell a great deal about a person by seeing the interior space that person calls home.

Attributes of Interior Design

Like painting or sculpture, an interior can be interpreted through the attributes of subject, form, and content, but first the fundamental relationships that determine the character of interior space must be understood.

483

483
For a way of life that includes weaving and other crafts, the living area incorporates a loom and work table into the total design. Owner-architect: Kipp Stewart. © by Morley Baer.

484
A house in Belvedere, CA, shows integration of landscape, architecture, and interior spaces. Designers: Callister, Payne & Bischoff.

485
The atrium, or inner courtyard.

486
The main living area.

An interior is not simply an enclosed area. It is space related to the *architecture* in which it is located and to the *landscape* in which the building is set. An interior surrounded by a busy city may attempt to shut out the larger environment, creating a peaceful corner into which the world cannot intrude. Other interiors, in a scenic setting or high above the city, include an expansive view as an important part of the life within. Architecture relates to active human use through *furnishings.* Interior space is shaped and given character by the furniture placed within it and by the colors and materials on ceilings, floors, and walls. These relationships—between structure, landscape, and furnishings—mold a space into a vital area around which our larger environment pivots.

The attributes of subject, form, and content can best be understood in reference to a specific example, such as the house in Figures 484, 485, and 486. The *subject* here is a home overlooking San Francisco Bay, in which all the elements of architecture, landscape, interior spaces, and furnishings have been integrated to achieve a composition of satisfying unity. In the

484

485

486

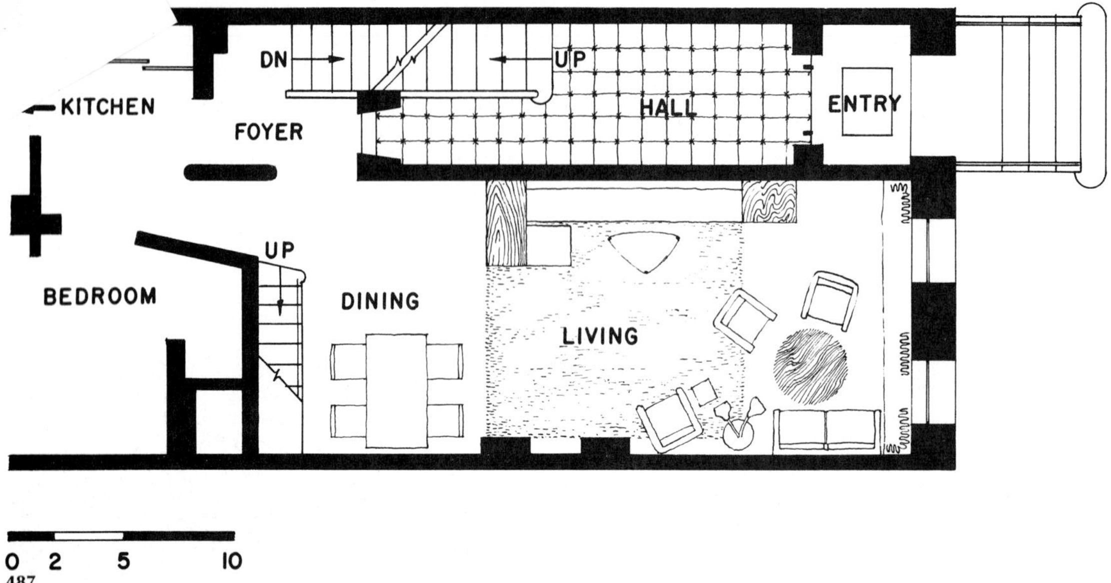

487

first view (Fig. 484) we see how the *form* of the house is in harmony with its setting as it nestles into the cliffside, with trees and plants providing a natural transition between building and terrain. A long, narrow swimming pool adjacent to the approach leads the eye along the edge of the cliff to the house itself. Indoor-outdoor harmony is carried over into the atrium (Fig. 485), an enclosed courtyard within the house, partially walled by a glassed-in gallery. Potted plants in the gallery blend with the plants in the atrium to create a natural indoor landscape. A huge skylight running the entire length of the room emphasizes again the relationship between landscape and interior space that defines the *content* of the dwelling. Low-lying furnishings accentuate the impression of a wide, unhampered space (Fig. 486). Covered with soft, colorful cushions, the low furniture helps to enhance the quality of leisure and comfort, which, pervading the entire house, becomes the keynote of its content.

The Manipulation of Space

The architect molds space by enclosing it, but the interior designer must manipulate space that is already defined by walls, and often by doors, windows, and other architectural features. The designer begins with documents—statements of purpose, of existing features, of requirements of the client, of preferences in colors, styles, and materials—and translates the three-dimensional space to be designed into a two-dimensional drawing. In Figure 487 we see a floor plan for a living-dining area in a New York City brownstone house. Such a house, attached on each side to similar houses, and facing directly on the sidewalk, offers one of the least flexible of interior spaces. Here the space has been skillfully designed, first by diagraming the area to scale, then by analyzing the activities that would take place within it, and, finally, by arranging the furniture, also drawn to scale, within each section of the area. The result is a compact design that effectively serves the needs of its occupants (Fig. 488).

487
Floor plan showing furniture arrangement for New York City brownstone house remodeled by Joseph Aronson for his family.

488
Interior view of Joseph Aronson brownstone house in New York City.

489
A textured panel gives drama to a high fireplace wall, at the same time balancing a window. Designer: Cindi Sands.

490
Silverstone residence near Taxco, Mexico. A partial wall of rough-hewn stone dramatically modifies a long, narrow space while echoing its mountainous site. Architects: Anshen + Allen.

As shown in Figure 485, space can be manipulated by expanding it horizontally with glass panels. Space can be extended vertically as well by using *line* to give an impression of great height. The fireplace wall in Figure 489 appears to soar dramatically as a result of the use of simple lines and the strategic placement of a textured panel on the left.

Long, narrow spaces can be broken by room dividers—bookshelves, a decorative screen, plants, or a partial wall of stone (Fig. 490). A square room, or one excessively large, can be made more livable by arranging the furniture into groupings for conversation, eating, watching television, or listening to music.

488

489

490

Elements and Principles of Interior Design

In no area are the elements and principles of design more obvious than in the design of interiors. We have mentioned *space* and *line*. *Color* and *texture* are also fundamental, for either element can totally transform the character of a room. Warm, bright colors tend to make a room seem smaller, whereas cool colors (blues and greens) appear to move the walls farther apart. Psychologically, warm colors are considered conducive to eating and entertaining, but the reaction to color is so intensely personal that it is impossible to establish rules. More important is the manner in which color is used, its orchestration and dramatization through *emphasis*. In Figure 491 dark ceiling beams give character to a predominantly pale room, emphasizing its existing architectural structure. In Figure 492 bold

491

491
A predominantly pale room is enlivened by dark ceiling beams.
Designer: Janet Schirn Interiors.

492
Dramatic contrasts give this room strong character. Owner-architect: Robert Fitzpatrick. Ezra Stoller © ESTO.

contrasts in furnishings transform an ordinary room into a striking composition displaying emphasis and *balance*.

Sometimes landscape or climate determines the use of color. In hot countries, white and cool hues provide relief from the heat; in the north gold and orange provide distraction from the dullness of dark forests and cold winters. Designer Mario Buatta believes color will become far more important as a decorating tool to relieve the drabness and monotony of city life.

Effective use of color does not necessarily mean a lavish use of bright hues. The color scheme of the living room in Plate 33 (p. 314) is predominantly off-white and earth tones accented by dramatic greenery. Such color harmony is in perfect balance with a semirural setting. This harmony is further enhanced by the balance of shapes and visual *textures* realized by the diamond-patterned floor and the angled shapes of ceiling beams.

492

493

494

493
A concrete wall can provide tremendous textural interest. Designer: Emile Norman.

494
Growing bamboo becomes the point of emphasis in this study of interior textures. Architect: Mark Mills.
© Morley Baer.

Balance of texture is especially important in interior design, since texture exerts an important influence on our adjustment to surroundings. Too much smooth texture can make a space seem cold and impersonal; too much rough texture can make us feel claustrophobic. Formal rooms generally use a minimum of *tactile* texture, relying upon smooth rich fabrics with lively visual patterns for a sense of well-being. In a room intended for relaxed comfort, on the other hand, tactile texture may be emphasized, through discreet use of shag rugs, rough stone, and unfinished wood. The textured concrete wall in Figure 493 is interesting because of its *variety* and *rhythm,* but it is effective as design because of its juxtaposition with a fireplace hood of smooth metal. Plants are an excellent means of providing textural interest, but they, too, are most effective when contrasted with large expanses of smooth wood or rough stone (Fig. 494).

Proportion and *scale* in a home are necessarily determined by the size of the people who live there. Tall people require not only long beds but high ceilings and high cabinets, as well as a feeling of adequate space in which to be comfortable, to stretch out. Furniture should be scaled both to the room size and to the people who will use it. Large people need sturdy furniture.

Plate 34
Banking Hall, Fribourg State Bank, Fribourg, Switzerland.
Marion Botta, architect.

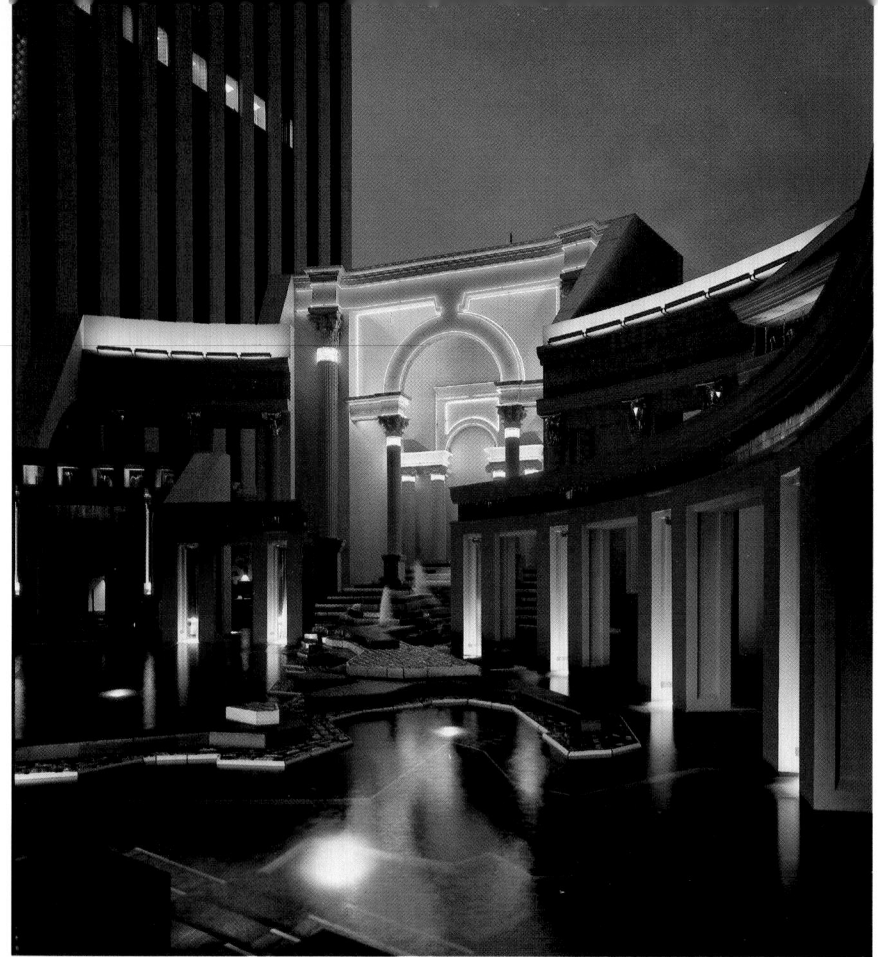

Plate 35
Piazza d'Italia, New Orleans.
Architects: Perez Associates, with Charles Moore, Ron Filson, Urban Innovations Group.

Plate 36
Nightlighting at Butchart Gardens near Victoria, B. C.

In Figure 489 we saw how the illusion of height can be given to a room by the use of line and a vertical panel reaching upward. In Figure 495 we see the opposite effect, as a horizontal panel brings a dominant living room wall into scale with the furnishings. The architect has used two bold devices to prevent the expanse of brick wall surrounding the fireplace from becoming monotonous and overpowering. First, the heavy ceiling beam forms a strong demarcation between wall and ceiling, both by virtue of its being dark and by its diagonal line, which cuts firmly across the horizontal lines of the brick and the opposing lines of the wooden ceiling decking. Second, the band of light concrete directly over the fireplace opening is exactly level with the tops of the furniture, thus bringing the fireplace wall into direct proportional relationship with the furnishings and, at the same time, providing dramatic emphasis as the natural focal point of the room.

Variety within a home is the result of textures, colors, and furnishings. The selection of objects of art—pottery, paintings, sculpture, wall hangings—can contribute both interest and variety. *Unity* may be the result of a color theme or themes that flow throughout the house, of similar carpeting and other textures used to some degree in every room. Focal points within a home may also exhibit variety and unity. In Figure 496 diverse elements have been grouped on a kitchen wall, with careful placement according to size, shape, and spacing. In dramatic contrast with the old iron, the light background serves to unite the varied pieces; the resulting composition is far more effective than any single piece would be.

495

496

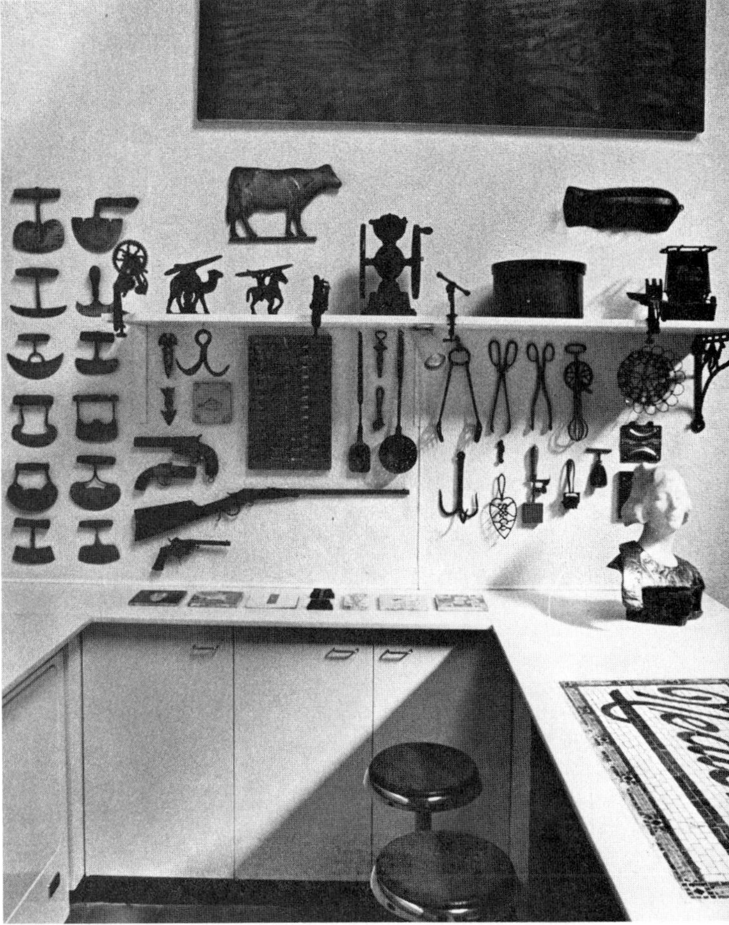

495
Dramatic accent relates the fireplace to the scale of the furnishings in a small living room. Architect: Aaron Green.

496
A collection of antique artifacts and kitchen utensils illustrates the principles of unity and variety in this New York loft-apartment.

497

498

Time, Motion, and Light

To be fully appreciated a home must be experienced night and day and over the seasons. Time is required to notice vistas from windows or views down hallways, to linger over groupings of plants, or to contemplate a wall of prints or paintings. There are homes in which one can look in any direction and see something attractive, even in the kitchen (Fig. 497).

Any space for living must incorporate design for comfortable and efficient *motion*. Traffic patterns in a house control the rhythms of daily life, providing space that makes it possible to move about. They allow dinner guests smooth passage from fireside to dining table and make it possible for occupants to hurry to a door or telephone without hitting a corner of a table. Traffic patterns are easier to arrange in large areas, of course, but they are less a matter of unlimited space than of careful planning.

Light as an artistic medium has unique qualities. We can neither touch nor feel it, yet it has the ability to transform a familiar environment into a place of mystery and magic. Adequate sunlight in a house is the result of good weather and wise orientation, but dramatic lighting at night is the result of effective design. Taking our cue from theatrical lighting, we can recess fixtures behind beams and soffits, causing a work of art or furniture grouping to be spotlighted. We can wash a wall with light from hidden fluorescent tubing or create a focal point with a striking lighting fixture (Fig. 498). Since light changes colors, the use of lamplight can transform walls and fabrics. Designers at Brunschwig and Fils, one of the most respected fabric design firms, make their fabrics in varying colors, taking into account the differences in light in different parts of the country. Light also changes textures, creating deep shadows that emphasize their roughness or highlight their smoothness.

497
Plants, an array of herbs and spices, and bright ceramic tiles all contribute to the visual interest of this kitchen. Designer: Paul Bradley.

498
A large wooden grill provides scale and character to the lighting in this dining room, faceting the light to make the furnishings sparkle. Architect: Alden Dow.

499
Home in Midland, MI. Architect: Alden Dow.

Time, motion, light—all of these are embodied in the design of the house in Figure 499. Time is necessary to enjoy the view through the tall windows, to wander out onto the terrace, and to explore the hanging balcony. Traffic patterns move one in and out and up and down, as well as along the balcony, which provides an intriguing view of the living room from overhead. Sunlight flows along the beams, dramatizing them. Spilling into the rooms below, it washes the fireplace wall, emphasizes the brick of the flooring, and gives sheen to the foliage.

499

500

Furnishings

Furnishings relate architecture to human use; they also give interior space its personality. Row houses and condominiums are eloquent proof: identical when empty, their interiors seem scarcely to have any similarity when furnished. Through furnishings we express our interests and our tastes.

Professional crafts organizations all over the world encourage members to produce one-of-a-kind pottery, furniture, baskets, and other utilitarian objects for sale. From Ireland to Indonesia, such organizations have played a vital role in economic development, at the same time providing a wide selection of treasures from which the homes of the world can be furnished. In the United States alone there are over 1200 of these organizations, and the galleries selling their work report such success that there can be no doubt of contemporary appreciation of handcrafted works (Fig. 500). Interior designers make extensive use of such sources, feeling that crafts give character to a room and that they supply an alternative to mass-produced consumer goods. Such works are not inexpensive but do offer great charm and distinction that will not be duplicated (Fig. 501).

Modular furniture affords a less expensive way to furnish a room in style. This furniture is designed according to a repeated pattern and can be fitted together in various ways. A good example is the modular unit in Figure 502, which consists of a desk, a bookcase, a chest of drawers, a closet, and a bunk bed with storage space underneath. The exposed bolts provide more than a decorative touch: when they are removed, the unit can be disassembled and set up in different ways. Other sections can be added as needed.

An ever-growing and ever-changing field of design, the subject of home furnishings offers limitless possibilities. We walk into an empty space and, through our choices of shapes, masses, textures, and colors, we create a special world that is an intimate reflection of ourselves and a source of comfort in our daily lives.

500
Wendell Castle. Leather-Topped Desk, 1977. Maple, leather; traditional joinery, stacked horizontal lamination, shaped; 2′5″ × 5′9″ × 2′2½″ (74 × 175 × 67 cm).

501
Michael Coffey. *Aphrodite,* rocking lounge-chair. Mozambique wood, laminated, shaped; 7′6″ × 2′4″ × 4′6″ (2.29 × .71 × 1.37 m).

502
KD6 modular furniture bolts together in many different combinations, depending upon the owner's needs and available space.

501

502

Public Interiors

Nearly every day most of us are exposed to offices, hallways, auditoriums, or other public spaces that exert some influence, however unconscious, on our mood or outlook. For a long time such areas were painted in "institutional" tan or gray, to give an unobtrusive background for a variety of people and activities. Hotel room walls were painted beige because it "went with everything." Then new trends took hold. Hotel managers realized that cheerful surroundings increased enjoyment and were more apt to lure guests into a second visit. Dining areas, in particular, have been immersed in warm colors to inspire conviviality and to stimulate the appetite. Dark paneling, soft lights, and a generous use of red in walls and furnishings are the design formula in many high-quality restaurants.

In the Fribourg State Bank (Pl. 34, p. 363), green is used with stunning effect. The natural color of the marble employed in walls and flooring is extended into wooden trim and panels, which are accentuated by natural wood tones and black leather furniture. The monochromatic color scheme provides elegance, a sense of coolness and order, and perhaps a subconscious association with the color of money. Though less personal than in the home, the use of color in public interiors can nevertheless exert significant influence through symbolic and psychological associations.

If color lends drama, so can total absence of color. Elevators, notoriously small, dark, and inviting claustrophobia, are the exact opposite in the San Antonio Museum of Art, whose architects conceived the elevators serving the two towers of the onetime brewery as dazzling kinetic sculptures (Fig. 503). Glass-walled cabs move up and down through hoistways of glass and mirror-finished steel, revealing chrome-plated counterweights, sheaves, and pit buffers. Rows of tiny lights mounted on the tops and bottoms of the cabs give a sense of fantasy to the elegant reflections of mass and movement. As the cabs move upward and downward, the paintings exhibited on nearby walls are clearly visible—far from being a sequestered interval, the elevator ride is an exciting viewing experience.

The design of public interiors includes such diverse spaces as courtrooms, dentists' offices, hospitals, and luxury liners. Some of these spaces are approached with happy anticipation; others are entered with foreboding. For the latter, designers use techniques they employ in homes. Now found in dentists' offices are nubby textures in fabric, paintings and plants, interesting artifacts, indirect lighting, and background music. A more homelike environment is intended to give the patient reassurance.

Reception areas of commercial or industrial buildings often provide the visitor with a first impression that may have lasting associations. Frequently the interior is designed by the architect, who envisions lighting and furnishings as part of his or her original conception. The reception area in Figure 504 is overwhelming in scale and makes use of geometric structural masses juxtaposed to form interesting patterns. There is also extensive use of texture in the walls. The interior has been dramatized by skillful use of lighting, plants, and carpeting. However preoccupied, any person entering this area must experience a feeling of respect.

Traditionally, the most sumptuous interiors are those devoted to public entertainment. Opera houses the world over have long been associated with elegance and luxury in echo of the days when musicians, sponsored by royalty, gave many of their most important recitals in palace drawing rooms. Opulent textures, rich colors, and dramatic lighting become the means by which a sense of festive anticipation is encouraged (Fig. 505).

503
Elevator in the San Antonio Museum of Art.

504
Paul Rudolph. Reception area of Burroughs, Wellcome & Co., building, North Carolina. Designed in concrete-aggregate and glass. 1974–1975.

505
Interior of La Scala Opera House, Milan, Italy. Original design, 1778, remodeled 1867 and 1921.

503

504

505

Contemporary Trends in Interior Design

Perhaps the most far-reaching influence on contemporary interior design is the fact that today people outside the profession have greater confidence in their own taste and want homes that reflect themselves as individuals. Most professional designers find this exciting: there are more choices, less emphasis on formulas, increased interest in the unusual. Designers often work with clients in informal partnership as the client refinishes antiques or builds innovative furniture that will become a focal point in the overall design (Fig. 506). Other designers are intrigued by innovation for its own sake. At the recent furniture fair in Milan (Il Salone del Mobile), the work of Italian furniture designers became a colorful explosion of imaginative designs (Fig. 507).

According to designer Noel Jeffrey, "The computer is going to have a very great impact on design. . . . The video boom will bring on a whole new wave of furniture designed to humanize media machinery and make it blend seamlessly into the home."[1] Already designers are marketing cabinets for home computer centers, as well as furniture to house electronic

[1] "What Top Decorators Across the Country See Ahead," *House Beautiful,* February 1982, p. 77.

506

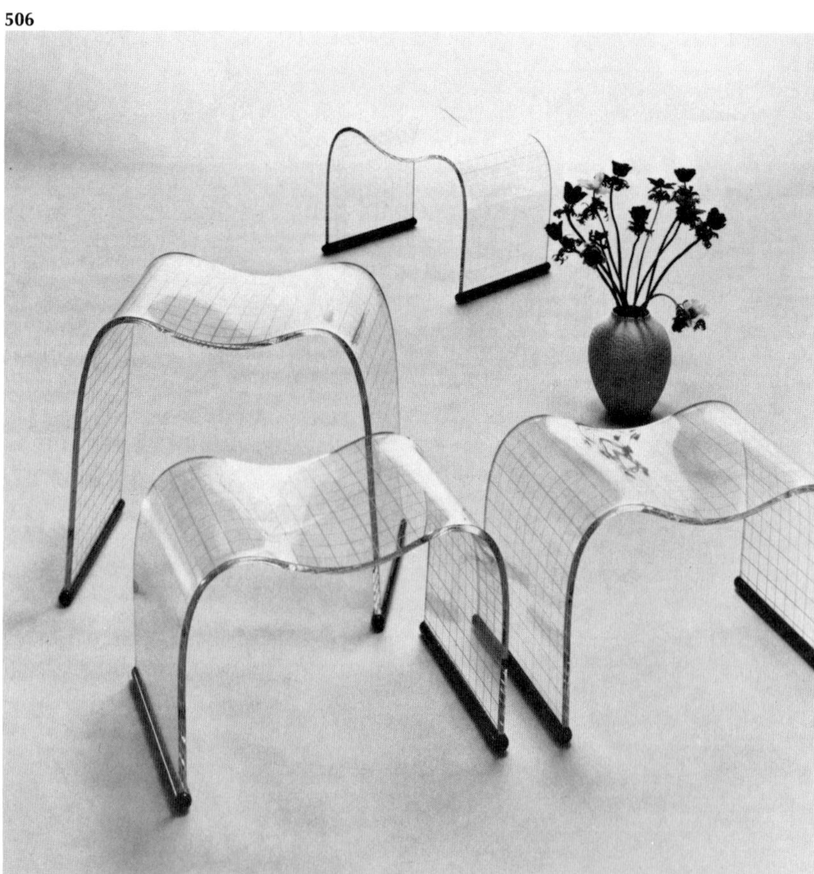

506
Vittorio Livi for Fiam of Italy. *Onda.* Etched glass with black lacquered wood frames, 22 × 13¾ × 17" (55 × 35 × 43 cm). The Pace Collection, Inc., New York.

507
Paolo Deganello. "Squash" love seat from Driade's Soft Series. Drawing by Stephen Keleman, Orient Point, New York.

507

equipment. One example is a television screen built into a chimney breast in a bedroom where a projector and video tape control unit are stored in a cabinet that is part of the design of the bed.

Aside from the impact of technology, interior design today is responding to the two basic pressures of contemporary life, overcrowding and industrialization. The result is special emphasis on two of the basic elements of design, *space* and *color*. People need attractive and flexible space in which to work, shop, dine, and carry out all the other activities of urban experience, and increasingly architects and interior designers are forming teams to fulfill this need. Second, in a world gray with industrialization, color has become both an inspiration and a necessity: contemporary interiors are bright with the colors of gardens or carnivals, or the more subtle hues of ripe fruit. Whether we are professional designers or individuals creating an intimate space for ourselves in an increasingly chaotic world, we can have no doubt that interior spaces exert a vital influence on the quality of our lives.

25 Architecture

Since the first inhabited cave, the ways in which space has been enclosed have manifested the effectiveness, the variety, and the richness of human life. The igloo, the skyscraper, the cathedral, and the tent all represent spatial enclosures for specific purposes. The interpretation and delineation of *space* has developed into the highly technical and immensely complex field of architectural design.

Architecture is a blending of art, creativity, and function. Increasingly the architect works with other designers—teams of fellow architects, interior designers, landscape architects, engineers—and with the public, to arrive at the most functional and aesthetic solution to a design project. In some ways architectural design is the most dominant and influential aspect of our environment, the buildings in which we live and carry out the many activities of human existence. To the city dweller, architecture *is* environment (Fig. 508).

Structural Design in Architecture

Although new methods and materials have expanded contemporary architectural processes far beyond those used in past centuries, any understanding of architectural design should be based on familiarity with the four traditional structural classifications: *post-and-lintel, arch, cantilever,* and *truss* (Fig. 509).

The Parthenon (Fig. 194) stands as the classic example of post-and-lintel construction. In this system two verticals are erected, and the intervening space is bridged by a beam, or lintel. This arrangement creates angular space within two walls and a flat roof (or any variation of the peaked roof) above the horizontal beams.

The development of the *arch* provided architects with a new concept: curved and circular space. First used by the Mesopotamians, the arch became a truly revolutionary element in the hands of the Romans. They repeated it in *arcades,* placed arches at right angles to one another to form *vaults,* and rotated the arch on its central axis to create the dome, thus providing succeeding centuries of architects all over the world with the tool for some of their most imposing landmarks (Fig. 510).

508

508
New York City skyline.

509
The four traditional structural systems: post-and-lintel, arch, cantilever, and truss.

510
St. Peter's Basilica, Rome.
Dome designed by Michelangelo. 1547.
Dome 140′ (42.7 m) in diameter.

511
Frank Lloyd Wright. Kaufmann House (*Falling Water*). Bear Run, Pa., 1936.
Cantilevered concrete balconies and rough walls of local stone.

The *cantilever* system came into prominence with the development of reinforced concrete—concrete poured over steel rods or mesh to give it support and stability. Having immense tensile strength, steel beams can span greater distances than either stone or wood. When this strength is combined with the strength of concrete under compression, a new and versatile material evolves. Beams imbedded in slabs of concrete and riveted or welded into place can support tremendous weights, even when extended into space. This extension provides a new concept of open space—an approach in which space is articulated rather than enclosed.

One of the best-known cantilever constructions was designed by Frank Lloyd Wright for the Edgar Kaufmann family in Pennsylvania, the house known as "Falling Water" (Fig. 511). Built on pylons or piers, anchored in a foundation of natural stone, the house has cantilevers of tawny-colored concrete projecting dramatically over the waterfall. The cantilevers, which

post and lintel

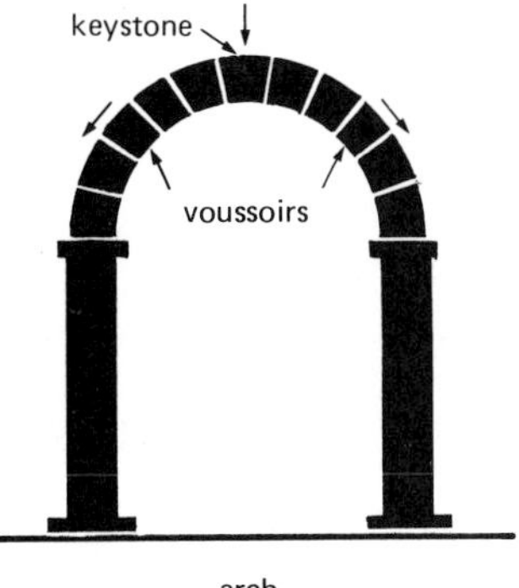

arch

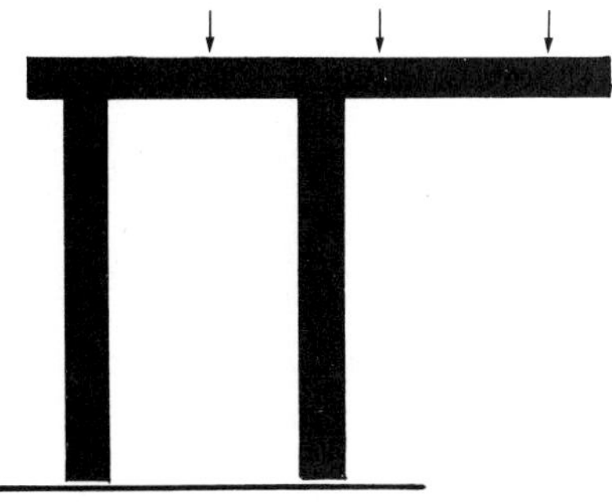

cantilever

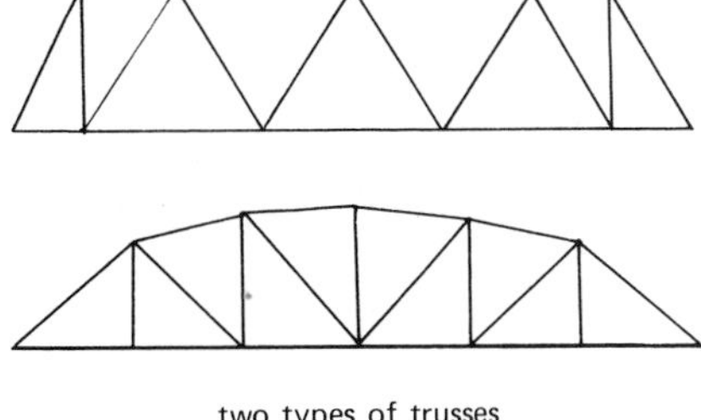

two types of trusses

509

510

511

512

also serve as terraces, have no support at one end. They form layers of solid structure counterbalanced by open space. Glass walls carry the feeling of space indoors, and contrast in texture with the stone of the chimney and the surrounding woods.

Trusses are employed when it is necessary to span longer distances than can be bridged by post-and-lintel construction. The truss consists of a rigid framework of bars, beams, or other material that is so strong it cannot be pushed out of shape. Trusses have long been used for steel bridges (see Fig. 209) as well as for large pavilions and aircraft fuselages.

The materials and technology of the twentieth century have added immeasurably to the vocabulary of structural design in architecture (Fig. 512). As we mentioned in Chapter 11, plastic foams and ferrocement have inspired flowing forms never before possible in structural design (see Figs. 226 and 233). A quite different approach is the *geodesic dome* patented by R. Buckminster Fuller in the 1940s. Just as a flat sheet of paper can be made into a dome by crumpling its surface into a series of small planes, an architectural dome can be created by the arrangement of small triangles combined with tetrahedrons (Fig. 513). This system makes it possible to cover much larger areas with a dome than had been possible with traditional construction. The triangular modules can be made of lightweight metal and the resultant structure covered with suitable material, such as plastic, cloth, or wood. An added advantage of the geodesic dome is its energy efficiency. Any domed ceiling reduces the volume of air at the ceiling, but the pockets of faceted surface hold warmth as well.

Another revolutionary concept in architectural design is *modular* construction, which depends upon prefabricated modules or units shipped intact to the building site, where they are attached to one another to form a building. The major advantage of this system is cost saving, since units mass-produced at a factory are much less expensive than on-site construction, and time spent in building is held to a minimum.

512
Environ A, architect Valerie Batorewicz' home in New Haven, CT, combines conventional building techniques with synthetic materials.

513
Bernard Judge's design for an experimental house of aluminum rods and plastic skin, Hollywood, CA. Based on the geodesic dome principle developed by R. Buckminster Fuller. 45′ (13.7 m) in diameter. 1958.

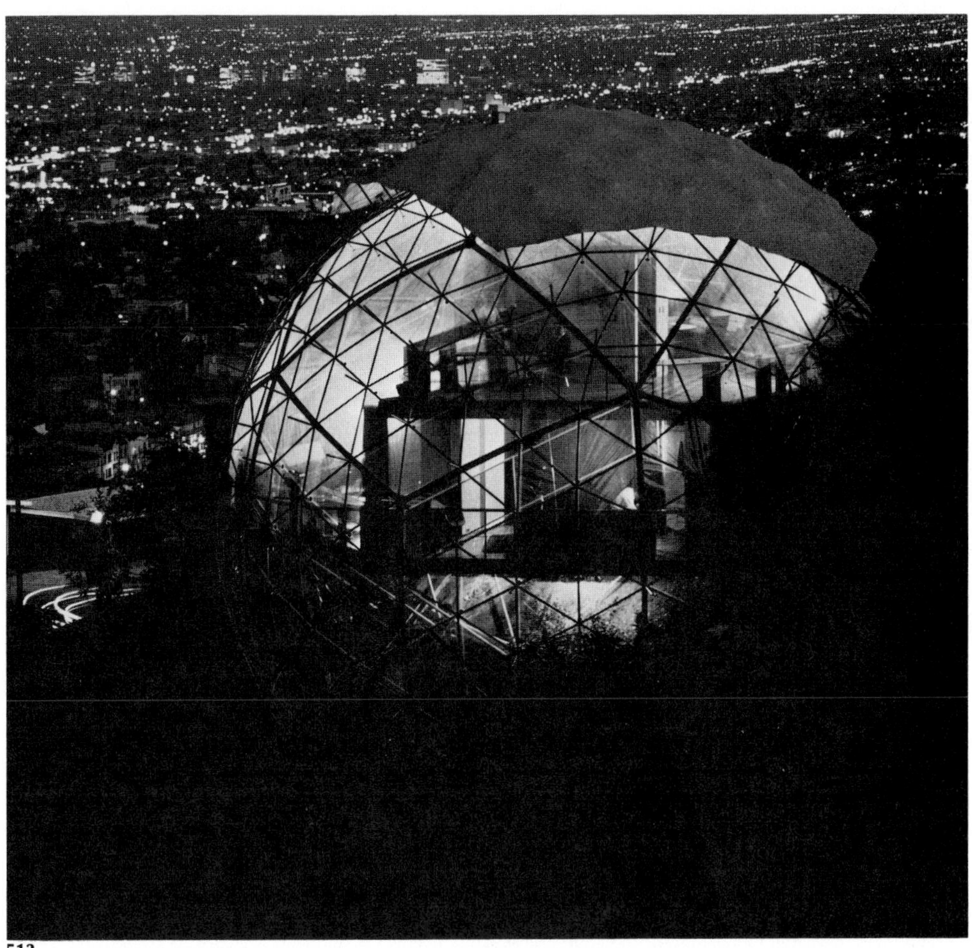

513

Attributes of Architectural Design

In a sense, the attributes of *subject, form,* and *content* chart the progress of an architect's work on any given project. As an example let us consider the Fribourg State Bank in Switzerland. *Subject* is stated in a set of specifications:

> Site: Flat triangular site, approximately 165,000 sq. ft. at the apex of a city block adjacent to the railroad station piazza.
>
> Program: Banking hall and offices, rental office space, restaurant, dance hall and underground parking. Three floors are underground, seven floors above, plus a penthouse level, more than 2 million cu. ft. altogether.[1]

Form becomes the architect's solution to the requirements stated in the "specs." Here architect Mario Botta has used reinforced concrete bearing walls and columns as his structural components, the vocabulary with which he expresses his aesthetic convictions concerning what is needed.

[1] Nory Miller, "Transfigurer of Geometry," *Progressive Architecture,* July 1982, p. 57.

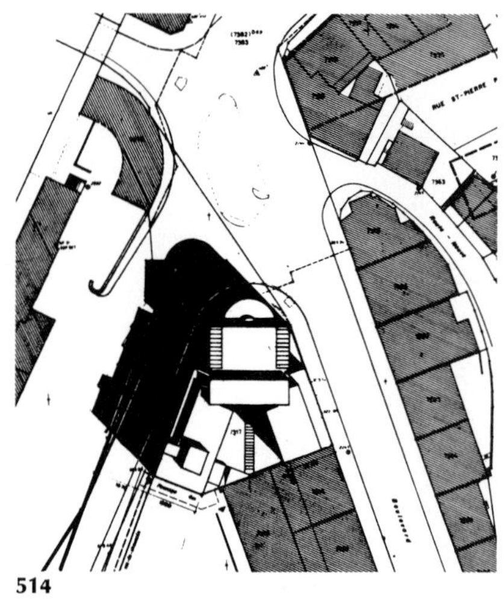
514

515

514
Mario Botta. Site plan of Fribourg State Bank, Fribourg, Switzerland. Completed 1982.

515
Façade of Fribourg State Bank.

516
Pruitt-Igoe housing project being blown up. Minoru Yamasaki, Pruitt-Igoe Housing. St. Louis, MO. 1952–1955.

517
Jørn Utzon and others. Opera House, Bennelong Point, Sydney Harbor. 1957–1973.

The first obvious need is a matter of urban *infill* or *retrofill,* that is, a blending of the new building with the established architecture that will surround it. In Figure 514 we see a drawing of the site plan in which two wings unite the new building with the adjacent houses along each of the two avenues that form the triangular site. Figure 515 shows the superb blending of the *façade* (the front surface) by the convex curving that maintains the corner yet is raised at the street level to allow for the passage of traffic. Barely discernible in the photograph is the reverse or concave curving at attic level (behind the metal railing), which echoes the shape of the piazza below. Although the bank has just been finished, it is already an unobtrusive part of its environment.

The interior is another matter (Pl. 34, p. 363), for here we find an undeniable sense of grandeur. Materials are traditional—green and gray marble, fine woods, and the more ordinary materials of basic construction. They are used in geometric *shapes* and varied *colors* and *textures,* distributed throughout the building in a balanced and rhythmic way. This is a bank of dignity and opulence, one that inspires immediate confidence. In this we find *content,* the manner in which the enclosed space meets the social goals for which it was intended.

Content in architecture cannot be accurately assessed until a building has been in use for some time. One of the most urgent social problems of the twentieth century has been overcrowded housing, particularly in city slum areas. Many solutions have been offered, and structures built accordingly, only to prove miserable failures. The outstanding example is the Pruitt-Igoe housing project built in St. Louis in 1952–55, a high-rise complex with all the proper formulas—separate pedestrian and vehicular traffic areas, play space, laundries and centers for gossiping, all in a clean, healthful environment. The *form* appeared the ideal solution to overcrowding and disease, and it was assumed by the planners that good health and improved behavior would result. Instead, the crime rate rose astronomically, exceeding that in all other housing developments. In 1972, after the buildings had been continuously vandalized, several of the slab blocks were blown up (Fig. 516). Architectural analysts attributed the failure of the project to the anonymity of the building, with its identical living cubicles, long corridors, and lack of controlled semiprivate space. The *subject* was admirable, the *form* was theoretically sound, but the *content* was a total failure.

Elements and Principles of Architectural Design

As noted in the discussion of the Fribourg State Bank, the elements and principles of design operate in architecture on a grand scale. *Mass* is indigenous to architecture, serving practical as well as symbolic purposes. In cities, cubical masses fit neatly together, conserving space, whereas ceremonial buildings have traditionally consisted of a cube combined with a cylinder culminating in an impressive dome, which symbolizes eternity (Fig. 510). The freedom extended by new materials and methods has resulted in imaginative masses (Fig. 517).

516

517

518

519

518
Naff (John M., Jr.) house, Pajaro Dunes, CA. Designed by William Turnbull of Turnbull Associates, MLTW, San Francisco, CA. Built in 1969. © by Morley Baer.

519
Church at Trampas, NM, adobe. 17th century.

520
Daon Centre, Vancouver, B.C. Architect: Musson Cattell & Associates.

Line and *shape* in architecture tell us much about a community or a person. Approaching a city dominated by the vertical lines and long rectangles of skyscrapers, we expect density of population, industrial activity, and a wide variety of commercial enterprises. New England villages dominated by the soaring triangle of a church steeple speak for the traditional character of the people who live there. The massive colonial-style mansions of the South, with their impressive vertical columns, imply interest in land, money, and prestige. A house that blends into its surroundings states clearly that the builder appreciates the beauty of the setting. The lines of the house in Figure 518 are horizontal and low to the ground to echo the lines of sea and dunes. Windows compose the wall facing the sea, and the natural finish of the wood weathers to the tones of sand and driftwood.

Beach grasses growing against the walls pull the structure into the natural vegetation. Line here is used as a continuation of landscape.

Color also has symbolic architectural associations—neat white farmhouses, red barns, New York's brownstone houses, the red brick Georgian homes in Philadelphia and Washington, D.C., the earth tones of adobe buildings in New Mexico (Fig. 519). The grayness of cities has been a cliché until recent years, when designers began seeing the cheerful possibilities in coordinating city blocks by color. Cities in Florida, California, England, and Italy are now sporting whole blocks in lavenders, reds, pinks, greens, and blues. Color coding also relates the buildings within a complex, thereby aiding in their identification.

Some builders have experimented with mirrored walls on skyscrapers, providing dramatic reflections of sky and surroundings that change throughout the day (Fig. 520). This innovation has its hazards, however; owners of mirrored buildings have been sued by their neighbors because in warm climates the mirrors reflect intense heat on adjacent buildings.

520

521

We have discussed the *texture* of architectural materials in several instances (note textures, both visual and tactile, in the Fribourg State Bank in Pl. 34). There are many types of glass blocks, concrete blocks, and decorative tiles that can provide textural accents. An unusual effect in cast brick gives the impression of bas-relief in Figure 521, relieving the monotony of light brick while retaining the *variety* and *unity* of the material.

Since we have used numerous architectural examples in our discussions of the principles of design in Chapters 8–10, perhaps it will be sufficient to summarize by analyzing a single building in which all of the principles can be identified. The apartment building in Figure 522 uses arches and balconies to provide *balance* and *rhythm,* lightening what could be an extremely heavy mass. Space flows in and out of the arches, vertical lines break the solid horizontality, and the color is a warm yet subtle rosy earth tone. Providing dramatic points of *emphasis,* the arches are in *scale* with the total building and in careful *proportion* to the textural areas between them. There is, of course, tremendous *variety*—in shape and texture—and yet the entire design is one of *unity.* Not all buildings are such obvious expressions of all the elements and principles of design, but careful analysis will reveal the working of these elements and principles in any successful architectural design.

522

521
School District 60 Administration Bldg. Pueblo, Co. Hurtig, Gardner & Froelich, Architects.

522
Les Arcades du Lac and Le Viaduc. Saint Quentin-en-Yvelines, France. Architects: Taller de Arquitectura/Ricardo Bofill, Barcelona. 1978.

523
Comparison of Doric and Ionic orders, which, with the more elaborate Corinthian (right), formed the basic design of Greek architecture of the Classic Period.

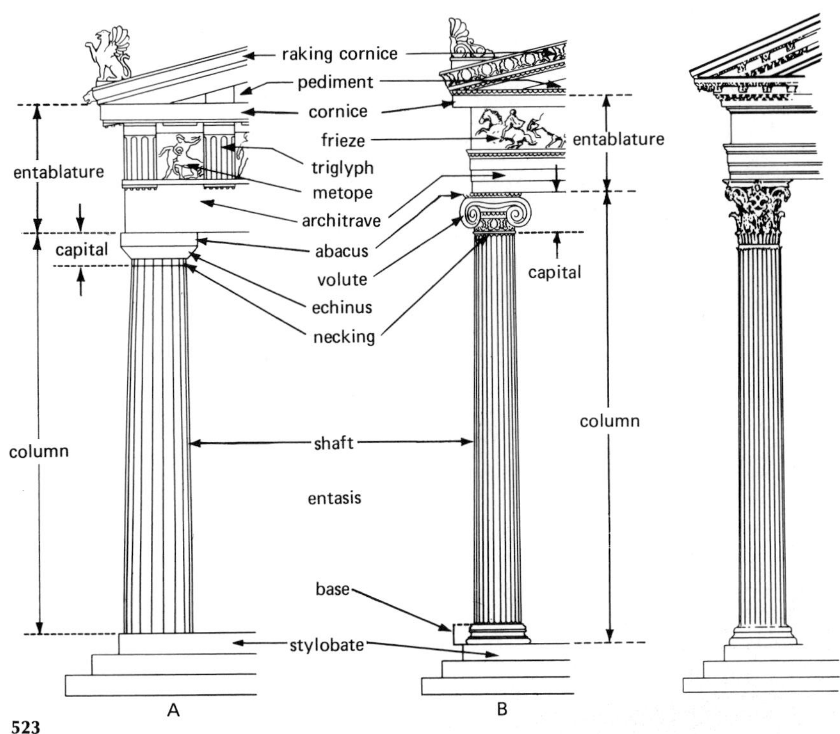

523

Development of Contemporary Architecture

In the broadest terms, artistic expression has been categorized traditionally in one of two ways: classical or romantic. We compared examples of classicism and romanticism in painting in Chapter 9: recall the symmetrical balance, intellectual approach, and clear, clean outlines of David's classical *Death of Socrates* (Fig. 184), and the asymmetrical balance, swirling color, and darkly emotional quality of Goya's *Executions of the Third of May, 1808* (Fig. 185), which is classified as romantic. *Classicism* dates from the so-called Golden Age of Greece (480–400 B.C.) and is epitomized in the architecture of the Parthenon (Fig. 194). Greek architecture of this period displayed the same symmetrical balance and clean lines that we saw in David's painting, and was based on one of three orders—the Doric, Ionic, and Corinthian—that determined the proportions as well as the amount and character of ornamentation (Fig. 523). There have been other notable architectural styles, particularly the Gothic, but the importance of the classical to us is the fact that it has been revived periodically and in various guises throughout architectural history. Its dignity has given it an imposing role in human experience, taking form in banks and law courts, triumphal arches and opera houses throughout the Western world. Partly as a result of Thomas Jefferson's enthusiasm for classicism, it was adopted as the prevailing style in the design of Washington, D.C.

The *romantic* style of architecture was born of the so-called Gothic novels of the late eighteenth century, in which the action took place among ruins of mysterious and fantastic character, redolent of melancholy and mysticism. Wealthy Englishmen put the settings into tangible form by building mansions replete with towers, turrets, and labyrinthine corridors. The trend flourished not only in novels but also in architecture. A well-known example is the Palace of Neuschwanstein (Fig. 524) built by King Ludwig II of Bavaria, an imaginative monarch known for his hallucinations. The romantic style in architecture can be characterized by several traits: *eclecticism* (the combining of several styles) with a strong Gothic flavor, an element of *fantasy,* and reference to a fanciful *past.* The Victorian period in America saw its development into a distinctive pattern sometimes referred to as "gingerbread houses" (Fig. 525).

The age of modern architecture was born with the first skyscraper, the Wainwright Building in St. Louis, built in 1890 (Fig. 526). The building's designer, Louis Sullivan, interpreted the slogan "form follows function" to mean that it did not matter what a building looked like as long as it fulfilled its function. The function of the skyscraper was to answer the need for commercial centralization in the Middle West. The Wainwright Building was hailed as a tremendous engineering feat made possible by steel-skeleton construction and the elevator. Although the skyscraper increases congestion in an already crowded area, it was seen as a proud and soaring expression of a technologically oriented people.

Sullivan's protegé, Frank Lloyd Wright, carried his own ideas into subsequent skyscrapers, but his most significant contribution was organic architecture, based on a philosophy uniting site, structure, material, and decoration (Fig. 511). His houses were integrated with the land by means of horizontal lines and indigenous materials, and the opening up of space, allowing rooms to flow into one another and outdoor and indoor areas to mingle. Glass was the key to space as it was expressed in the *International Style* that took form in Germany in the work of Walter Gropius.[2] In this style, basic steel and glass boxes opened the interior visually but kept interior spaces in traditional rectangular configurations.

524

Contemporary Directions in Architecture

The dominant trend in architecture today is *Post-Modernism.* As in painting, the term is indicative not of a specific style so much as a turning away from what has gone before. The International Style of architecture, with its glass and steel boxes, interpreted function as structural capability, failing to recognize that its indiscriminate use made homes, filling stations, and office buildings all look very much alike, the sameness of which penetrated into the fabric of everyday living. The failure of Pruitt-Igoe (Fig. 516) represents the explosion point of tensions that had been building for several decades in a world unable to satisfy the aesthetic and spiritual needs of its inhabitants.

Where does architecture turn under such circumstances? First, it turns to the past, to symbols that revive human terms and provide meanings linking people to their ancestors, their memories, and the springs that feed their aspirations. Post-Modernism, then, begins with *revivals of past styles.* A pure revival never satisfies a later period, however, so many styles and

524
King Ludwig II of Bavaria. Palace of Neuschwanstein. 1869.

525
S. and J. C. Newson. William Carson Residence, Eureka, CA (now the Ingomar Club). 1884.

526
Louis Sullivan. Wainwright Building, St. Louis, MO. 1890–1891.

[2]Walter Gropius, *The New Architecture and the Bauhaus* (Cambridge, Mass.: MIT Press, 1968).

525

526

527

influences are combined, in a *radical eclecticism.* Eclecticism, the blending of many influences, can result in a watering down of previous styles. As implied by the term *radical,* however, the Post-Modernists seek not to imitate but integrate the meanings and associations of diverse historical elements, set in modern form. This results in the keynote of Post-Modern architecture, dual or double "coding," the use of architectural symbols on two levels, by which traditional metaphorical meaning is assigned to contemporary elements. Houses traditionally have looked like faces, with their windows as eyes and the door as mouth. The International Style denied this animistic expression with expanses of glass or concrete and disguised entryways (Fig. 527). But the Post-Modernist has sought not only to return to symmetry but to emphasize a recognizable physiognomy. In the house in Figure 528 it is almost as though the front wore a benign expression. To the contemporary coding of simple, clean lines is added an assortment of elements that can be interpreted symbolically according to the associations of the viewer—columns set at heights and distances to emphasize the door; the shape of an Assyrian ziggurat, or temple; a smokestack, the use of moldings to accentuate windows and to outline the roof against the sky.

Post-Modernists have also developed a new conception of space, which is in distinct opposition to the tight geometry of the Modern conception. Post-Modern architecture is almost metaphysical, with spaces that seem to lead somewhere, but to a place not yet clearly defined. There is a feeling of affinity to the body and its movements, rather than a sense of constraint within immovable walls.

The rich symbolic and spatial language of Post-Modernism is impressively articulated in the work of architect Charles Moore. Widely traveled and of broad architectural experience, Moore exemplifies the Post-Modernist architect. Teaming with two architects who supplied a store of cultural knowledge, he designed the *Piazza d'Italia* in New Orleans, a focal point commemorating the contribution of the Italian community to the

527
Christopher Owen's design for a house in New York's suburbs is a contemporary version of the International Style of Architecture. 1975.

528
Michael Graves. Schulman House, Princeton, N. J. 1976–1978.

529
Charles W. Moore with Urban Innovations Group, August Perez and Associates.
Piazza d'Italia, New Orleans, LA. 1976–1979. Aerial view.

528

culture of the city. This design demonstrates the flexible language characteristic of Post-Modernism. It also exemplifies the characteristic civic requirements that have made that language both possible and necessary.

The structure had to be fitted into an existing neighborhood of mixed architectural styles, bordered on one side by a skyscraper. Its intended function was as a focal point in a busy city, where once a year the Italian community could dramatize its presence with an exuberant celebration of St. Joseph's Day, honoring their patron saint with sales of Italian specialties, exhibits of Italian arts and crafts, and all the jubilation of native songs and dances. The setting for such a celebration had to be rich in indigenous symbols recalling the origins of the celebrants. The aerial view in Figure 529 shows the subtle adjustment to setting, the domination of the rectangular neighborhood by the predominant circle, and the transitional arcs and curves in the buildings, rings of pavement, and arched entryway. The circular form extends out into three streets, giving the passerby a cue that something unusual is transpiring behind the existing buildings. What transpires is a totally unpredictable use of space. Instead of focusing in on the circle as a kind of bull's-eye, the space is broken by partial discs, screens of columns that spin asymmetrically on a diagonal axis. The diago-

529

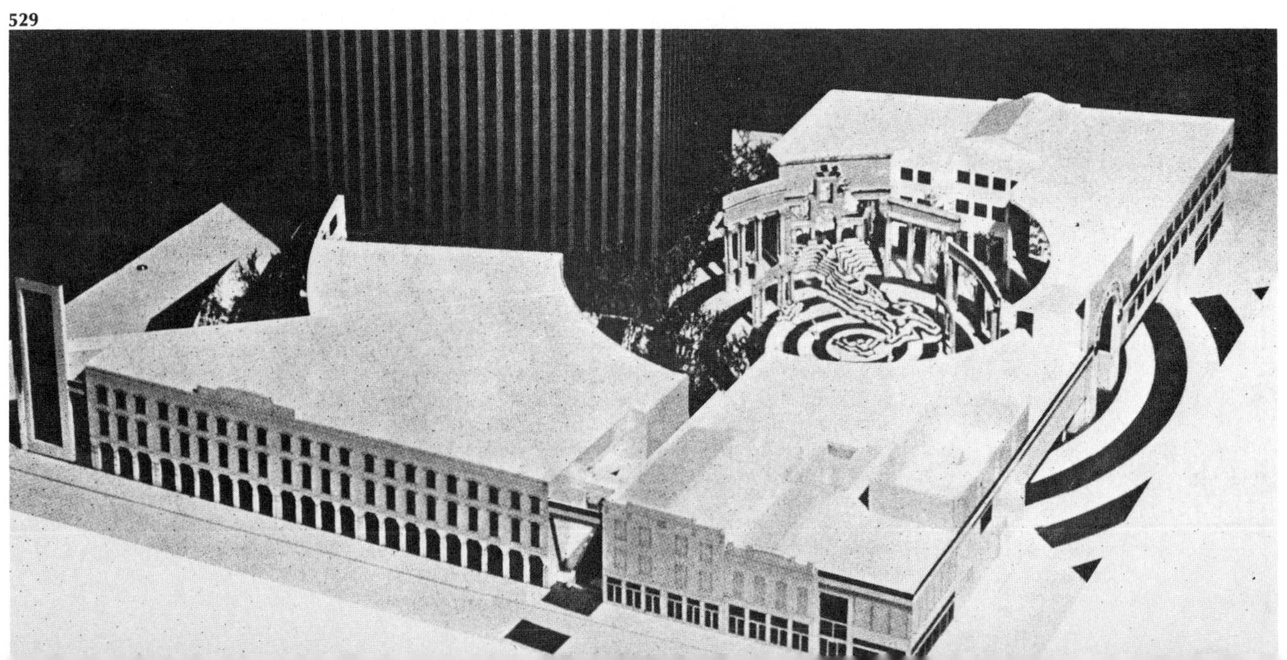

530

nal is reenforced by a cascade of varied forms: the boot of Italy rising toward the northern Alps, the five orders of Italian columns, a pergola adjacent to the circle, and a campanile (bell tower) at the far corner. Space threads and flows until it culminates in the fountain, where all the symbols of Post-Modern architecture erupt in joyous movement. Capitals, moldings, and columns all appear to be made of water. Water washes over a stainless steel arch, down stucco walls, and over an 80-foot (24.3-meter) three-dimensional map of Italy, flowing into two basins representing the Tyrrhenian and Adriatic seas. Color is used symbolically. There are focal points of black-and-white to echo the adjacent skyscraper, and there are the rich earth tones of the Italian soil and areas of gold the color of Italian sunlight. The essence of Post-Moderism is reached at night, when all the traditional symbols of past centuries are outlined in colored neon lights (Plate 35, p. 364).

Eclecticism is usually considered a characteristic of Romantic architecture, but the Post-Modernists belie that association with a style they label the New Classicism. We have mentioned the periodic revival of Classical architecture throughout history—in the Italian Renaissance of the fourteenth century, which was considered the literal "rebirth" of all things classical, in seventeenth-century England under the architect Inigo Jones, and again in the Georgian style (named for the reign of the four Georges in England) that distinguished American colonial architecture. Napoleon commissioned classical architecture all over Paris as the only style worthy of his aspirations, and Hitler and Stalin both used it as a symbol of power and stability and lasting values. Today it provides a symbol of universal order and eternal values in a continually changing world.

The New Classicism is treated in two ways: the traditional historic approach and the approach in which classical elements are applied in a free, nontraditional way. The new courthouse in Manchester, Connecticut (Fig. 530), illustrates the latter. Remodeled upon the shell of a 1962 supermarket, the building retains the original white wings at either side and concentrates the Classical elements on the front. In accordance with Classical tradition, the façade is symmetrical, with the entrance firmly in the center and the arched windows, flagpoles, and inscription balanced at the sides. The cornice over the door is Greek (see Fig. 523); the large stones at either side and at the corners of the building, a treatment known as *rustication,* echo old Roman city gates. Inside, the barrel-vaulted ceiling forms a half-cylinder above the floors of terrazzo (small marble chips set in concrete and polished). The original supporting columns are sheathed to become Tuscan in style after one of the old Roman orders, and Classical details embellish walls and doorways. There is a clarity and order about the building that is eloquent testimony to its purpose. It is not monumental in style but human, emphasizing its relationship to the community, as is characteristic of the Post-Modern approach.

530
Courthouse at Manchester, CT. Architects: Allan Greenberg, with Peter Kosinski Associates. 1980.

531
Grain storage barn in the hamlet of Holleren in the Emmental-Berne area of Switzerland.

Vernacular Architecture

We tend to think of architecture as impressive buildings designed by experts, yet on a worldwide scale this is true of only 5 percent of all buildings. The rest are built by individuals for their own use, often without drawn plans or written specifications, expressing their own tastes and needs, and with no pretensions to aesthetic design. This is vernacular architecture, which is the folk music of architectural design, carrying its own integrity and validity.

Vernacular architecture has several distinguishing characteristics. In its *directness* and total *lack of self-consciousness,* it becomes a basic expression of a culture, of the dreams and values of a people. There are no criteria imposed by professional designers, and there is usually no concern for expressing status. In its simplest form, the house was built by the owner, but later, building tradesmen took part, providing specialized skills. Building was done in a traditional manner, *within traditional models,* with adjustments being made to suit individual needs.

Vernacular building is usually *done with the site and the climate in mind,* working with nature rather than imposing upon it. It respects the work of other people and *their* houses, blending with the total environment. Although its adherence to traditional models limits its modes of expression, *it can fit into many situations,* and *it can accept additions and changes* that would destroy the design of a high-style structure.

Examples of vernacular architecture could begin with the first shelter of tree branches and continue to the present day. The adobe church in Figure 519 is an example of a vernacular style that has existed in the United States for more than three centuries, being built of the very mud upon which it stands, patted with straw into bricks and dried in the sun, then plastered with the same mud after the building has been constructed. Similarly ancient is the tradition of building storage barns in Switzerland from the wood and stone of the surrounding mountainsides. Such buildings were frequently decorated with designs and inscriptions indicative of the vital role cattle played in alpine existence (Fig. 531).

531

Present-day vernacular is not so much a matter of homes as of *types* of buildings unique to the twentieth century—the motel, the gas station, the diner, and the drive-in. These fill a specific function and are built by construction firms, in collaboration with the developer or potential owner. There are vernacular homes, however. A small number of people are building homes by hand, tilling the land, and becoming self-sufficient. Although this style of life represents a self-conscious choice, the homes thus built echo the authentic beginnings of vernacular architecture.

Architecture Today

Architectural design today is in a state of flux as architects and builders search for a style that will be a true expression of our time. Many of the reasons for the lack of a current style are not aesthetic. The energy crisis has negated some of the characteristics most cherished in recent generations: open flowing space, walls of glass, and rooms that seem to mingle with the out-of-doors. When contemporary designs use glass, it is often in connection with solar heating.

The house in Figure 533 is one of a series of natural-convection houses using under-floor rock beds heated entirely by the sun (Fig. 532). Utilizing no fans, pumps, or blowers, they maintain almost constant temperatures day and night, generating essentially 100 percent of the heat needed for a 2000-square-foot structure, with a temperature swing of only 4.2 degrees Fahrenheit. Other innovations include the use of rammed earth, soil tamped by pressure into forms to create walls and other structural components. Rammed earth soaks up heat during mild winter days, giving it back to the interior on cold nights. Still other architects use sod roofs for insulation, and many are building entirely underground to conserve energy (Fig. 534).

532

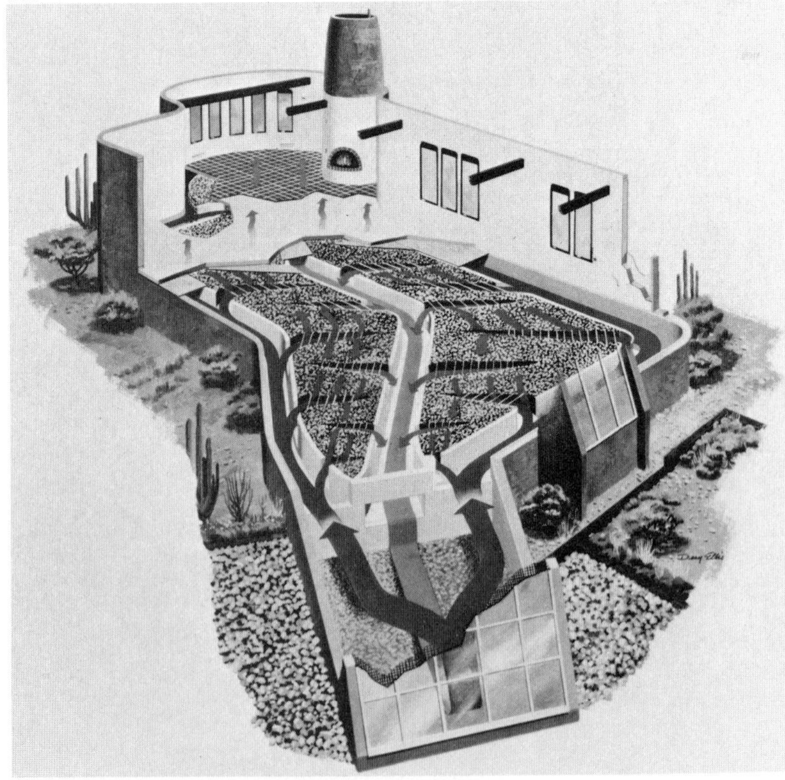

532
Design for siphon collector for solar heat. Illustration by Dean Ellis.

533
Horizontal rock bed for solar heating system.

534
William Morgan, Architect. Atlantic Beach Dunehouses. Sprayed concrete granite, two one-bedroom apartments, each 750 square feet (228.8 m). Completed 1975.

533

534

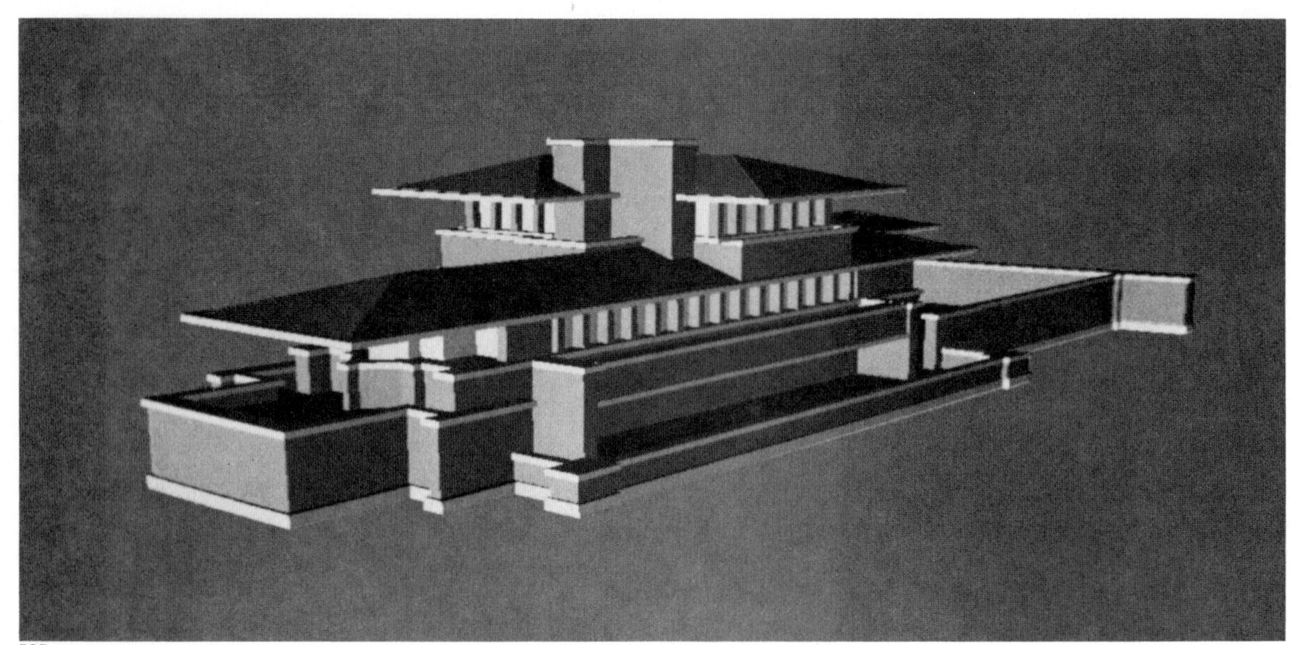
535

The computer, mentioned in Chapter 12 as a means of drawing plans, is also being employed in systems by which the viewer simulates the experience of walking toward a projected building from various angles. Using a color television set as the output device, abstract opaque planes are "painted" on the screen in such a way that a three-dimensional reproduction of a proposed building can be projected in different views (Fig. 535).

The architectural designer has always carried a heavy responsibility, but today the burden becomes increasingly complex. Our environment is cluttered with past mistakes, bad taste, and the results of generations of experimentation and changing styles. New buildings must be *contextual,* that is, they must fit in with the existing neighborhood, and they must also exhibit *retrofit* in their relationships with contiguous structures. The public is better educated and more outspoken than ever before regarding any impact on the environment. It is a time not just of changing styles but of radically changing outlooks and patterns of living, and architects must be sensitive to the spirit of the past as a thread in the human continuum while building for a complex, challenging, and frequently unpredictable future.

535
Computer-generated image of Frank Lloyd Wright's Robie House, displayed on a 1000 × 1000 raster display. The geometry was modeled using an input routine designed by Wayne Robertz, the modeling was performed by Dan Ambrosi. Cornell University, New York, Program of Computer Graphics, Dr. Donald P. Greenberg, Director.

26 The Total Environment

Thus far we have discussed environment in terms of a world that can be designed to serve and express human life. Beyond our own walls, however, there is the larger world composed of a network of communities, each with its unique flavor and needs. These may be states, cities, counties, towns, or villages. A nation is an entity with broad national goals, but it is within the communities that any significant changes in environmental quality must occur.

It is communities that apply for designations of wilderness areas or historic preservation, and it is community effort that makes possible the success of landscape designers in developing their designs. Communities rebel against the building of atomic power plants or establishment of prisons in their midst, or the transformation of the landscape because of drilling for oil (Fig. 536). They do not always succeed in their efforts, of course. Entire towns have disappeared under water when dams and power plants have been built. Other communities in secluded and beautiful areas have changed character when tourists surged in, building summer homes and demanding the amenities of the urban areas they left behind. Even in such drastic situations, however, it is the community that must determine the form its adaptation to outside influences must take.

Landscape Design

In a sense, community planning begins and ends with landscape design. If there are to be parks and other decorative plantings, the space for them must be designated before any building is started. The actual planting, on the other hand, takes place after construction is completed.

536

536
Former wheatfields near Hays, KS, dotted with oil rigs.

537

Although we have records of gardens from biblical times to the present, the origin of *landscape architecture* is attributed to André Le Nôtre, who designed the gardens at the Palace of Versailles for Louis XIV. The term was an accurate one, for the gardens stretched for miles and became an extension of the palace, a series of outdoor rooms that served as a setting for elaborate entertainment. Magnificent fountains, waterways, and sculpture accentuated the formal plantings, which included the *parterre,* or designed flower bed (Fig. 537). Foliage, sculpture, and water were coordinated into a rhythmic and unified design in which the palace became the point of emphasis. It is fitting that contemporary landscape designers use the term *landscape architecture* to describe their work, since the landscape is so much a part of city planning, involving a combination of buildings, thoroughfares, and plantings similar to that encountered at Versailles.

Since the first step in any design is an analysis of the project, landscape design begins with *site analysis.* Analysis of landscape includes a map showing topography, access routes, existing structures, and planted areas. Details of drainage and water sources are noted and geological variations assessed. In some cases the angle of sunlight is important throughout the seasons of the year. When the original analysis has been made, the designer draws up plans for the renovation. The work is carried out in the same way as that of any architect, with drawings of both plan and elevation. Figure 538 shows two of the drawings made in the process of restoring a sixty-year-old country estate in Michigan. The city of Flint has grown up around the estate. The project was to restore it for present-day living, with the idea ultimately of opening it to the public as an example of the gracious living of an earlier era.

The *contour of the land* can be a fundamental issue, particularly in new projects. Buildings require level sites, but the charm of a landscape may rely on hills, ravines, or waterways. Much can be done with heavy equipment. Knolls can be leveled and berms (artificial hills) can be built up. Steep slopes can be terraced into a series of flat areas or can be planted with vines and low shrubs to prevent erosion. Lakes, ponds, streams, and waterfalls can all be built artificially (Fig. 539).

537
André Le Nôtre. Palace Gardens, Versailles. 1662–1688.

538
C. S. Mott Estate. Sketch by Carl D. Johnson. Graphics by Johnson, Johnson & Roy, Ann Arbor, MI.

539
A pond and waterfall can be built in a small area, providing beauty of sight and sound.

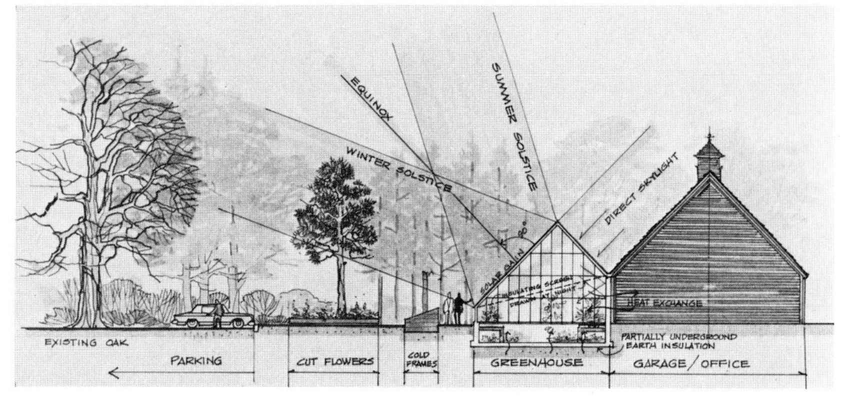

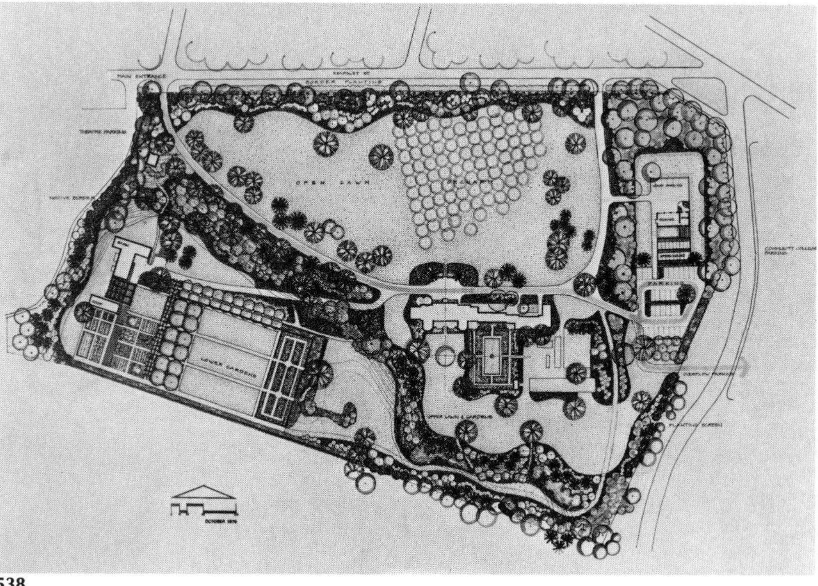

538

539

Soil is important not only in planting but in the building of ponds and streams. A pond cannot be expected to survive if the bottom is so porous the water drains out. Most plants, on the other hand, cannot survive in soil without drainage. In creating a new landscape, it is not unusual to bring in a complete complement of topsoil mixed to specification.

One of the fundamental tools of the landscape designer is a *knowledge of botanical forms and their needs.* These forms vary widely in their climatic requirements, so it is vital to select planting materials accordingly. Severe winters automatically eliminate a large body of plants from consideration, while hot summers make it impossible for another group to survive. Altitude can be a factor, and amount of moisture is crucial. Trees vary widely in their habitat. Acid or alkaline soils are a factor that must be assessed for many plants to thrive. Although climate can be controlled to some extent by the creation of shady areas or pockets of warmth, the difficulty of maintenance is greatly increased when plants are in situations that are basically incompatible.

540

540
Circular segments of clay pipe held tightly in painted wood frames create an airy screen for privacy. *House & Garden Garden Guide,* © 1968 by the Condé Nast Publications, Inc., New York.

541
Fan-patterned paving. De Dam, Amsterdam.

There is another aspect to the relationship between plants and climate, however. In many historic gardens in Italy and Spain, plants were used to *control* climate. Trees and hedges protected courtyards and open rooms from the summer sun, yet allowed the low rays of winter sun to penetrate. To provide a cooling system shade was often combined with water that splashed from fountains onto tiled walks. Allées (corridors between plantings) of trees and bosks (thick clumps of trees) directed breezes and screened the sunlight. Contemporary landscape architects are finding these devices even more applicable to urban areas. Trees produce oxygen and act as air purifiers in addition to their role in screening and cooling.

We usually think of plantings as the most aesthetic elements in landscape design, yet there are other *aesthetic aspects* that heighten the effect of the plantings. Among these are *enclosures, embellishments,* and *lighting.*

Using a garden wall as an *enclosure* is a classic means of secluding a quiet spot from the outside world. In city planning, variations of the garden wall abound. These are used to screen landscaped areas from unsightly buildings and traffic noise, or simply to demarcate decorative and commercial sections. On a city block, even a tiny plot of ground can be made private by skillful use of an enclosure (Fig. 540). Enclosures can consist of plantings, as mentioned above—hedges, allées, bosks, and vine-covered trellises, all of which act as coolers and air filters. Walls of stone, brick, or adobe can serve as solar heat collectors, giving back warmth in the cool of evening; however, they must have openings for air circulation if plants are to thrive within. Walls or fences of less massive material can take many forms. Decorative building blocks of concrete, pumice, tile, or glass come in many designs, and wooden fences can be built in a variety of heights and patterns.

Embellishment is a broad term covering any artificial device added to a landscaping project for decorative purposes. Statuary and waterways, including pools, fountains, and waterfalls, are time-honored embellishments. Benches, arbors, and gazebos form another group, designed for human enjoyment and serving the element of *time,* which is fundamental to experiencing landscape design. Still another approach to embellishment is texture. Plantings provide texture of immense diversity, but additional interest can be supplied by imaginative paving (Fig. 541).

Lighting extends the time of enjoyment of a landscape dramatically. A lighted garden has two temporal aspects: its daytime character, with details of plants clearly visible, and its nighttime disposition, filled with the mystery of light and shadow and lively with fanciful forms. Lighting in landscape is an art as technical as theatrical lighting and with many of the same purposes. A plant can be spotlighted, an allée or a fountain can be floodlighted, and indirect lighting among rocks and shrubbery can transform an already lovely view into sheer enchantment (Pl. 36, p. 364).

541

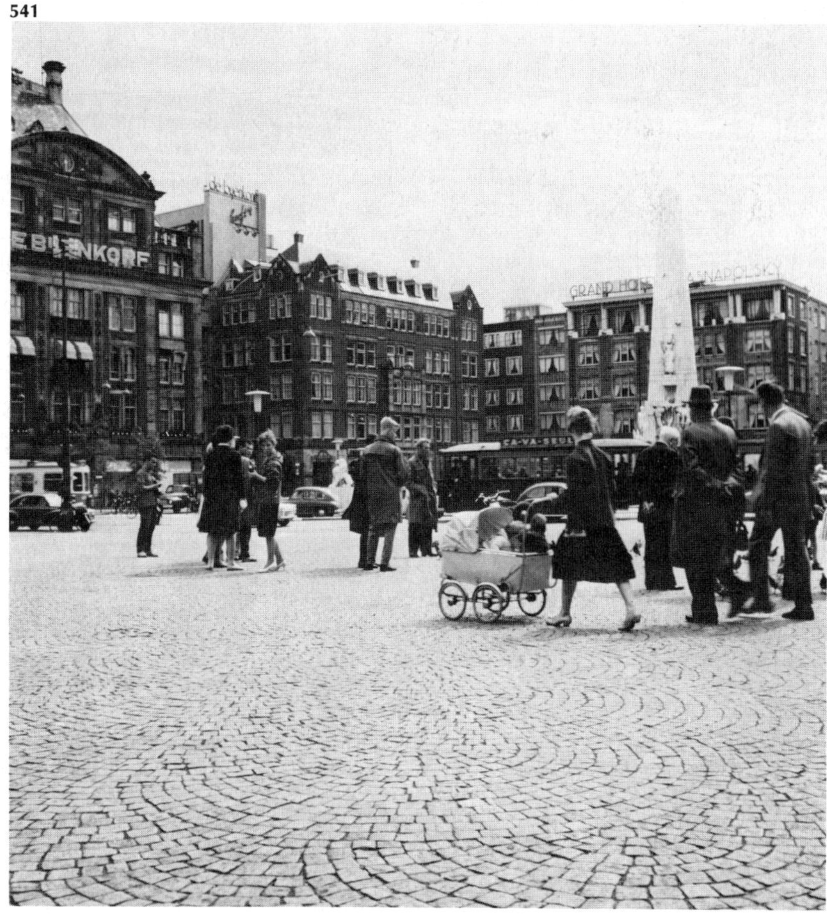

Community Design

As cities become increasingly complex and impersonal, the community within the city acquires a role of ever greater importance. People who have grown up within large cities tell us this has always been so, that within the bustling metropolis, the individual has found a support system within the smaller unit, perhaps an ethnic group or just the neighbors bound together by the mutual problems of living on the same block. The *physical* division of the American city into neighborhoods came following World War II, when *decentralization* became the revolutionary solution to problems of crowded downtown areas, lack of parking space, and the impersonal concrete and glass of the average city. For generations the population had been gravitating from rural areas to the cities; then the flow reversed as people poured from downtown areas into suburban developments. The suburban shopping center became a leading area for architectural design as merchants banded together in attractive settings with ample parking space and an atmosphere conducive to relaxed, casual shopping. Centers developed into elaborate replicas of European settings with fountains, waterfalls, statuary, flower beds, theaters, and restaurants in addition to every conceivable variety of shop. In many such centers, vehicular traffic was abolished (Fig. 542).

As with many solutions, this one gave rise to a new set of problems. Downtown areas with their big stores and high buildings now became a new variety of ghost town as merchants found that business had moved to the suburbs. The obvious solution was the branch store in the shopping center, in a sense a self-defeating measure, since branch stores left the large downtown establishments virtually empty. The seventies saw the birth of a kind of hybrid environment: the earmarks of suburbia were transplanted downtown as streets were closed off and converted into malls; plantings and other landscaping devices blossomed among the old buildings, smaller and more exotic shops appeared, and transportation by public conveyance was encouraged as a means of luring the population back downtown. Thus the American city planner discovered a solution that had been proven in Milan, Italy, a hundred years before.

In 1860 the city of Milan staged a competition inviting all citizens to submit designs for a covered galleria, to be built in the center of town. The winning plan was that of Giuseppe Mengoni, and in 1867 the Galleria Vittorio Emanuele was officially opened to the public (Fig. 543). It consists

542

542
The Plaza, Place Ville Marie, Montreal.

543
Giuseppe Mengoni. Galleria Vittorio Emanuele, Milan. Completed 1867.

544
Larimer Square in Denver is graced by intersecting arcaded walkways and attractive shop fronts.

543

of two covered streets, 643 and 344 feet long, respectively, intersecting in the form of a Latin cross. The glass roof soars to a height of 88 feet and culminates in a central cupola 160 feet above the ground. Within this spectacular enclosure are nearly a hundred smart shops, plus elegant restaurants and cafés. Since its inception, the Galleria has been a meeting place for artists, writers, and musicians, as well as a gathering point for the entire population of Milan. In summer the airy coolness of the Galleria attracts throngs of tourists. The structure was heavily damaged in World War II, but it was completely rebuilt within twelve years. Today it stands as a monument to intelligence and foresight in city planning.

Redesign of an existing area often begins with the desire to eliminate urban blight. Larimer Street was the "skid row" of Denver until a group of inspired citizens formed the Larimer Square Association and renovated a block-long segment of the area (Fig. 544). Oldtime façades were retained, while arcades leading into courts and walkways encouraged artists and shopkeepers to establish galleries. Such oases have blossomed throughout the United States—Old Town in Chicago, Pioneer Square in Seattle, Ghirardelli Square in San Francisco, and many others. Renovation of this kind represents community design at its best, the cooperation of local vision and abilities to transform an eyesore into an attraction.

544

545

Design for rebuilding usually follows some natural or man-made disaster, as in San Francisco after the great earthquake and fire of 1906; in London after the catastrophic fire of 1666 leveled the city; and in most of Europe following World War II. A striking example of urban reconstruction can be seen in Rotterdam, where the core of the city had to be entirely rebuilt (Fig. 545). The Town Hall, one of only two major buildings that survived the bombing, today stands as the focal point of a new pedestrian mall and town center. A disaster area was converted into a model city that has provided inspiration to people in all parts of the world.

A major solution to the problem of *preserving* the city has been undertaken in Norfolk, Virginia. Old Ghent, a rundown former residential community, has been rehabilitated by the Norfolk Rehabilitation and Housing Authority. This agency uses private funds to provide low-interest loans for conserving and rebuilding the big, comfortable houses of a former era, which have come into great demand (Fig. 546). The success of the venture has inspired the renovation of a blighted area adjacent to Old Ghent and extending into the downtown area, a development known as Ghent Square. Slum land was cleared and rezoned to accommodate more than four hundred middle- and upper-income houses, as well as specialty shops and boutiques. Textures and materials are consistent in both developments. A Colonial lighting system and extensive use of maples and magnolias in parks and malls unify Old Ghent and Ghent Square.

545
Town Hall of Rotterdam, seen from the Lijnbaan shopping center, the first post-war pedestrian mall and town center in Europe.

546
Renovated attached houses in Old Ghent, a residential community in Norfolk, VA.

547
View of Siena, Italy.

548
Le Corbusier and Pierre Jeanneret's Voisin Plan (1925), which would have redesigned the center of Paris to provide skyscraper housing and much open space.

Design for Cities

The city originated as a solution to the problem of defense. When medieval cities were built, they consisted of clusters of people gathered together for mutual protection. Strong walls encircled the houses and shops, and as the population grew, outer walls were erected, creating the faubourg or "false city" between the two walls. Central areas grew up around plazas, civic buildings, and churches (Fig. 547).

The advent of the machine in the eighteenth and nineteenth centuries

546

547

brought dramatic changes to the city—new developments in transportation that revolutionized commerce and the beginnings of industry that would eventually transform the world. It also brought the metropolitan slum and the industrial factory district, which rapidly became breeding places for civic turmoil. In the two centuries since the Industrial Revolution began, the situation in the cities has become so critical that many plans have been formulated to correct it.

Among the first designers to take an interest in rebuilding the twentieth-century cities was Le Corbusier, a Swiss architect who in 1925 designed a model for the reconstruction of Paris (Fig. 548). This model, known as the Voisin (neighbor) Plan, embodied his theory that most cities need sweeping renovation rather than small and often uncoordinated reforms. In this plan, housing was to be centralized in sixteen glass-walled skyscrapers in the heart of the city, thus stacking houses vertically instead of allowing them to spread horizontally. Such a system would lift people above the fumes and noise of the city, as well as conserve land area. The keynote of Le Corbusier's plan was balance. Each building was to be designed in such a way that the negative space surrounding it would at least equal the positive area of the building, providing each of four wings with air, sunlight, and a view of the city. Landscaped areas were to surround the buildings, balancing the structures with the soft textures and colors of nature.

548

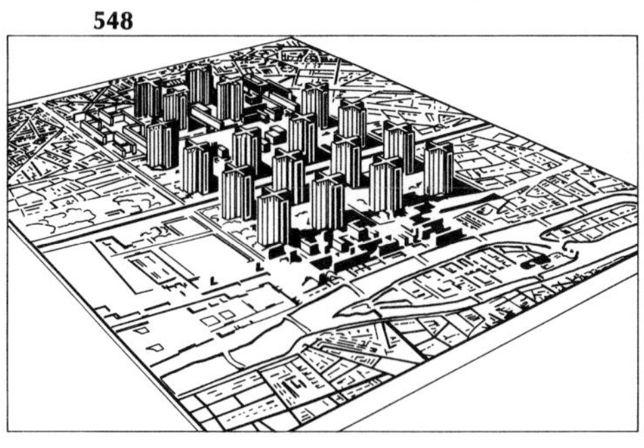

The plan did not materialize in Paris, but it served as a model for many other cities. Unfortunately, the results were disastrous. The high apartment buildings in their own landscaped areas removed people from the shared public space, the street, which is the essential artery of the city. With forty nearly identical apartments on one floor, no one knows nor cares who lives down the hall or who writes the obscene graffiti on the walls. The sense of isolation erodes the sense of responsibility, and crime increases. The next attempt to solve the problem of city housing was directed toward low-rise high-density buildings, such as Pruitt-Igoe (p. 378). The complexity of influences in city life makes it doubtful that any architectural project alone would resolve all the difficulties. Underlying aesthetic and sociological efforts is the problem of financing. In New York in the 1970s there

549

occurred the world's biggest boom in office space, simply because such space was dependably profitable. Experimental housing was not.

Cities all over the world have found it necessary to deal with delapidated sections that would inevitably become slum areas and pockets of crime. Often, rebuilding old sections of a city, or *urban renewal,* is far more expensive than erecting a new city would be. Financially and aesthetically, the renewal of the city has been one of the great challenges of the twentieth century. Such projects require a high degree of community accord in order to find the appropriate aesthetic solution and the financial backing to realize it.

Such a solution was developed by the city of San Antonio, Texas, whose river, winding through the downtown area, had become a city dump, its banks lined with trash, old tires, and rusting automobiles. Because the San Antonio River brought periodic devastation by flooding, city planners suggested covering it with concrete and using it as a sewer. Farsighted citizens saw it instead as a focal point for the city. After 23 years of study, they set up a River Walk Commission to prepare a master plan for the development of the river as a scenic attraction. Today the Paseo del Rio is a thriving business area, lined with shops and exotic restaurants, featuring beautifully landscaped vistas that serve as a center of attraction for both residents and visitors (Fig. 549).

The revitalization of a decaying downtown area in Baltimore has centered around the Inner Harbor Program, which involves renewal of 240 acres surrounding the harbor basin where the city originated (Fig. 550). Planned in several stages, a thirty-year program for redevelopment of the area was unveiled in 1964. It includes major office buildings, apartments, and luxury hotels, with low pavilion structures housing restaurants, shops, theaters, and other visitor attractions. Although 52 major buildings have been constructed in the downtown renewal projects, some older buildings have been retained, and structures in nearby neighborhoods are being restored to maintain the historic Baltimore flavor, many of them being sold for a dollar to people who promise to invest their own effort in restoration. Among the new attractions are a World Trade Center; a convention center; the Maryland Science Center, where guests are encouraged to take part in exhibits by pushing buttons and turning wheels; and an Outdoor Concert

549
The Paseo del Rio, or River Walk, is the focus of downtown San Antonio, TX.

550
View of Harborplace in Baltimore, MD.

551
Drawing of Harborplace in Baltimore, MD.

Pavilion featuring everything from rock to symphony concerts. A hundred neighborhoods in the city now hold their own festivals, and sixteen ethnic groups make use of the facilities at Harborplace in the Inner Harbor for their celebrations. The city that was once worn out and decrepit has become a bustling hub, truly responsive to the needs and goals of its people, a result that has come about largely through the efforts of the people themselves (Fig. 551).

European visitors sometimes feel that American cities have an unfinished look; this is another way of saying they lack the aesthetic unity of cities in older cultures. Reasons given have to do with American individuality. Both builders and designers have been impressed with the urgency of creating something new and different, of exhibiting originality and innovation in a style that would be American in flavor. Contemporary city designers stress *contextualism,* designing individual buildings in accordance with an overall plan, placing each new building *in context* with its setting. A building can stand out because of the excellence of its design, but it retains its primary role as a unit in the total conception of how the city should look. This does not mean building only in the predominant style of older buildings. It means adaptation and a sensitivity to both historical and contemporary forms.

550

551

552

There are numerous examples of contextualism on college campuses, where the peak enrollment of the sixties made it necessary to expand buildings, from libraries to dormitories. Many of the classroom buildings were in traditional styles modeled after European universities, as was the practice in the late nineteenth and early twentieth centuries. Contemporary American architects felt a certain dishonesty in mimicking the original style. The solution to the problem was usually an adaptation in a modern vein, such as the one given a new wing to the Boston Public Library (Fig. 552). The original building had been designed by the famed architectural team of McKim, Mead, and White and was a respected landmark in the city. Philip Johnson was commissioned to design the new wing, in which he kept the spirit of the 1895 building but used thoroughly contemporary lines. Maintaining a height no greater than the original one, he designed the new wing with three large arcades that suggest but do not mirror the arched windows of the old building. The design offers striking variety, yet maintains the unity of Copley Square.

As modernization and urban renewal cut great swaths through existing cities following World War II, concerned citizens took steps to preserve representative homes and other buildings for their educational and historical value to future generations. In 1949 Congress chartered the National Trust for Historic Preservation for this purpose, listing landmarks in the National Register and allowing tax benefits for restoration and maintenance. Anyone can suggest a landmark for such listing and, as a result, well over twenty thousand landmarks are now included in the Register, ranging from covered bridges to Indian petroglyphs. Even earlier, however, farsighted individuals had begun restoring whole communities. The most generally known is Colonial Williamsburg, where renovation began in 1927, financed by John D. Rockefeller, Jr. Carried out with painstaking research, this project restored more than 75 colonial buildings and rebuilt on the original foundations more than 185 others, including the capitol, the Governor's Palace, and Bruton Parish Church. People who live in the town wear colonial dress, and colonial crafts such as blacksmithing, candlemaking, and ironwork are carried on as they were in colonial days. Gardens are meticulously kept, and special holidays such as Christmas draw great crowds of visitors. Similar colonial settlements can be found in New England. Other districts have been restored simply as examples of architectural styles. The Vergennes Historic District in Vermont (Fig. 553) encompasses 80 buildings in which all the significant styles of the nineteenth century are represented. Restored sections of cities are frequently listed as historic districts because of similar architectural interest.

With established cities so fraught with problems, the designing of a complete *new city* can represent the ultimate challenge. In the Depression

552
Philip Johnson, John Burgee, and Architects Design Group. The Boston Public Library Addition, on Copley Square. Original building by McKim, Mead, & White, 1888–1892. New Wing completed 1973.

553
Vergennes Historic District, VT.

554
An architect's drawing of the city of Greendale, WI, shows a balance between structures and open green areas.

553

years of the 1930s the U.S. Federal Government purchased land near three large cities for the purpose of creating jobs by building model communities. The new towns would house workers near industrial areas, yet give them an attractive and satisfying life away from the noise and overcrowding of the city. The three towns constructed were Greenbelt, Maryland; Greenhills, Ohio; and Greendale, Wisconsin. The planners followed the examples set earlier by Radburn, New Jersey, the first community in the United States to separate traffic from residential areas in such a way that the pedestrian could move about easily and safely.

Typical of this design concept is Greendale (Fig. 554), where open areas and belts of trees curve in biomorphic shapes, which soften the rectangles of the residential streets. These shapes are integrated throughout the community in such a way that all living areas face parks or open country.

554

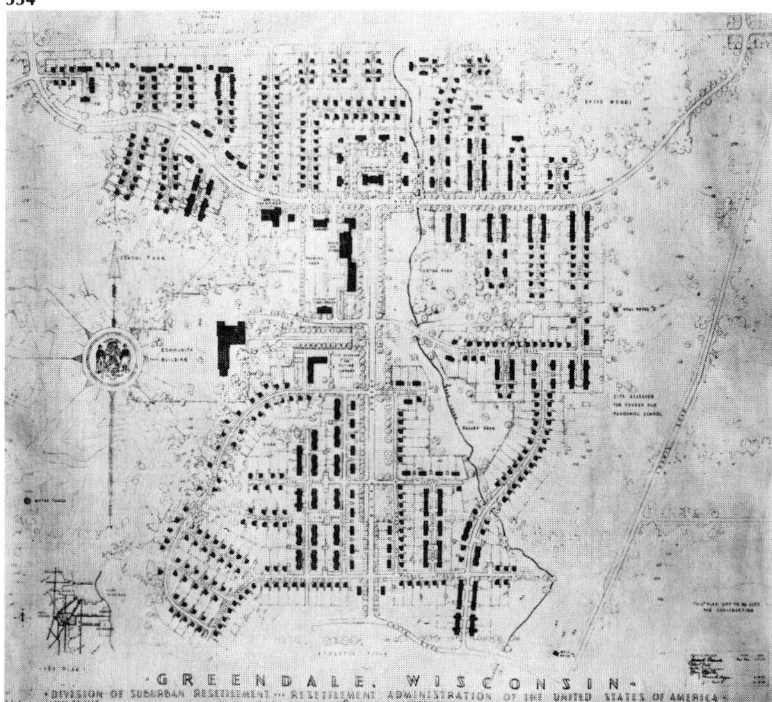

Kitchens and utility rooms open onto quiet service roads so that daily chores can be carried out in an unobtrusive manner, and each house is set on a plot of ground large enough to ensure real privacy. The individual home is more important than any arbitrary consistency of line along a street. Many residential streets terminate in dead ends or curve to join other streets adapted to the topography of the land. Wherever possible, sidewalks cross thoroughfares by means of underpasses. Materials for houses were chosen with variety in mind, and paint colors were selected to make each home as individual as possible.

Fulfilling the original designers' hopes, Greenbelt, Greenhills, and Greendale have provided inspiration to other cities seeking to escape the deadly monotony of the usual suburban patterns and to find a means of establishing a full and attractive community life. Similar experimental cities have since been built in other localities, with these same goals in mind.

The Total Environment

Encompassing the cities, our homes, and all the accoutrements of our lives is the total environment. Included is every example we have shown throughout this book—every delicately designed flower or seashell, every work of human hands, every mountain, meadow, and ocean wave. Each of these carries its own complement of the elements and principles of design, but when we view the totality, we see the elements and principles with a broader perspective.

Visually, as we noted at the beginning, line, shape, mass, space, texture, and color are all around us, in vegetation, geological structure, biological forms, and the physical characteristics of the landscape. The cities provide patches of dense texture, the mountains rough ones, and the lakes and prairies are smooth shapes among textured forests. The entire color wheel operates about us continually in flowers, sky, water, the pigments applied to various substances by human hands, and, in its total spectrum, in sunlight and the rainbow. Everywhere are the rhythms of the seasons and of daily living, but there are also the rhythms of transportation systems—highways, railways, rapid transit, flight patterns, waterways, and harbor facilities. The accelerated rhythms and dense texture of cities make them focal points of emphasis in the landscape. Variety is infinite. Proportion and scale are seen in the comparison of mountains and oceans, human beings, and the intimate environment people have designed specifically for their own use. Over all, the vastness of the universe dwarfs even the most monumental masses on the Earth (Fig. 555).

The elements and principles are all there, most of them operating independently of human consciousness. Two principles deserve and require our special attention: unity and balance in the total environment.

When human beings discovered fire, they began to control the environment instead of adapting to it, and to counterbalance the effect of environmental forces. Now, thousands of years later, the balance has swung precariously in the direction of overcontrol of the environment. It is estimated that if recent population trends continue, by the year 2600 each person will have less than a square yard of the Earth's surface in which to live and move. We continually disrupt environmental unity, demolishing landscape to create cities, dumping our wastes into air and water, devastating geological balance when we build dams, drill for oil, and lower the ground

555
Aerial view of Western Himalayan Range near Ladakh, India.

level by pumping water for industrial uses, removing substances important to the firmness of the Earth. Forests have been destroyed all over the world for immediate human use, causing rain to leach nutrients from the soil so nothing but desert remains. Hurricanes are believed to be influenced by unstable ground levels, and dust storms result from overplowed fields. Imbalance of the physical environment leads to imbalance and disunity among the peoples of the Earth, who struggle for control over natural resources in order to exert power over other people. A crucial point has been reached in the total environment at which the survival of the Earth and its inhabitants is at stake. Embracing all fields of design, design for total environment is not only a reflection of human creativity and ingenuity but also a challenge to human integrity and purpose.

Contemporary Trends in Environmental Design

The return of the human element to the arts, with its personal mythology and emotional content, is a major trend in contemporary environmental design, and in its philosophical and practical significance lies our greatest hope for the future. Computers make environmental assessments, projecting population growth, densities, and relationships between the natural environment and that shaped by human beings. Such assessments are used in making national decisions that are politically enforceable, socially acceptable, economically feasible, and technically possible. Yet when government threatens to wipe out beautiful wilderness areas in order to develop sources of energy, it is people who make the outcry that reverses the decisions. It is people who support the expenditure of more than twenty million dollars annually to clean up the streams and rivers of the world. There have been numerous protests against environmental damage caused by industry, many of them with far-reaching results.

The contemporary attitude toward the city reflects the return to the human element, in a rethinking of the city, not as a den of vice and materialism, but as a center, in the words of Aristotle, "to make man happy and safe." The emphasis in the eighties is away from the malls and suburbia that cut into the life of the city by dissipating it, separating people from the vital center of city life.

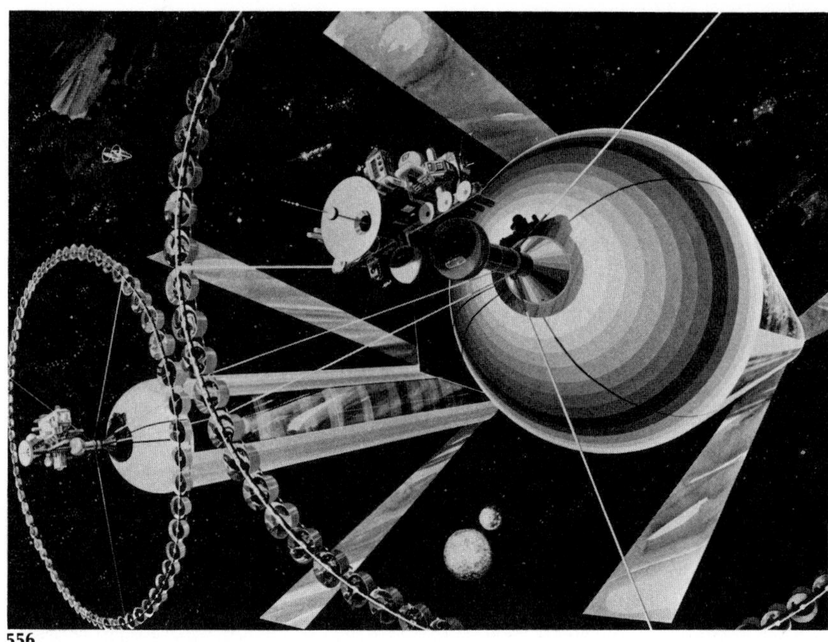

556

Contemporary landscape architects also are moving toward a personalization of the landscape. Formal plantings are not so important as livable ones, and gardens are designed for easy upkeep rather than impressive display. The sounds of water and the play of lights are reappearing in landscape design, not in castle grounds and historic gardens, but in the middle of cities where the greatest number of people can enjoy them.

Design for the Future

The essence of contemporary trends in environmental design is conservation and preservation of the best of our present environment for future generations. With the advent of the space age, designers can allow their fantasies full play and still produce designs that are well within the realm of possibility. Principal among concerns of such designers is the threat of overpopulation. Suggestions have been made for platform cities with traffic moving in corridors underground, and for multitiered cities a mile wide and twenty miles long, which eventually would join city to city. Plans have been drawn for satellite cities to be situated in "rural rings" around existing metropolises, and for cellular cities and towns in which a number of community units are placed around a central or urban core. Floating cities have been designed as a solution to the decreasing availability of land, and we hear much of possible space cities, orbiting communities as well as fixed extraterrestrial towns (Fig. 556).

556
Design for a 20th-century space colony orbiting between the earth and the moon. The cylinder is 19 miles long and 4 miles in diameter, with a potential to accommodate a population ranging between 200,000 and several million people.

Never before has the world seemed so complex. Whether we are designers or simply citizens making daily choices about our quality of life, the range of possibilities is truly unlimited. It is only in a solid grounding of design principles that we can hope that our choices will be the wisest for ourselves and for our environment, and for those who will inherit it from us.

Glossary

Terms italicized within the definitions are themselves defined in the Glossary.

Abstract Expressionism An art style, also called "New York School," that emerged after World War II, and which emphasized *nonobjective* form, spontaneous invention, and frequently evidence of energetic activity on the part of the artist, leading to the term "Action Painting."
abstraction Originating with a recognizable form but simplified or distorted into a new entity.
achromatic Having no color, a *neutral* such as black, white, or gray.
acrylic A *plastic* which in solid form is usually rigid, clear, and transparent; also, a binder for pigments used in painting.
additive Descriptive of a sculptural method in which *form* is created by building up materials, as by modeling or welding. Compare *subtractive*.
additive primary colors In light, those primary colors—red, blue, and green—which in theory can be blended to add up to white light.
aesthetic From Greek *aisthetikos,* "pertaining to sensory perception."
after-image A physiological phenomenon in which the retina of the eye becomes fatigued after viewing any *hue* for a sustained period of time, causing the *complementary color* to be seen.
allée A corridor between plantings of trees.
alloy A combination of two or more metals fused in the molten stage to form a new metal.
analagous Referring to adjacent colors on a color wheel.
appliqué A fabric-decorating technique in which various shapes, colors, and types of material are stitched onto a background to create a design.
aquatint In *printmaking,* a variation of the *intaglio* method in which a porous ground of resin is applied to a plate, after which the plate is dipped by stages into an acid bath to create a range of tonal values.
arcade A series of *arches* supported by piers or columns to form an open passageway.
arch A structural device, generally any opening spanned by a curved top supported by two uprights. The true arch consists of wedge-shaped blocks converging on a *keystone* at the center of the opening.
Art Nouveau A decorative style of the 1890s, based primarily on flowing, curvilinear plant and animal forms.
assemblage The act of creating a work of art by joining together fragments of objects that often serve some other purpose; also the work so created.
asymmetrical balance Balance in which the two imaginary halves of a composition have equal weight but are disposed unevenly.
atmospheric perspective The effect of an intervening body of air between an object and a viewer, causing a softening of outlines, blurring and cooling of colors, and loss of detail at the horizon; the simulation of depth in two-dimensional art by the portrayal of this effect.
bas-relief or **low-relief** Sculpture in which the figures are attached to a background and project only slightly from it.
batik A form of resist dyeing for fabric in which nonprinting portions of a design are "stopped out" with wax to prevent color penetration.
Bauhaus A school of design founded in Germany, in 1919, known for its adaptation of design principles to mass production; also descriptive of the works, especially furniture, designed by the staff.
berm An artificial ridge or hillock built up to provide privacy or interest in a landscaped area.
bilateral symmetry A type of design balance in which the two halves of a composition, formed by a bisector, are mirror images of each other.
binder A substance in paints that causes the pigment particles to hold together, to a *support*.
biomorphic Taken from nature, from the Greek meaning "structure based on life."
bisque Clay that has been fired but is not to be glazed.
bosk A thick clump of trees.
calligraphy The art of beautiful writing.
cantilever A structural member, as in architecture, projecting from an upright, and unsupported at the opposite end.

cartoon A drawing made to scale on paper, used in transferring designs as a basis for painting, mosaic, or tapestry.
casein A painting medium in which the pigment is bound with milk curd.
casting The process of forming a liquid or plastic substance into a specific shape by pouring it into a mold and allowing it to harden.
cauterium A metal instrument used in modeling *encaustic*.
chasing A decorative technique for metal in which the exterior surface is repeatedly struck by a rounded tool propelled by a hammer.
chiaroscuro The use of light and dark value areas in a painting to imitate effects of light and shadow found in nature.
china A commercial white ceramic ware similar to *porcelain*, firing in higher temperature ranges.
chroma See *intensity*.
cire-perdue or **lost wax** A method of *casting* metal in which a model is coated with wax and a mold built around it. When heated, the wax melts and flows out, leaving a cavity into which molten metal can be poured and allowed to solidify.
cloisonné An *enameling* technique in which color or design areas are separated by thin metal wires fused to a metal base.
closure The process by which perceptions are unified to acknowledge a specific shape.
coiling A forming method by which rolls of clay, in the plastic state, are built up and joined together.
collage A predominantly two-dimensional work of art on which pieces of paper, cloth, or other materials are pasted. Loosely, any assembly of materials to create a design.
collagraph A print made from a surface that has been built up in the manner of a *collage*.
Color Field painting Works in which the viewer is meant to experience colors directly, without reference to form or emotional and psychological content.
color wheel A circular arrangement of colors that expresses their relationships according to a particular color theory.
complementary colors Colors opposite one another on a *color wheel*, which, when mixed together in equal parts, form a neutral, or, in the case of light, form white.
composition An ordered relationship among parts or elements of design.
conceptual art A work of art or an event that depends on an intellectual concept of the artist.
conceptual imagery Imagery derived from imagination, emotion, dreams, or other internal sources; compare *perceptual imagery*.
content The substance of a work of art, including its emotional, intellectual, symbolic, thematic, and narrative connotations.
contextualism Architecture designed to blend in with its surroundings, particularly in established city areas.
contour In two-dimensional art, a line that represents the edge of a form or group of forms.
cross-hatching A series of intersecting sets of parallel lines used to indicate shading or volume in a drawing.
Cubism An art style developed by Pablo Picasso and Georges Braque, beginning in 1907, characterized by faceted forms, flattened *pictorial space*, and *figure-ground ambiguity*.
decorative design Embellishment or surface enrichment of an object. Decorative design may be inherent in structure or may be applied to a completed structure.
Deutscher Werkbund An organization founded in Munich in 1906, with the idea of incorporating aesthetic design in mass-produced products. A forerunner of the *Bauhaus*.
dome A hemisphere or inverted cup, theoretically the result of rotating an arch on its axis.
drypoint A method of *intaglio printmaking* in which a metal plate is needled with a sharp point that raises a burr, or curl of metal. The burr gives drypoint its characteristic soft, velvety quality.
dual coding The combining of traditional and modern architectural styles so a structure can be experienced on two levels of association.
ductility The capacity of metal for being hammered thin or drawn out, without breaking.
earthenware A coarse, porous, usually reddish ceramic ware fired in low temperature ranges.
eclecticism The combining of many different styles and influences in one work.
embroidery The technique of decorating fabric with colored threads worked in a variety of stitches.
enameling The art of creating designs in colored glassy materials which are fused to metal.
encaustic A type of paint in which the *binder* is wax.
engraving A technique in which an image is created by scratching into metal, wood, or other materials, with a sharp tool. Also, the *print* that results when ink is placed in the depressions and paper forced in to make an impression.
etching A *printmaking* process in which acid acts as the cutting agent. A metal plate is coated with acid resist; the resist is scratched away in image (or printing) areas, and then the plate is dipped in acid.
Expressionism An early twentieth-century art movement that emphasized the artist's emotional response to experience, especially through the use of color and symbolic imagery.
façade The exterior, usually the front, of a building.
Fauvism A movement in painting, originating in France in

1905, characterized by the unconventional, apparently arbitrary use of bright, contrasting colors.

felting A method of making cloth by interlocking loose *fibers* together through a combination of heat, moisture, and pressure.

fiber A natural or synthetic material capable of being made into yarn or thread.

figure-ground A relationship, usually in two-dimensional art, between a form and its background or surroundings. Figure-ground ambiguity refers to an inability to distinguish between the two.

focal length The distance between the lens and the film in a camera.

foreshortening A device used in two-dimensional art to portray forms in such a way that they appear to project or recede from the picture plane; a means of creating spatial depth in figures.

form 1. The underlying structure or *composition* in a work of art. 2. The shape or outline of something. 3. The essence of a work of art—its medium or mode of expression. 4. The substance of something, as in "solid or liquid form."

fresco A painting *medium* often used for murals in which the paint is applied to a *ground* of wet plaster.

general illumination Lighting in a stage set that makes all action visible at once.

geodesic dome A dome, first devised by R. Buckminster Fuller, composed of small modules based on the triangle.

gesso A mixture of white pigment, glue, and plaster or gypsum that serves as a *ground* for tempera.

Gestalt A term referring to the totality of unified configurations with which we seize our visual experiences, from the German word for "form."

glaze A glassy vitreous coating fired onto ceramic ware for decoration and/or waterproofing. Also, a thin layer of paint, applied to canvas or other base in one or more layers, to achieve transparency or luminosity in a painting.

gouache Opaque watercolor paint in which the *binder* is gum arabic and a paste of zinc oxide.

graphic Descriptive of the arts involving drawing or writing. "Graphic design" usually means design for a printed format, such as advertising, books, magazines, and packaging.

gray scale A series of *value* gradations between white and black.

greenware Clay vessels that have not been fired.

grisaille An enameling technique using only black, white, and shades of gray. Thin layers of white are applied to a dark background for shading. A similar technique is used in stained glass.

ground 1. A preliminary material applied to a *support* as preparation for the drawing or painting *medium*. 2. The background or general area of a *picture plane* as distinguished from the forms or figures. See *figure-ground*.

grout Thin mortar or paste used to fill in around the *tesserae* in a mosaic.

hatching A series of closely spaced parallel lines used to indicate shading or volume in a drawing.

haut-relief or **high relief** Sculpture in which forms project from a background to considerable depth.

hue The pure state of any color; the name by which a color is called.

iconography 1. The visual imagery used to convey the meaning of a work of art, and the conventions governing such imagery. 2. The study of various forms of meaning found in pictorial representations. 3. Loosely, the "story" behind a work of art, especially religious or mythological symbolism.

ideographic A term for writing in which the characters are abstracted images of the objects they represent.

illumination The art of decorating manuscripts with scrolls, miniature paintings, and symbolic embellishments.

imagery The art of making images or pictures to represent or evoke a particular thing. See also *perceptual imagery, conceptual imagery*.

impasto The thick application of paint to a *support;* also, the three-dimensional surface that results from such application.

Impressionism An art style, originating in France in the 1870s, in which artists sought to represent, in paint, transitory effects of light, shade, and color that occur in nature.

infill The designing of new buildings within a city, or adding to existing structures, so that new construction blends with the older buildings.

inlay A method of decorating wood (and sometimes other materials) by inserting small, and often contrasting, pieces of material into a backing to form a design.

intaglio 1. A printmaking method in which the image area is recessed below the surface of the plate. Compare *relief*. 2. Any depressed image created by carving, cutting, or incising.

intensity The relative purity or grayness of a color. Colors that are not grayed have "high intensity" whereas grayed colors have "low intensity."

interior decoration The arranging of interior furnishings to satisfy a specific taste.

iridescence The rainbow effect by which a material or surface seems to reflect all the hues of the spectrum, as a result of light playing on it.

kinetic Relating to or produced by motion.

lamination Gluing together of thin sheets, as in wood or plastic.

leather hard The stage at which drying clay can be carved or incised.

linear perspective A system for depicting three-dimensional depth on a two-dimensional surface, dependent on the illusion that parallel lines receding into space converge at a point, known as the *"vanishing point."*

lithography A *planographic* or flat-surface *printmaking* technique, in which the image areas are neither depressed nor raised. (Compare *relief* and *intaglio.*) Printing depends upon the mutual antipathy of grease and water.

local color The color of things seen under standard light without shadows; the "real" color of objects in the natural world.

logo An insignia adopted by a commercial concern for visual identification in the eyes of the public.

lost-wax casting See *cire-perdue.*

luminal art Art, especially sculpture, of which light is an element.

Luminists A group of painters who interpreted the effects of light on colored objects.

luminosity The actual or illusory effect of giving off light.

luster The glow of reflected light.

macramé A fiber-construction technique in which *form* is achieved by knotting strands into varied patterns.

malleability The capacity of materials for being manipulated by tools.

marquetry Wood inlaid with other materials, such as ivory, shell, or contrasting wood, to form decorative designs in furniture.

medium 1. The material used for a work of art. 2. The basis for a type of paint, such as oil. 3. The form of expression in a work of art, such as painting or printmaking.

mezzotint An *intaglio printmaking* process in which the plate is initially roughened with a tool called a rocker, then gradually smoothed for intermediate values, working from dark to light.

Minimal Art A style of painting and sculpture, originated in the mid-twentieth century, in which *form* is achieved by the barest means—contour shape, flat surface, and sometimes pure unmodulated color. Minimal works tend to be geometric in their precision.

modeling 1. Shaping objects from *plastic* material, such as clay. 2. In drawing or painting, effects of light and shadow that create the illusion of three-dimensional volume.

modular Characterized by repetitive and/or interconnecting units that can be assembled in different ways, especially in furniture or architecture.

monochromatic Having only one hue, possibly with gradations of value or intensity.

monoprint A one-of-a-kind *print* made by transferring to paper an image drawn on a plate, usually of glass.

mosaic An art form in which pieces of glass, ceramic tile, or other materials are fitted together to form a design and then glued or cemented to a background.

motif An element, frequently the theme, of a work of art, which may be repeated or elaborated on.

negative space The space surrounding or flowing through the shapes and masses delineated by the artist. See *positive space.*

neutral A color not associated with any particular *hue,* for instance, gray or tan.

New Classicism A contemporary revival of classical forms in architecture, either with a traditional historical approach or in a nontraditional way.

niello A technique of decorating metal with black pigment forced into incised lines.

nonobjective Having no resemblance to natural forms or objects.

nonrepresentational See *nonobjective.*

normal value The value of any color when it is in its pure unmixed state.

Op Art An art style of the mid-twentieth century, concerned with optical stimulation and manipulation, including the creation of optical illusions, a sense of vibration, and *afterimages.*

palette 1. The range of colors used for a painting. 2. The range of colors characteristic to a single artist or group of artists. 3. The surface on which an artist mixes paint.

parquetry Wood, often of contrasting colors, worked into an inlaid mosaic, especially on a floor.

parterre A garden in which the beds and paths are arranged to form a pattern, usually geometric.

patina A surface coating on metal that results from natural oxidation or from the application of certain chemicals.

perceptual imagery Imagery derived from experience or perception of the natural world.

Photorealism An art style of the mid-twentieth century, in which objects or people are depicted with photographic accuracy.

piazza An open square in a town or city.

pictorial space In a painting, the apparent or illusionary space that appears to recede backward from the *picture plane.*

picture plane An imaginary flat surface assumed to be at the front surface of a painting.

pigment A colorant ground into a fine power and used to color paints or dyes.

pile weave A weave characterized by protruding tufts or loops of fiber.

pinching A method of shaping clay with the fingers.

plain weave A basic weave characterized by a regular alternating sequence of one-up, one-down interlacing of *warp* and *weft* yarns.

planography A *printmaking* method in which the printing surface is flat, neither raised nor recessed. See *lithography.*

plastic 1. Capable of being molded or shaped. 2. Solid, sculptural, three-dimensional. 3. Any of numerous synthetic substances composed principally of carbon compounds in long molecular chains.

plasticity The ability of a material to be molded or shaped; solidity, three-dimensionality.

plique à jour An enameling technique similar to cloisonné, but with the metal base removed, after firing, for a translucent effect.

plywood Laminated wood in which the grain of alternate layers is at right angles to that of the layers between.

pointillism A technique of applying tiny dots of color to canvas. The term is used especially in connection with the work of Georges Seurat.

polychrome Painting in many colors, as in wood or ceramic sculpture.

Pop Art An art style dating from the mid-1950s that takes as its subject matter popular, mass-produced symbols.

porcelain A pure white, hard ceramic ware that fires at very high temperatures, used especially for fine dinnerware and figurines.

positive space Space occupied by the shapes or masses delineated by the artist. See *negative space.*

post-and-lintel A structural system in architecture in which beams or lintels are placed horizontally across upright posts.

Post-Impressionism A loose term to designate the various painting styles following *Impressionism,* during the period from 1885 to 1900. The term is applied primarily to the works of Van Gogh, Cézanne, Gauguin, Seurat, and their followers.

Post-Modernism A twentieth-century style of painting and architecture that combines modern simplicity with traditional decorative elements.

primary color One of the basic colors on any *color wheel,* which it is assumed cannot be mixed from other colors, and which serves as a basis for mixing all combinations on the wheel.

print An impression made on paper from a master plate, stone, or block created by an artist, usually repeated many times for multiple images that are identical or similar. Also, a similar process applied to cloth.

printmaking The art of making prints.

proportion Size or weight relationships among structures or among elements in a single structure. Compare *scale.*

quilting The process of sewing together small pieces of cloth (in a pattern or at random) to form a design, and then stitching to create a puffed surface.

radial symmetry Balance achieved by the arrangement of elements in a circular pattern around a central core.

radical eclecticism The pulling together of many architectural influences into an integrated style.

raked set A stage set in which the axis is not parallel to the footlights.

refraction The bending of a ray of light as it passes through a prism or lens.

relief 1. A *printmaking* process in which portions of the image to be printed are raised above the surface of the plate or block. Compare *intaglio.* 2. Any raised image, as in sculpture.

relief sculpture Sculpture attached to a background from which it projects. See *bas-relief, haut-relief.*

repoussé A forming technique for metal in which punches driven by hammers push the metal out from its reverse side to create a low *relief* design on the front.

retrofill See *infill.*

Romantic architecture Architecture with a flavor of fantasy, often Gothic in derivation.

saturation See *intensity.*

scale Size or weight relationships in a structure or between structures, especially as measured by some standard, such as the human body.

secco A method of painting in which plaster is applied to dry plaster walls.

secondary color A color created by mixing two primary colors on any *color wheel.*

serigraphy A printmaking process based on stencils or screens. See *silk screen.*

shade A variation of any color that is darker than its *normal value.*

silk screen A *printmaking* method in which the image is transferred to paper or cloth by forcing ink through fine mesh screens, usually of silk, on which nonprinting areas are "stopped out" to prevent color penetration.

simultaneous contrast The tendency of *complementary* colors to intensify each other when placed side by side.

slab construction A method of forming clay by rolling it into flat sheets and then joining the sheets to each other or to other forms.

slip Liquid clay, the consistency of cream, usually used for casting.

specific illumination Lighting in a set that molds and models to control audience reaction.

split complement A combination of colors involving one *hue* and the hues on either side of its *complement* on a *color wheel.*

stained glass Glass that has been colored and arranged in pieces to create a design or pattern. Often the pieces are joined by strips of lead.

stitchery Any fabric-decorating technique in which the thread stitches predominate on the surface and carry the major design.

stoneware A relatively hard, vitreous ceramic ware, usually gray or tan, that fires in the middle-range temperatures.

structural design Design concerned with the creation of

basic *form* in an object, as distinguished from surface enrichment.

stylization The simplification of a form to emphasize its design qualities.

subtractive Descriptive of a sculptural method in which *form* is created by carving or cutting away material. Compare *additive*.

subtractive primary colors The colors—cyan (turquoise), magenta, and yellow—which subtract from white light the wavelengths for all colors except the one seen.

successive contrast The phenomenon by which the *afterimage* of a visual impression appears to the closed eye, in the complementary colors of its original.

support In two-dimensional art, the material to which the drawing or painting *medium* is applied, as a canvas.

Surrealism An art movement, originating in the early twentieth century, which emphasized intuitive and nonrational ways of working as a means of recreating the chance relationships and symbols that often occur in dreams.

tapestry A type of *weaving* in which the *weft* yarn carries the design and appears on the surface of the fabric only in certain areas.

tempera A painting *medium* in which the pigment is bound together with egg yolk or with animal or vegetable glue.

tensile strength A characteristic of metal, or other materials, whereby it can be stretched or extended without breaking.

terrazzo Small marble chips set in concrete and polished.

tesserae Small pieces of glass, tile, stone, or other material used in a *mosaic*.

thermoplastic Descriptive of *plastics* that can be reheated and reshaped without undergoing chemical change.

thermosetting Descriptive of plastics that undergo a chemical change during curing and become permanently shaped.

tint A variation of any color that is lighter than its *normal value*.

tonality The quality of lightness or darkness, brightness or grayness in a work.

tone A softened color achieved by mixing a pure *hue* with gray or with its *complement*.

triad Any group of three colors equidistant from each other on a *color wheel*.

trompe-l'oeil French for "fool-the-eye," a two-dimensional visual representation so carefully contrived that it gives the illusion of a three-dimensional object or space.

truss A structural form in architecture consisting of rigid bars or beams arranged in a system of triangles joined at their apexes, especially common in bridge design.

value The lightness or darkness of a color.

vanishing point In *linear perspective,* the point at which lines or edges parallel in nature converge at the horizon line.

vault An *arched* roof, usually of stone or concrete, created by two intersecting arches.

vehicle See *binder*.

veneer A thin layer of fine wood applied over a base of stronger, less decorative wood. Also applies to marble and other materials.

vernacular architecture Architecture designed by the people who will use it, using native materials, and having no pretensions to architectural style.

visual texture Surface variety that can be seen but not felt with the fingers.

warp In *weaving,* the lengthwise yarns held stationary on the loom and parallel to the finished edge of the fabric.

watercolor A painting *medium* in which the *binder* is gum arabic.

weaving The process of interlacing two sets of parallel threads, held at right angles to each other, to form a fabric.

weft In *weaving,* the crosswise yarns that intersect the *warp* to create a fabric.

woodcut See *relief*.

Bibliography

CHAPTERS 1–10 *Elements and Principles of Design*

Albers, Anni. *On Designing.* Middletown, Conn.: Wesleyan University Press, 1971.

Albers, Josef. *Interaction of Color.* New Haven: Yale University Press, 1975.

Arnheim, Rudolf. *Visual Thinking.* Berkeley: University of California Press, 1969.

Birren, Faber. *Light, Color, Environment.* New York: Van Nostrand Reinhold, 1969.

Collier, Graham. *Form, Space, and Vision.* 3rd ed. Englewood Cliffs, N.J.: Prentice-Hall, 1972.

Evans, Helen Marie. *Man the Designer.* New York: Macmillan, 1973.

Faulkner, Ray, and Edwin Zeigfeld. *Art Today.* 5th ed. New York: Holt, Rinehart and Winston, 1969.

Grillo, Paul. *Form, Function, and Design.* New York: Dover, 1975.

Itten, Johannes. *Design and Form.* 2nd rev. ed. New York: Van Nostrand Reinhold, 1975.

——— *The Art of Color.* New York: Van Nostrand Reinhold, 1974.

——— *The Elements of Color.* New York: Van Nostrand Reinhold, 1970.

Kepes, Gyorgy. *Language of Vision.* Chicago: Paul Theobald, 1969.

Knobler, Nathan. *The Visual Dialogue.* 3rd ed. New York: Holt, Rinehart and Winston, 1980.

Libby, William Charles. *Color and the Structural Sense.* Englewood Cliffs, N.J.: Prentice-Hall, 1974.

McHarg, Ian. *Design with Nature.* Garden City, N.Y.: Natural History Press, 1969.

Nelson, George. *Problems of Design.* 3rd ed. Whitney Library of Design, 1974.

Ocvirk, Otto G., Robert O. Bone, Robert E. Stinson, and Philip R. Wigg. *Art Fundamentals: Theory and Practice.* 4th ed. Dubuque, Iowa: Wm. C. Brown, 1981.

Pearce, Peter. *Structure in Nature is a Strategy for Design.* Cambridge, Mass.: MIT Press, 1978.

Russell, Stella Pandell. *Art in the World.* New York: Holt, Rinehart and Winston, 1975.

Stix, Hugh, et al. *The Shell: Five Hundred Years of Inspired Design.* New York: Ballantine, 1972.

Strache, Wolf. *Forms and Patterns in Nature.* New York: Pantheon, 1973.

Vasarely, Victor. *Notes Brutes.* Venice, Alfieri, 1970.

Wong, Wucius. *Principles of Three-Dimensional Design.* New York: Van Nostrand Reinhold, 1977.

CHAPTERS 11–14 *Materials and Processes*

Wood

Brodatz, Philip. *Wood and Wood Grains: A Photographic Album for Artists and Designers.* New York: Dover, 1972.

Constantine, Albert. *Know Your Woods.* New York: Charles Scribner, 1972.

English, Kevin. *Creative Approach to Basic Woodwork.* San Francisco: Cowman, 1969.

Fendelman, Helaine. *Tramp Art: An Itinerant's Folk Art.* New York: E. P. Dutton, 1975.

Forgione, Joseph, and Sterling McIlhany. *Wood Inlay.* New York: Van Nostrand Reinhold, 1973.

Hayward, Charles H. *Complete Book of Woodwork.* New York: Drake, 1972.

Joyce, Ernest. *The Encyclopedia of Furniture Making.* New York: Drake, 1971.

Piepenburg, Robert. *Designs in Wood.* New York: Bruce, 1969.

Willcox, Donald. *New Design in Wood.* New York: Van Nostrand Reinhold, 1970.

Metal

Almeida, Oscar. *Metalworking.* New York: Drake, 1971.

Carron, Shirley. *Modern Pewter: Design and Technique.* New York: Van Nostrand Reinhold, 1973.

Clarke, Carl D. *Metal Casting of Sculpture and Ornament.* Butler, Maryland: Standard Arts, 1980.

D'Allemagne, Henry R. *Decorative Antique Ironwork.* New York: Dover Publications, 1968.

Forms in Metal: 275 Years of Metalsmithing in America. New York: American Crafts Council, 1975.

Glass, Fred J. *Metal Craft.* Felton, Calif.: Paragraph Press, 1971.

Hover, Otto. *Wrought Iron.* New York, Universe Books, 1969.

Metal: A Bibliography. New York: American Crafts Council, 1977.

Morton, Philip. *Contemporary Jewelry.* 2nd ed. New York: Holt, Rinehart and Winston, 1976.

Silvercraft. Elmsford, N.Y.: British Book Center, 1977.

Southwork, Susan and Michael. *Ornamental Ironwork.* Boston: David Godine, 1978.

Stone

Evans, Joan. *Pattern: A Study of Ornament in Western Europe.* 2 vols. New York: Da Capo Press, 1976.

Murphy, Seamus. *Stone Mad: A Sculptor's Life and Craft.* Boston: Routledge and Kegan, 1976.

Clay

Atil, Esin. *Ceramics from the World of Islam.* Baltimore, Garamond/Pridemark Press, 1973.

Barry, John. *American Indian Pottery.* Florence, Alabama: Books Americana, 1981.

Berenson, Paulus. *Finding One's Way with Clay*. New York: Simon and Schuster, 1972.
Bunzel, Ruth. *The Pueblo Potter*. New York: Dover Publications, 1972.
Cooper, Emmanuel. *A History of World Pottery*. New York: Larousse, 1981.
De Jonge, C. H. *Delft Ceramics*. New York: Praeger, 1970.
Espejel, Carlos. *Mexican Folk Ceramics*. Barcelona: Editorial Blume, 1975.
Fujioka, Ryoichi. *Shino and Oribe Ceramics*. New York: Kodansha International and Shibundo, 1977.
Leach, Bernard. *A Potter's Book*. Levittown, N.Y.: Transatlantic Arts, 1965.
Medley, Margaret. *The Chinese Potter*. New York: Charles Scribner, 1976.
Miserez-Schira, Georges. *The Art of Painting on Porcelain*. Radnor, Pa.: Chilton, 1974.
Nelson, Glenn. *Ceramics*. 4th ed. New York: Holt, Rinehart and Winston, 1978.
Paak, Carl E. *The Decorative Touch*. Englewood Cliffs, N.J.: Prentice-Hall, 1981.
Rhodes, Daniel. *Clay and Glazes for the Potter*. Rev. ed. Philadelphia: Chilton, 1973.
Riegger, Hal. *Raku: Art and Technique*. New York: Van Nostrand Reinhold, 1970.
Shafer, Thomas. *Pottery Decoration*. New York: Watson-Guptill, 1976.
Wildenhain, Marguerite. *Pottery: Form and Expression*. New York: Reinhold, 1962.
Yoshida, Mitsukuni. *In Search of Persian Pottery*. New York: Weatherhill, 1972.

Glass

Bernstein, Jack. *Stained Glass Craft*. New York: Macmillan, 1973.
Bovini, Giuseppe. *Ravenna Mosaics*. Greenwich, Conn.: New York Graphic, 1968.
Chagall, Marc. *The Jerusalem Windows*. New York: Braziller, 1967.
Gardner, Paul V., and James S. Plant. *Steuben: Seventy Years of American Glassblowing*. New York: Praeger, 1975.
Hutton, Helen. *Mosaic Making Techniques*. New York: Charles Scribner, 1977.
Johnson, James Rosser. *The Radiance of Chartres*. New York: Random House, 1965.
Metcalf, Robert, and Gertrude Metcalf. *Making Stained Glass*. New York: McGraw-Hill, 1972.
Tiffany. Intro. by Victor Arwas. New York: Rizzoli International, 1979.

Fiber

Albers, Anni. *On Weaving*. Middletown, Conn.: Wesleyan University Press, 1965.
Amir, Ziva. *Arabesque*. New York: Van Nostrand Reinhold, 1977.
Bath, Virginia. *Needlework in America*. New York: Viking Press, 1979.
Beagle, Peter. *American Denim*. New York: Harry Abrams, 1975.
Bishop, Robert, and Elizabeth Safanda. *A Gallery of Amish Quilts*. New York: E. P. Dutton, 1976.
Bress, Helen. *The Weaving Book*. New York: Charles Scribner, 1981.
Brown, Rachel. *The Weaving, Spinning and Dyeing Book*. New York: Alfred A. Knopf, 1978.
Bunting, Ethel-Jane W. *Shindi Tombs and Textiles: The Persistence of Pattern*. Albuquerque: The Maxwell Museum of Anthropology and the University of New Mexico Press, 1980.
Constantine, Mildred, and Jack Lenor Larsen. *Beyond Craft: The Art Fabric*. New York: Van Nostrand Reinhold, 1972.
D'Harcourt, Raoul. *Textiles of Ancient Peru and Their Techniques*. Seattle: University of Washington Press, 1974.
Elson, Vickie G. *Dowries from Kutch*. Los Angeles: Museum of Cultural History, 1979.
Gittinger, Mattiebelle. *Splendid Symbols: Textiles and Tradition in Indonesia*. Washington, D.C.: The Textile Museum, 1979.
Gostelow, Mary. *A World of Embroidery*. New York, Charles Scribner, 1975.
Held, Shirley E. *Weaving: A Handbook of the Fiber Arts*. 2nd ed. New York: Holt, Rinehart and Winston, 1978.
Holstein, Jonathan. *The Pieced Quilt*. Boston: The New York Graphic Society, 1973.
Kahlenberg, Mary Hunt, and Anthony Berlant. *The Navajo Blanket*. New York: Praeger, 1972.
Kahlenberg, Mary Hunt. *Textile Traditions of Indonesia*. Los Angeles: Los Angeles County Museum of Art, 1977.
Klimova, Nina T. *Folk Embroidery from the U.S.S.R.* New York: Van Nostrand Reinhold, 1981.
Kmit, Ann, Johanna and Loretta Luciow. *Ukranian Embroidery*. New York: Van Nostrand Reinhold, 1978.
Krevitsky, Nik. *Batik: Art and Craft*. New York, Van Nostrand Reinhold, 1973.
Larsen, Jack L., and Alfred Buhler. *The Dyer's Art*. New York: Van Nostrand Reinhold, 1977.
——— *Stitchery: Art and Craft*. New York: Van Nostrand Reinhold, 1973.
Ley, Sandra. *Russian and Other Slavic Embroidery Designs*. New York: Charles Scribner, 1976.
Mackie, Louise W. and John Thompson. *Turkmen: Tribal Carpets and Traditions*. Washington, D.C.: The Textile Museum, 1980.
Petrakis, Joan. *The Needle Arts of Greece*. New York: Charles Scribner, 1977.
Pfannschmidt, Ernest Erik. *Twentieth Century Lace*. New York: Charles Scribner, 1975.
Picton, John, and John Mack. *African Textiles*. London: The British Museum Publications, 1979.
Ramazanoglu, Gulseren. *Turkish Embroidery*. New York: Van Nostrand Reinhold, 1976.
Rossbach, Ed. *The Art of Paisley*. New York: Van Nostrand Reinhold, 1980.
Rowe, Ann Pollard. *A Century of Change in Guatemalan Textiles*. New York: Center for Inter-American Relations, 1981.
Thorpe, Azalea S., and Jack Lenor Larsen. *Elements of Weaving*. Garden City, N.Y.: Doubleday, 1978.
Wasserman, Tamara E., and Jonathon Hill. *Bolivian Indian Textiles: Traditional Designs and Costumes*. New York: Dover Publications, 1981.
Westphal, Katherine. *Dragons and Other Creatures: Chinese Embroidery*. Berkeley: Lancaster-Miller Publishers, 1979.
Yugoslavia/Croatian Folk Embroidery. New York: Van Nostrand Reinhold, 1976.

Plastics

Hollander, Harry. *Plastics for Jewelry*. New York: Watson-Guptill, 1974.
Newman, Jay, and Lee Newman. *Plastics for the Craftsman*. New York: Crown, 1973.
Newman, Thelma. *Plastics as Design Form*. Philadelphia: Chilton, 1972.
Plastic as Plastic. New York: Museum of Contemporary Crafts, 1969.
Quarmby, Arthur. *Plastics and Architec-*

ture. New York: Praeger, 1974.
Rees, David. *Creative Plastics*. New York: Viking, 1973.

CHAPTER 15 *Symbolism*

Appleton, Leroy. *American Indian Design and Decoration*. New York: Dover Publications, 1971.
Bailey, Henry T., and Ethel Pool. *Symbolism for Artists*. Detroit: Gale, 1973.
Beurdely, Jean-Michel. *Thai Forms*. New York: John Wetherhill, 1980.
Gerhardus, Maly, and Dietfried Gerhardus. *Symbolism and Art Nouveau*. New York: E. P. Dutton, 1979.
Gombrich, E. H. *Symbolic Images: Studies in the Art of the Renaissance*. New York: E. P. Dutton, 1972.
Hulme, Edward. *Symbolism in Christian Art*. New York: Sterling, 1979.
Murray-Aynsley, Harriet G. *Symbolism of East and West*. Detroit: Gale, 1971.
Quong, Rose. *Chinese Written Characters: Their Wit and Wisdom*. New York: Cobble Hill Press, 1968.

CHAPTER 16 *Painting*

Gardner's *Art Through the Ages*. 7th ed. Rev. by Horst de la Croix and Richard G. Tansey. New York: Harcourt, Brace, Jovanovich, 1980.
Gaunt, William. *The Impressionists*. New York: Weathervane Books, 1975.
Janson, H. W. *History of Art*. 2nd ed. Englewood Cliffs, N.J.: Prentice-Hall, 1977.
Mendelowitz, Daniel M. *A History of American Art*. 2nd ed. New York: Holt, Rinehart and Winston, 1973.
Myers, Bernard S. *The German Expressionists: A Generation in Revolt*. New York: Praeger, 1957.
Muller, Joseph-Emile. *Fauvism*. Trans. by S. E. Jones. New York: Praeger, 1967.
Parola, René. *Optical Art: Theory and Practice*. New York: Van Nostrand Reinhold, 1969.
Rosenblum, Robert. *Cubism and Twentieth-Century Art*. New York: Abrams, 1966.

CHAPTER 17 *Sculpture*

Barbara Hepworth. London: The Tate Gallery, 1968.
Brommer, Frank. *Sculptures of the Parthenon: Metopes, Frieza, Pediments, Cult Statue*. New York: Thames Hudson, 1979.
Irving, Donald J. *Sculpture: Material and Process*. New York: Van Nostrand Reinhold, 1970.
Kelly, J. J. *The Sculptural Idea*. Minneapolis: Burgess, 1970.
Kidson, Peter. *Sculpture at Chartres*. New York: St. Martin's, 1975.
Kowal, Dennis, Jr., and Dona Z. Meilach. *Sculpture Casting*. New York: Crown, 1972.
Krauss, Rosalind. *Sculpture of David Smith: A Catalogue Raisonné*. New York: Garland, 1977.
Legg, Alicia, ed. *Sculpture of Matisse*. New York: Museum of Modern Art, 1972.
Moore, Henry. *Sculpture and Drawings 1964–73*. New York: Wittenborn, 1977.
Richter, Gisela M., ed. *Sculpture and Sculptors of the Greeks*. 4th ed. rev. and enl. New Haven: Yale University Press, 1971.
Roukes, Nicholas. *Sculpture in Plastics*. New York: Watson-Guptill, 1978.
Stone, Anna. *Sculpture: New Ideas and Techniques*. Levittown, N.Y.: Transatlantic, 1977.
Wittkower, Rudolf. *Sculpture: Processes and Principles*. New York: Harper and Row, 1977.
Wood, Jack C. *Sculpture in Wood*. New York: Da Capo, 1977.

CHAPTER 18 *Printmaking*

Artist's Proof: The Annual of Prints and Printmaking. New York: Pratt Graphics Center and Barre Publishers. Annually.
Eichenberg, Fritz. *The Art of the Print*. New York: Abrams, 1976.
Escher, M. C. *The Graphic Works of M. C. Escher*. New York: Ballantine, 1971.
Mayor, A. Hyatt. *Prints and People*. New York: The Metropolitan Museum of Art (dist. New York Graphic), 1971.
Peterdi, Gabor. *Printmaking*. New York: Macmillan, 1971.
Robertson, Ronald G. *Contemporay Printmaking in Japan*. New York: Crown, 1965.
Ross, John, and Clare Romano. *The Complete Printmaker*. New York: The Free Press, 1972.
Saff, Donald and Deli Sacilotto. *Printmaking: History and Process*. New York: Holt, Rinehart and Winston, 1978.
——— *Screenprinting: History and Process*. New York: Holt, Rinehart and Winston, 1979.

CHAPTER 19 *Graphic Design*

Clarke, Beverly. *Graphic Design in Educational Television*. New York: Watson-Guptill, 1974.
Croy, Peter. *Graphic Design and Reproduction Techniques*. Rev. ed. New York: Focal Press, 1972.
Douglass, Ralph. *Calligraphic Lettering*. 3rd ed. New York: Watson-Guptill, 1975.
Ehmcke, R. H. *Graphic Trade Symbols by German Designers*. Magnolia, Mass.: Peter Smith, n.d.
52nd Annual of Advertising Editorial and Television Art and Design with the 13th Annual Copy Awards. New York: Watson-Guptill, 1973.
Graphic Design International. Philadelphia: Hastings, 1977.
Jeffares, Katherine. *Calligraphy: The Art of Beautiful Writing*. No. Hollywood, Calif.: Wilshire, 1978.
Lam, C. M., ed. *Calligrapher's Handbook*. New York: Taplinger, 1976.
Phillips, Dave. *Graphic and Optical Art Mazes*. New York: Dover, 1976.

CHAPTER 20 *Photography*

Adams, Ansel. *Ansel Adams: Images 1923–1974*. Greenwich, Conn.: New York Graphic, 1974.
Caponigro, Paul. *Paul Caponigro*. Millerton. N.Y.: Aperture, 1972.
Cartier-Bresson, Henri. *The World of Henri Cartier-Bresson*. New York: Viking, 1968.
Dixon, Dwight R., and Paul B. Dixon. *Photography: Experiments and Projects*. New York: Macmillan, 1976.
Eisenstadt, Alfred. *Witness to Nature*. New York: Viking, 1971.
Haas, Ernst. *The Creation*. New York: Penguin, 1978.
Life Library of Photography. New York: Time-Life Books, 1970–1971.
Swedlund, Charles. *Photography*. 2nd ed. New York: Holt, Rinehart and Winston, 1981.
Varney, Vivian. *Photographer as Designer*. Worcester, Mass.: Davis Mass, 1977.

CHAPTER 21 *The Performing Arts*

Allensworth, Carl, with Dorothy Allensworth and Clayton Rawson. *The Complete Play Production Handbook.* New York: Harper and Row, 1982.

Bay, Howard. *Stage Design.* New York: Drama Book Specialists, 1974.

Burris-Meyer, Harold, and Edward C. Cole. *Scenery for the Theater.* 3rd ed. Boston: Little, Brown, 1972.

Parker, W. Oren, and Karvey K. Smith. *Scene Design and Stage Lighting.* 4th ed. New York: Holt, Rinehart and Winston, 1979.

Pecktal, Lynn. *Designing and Painting for the Theatre.* New York: Holt, Rinehart and Winston, 1975.

Russell, Douglas. *Stage Costume Design: Theory, Technique, and Style.* New York: Appleton-Century-Crofts, 1973.

Schubert, Hannelore. *The Modern Theatre: Architecture, Stage Design, Lighting.* New York: Praeger, 1971.

CHAPTER 22 *Apparel*

Greenwood, Kathryn M., and Mary F. Murphy. *Fashion Innovation and Marketing.* New York: Macmillan, 1978.

Hamburger, Estelle. *Fashion Business: It's All Yours.* New York: Harper and Row, 1976.

Kohler, Carl. *History of Costume.* Magnolia, Mass.: Peter Smith, n.d.

Mathisen, Marilyn. *Apparel and Accessories.* New York: McGraw-Hill, 1979.

Peltz, Leslie Ruth. *Fashion Color, Line, and Design.* Indianapolis: Bobbs-Merrill, 1971.

Salomon, Rosalie K. *Fashion Design for Moderns.* New York: Fairchild, 1976.

Sproles, George B. *Fashion: Consumer Behavior Toward Dress.* Minneapolis: Burgess, 1979.

CHAPTER 23 *Industrial Design*

Ambasz, Emilio, ed. Italy: *The New Domestic Landscape.* New York: The Museum of Modern Art, 1972.

Carrington, Noel. *Industrial Design in Britain.* Winchester, Mass.: Allen Unwin, 1976.

Drexler, Arthur. *Design Collection: Selected Objects.* New York: Museum of Modern Art, 1970.

Itten, Johannes. *Design and Form: The Basic Course at the Bauhaus.* 2nd rev. ed. New York: Van Nostrand Reinhold, 1975.

Loewy, Raymond. *Industrial Design.* New York: Overlook Press, 1980.

Portable World. New York: Museum of Contemporary Crafts, 1973.

CHAPTER 24 *Interiors*

Ball, Victoria Kloss. *Opportunities in Interior Design.* Skokie, Ill.: National Textbook, 1977.

Faulkner, Sarah. *Planning a Home.* New York: Holt, Rinehart and Winston, 1979.

Faulkner, Ray, and Sarah Faulkner. *Inside Today's Home.* 4th ed. New York: Holt, Rinehart and Winston, 1975.

Floethe, Louise L. *Houses Around the World.* New York: Charles Scribner, 1973.

Harling, Robert, ed. *Dictionary of Design and Decoration.* New York: Viking, 1973.

Hatje, Gerd, and Peter Kaspar. *1601 Decorating Ideas for Modern Living.* New York: Abrams, 1974.

Larsen, Jack L., and Jeanne Weeks. *Fabrics for Interiors.* New York: Van Nostrand Reinhold, 1975.

Magnani, Franco, ed. *Living Spaces: 150 Design Ideas from Around the World.* New York: Whitney Library of Design, 1978.

Philip, Peter. *Furniture of the World.* New York: Mayflower, 1978.

Phillips, Derek. *Planning Your Lighting.* New York: Quick Fox, 1978.

Stoddard, Alexandra. *Style for Living.* Garden City: Doubleday, 1974.

Zakas, Spiros. *Lifespace and Designs for Today's Living.* New York: Macmillan, 1977.

CHAPTER 25 *Architecture*

Bloomer, Kent C., and Charles W. Moore. *Body, Memory and Architecture.* New Haven: Yale University Press, 1977.

Boericke, Art, and Barry Shapiro. *Handmade Houses: A Guide to the Woodbutcher's Art.* San Francisco: Scrimshaw, 1973.

Giedion, Siegfried. *Architecture and the Phenomena of Transition: The Three Space Conceptions in Architecture.* Cambridge, Mass.: Harvard University Press, 1971.

Gombrich, E. H. *The Sense of Order.* Oxford: Phaidon, 1979.

Gropius, Walter. *The New Architecture and the Bauhaus.* Cambridge, Mass.: MIT Press, 1968.

Hoyt, Charles King. *More Places for People.* New York: McGraw-Hill, 1982.

Jencks, Charles. *The Language of Post-Modern Architecture.* New York: Rizzoli, 1977.

Johnson, Timothy E. *Solar Architecture: The Direct Gain Approach.* New York: McGraw-Hill, 1982.

Moholy-Nagy, Sibyl. *Native Genius in Anonymous Architecture in North America.* New York: Schocken, 1976.

CHAPTER 26 *The Total Environment*

Bacon, Edmund N. *Design of Cities.* New York: Penguin, 1976.

Bring, Mitchell, and Josse Wayembergh. *Japanese Gardens: Design and Meaning.* New York: McGraw-Hill, 1982.

Diekelmann, John, and Robert Schuster. *Natural Landscaping.* New York: McGraw-Hill, 1982.

Eckbo, Garrett. *Home Landscape: The Art of Home Landscaping,* rev. and enl. ed. New York: McGraw-Hill, 1982.

Gruen, Victor, and Larry Smith. *Centers for Urban Environment.* New York: Van Nostrand Reinhold, 1973.

Kepes, Gyorgy, ed. *Arts of the Environment.* New York: Braziller, 1972.

Kurtz, Stephen A. *Wasteland: Building the American Dream.* New York: Praeger, 1973.

Le Corbusier. *Towards a New Architecture.* New York: Praeger, 1970.

Lynch, Kevin. *Managing the Sense of a Region.* Cambridge, Mass.: MIT Press, 1976.

Mumford, Lewis. *Culture of Cities.* New York: Harcourt, Brace, Jovanovich, 1970.

——— *Roots of Contemporary American Architecture.* New York: Dover, 1972.

Index

Photographic credits

The author and publisher wish to thank the custodians of the works of art for supplying photographs and granting permission to use them. Photographs have been obtained from sources listed in the captions, unless listed below.

A/AR: Alinari/Art Resource, New York
AMNH: American Museum of Natural History, New York
BN: Bibliothèque Nationale, Paris
G: Giraudon, Paris
H: Hirmer, Munich
HB: Hedrich Blessing, Chicago
HRV: H. Roger Violett, Paris
M: Marburg, Marburg/Lahn
NYPL: New York Public Library
NmcG: Norman McGrath, New York
PM: Philip Molten, Tiburon, California
PR: Photo Researchers, New York
RS: From *Crafts of the Modern World,* by Rose Slivka with the World Arts Council, and Horizon Press, © Rose Slivka.
S/AR: Scala/Art Resource, New York
WS: Willard Stone

References are to boldface figure numbers.

Color Plates:
Plate 3: Eric Pollitzer, Plate 4: Ampliaciones y Reproduciones, Barcelona. Plate 6: G. Plate 7: The Vasarely Center, New York. Plates 17 and 18: Phaidon Press Ltd., Oxford, The Bridgeman Art Library, London. Plate 20: Service de Documentation Photographie de la Réunion des Musées Nationaux, Paris. Plate 21: Lester Kierstead Henderon, Cover Illustration of *The Sublime Heritage of Martha Mood, Volume II,* Published 1983 by Kierstead Publications, Monterey. Plate 22: Evelyn Hofer, New York. Cleve Gray. Plate 23: R. Sheppy Moore, The American Federation of the Arts, New York. Plate 25: André Emmerich Gallery, New York. Plate 28: Robert Miller Gallery, New York. Plate 30: © Bert Stern, New York. Plate 31: Martha Swope, New York. Plate 32: Dominique Issermann/Sygma, Inc., New York. Plate 33: Russell McMasters, New York. Plate 34: Alo Zanetta, Vacallo, Switzerland. Plate 35: © NG. Plate 36: PR.

Chapter 1 2: AMNH. 5: A/AR. 6: Grant M. Haist/National Audubon Society, PR. 8: Fotocielo, Rome. 11: Bulloz, Paris. 13: A/AR. 14: Photograph by David Smith at his home. 17: Docutel/Olivetti Corporation, New York. 18: Canadian Government Office of Tourism, Ottawa. 20: AMNH. 21: Dr. Howard E. Bigelow, University of Massachusetts, Amherst.
Chapter 2 26: Gladys Walker, Seattle. 27: Hoffritz International, Hammond/Keehn, Inc., New York. 29: Geary's, Beverly Hills. 32: Malcolm Grear Designers, Inc., Providence. 33: Walt Quade, Eastsound, Washington. 36: Markline Company, Waltham, Massachusetts. 37: Robert Walsh, New York. 39: AMNH. 42: Ken Karp, New York. 43: General Electric Company, Bridgeport. 44: US Suzuki Motor Corporation, Brea, California.
Chapter 3 45: Shigeo Anzai, Tokyo. 47: NYPL. 49: From *Forms and Patterns in Nature,* by Wolf Strache, Random House, New York. 50: Charles Moore, Black Star, New York. 52: Asian Art Photographic Distribution, New York. 53: Walt Quade, Eastsound, Washington, From *Chinese Written Characters: Their Wit and Wisdom,* by Rose Quong, Cobble Hill Press, 1968, New York. 59: Roger Marschutz, Los Angeles. 60: Massachusetts Institute of Technology.
Chapter 4 71: The British Tourist Authority, New York. 72: AMNH. 74: Antonia Graeber, Los Angeles. 75: Leo Castelli Gallery, New York. 76: George Jennings, Jr., Norwich, Conn. 77: RS. 78: Tung Yah Asian Arts, La Jolla, California. 82: Jan Lukas, PR. 88: Helmsley Spear, Inc., New York. 90: Nat Norman, PR. 91: Roger Werth for *Longview Daily News,* 1980, Woodfin Camp, New York. 97: Russell Dixon Lamb/PR.
Chapter 5 103 and 104: WS. 112: Magnum, New York. 113: Julius Shulman, LA. 114: AMNH. 115: Caisse Nationale des Monuments Historiques et des Sites, Paris. 118: Kissarvik Cooperative, Rankin, N.W.T. Canada. 121: A/AR. 124: Harry Murphy + Friends, Mill Valley, CA. 125: The Vasarely Center, New York.
Chapter 6 128: ARCO Center for Visual Art, LA. 135 and 136: © NM. 139 and 140: RS. 141: Asian Art Photographic Distribution, New York. 143: H. 144: From *The New Churches of Europe,* by G. E. Kidder Smith. 146 and 147: Antonia Graeber, LA. 152: RS.
Chapter 7 155: From Munsell: *A Grammar of Color* copyright © 1969 by Reinhold Publishing. Reprinted by permission of Van Nostrand Reinhold Company, New York. 159: LWT International, London. 160: AMNH
Chapter 8 160 and 163: AMNH. 167: © 1982 Trustees of Princeton University. 171: Anne Odom, Washington, D.C.
Chapter 9 172: Myron Wood, PR. 175: Henri Cartier-Bresson, Magnum. 178: S/AR. 183: Nathan Rabin, New York. 189: RS.
Chapter 10 191: Allen Mewbourne, Houston. 192: The Bettmann Archive, Inc., New York. 194: Alison Frantz, Princeton, New Jersey. 198: Eastman Kodak Company, Rochester, New York. 200: A/AR. 201: AMNH. 202: Dick Kruger, Brand Advertising, Inc., Chicago. 203: Robert d'Estrube, Stephen Lowe Art Gallery, Victoria, B.C. 207: Wilhelm Rauh, The Bayreuth Festival, Bayreuth, West Germany.
Chapter 11 209: Amwest Picture Agency, Denver. 210: Bill Apton, Brook Haven. 211: The Innuit Gallery of Eskimo Art, Toronto; Paleeajook Cooperative, Ltd., Spence Bay, N.W.T. 214: M. 216: Richard di Liberto, New York. 219: Edmund V. Gillon, Brooklyn. 220: George Flamming, Birmingham. 224: HRV. 226: Studio Ing. Nervi, Rome. 227: *"Crafts" Magazine,* Crafts Council, London. 231: The Pace Gallery, New York. 233: Roberts Commercial Photos, Boulder.
Chapter 12 236: ConStruct, Chicago. 239 Evon Streetman, Florida. 244: WS. 247: Meyers Walker, New York. 248: Marc Slivka, New York. 249: "The Craftsman Gallery," Scarsdale, New York. 256–258: From *Weaving as an Art Form* by Theo Moorman. Copyright © Van Nostrand Reinhold Company. Reprinted by permission of the Publisher. 260: John Clemmer, New York. 263: "NBC Nightly News,"/Digital Effects, Inc., New York, 1982.
Chapter 13 264: Jack Lenor Larsen, New York. 267: Hector R. Aoebes, PR. 268: Australian Tourist Commission, New York. 269: © NM. 274: Georg Jensen Silversmiths, Denmark. 275: The Allrich Gallery, San Francisco. 276. Arras Gallery, New York. 277: Royal Leerdam, Leerdam, the Netherlands. 278: British Authority, New York.
Chapter 14 280: Indonesian Collection of the Rijksmuseum voor Volkenkunde, Leiden, Netherlands. 281: Reproduced by courtesy of the Trustees of the British Museum, London. 283: Ampliaciones y Reproduciones, Barcelona. 285: A/AR. 287: Ernst Haas, New York. 288: German Information Center, New York. 289: Guild of Bookworkers, New York. 292: A/AR. 293: RS. 295: Piedmont Craftsmen, Inc., Winston-Salem, N.C. 297: Blake Praytor, San Francisco.
Chapter 15 309: Eliot Elisofon, *Life Magazine,* © Time, Inc. 311: Jewish Museum, AR. 313: M. 323: Cotton Incorporated, New York. 327: Photogravure de Schutter, Antwerp.
Chapter 16 333: Nancy Hoffman Gallery, New York. 341: Leo Castelli Gallery, New York. 344: Photo by Eeva-Inkeri, The Allan Frumpkin Gallery, New York. 345: Willard Gallery, New York. 346: Haber Theodore Gallery, New York.
Chapter 17 347: André Emmerich Gallery, New York. 348: From *The Modern Blacksmith,* by Alexander G. Weygers, Copyright © 1974 by Van Nostrand Reinhold Company. Reprinted by permission of the Publisher. 349: A/AR. 352: A/AR. 355–356: A/AR. 357: La Federation des Cooperatives du Nouveau Québec, Montreal. 359: Blum Helman Gallery, New York. 364: Holly Solomon Gallery, New York, Eyris Production, New York. 367: John Weber Gallery, New York. 368: Diverse Dimensions Art, New Rochelle.
Chapter 18 370: From *Collograph Printmaking* by Donald Stoltenberg. Davis Publications, Inc., Worcester, 1975. 372: NYPL, Prints Division, The Astor, Lenox and Tilden Foundations. 374: From *Collograph Printmaking* by Donald Stoltenberg. Davis Publications, Inc., Worcester, 1975. 384: Petersburg Press, London. 386: Parasol Press, New York. 387: Jack Rutberg Fine Arts, LA. 390: Castelli Graphics and Multiples, Inc., New York. 391: Rosa Esman Gallery.
Chapter 19. 393: Biblioteca Vaticana, Rome. 394: *Redbook Magazine,* May 1981. 396: Frank Moscati, Push Pin Lubalin Peckolick, New York. 397: Illustration by Gyo Fujikawa; reprinted by permission of Grosset & Dunlap, Inc., From *My Favorite Thing,* © 1978 by Gyo Fujikawa. 401: Reid Miles, CBS Records. 402: Joseph Abeles, New York. 403: Reproduced with permission of AT & T, New York. 405: Howard Krieger, Simmons USA, Atlanta. 407: Vance Henry, PR. 409: Williams & Associates, South Lynnfield, Mass.
Chapter 20 411: Enrico Ferorelli, Wheeler Pictures, New York. 412: Art Kane, New York. 421: *Life Magazine,* © Time, Inc. 424: United Press International, New York. 425: Chermayeff & Geismar Associates, New York. 426: Creative Art Images, LA.
Chapter 21 431: Jan Lukas, PR. 432: Columbia Artists Management, New York. 433: The Greek National Tourist Organization, New York. 434: NYPL, The Astor, Lenox and Tilden Foundations. 437 and 438: From *The Complete Play Production Handbook,* Revised Edition by Carl Allensworth; reprinted by permission of Harper & Row, Publishers, Inc., New York. 483: Courtesy of the ANTA Collection in the Hampden-Booth Theatre Library at The Players, New York. 440 and 441: Virginia Museum Theatre, Richmond. 445: Joseph Abeles, New York. 446: Fred Fehl, New York. 447: XXth Century Ballet, Brussels.
Chapter 22 448: AMNH. 449: Frederick Ayer, PR. 450: Gordon Munro Studio, Inc., New York. 451: NASA. 452: George Stavrinos, Larchmont. 454: Max Petrelius, Helsinki. 455: General Mills, Inc., Minnesota. 456: E. I. DuPont de Nemours and Company, Inc., New York. 457: Bill Blass, New York. 458: Wide World Photos, New York. 459: Mary MacFadden, New York. 460: Gordon Munro Studio, Inc., New York. 462: E. I. DuPont de Nemours and Company, Inc., New York. 463: Max Petrelius, Helsinki. 464: Gamma Liaison. 465: Copyright © 1974 by Newdon Company; all rights reserved; courtesy of Paramount Pictures Corporation. 466: Elizabeth Arden, Inc., New York.

Chapter 23 467: Knoll International, New York. 468: The Coca-Cola Company, Atlanta. 469: Burson-Marsteller, New York. 470: Contourpedic Corporation. 472: Sport Kites, LA. 473: Apple Computer Inc., Cupertino, California. 474: Renault, USA, N.Y. 475: CBS Television, New York. 476: Ford Motor Company, New York. 477: American Telephone and Telegraph Company, New York. 479: Brionvega Radio and TV Company, Milan. 481 and 482: WS.
Chapter 24 484–486 and 489: PM. 490: Maynard L. Parker, LA. 491: Hedrich Blessing, Chicago. 495: Maynard L. Parker, LA. 496: Michael Geiger, New York. 497: PM. 498 and 499: Hedrich Blessing, Chicago. 500: American Craft Museum of the American Craft Council; from the exhibition *New Handmade Furniture,* 1979; Bob Hanson for American Crafts Museum. 501: Photo by Baldinger, Poultney, VT. 503: © Nick Wheeler, 1981. 504: Greg Plachita, Burroughs Wellcome Company, Research Triangle Park, N.C. 505: George Haling, Wheeler Pictures, New York. 506: The Pace Collection, New York. 507: Steven Kelemen, Orient Point, New York.
Chapter 25 508: © Evelyn Hofer, Archive Pictures, Inc., New York. 510: A/AR. 511: Bill Hedrick, Hedrich Blessing, Chicago. 512: Valerie Batorewicz, New Haven. 513: Julius Shulman, LA. 514 and 515: Alo Zanetta, Vacallo, Switzerland. 516: *St. Louis Post-Dispatch.* 517: Australian Information Service, New York. 519: Library of Congress, Wash. D.C. 520: Caldwell, Bartlett, Wood, Inc., Memphis. 521: Pella, Rolscreen Company, Minneapolis, Minn. 522: Deidi van Schaewen, Paris. 524: German Information Center, New York. 525: PM. 526: HB. 527: © NM. 528 Michael Graves, Princeton. 529: © NM. 530: Benjamin T. Rogers. 531: Swiss National Tourist Office, New York. 532: Reprinted from *Popular Science* with Permission, © 1983, Times Mirror Magazines, Inc. 534: Alexander George, William Morgan Architects.
Chapter 26 536: © David Plowden, 1977, PR; Freelance Photographers Guild, New York. 539: Maynard L. Parker. 540: *House & Garden,* New York. 541: Lawrence Halprin, San Francisco. 542: Frizer Corporation, Ltd., Calgary, Alberta. 544: McAllister of Denver. 545: The Consulate General of the Netherlands. 543: Brogi, AR. 546: the Norfolk Redevelopment and Housing Authority, Norfolk. 547: A/AR. 549: San Antonio Convention & Visitors Bureau, San Antonio, Texas. 550: M. E. Warren Annapolis, Charles Center-Inner Harbor Management, Inc., Baltimore. 551: Charles Center-Inner Harbor Management, Inc. Baltimore. 552: Johnson, Burgee architect and architects Design Group, New York. 553: Terry Winters, Vermont Division for Historic Preservation, Montpelier. 554: © Lynn McLaren, Rapho/PR. 556: NASA.